375c

...ssion ac...
...oks at...
. Bagchi,
...mment.

hese central st...
...onomic growth
ports by the six
ssions of the Co
scussions of thei
atthews, whose
Past Economic
d H. Giersch
Factors of Ec
"Resource
atchaturo
owth"; S
owth."

Economic Growth and Resources

Volume 1: The Major Issues

International Economic Association publications

THE GAP BETWEEN RICH AND POOR NATIONS
ECONOMIC RELATIONS BETWEEN EAST AND WEST
ECONOMETRIC CONTRIBUTIONS TO PUBLIC POLICY
APPROPRIATE TECHNOLOGIES FOR THIRD WORLD DEVELOPMENT
ECONOMIC GROWTH AND RESOURCES

Economic Growth and Resources

Volume 1: The Major Issues

Proceedings of the Fifth World Congress of the
International Economic Association
held in Tokyo, Japan, 1977

Plenary Sessions

Edited by

EDMOND MALINVAUD

President 1974–7

St. Martin's Press New York

ISBN 0-312-23314-0

Library of Congress Cataloging in Publication Data

International Economic Association.
  Economic growth and resources.

  Includes bibliographies and indexes.
  CONTENTS: v. 1. The major issues, edited
by E. Malinvaud. – v. 2. Trends and factors,
edited by R. C. O. Matthews. – v. 3. Natural
resources, edited by C. Bliss. [etc.]
  1. Economic development – Congresses.
2. Economic policy – Congresses. 3. Natural
resources – Congresses. 4. Japan – Economic
conditions – 1945 -   – Congresses. I. Title.
HD82.I45   1979a   330.9   79-4430

ISBN 0-312-23314-0 Volume I. The Major Issues
ISBN 0-312-23315-9 Volume II. Trends and Factors
ISBN 0-312-23316-7 Volume III. Natural Resources
ISBN 0-312-23317-5 Volume IV. National and International Policies
ISBN 0-312-23318-3 Volume V. Problems Related to Japan

Contents

Acknowledgements

The holding of the Fifth World Congress of the International Economic Association was made possible by the magnificently generous grants made for it by the Science Council of Japan and by the help of the two other sponsoring bodies, the Union of National Economic Associations in Japan and the Institute of Statistical Research. The Association has reason to be extremely grateful to Professor Shigeto Tsuru, now its President, for all that he did to make this possible, to Professor Ochi of the Science Council, to Professor Uchida, President of the Union of National Economic Associations, and to Professor Nakayama, President of the Institute of Statistical Research, who did everything within their power to ensure the success of the Congress.

Apart from our Japanese hosts, our gratitude is also due to the two bodies, UNESCO and the Ford Foundation, which have long supported and made possible our work and whose funds contributed to this Congress.

List of Contributors to this Volume

Professor Moses Abramovitz, Stanford University, USA
Professor Irma Adelman, University of Maryland, USA
Dr Odd Aukrust, Central Bureau of Statistics, Oslo, Norway
Professor Edmar L. Bacha, University of Brasilia, Brazil
Professor A. K. Bagchi, Centre for Studies in Social Sciences, Calcutta, India
Professor Wilfred Beckerman, Oxford University, UK
Professor Bela Balassa, World Bank, Washington, USA
Professor Oleg Bogomolov, Institute of Economics of the World Socialist
    System, Moscow, USSR
Professor Mogens Boserup, University of Copenhagen, Denmark
Professor Martin Bronfenbrenner, Duke University, North Carolina, USA
Dr Nicholas Bruck, Washington, USA
Professor Béla Csikós-Nagy, Budapest, Hungary
Professor D. Delivanis, University of Thessaloniki, Greece
Dr Uka I. Ezenwe, Ahmadu Bello University, Zaria, Nigeria
Academician N. P. Fedorenko, Academy of Sciences, USSR
Professor Herbert Giersch, Institut für Weltwirtschaft, Kiel, F.R. of Germany
John Hardt, Congressional Research Service, Washington DC, USA
Professor Geoffrey Heal, University of Sussex, UK
Professor Hendrik Houthakker, Harvard University, USA
Dr Madhur Srinivas Iyengar, Delhi, India
Mr Michael Kaser, Oxford University, UK
Professor John W. Kendrick, US Department of Commerce, Washington DC,
    USA
Academician T. S. Khachaturov, Association for Soviet Economic Scientific
    Institutions, Moscow, USSR
Professor Irving B. Kravis, University of Pennsylvania, USA
Dr Constantino Lluch, World Bank, Washington, USA
Professor Edmond Malinvaud, President IEA, Paris, France
Professor Evgeni Mateev, Sofia, Bulgaria
Professor R. C. O. Matthews, Clare College, Cambridge, UK
Professor Franco Modigliani, Massachusetts Institute of Technology,
    Cambridge, USA
Professor Costin Murgescu, Academy of Social Sciences, Bucharest, Romania
Professor Tasuku Noguchi, Keio University, Tokyo, Japan
Professor Kazushi Ohkawa, Hitotsubashi University, Japan
Professor Józef Pajestka, Planning Commission, Warsaw, Poland
Dr K. N. Raj, Centre for Development Studies, Ulloor, Kerala, India

Professor Zdzislaw Sadowski, Institute of Planning, Warsaw, Poland
M. Christian Sautter, Institut National de La Statistique et des Etudes Economiques, Paris, France
Professor Tibor Scitovsky, London School of Economics, UK
Professor Richard Stone, Cambridge University, UK
Professor Akira Takayama, Purdue University, USA
Professor Shigeto Tsuru, Hitotsubashi University, Japan
Professor Victor Urquidi, El Collegio de Mexico, Mexico
Professor Georg Winckler, University of Vienna, Austria

Introduction

Edmond Malinvaud

PRESIDENT IEA, PARIS, FRANCE

This volume publishes part of the work done for and during the Congress held in Tokyo in the summer of 1977 by the International Economic Association. More exactly, it gives the full proceedings of the plenary sessions, whereas four other volumes will publish a selection of the papers presented in specialised sessions.[1]

A congress, intended as a gathering of a great number of economists coming from distant countries and distant subdisciplines, should ideally have a rather broad programme and should be concerned with questions arousing a wide interest both for research and for decision-taking. Economic growth undoubtedly meets this requirement; moreover, in the 1970s one could not speak of economic growth without paying some attention to the use of the resources that make it possible.

On the other hand, the subject could easily have become too broad, have finally covered almost the whole of economics and have been so diluted as to leave too few opportunities for profound scientific interchange. Hence, some delimitation had to be chosen so as to avoid this risk.

The book begins with the search for an explanation of why economic growth has been so rapid in the developed capitalist countries during the three decades following the last world war. Then two more specific questions of great interest are taken up successively: the changes in inequality and the prices of exhaustible resources. The planning of economic growth comes next, but of course a special main article and discussion is devoted more particularly to the growth policies of developing countries. Finally, it was thought the Congress should seriously consider the present misgivings about what economic growth achieves for the people of the world; such is the purpose of the last main article.

The book ends with six short reports given during the last day of the Congress and respectively presenting the work done in six groups of specialised sessions.[2] The themes of these groups were:

(1) past economic growth and its measurement;

[1] See R. C. O. Matthews (ed.), *Economic Growth and Resources: vol.2: Trends and Factors*; C. Bliss and M. Boserup (eds.), *Economic Growth and Resources: vol.3: Natural Resources*; I. Adelman (ed.), *Economic Growth and Resources: vol.4: National and International Policies*; S. Tsuru (ed.), *Economic Growth and Resources: vol.5: Problems Relating to Japan.*

[2] The full programme of these sessions is given at the end of the book, pp. 264–72.

(2) factors of economic growth;
(3) resources for future economic growth;
(4) prospects of economic growth, economic policies and regulations;
(5) international division of labour and co-operation in economic development;
(6) growth and resources problems related to Japan.

These six reports give to the present book a breadth that would have been lacking otherwise; they exhibit the wide range of topics that economists consider in order to permit a better knowledge and better control of economic growth; they present the views that were entertained in 1977 on these various topics.

In the opening paper Moses Abramovitz scrutinises the postwar economic growth of capitalist countries. He argues that a special set of circumstances made the potential for productivity growth strong and enabled developed countries to exploit that potential rapidly, in concert and over a long period. Some of these circumstances were transitory and have now weakened or, in some cases, disappeared. The prospects for an early renewal of the postwar growth drive at the same rapid pace has, then, become uncertain and dubious.

The discussion of this paper bears both on our understanding of the past thirty years and on its implication for future growth in capitalist countries. Pointing to the fact that growth was also rapid in the developing countries and in Eastern Europe, Richard Stone questions whether the special circumstances experienced in the west were really the determining factor. Kazushi Ohkawa's contribution leads us to realise that we know still very little about the factors explaining the 'social capabilities' of a country and that variations in these capabilities may play an important role both in explaining the past and in forecasting the future. Notwithstanding minor differences of appreciation, all the contributors agree that, whereas growth is very likely to be slower in the coming decades, it still will be fast by prewar historical standards.

Edmar Bacha approaches the difficult question of knowing how economic growth is related to changes of inequalities, more precisely to changes in the size distribution of incomes. The first part of his paper surveys the many empirical studies that have recently been made on this question and shows that they validate the 'Kuznets curve' as a rough relation between income inequality and average real income per head (inequality tending to first increase with average income, then decrease with it); moreover the maximum of the curve seems to have drifted toward higher real income levels. The second part of the paper considers some explanations that have been offered for this phenomenon. Is it a reflection of the first increasing then decreasing dualism experienced by an economy through its development, as the structuralist school claims? Or a reflection of the development of education, as is argued by proponents of the human capital theory? Or is it a purely accidental statistical regression between national experiences that vary greatly according to the policies followed? Or should the explanation of this regression be found outside of economics, namely in wars and revolutions, the only significant determinants of important distributional changes?

The discussion takes up the two parts of the paper. On the statistical regressions, caution is required because the data used suffer from a number of pitfalls (incomplete coverage or reporting, lack of international or inter-temporal comparability, and so on) and the picture that emerges is certainly not as simple as a curve would suggest. As to the explanation, it would be very difficult to obtain a consensus among economists at present, except on a general statement to the effect that the mechanisms at work are complex, and involve not only economics but also politics and vary a great deal over time as well as among countries. But this is a lively field in which the present accumu-lation of better data and the intellectual efforts to analyse them are promising.

In his study of the long-run movement of prices of exhaustible resources, Geoffrey Heal starts from abstract theory and then confronts it with actual data. The theoretical literature, which is now well-developed, leads to simple and clear conclusions if perfect competition is assumed. For energy resources and basic minerals such an assumption is often particularly inappropriate. But it turns out that various specifications of imperfect competition lead to the same qualitative result, namely that the price of the resource should rise, and this at a rate which is dependent upon the rate of return on other assets.

However, the historical series of the real prices of resources during the last century exhibit considerable instability and do not show a clear upward trend. To reconcile theory and facts, the author only needs to consider, first, dis-equilibrium behaviour, and, second, changes in expectations associated with increases in known stocks and unanticipated cost reductions in extraction or in the production of substitutes. The presence of arbitrage between resources and other assets can be well tested on series for the 1960s and 1970s. The results are again not quite those the theory would predict; the principal cause of difference seems to be found in the manner in which expectations are formed.

The discussion permits some clarification on a number of points: how should the basic formula on the rate of increase of the price be revised when account is taken of the fact that the extraction cost of the resource is not *a priori* given? To what extent does the actual instability of resource prices depend on the way in which expectations are formed? What are the sources of bias in the historical series on the real price of resources?

The discussion also raises broader issues. In particular, motivated by the concern for a new economic order in the trade relations between developing and developed countries, B. Csikós-Nagy addresses some of his comments to those who attempt to forecast the price developments up to the end of this century. Pointing to the role of monopolies in the pricing of primary products, he insists that the respective political powers of producers and consumers will play an important role.

After a long introduction on the past achievements of the Soviet Union, T. Khachaturov and N. Fedorenko approach the important topic of planning the future utilisation of existing resources. They forcefully argue for a reduction in the large-scale waste of energy and materials that occurs with present methods of production. They show that such a reduction has already occurred to some extent. They exhibit the prospects for quite substantial further progress in this respect, thus contradicting the pessimism of the famous Meadows report. But they state the necessity of appropriate planning for a realisation of these prospects.

The discussants agree that doomsday resource pessimism is ill-founded because great possibilities still exist for new discoveries, for technical progress and for more economical production or consumption patterns. The necessity of the form of central planning now existing in Eastern Europe is, however, questioned by some economists; doubts are raised about its efficiency in resource saving. Michael Kaser voices a plea for studies assessing the relative efficiencies in this respect of various economic systems.

Two discussants devote their comments to the contribution that theoretical economists can make to a better planning of resource use. A. Takayama shows that the theory of optimal growth can throw light not only on the choice of the rate of exhaustion of depletable resources but also on the allocation of labour to research activities; he builds and solves two models exhibiting the optimal strategy in this respect. J. Pajestka argues that development analysis should not draw only on economics narrowly understood, but should study also socio-economic linkages as well as societal goals.

Writing about the 'barriers to development', K. N. Raj focuses his attention on the poorest countries of Africa and Asia. He notes that there is considerable agreement that 'the cards are stacked against them both internally and externally'. The internal obstacles to development come partly from the pressure of population on land and from the importance of the institutional changes required for raising productivity in agriculture, but mainly from the economic and power structure, from the interests and values it upholds, and from the limitation of choices that can be effectively made within such a framework. The external obstacles result from the fact that, since the Second World War, the already developed countries have become their own best customers and suppliers; expansion of world trade cannot be depended on to promote growth in the underdeveloped world to anything like the same degree as was possible earlier for most of the now developed countries. In the ultimate analysis, the internal and external barriers to development are basically political in nature.

While all are in agreement with this last statement, the discussants exhibit a rather wide spectrum of opinion. Several of them accept V. L. Urquidi's argument showing that the pressure of population on land is not an absolute negative factor and can be successfully faced by integrated rural development projects. Some discussants feel more generally that K. N. Raj overestimates the internal obstacles following from the present technologies of production or consumption and that national efforts can overcome these obstacles.

But the largest part of the discussion of this chapter concerns external barriers. B. Balassa argues that the poor performance of many less developed countries results from a bad policy choice favouring import substitution in manufacturing at the expense of agriculture; he points to the success of the few countries that have followed export-oriented policies during the past two decades; he stresses the scope for further increase of exports from the third world with accompanying progressive changes in comparative advantages. Other discussants are less optimistic, feeling that the developed countries may become more protectionist in the future, this being particularly likely if many other developing countries adopt export-oriented policies.

Dealing with the costs of growth — that is with the unfavourable implications of modern economic growth — E. Malinvaud tries to see what is the nature of these effects and to explore whether and how some of them might be avoided, even if this would mean slower growth. He considers, first, the costs associated with changes in the physical produced and non-produced resources (physical costs); second, the costs associated with labour mobility, social inequality and concentration (social costs); and, third, the appropriate balance between costs and satisfactions, some of the latter turning out to be illusory.

The discussion reveals the wide range of different meanings that is given to the catch-words 'costs of growth'. S. Tsuru examines how our current measures of output (GNP) should be revised so as to better estimate the *net* result of production. A. K. Bagchi argues that the growth of the now developed countries was made at the cost of the rest of the world. R. Matthews makes a plea for active research on the nature and extent of social externalities in consumption. The discussion also reveals that these are subjects about which objective knowledge definitely lags behind public concern. But the already existing body of theory is often relevant and should not be neglected either, as is forcefully demonstrated by F. Modigliani.

Among the topics that were not considered, two are particularly worth mentioning. First, studies of the trade cycle, or more generally of short-term economic trends, were deliberately omitted; this meant that policies for the regulation of business conditions could not be dealt with either, notwithstanding their crucial importance at the time when the Congress was held (they were occasionally touched upon, nevertheless, in the specialised sessions dealing with economic policies). Second, human resources were not considered, and attention concentrated on natural resources (a paper on population forecasts in a specialised session was regarded as necessary in relation to the evaluation of food and energy requirements). The economics of human resources is, of course, an important and lively area of study — so much so that it has been selected as the subject for the next Congress to be held in Mexico in 1980.

Ideally, the plenary sessions should have covered the full range of questions concerning economic growth so delimited and the use of natural resources that were particularly topical in the mid-1970s and attracted research from a large number of economists. It was, however, a strong constraint to try to achieve this aim within the format of only six main papers. Moreover, the choice of themes and of speakers may have in practice reflected to some extent the views of the Programme Committee[1] and has been subject to such random circumstances as always occur in human undertakings.

The study of economic growth has both positive and normative aspects. Its purpose may be to understand and explain the facts; or it may be to decide and implement a policy. In this field, much better than in the study of short-term trends, the literature usually distinguishes the two aspects. Indeed, within this volume the first three main papers are oriented toward the answering of positive questions, while two out of the three remaining main papers concern economic policies, with the last having both a positive and normative purpose.

It is out of the question to summarise here the six reports published at the end of this book, because each one of them is already a brief summary of a substantial number of papers and of the discussions that followed their two-day presentation. But so as to present an overview of what was discussed at Tokyo within the specialised sessions, it may be appropriate to list the main topics considered, roughly in the order in which they appear in the first five reports, and then to make brief reference to the work concerning Japanese growth.

This leads to the following list:

(1) the measurement of aggregate growth; why, notwithstanding its inadequacies or inaccuracies, the GNP is not likely to be displaced in its role as such a measure;

(2) phases of capitalist growth; why one should expect growth to be slower now than during the 1950s and 1960s;

(3) growth in the third world; the weaknesses of the statistical documentation in this field; the diversity of experiences, many of them rather disappointing; theories to explain them;

(4) the interrelationship between inequalities and development; the appropriate policies for reducing inequalities;

(5) why the accumulation of capital, both material and human, remains a determining factor of economic growth;

(6) the structural changes that are required in various regions of the world in order to permit future growth;

(7) how agricultural progress can be stimulated in developing countries;

(8) the crucial role of technical progress; how it can best be promoted by public support or by price incentives;

(9) the long-term transition from fossil to non-fossil sources of energy; why collaboration between physicists and economists is required;

---

[1] Chaired jointly by E. Malinvaud and S. Tsuru, the Programme Committee consisted of M. Abramovitz, S. Chakravarty, T. Khachaturov, A. Lindbeck, R. C. O. Matthews, Z. Sadowski, R. Solow, O. Sunkel, H. Uzawa and C. von Weizsäcker.

(10) the reorientation of consumption toward resource-saving patterns;

(11) appropriate macroeconomic and structural policies to face the difficulties that growth will now encounter;

(12) international conditions of growth; can the major impetus to development of poor nations come from the inside or does it depend on outside transfers and circumstances?

(13) what is the nature of the demand for a new international economic order? What can be expected from various proposals concerning this new order?

A good many of these topics were again discussed in the sessions concerned with growth within one particularly interesting country, Japan. Attention was also in this case devoted to environmental problems, which perhaps did not receive elsewhere in the Congress the place they should have had. Above all, the quality of these discussions must be noted. Not only has Japanese growth attracted the interest of a number of leading economists throughout the world, but also economic research on this subject within Japan has been booming. The debates exhibited a high scientific and cultural maturity, not less so when Marxists confronted their views or analyses with those of their more classical colleagues.

Looking at this book as a whole and more generally at the work done during the Tokyo Congress, one may of course deplore that some lines of research were not given more attention. In each case the questions then arise: was it because the Programme Committee did not think this particular line had a relevance to the Congress? Or was it because there was very little worth reporting, so that economic research has been unable to make significant progress?

I shall not try to survey the whole field here and to give for each case my personal answers to these challenging questions. I must, however, make a brief reference to the abstract theory of growth, which was almost entirely absent from the Congress. It is fair to say that this was a deliberate choice of the Programme Committee. Since the Congress was intended as a gathering of economists with very varied interests, it seemed wise to concentrate on sub-stantive issues and to neglect, on this occasion, the current research on fundamental abstract theories. Such research is the work of a few mathematical economists and pure theoreticians who have their own meetings. Perhaps one or two survey papers evaluating this work would have been welcome. They will have to be found elsewhere.

As it is, the book well testifies that growth is now a popular subject among economists, that they have succeeded in identifying a number of sub-fields within the study of this general subject and that, on each of the main topics, a methodology exists, as well as substantive results, which can be explained to the layman.

1 Rapid Growth Potential and its Realisation: The Experience of Capitalist Economies in the Postwar Period[1]

Moses Abramovitz
STANFORD UNIVERSITY, USA

Dramatic statements about the remarkable growth of the industrialised market economies are by now superfluous. The forces which account for this notable experience, however, still challenge explanation. And without a well-tested explanation, we are in a poor position to say whether rapid growth has now come to an end or whether it is likely to be resumed. Equally, we are in a poor position to suggest what policies might regenerate and sustain rapid growth were that an agreed aim of public policy.

Although, as said, we do not as yet have a well-tested explanation, a good deal of ground has been cleared, and the elements of a general understanding of the causes of rapid growth have begun to come into view. This being the case, I think it will be useful to try to draw these together as well as I can. This may help us discover how much agreement there is about the factors underlying postwar growth. And it may help us see where the empirical basis of our theories is especially weak and where, therefore, future work ought to be directed.

Both the breadth of this assignment and the limits of my own competence require that I restrict attention to the experience of the industrialised market economies as a group, and, correspondingly, to the common causes which I see behind it. A general view of this experience should help us understand the

[1] I should like to acknowledge the help I have had from Paul David. This paper has benefited not only from his critical reading, but also from his insights, shared during a long collaboration.

I must also acknowledge special intellectual debts to many contributions to the postwar growth literature. These include the growth-accounting calculations of John Kendrick, Edward Denison, Dale Jorgenson and others; the historical and analytical studies of Europe and Japan by Angus Maddison, of Japan by Ohkawa and Rosovsky, of France by Carré, Dubois and Malinvaud, and of Italy by G. Fuá, as well as still unpublished studies of the UK by Matthews, Feinstein and Odling-Smee, of Sweden by R. Bentzel and of Germany by Bombach and Gerfin; also the studies of structural change and the role of labour supply by Kuznets, Kindleberger and Kaldor and the collaborative Brookings volumes on the postwar economies of Britain and Japan.

differences among countries in their rates of growth, in so far as those differences have a systematic character. But I do not try to account for the utterly extraordinary speed of Japanese expansion or what is, from some perspectives, the equally divergent relative slackness of the British pace.

In this paper, I confine attention to one aspect of growth: namely, labour productivity as measured by output per worker. I treat the forces determining rapidity of productivity growth as falling into two classes: those governing the potential for productivity growth during the postwar era and those controlling the pace at which that potential was exploited. By the potential for productivity growth, I mean, first, the opportunity for progress which is presented by the enlargement in technological and organisational knowledge which took place in the course of the postwar period. I mean, second, the opportunity for productivity growth which exists when a country, relatively advanced in the state of its political, commercial and financial institutions and in its degree of technical competence, nevertheless finds itself behind the industrial leader in the level of achieved productivity. In that case, the country's degree of initial backwardness in productivity can be regarded as the rough measure of a gap between existing and potential productivity, and therefore, of the advance potentially open to it in the course of capital turnover and expansion and accompanying economic reorganisation. On the other hand, the absorption and application of potential advances in productivity — whether these are contemporaneously generated or available from a pre-existing, still unexploited stock of knowledge — involve several responsive economic actions: accumulation of both tangible and human capital per worker, together with a change in design of structures and equipment and content of education; enlargement of the scale of production, accompanied by greater specialisation of productive establishments, worker tasks and machine designs; change in the industrial distribution of labour, capital and output; and research and development effort to adapt new techniques to the resource endowments and scale constraints of particular markets and economies. The pace of exploitation of potential productivity growth should, therefore, be viewed as controlled by the speeds at which these economic responses take place and, at the next remove, by the conditions governing those speeds of response.

My paper's general thesis is simply stated. A special, but transitory, set of circumstances made the postwar potential for productivity growth strong and enabled developed countries to exploit that potential rapidly, in concert and over a long period. Some of the favouring circumstances arose from the Second World War itself, some from the frustation of normal growth caused by war, political upheaval and depression during the longer period beginning in 1914; some reflected the stage of development which a number of industrialised countries had reached; and some rested on national and international political and economic arrangements which have now broken down. Of course, there are other forces — an expanding technological frontier, rising education, growing managerial competence — which continue to work steadily for material progress. However, the importance of the essentially transitory influences in postwar development and the fact that these have now weakened and, in some cases, disappeared make the prospects for an early renewal of the postwar growth drive at the same rapid pace uncertain and dubious. Though it is not directly argued in the present paper, that seems to me to be the somewhat gloomy implication of my analysis. Are those prospects more dubious and uncertain than they were in 1950? That is, in a sense, the more hopeful question which our considerable ignorance still permits us to entertain.

I POSTWAR POTENTIAL

As already said, the potential for productivity growth during a period has two elements: first, the current pace of advance of productive knowledge; and, second, the initial gap between existing and best practice. I take these up in order.

A Acceleration in the growth of productive knowledge

There are no direct measures of the stock of productive knowledge, so no one can make secure judgements about its rate of advance. It is a question basic to our subject, however, and one must adopt some view about it, however provisional. In this very tentative spirit, I argue that the pace of progress in productive knowledge during the postwar years was at least as fast as in any earlier, comparably long period. Indeed it may well have been more rapid. Two sorts of considerations support this position.

First, it is consistent with many impressions and observations about the contemporary world – that there has been a speed-up in the pace of scientific progress generally; that levels of education are higher; that the numbers and proportions of scientists and engineers in industry or concerned with industrial applications have grown; that science-based industry has become more important; that business administration has become more systematic and is staffed with better-trained people; that the enlarged scale of economic activity, in the postwar period itself provided a wider basis of experience and, therefore, of improvement.

Second, it is consistent with the only aggregate measures we have – indirect and uncertain as these may be – namely, the residuals in the growth-accounting calculations. For this purpose, the relevant accounts are those for the USA. That is not because America is the source of all technological progress, but because, as Denison and Chung say, 'it seems unlikely that in the U.S. economy . . . the rate at which advances were incorporated departed much from the worldwide rate of new advance'.[1]

Proceeding from this assumption, we may note, first, that estimates for 'conventional'[2] total factor productivity growth, made with different bodies

[1] Edward F. Denison and Wm. K. Chung, *How Japan's Economy Grew So Fast* (Washington, DC: Brookings Institution, 1976) p. 79.

[2] By 'conventional' total factor productivity I mean an estimate of output per unit of total factor input in which inputs are not adjusted for differences in 'quality'.

of data and by different students, suggest that such advance was distinctly faster in the postwar period or, more generally, since the 1920s than it was before the First World War.[1] Denison's growth accounts, which go further and allow for intensity of work, longer schooling, better resource allocation and economies of scale, also suggest a similar acceleration in his final residual which he himself names 'Advances of Knowledge'.[2] The difference is of the

[1] USA GROWTH RATES OF TOTAL FACTOR PRODUCTIVITY, PRIVATE DOMESTIC ECONOMY (% per annum)

	Kendrick			Abramovitz-David
	Compound Rates			
	Net weighted	*Net unweighted*	*Gross weighted*	*Gross unweighted*
	(1)	*(2)*	*(3)*	*(4)*
1889–1919	1·3	1·65		1800–55	0·3
1919–48	1·8	2·03		1855–1905	0·5
1948–66	2·5	2·84		1905–27	1·5
				1927–67	1·9
TREND RATES				
1889–1916	1·03			
1916–29	2·29	2·2		
1936–66	2·33	2·7	2·09	
1948–66	2·33	2·6	2·09	

Sources: Columns (1), (3) and trend rates Column (2): Kendrick, *Postwar Productivity Trends in the United States, 1948–1969* (New York: Columbia University Press for NBER, 1973) Tables 3–2 and 3–4. Compound rates Column (2), *ibid.*, Table A–19b, extrapolated on the basis of Kendrick, *Productivity Trends in the U.S.* (NBER, 1961) Table A–XXII, Supplement. Column (4), M. Abramovitz and P. A. David, 'Economic Growth in America: Historical Parables and Realities,' *De Economist*, 121, no. 3 (1973) Tables 1 and 2.

'Net' figures combine labour and capital inputs with net share weights; 'gross' figures use gross share weights; 'weighted' figures combine labour and capital inputs by industry with weights proportionate to average net compensation per unit; unweighted figures are based on simple aggregations of man hours and net capital stock.

[2] Making use of Edward F. Denison's estimates for 1909–29, 1929–48, and 1948–69 and adjusting them for comparability yields the following estimates of the effect of advances in knowledge actually incorporated into production in the USA on the growth rates of national income per worker (figures in per cent per annum)

Line:	1909–29	1929–48	1948–69
(1) Denison-based estimates	0·15	0·62	1·19
(2) Alternative estimates	0·82	1·36	1·72

Source: Line (1): For 1929–48 and 1948–69, the figures are from E. F. Denison, *Accounting for U.S. Economic Growth, 1929–69,* (Washington, DC: Brookings Institution, 1974) Table 9–4, Columns 2 and 3. For 1909–29, the original figures were

order of 1 percentage point or somewhat more in comparisons between the postwar years and the decades immediately preceding either the 1920s or the First World War. And since, for most of the western industrialised countries, the intervening years constituted something of a growth hiatus imposed by great wars, political upheaval and major depression, this is the relevant comparison.

It is perhaps unnecessary to recite all the reasons which make such residuals unreliable measures of technological progress.[1] So far as they go,

[1] I have in mind not only the sensitivity of residuals to errors in reported data, but also serious uncertainties of principle. Are Denison's estimates of gains from longer schooling or better allocation sound? How much should really be allowed for economies of scale, and should the allowance be constant over time? Do Denison's figures allow adequately for the effect of change in the composition of capital by durability and other characteristics affecting true social rates of return? (Cf. L. R. Christensen and D. W. Jorgenson, *Measuring the Performance of the US Economy, 1929–69*, Social Systems Research Institute, University of Wisconsin, February 1973.) How much of the contribution of technological progress itself is hidden because the estimates rely on an assumption that such progress is Hicks neutral? (Cf. Abramovitz and P. A. David, op. cit.)

taken from Denison's *The Sources of Economic Growth in the US* (New York: Committee for Economic Development, 1962) Supplement Paper No. 13, Table 32, Column 1. These were adjusted by the present writer to make them comparable with the estimates for later years. For this purpose, I made use of a comparison provided by Denison for 1929–57 between estimates of sources of growth based respectively on the data and procedure used in his earlier volume and those used in his later volume (see, *Accounting for US Economic Growth*, Appendix S and Tables S–1 and S–3).

Line (2): The 'Alternative estimates' in this line are intended to test whether the acceleration of knowledge indicated by the Denison-based figures derive from some of the more controversial elements in the Denison calculations. The 'Alternative', first, eliminates his 'efficiency offset for decline in hours' (including his 'shift offset to hours decline'). Next, Denison's estimates of the contribution of longer schooling continue to be questioned. Recent work (cf. Paul Taubman and T. Wales, *Higher Education and Earnings,* New York: NBER General Series 101) implies that the Denison figures overestimate the contribution of education by failing to make enough allowance for the effect of differences in 'ability' and other correlates of education. The 'screening model' presents a rival theory which makes educational earnings differentials a basis for a private return to longer schooling but not for a social return. My 'alternative' recognises these doubts by reducing the Denison-based contribution by one-half. Third, doubts have been raised as to whether the contribution of economies of scale are to be associated only with output growth due to factors other than advance of knowledge itself or whether, as Denison contends, they should be associated equally with output growth from all sources. The 'alternative' reduces the contribution of scale economies. Finally, the 'alternative' recognises that, for the period 1909–29, there is a rival figure for the growth rate of national income based on the estimates of John Kendrick, who built on Kuznets' earlier work. The Kendrick-based growth rate is significantly higher than the Department of Commerce figures used by Denison. (See Denison, *The Sources of Economic Growth in the US,* Table 32, Footnote 1.) I do not contend that the 'alternative estimate' of the contributions of advance of knowledge is better than the Denison-based figures. I merely note that adjustments of the latter to allow for controversial elements do not change the conclusion to which they point: the increase in the effect of advance of knowledge on output growth between 1909–29 and 1948–69 remains approximately 1 percentage point.

however, they are not contradicted by other evidence, and they are consistent with the idea that contemporaneously generated productive knowledge helped provide a strong potentiality for rapid postwar productivity growth among industrialised countries.

B Greater 'backwardness' in Europe and Japan

When the postwar period opened, the actual levels of labour productivity in Japan, north-west Europe and Italy were especially low compared with those which their technological tradition, human skills and governmental, commercial and financial institutions were capable of supporting. This gap between capability and achievement constituted a second source of potentially rapid postwar growth.

To establish orders of magnitude, we can compare labour productivities in the various industrialised countries with that in the USA. One can determine the relative levels in 1950 on the basis of two closely related sets of figures. One set, provided by Denison,[1] is based on the well-known OECD/Gilbert comparisons of output with uniform US 1955 price weights. This set includes the USA and eight European countries. The other is an extrapolation back to 1950 from a 1965 comparison by Angus Maddison[2] which is itself an extension of the same OECD/Gilbert data. This set includes the same countries covered by Denison plus Japan and Canada. Differences between the two sets of figures for 1950 are negligible for the kinds of uses to which I put them.

Since the Maddison data cover two additional countries, I have used them as the basis for further extrapolation back to 1913 and forward to 1970 using figures for output per man in which outputs are aggregated with national price weights.[3] See Table 1:1.

According to these figures, the average labour productivity of the ten other countries in 1913 was about 60 per cent of the US level. The variance was

[1] Edward F. Denison, *Why Growth Rates Differ* (Washington, DC: Brookings Institution, 1967) Table 2–5, p. 23.

[2] Angus Maddison, 'Comparative Productivity Levels in the Developed Countries', *Banco Nazionale del Lavoro Quarterly Review*, no. 83 (December 1967).

[3] I have developed tables of relatives of output per worker based on US price weights starting from the Maddison estimates on two bases. One starts from Maddison's 1965 figures in which his estimates for employment are adjusted to make the proportion of women employed in agriculture conform to the female share of employment in non-agricultural industries (op. cit., Table 16). These are the basis for the summary figures in Table 1:1 of this text. The other starts from Maddison's 1965 relatives based on unadjusted employment data (op. cit. Table 9, with relatives converted to the base, US = 100). Maddison obtained his 1965 productivity relatives by extrapolating the OECD/Gilbert 1955 figures for output with US price weights according to the movement of output with national price weights as estimated by OECD, and then dividing by estimates of employment based on figures from OECD sources. I moved the Maddison 1965 figures back to 1960, 1955 and 1950 and forward to 1970 according to the movements of OECD output with national price weights and OECD employment data. The results of further extrapolations to 1913, shown in Table 1:1 of this volume were based on output and employment figures from national sources.

wide. These figures reflect the high level at which the USA had started its own industrialisation some 75 to 100 years earlier and the varying number of decades which then intervened before the industrialisation process had become well launched elsewhere. Between 1913 and 1950, the average productivity relative fell by about 20 per cent as a result of the combined effects of the First World War, the Second World War and the political and economic disturbances in the immediate aftermath of both wars. The rise in the relative during the Depression was illusory gain. Compared with potential, progress in almost all countries slowed down, but since under-utilisation of manpower was so much greater in the USA than elsewhere, there is a false

---

Denison (*Why Growth Rates Differ*, Tables 2–5) has worked out a third set of estimates of output per employed worker with 1955 US price weights for 1950, 1955, 1960 and 1964. Denison used the OECD/Gilbert *et al.* estimates of output for 1950 and, with the exception of consumer goods, also for 1955. He provides the following description of his method of deriving the proper figures for consumer goods output in 1955 and for total GNP in 1960 and 1964:

> Gilbert and Associates brought their 1950 estimates in United States prices forward to 1955 by a quite summary procedure. The 1950 national product in United States prices of each of the European countries was divided into twelve broad product categories including a five-way breakdown of consumption. For each category they assumed the percentage change from 1950 to 1955 to be the same in constant United States prices as in the constant prices of the country concerned. I have used their methodology in this study to obtain estimates for 1960 for components other than consumption. Instead of reweighting consumption on a five way basis, I used an indirect procedure to approximate the difference between the 1950–60 movement of consumption valued in United States and in national prices [Denison, *Why Growth Rates Differ*, p. 20; his 'indirect procedure' is described in his Section II, Chapter 17].

The three sets of figures are much alike. The rank order correlation coefficients between the relative standings of the several countries in 1950 according to the several sets of estimates are, as follows:

	Coefficient
Maddison-based adjusted and unadjusted	0·97
Denison and Maddison-based unadjusted	1·0
Denison and Maddison-based adjusted	0·95

At the same time, the levels and movements of the three sets of relatives were very similar. The figures in the table that follows show the unweighted means of the relative of the various countries and, in parentheses, the relative variance among the relatives. The USA is excluded uniformly.

	1950	*1960*	*1970*
Ten countries			
Maddison-based adjusted	48·4 (0·096)	57·0 (0·053)	69·8 (0·014)
Maddison-based unadjusted	47·4 (0·109)	55·5 (0·058)	67·6 (0·014)
Eight countries			
Denison	49·9 (0·040)	56 (0·017)	–
Maddison-based adjusted	49·2 (0·029)	57·5 (0·017)	70·4 (0·017)
Maddison-based unadjusted	48·1 (0·036)	56·2 (0·017)	68·5 (0·012)

TABLE 1:1 OUTPUT PER WORKER IN 1965 $US MEASURED AT US RELATIVE PRICES, 1913–70
(Means and Relative Variance of the Relatives of Nine or Ten Countries Compared with the USA (USA = 100))

	1913	1929	1938	1950	1955	1960	1965	1970
9 countries excl. Japan								
Mean	65·1			51·7	53·9	59·8	62·3	70·6
Relative variance	0·053			0·048	0·044	0·026	0·017	0·014
9 countries excl. Germany								
Mean	59·8	54·3	58·5	48·5				
Relative variance	0·102	0·068	0·036	0·109				
10 countries								
Mean	61·2			48·4	50·8	57·0	60·1	69·8
Relative variance	0·096			0·096	0·078	0·053	0·029	0·014

Source: See Footnote 3, pp. 6–7. Maddison-based table of relatives with employment of women in agriculture adjusted to share in non-agriculture.

Means and variances calculated excluding the USA.

appearance of catch-up.

The measured decline between 1913 and 1950 in productivity relative to potential was, in a sense, greater than these measures suggest. The US advantage in 1913 rested in part on a favourable man-land ratio which other countries, except Canada, presumably could never match. By 1950, proportions of employment devoted to farming had become smaller throughout the group and very much smaller in the USA.[1] The US productivity advantage in 1950, therefore, rested more nearly completely on its larger stock of reproducible capital per man and on the various elements underlying the efficiency of labour and capital in regard to which it is open to other countries to overtake it sooner or later.

The figures, next, carry the strong suggestion that the large productivity gap of 1913 and its enlargement during the disturbed years between then and 1950 did, in fact, constitute a strong potentiality for rapid postwar growth in the less advanced countries. In the next twenty years, these countries' productivity grew distinctly more rapidly than did that in the USA, although American labour productivity was rising as fast as ever and much more rapidly than before 1913. The mean productivity relative of the other countries rose from about 50 per cent to about 70 per cent of the US level between 1950 and 1970. At the same time, the variance among the follower countries declined by more than five-sixths (by seven-tenths excluding Japan). In general, the less productive the country in 1950, the more rapidly its productivity rose.[2]

[1] The share of workers engaged in agriculture in the USA fell from 32 per cent in 1910 to 12 per cent in 1950 (Kuznets, *Modern Economic Growth*, Table 3.2). The average share in nine other advanced countries fell from 35 per cent at various dates in the first decade of the century to 21 per cent at various dates between 1947 and 1952 (ibid., except Japan, for which see Ohkawa and Rosovsky, *Japanese Economic Growth*, Basic Statistical Table 15).

[2] The rise in the mean relative standing, as measured in Table 1:1, may exaggerate somewhat the true rise as this would appear in figures consistently valued at constant US relative prices, but the qualitative conclusion holds.

In Table 1:1 the relative productivity standings of 1950 with output measured with US price weights are, in effect, extrapolated to 1970 by the movement of national productivity figures with national price weights. Since, in general, the output growth rates of poorer countries with output weighted with national price relatives are higher than those calculated from output weighted consistently with US price weights, the rise in the productivity relatives as shown in Table 1:1 is biased upwards. We can get an idea of the importance of the bias from the results of the new study by Kravis and Associates *(A System of International Comparisons of Gross Product and Purchasing Power*, Baltimore: Johns Hopkins University Press, 1975, Table 1.6) which, for three of the countries of concern to us, repeats for 1970 the work of Gilbert and Associates for 1950. The new study provides a comparison of relatives of output *per capita* in 1950 and 1970 with outputs measured with own price weights and US weights respectively. The percentage increase in the average of the *per capita* relatives for France, Germany and Italy with US weights was 69 per cent of the increase with outputs measured in own weights. (The Kravis study also provided information for the UK, but since its change was so small, it seemed better to neglect it.) We may use this ratio to adjust the rise in

The same results emerge from measures of rank correlation between countries' labour productivity growth rates during successive periods and their initial relative productivity levels. The association is highest ($\rho_r = -0.9$) for the two decades 1950–70 taken together, somewhat less high ($\rho_r = -0.8$) for 1950–60 and lower ($\rho_r = -0.6$) for the 1960s alone. (See Table 1:2.)

That the association should be closer over two decades than over either one is not hard to understand. Some countries recovered from the war and its ιftermath more quickly and launched themselves into their postwar growth process sooner than others. Those which did relatively less well in the first decade by comparison with their initial standing tended to do better in the next. That the association of growth with initial standings should have been weaker in the 1960s than in the 1950s is again what one should expect. The potentiality which backwardness affords for growth may be thought to weaken as catch-up proceeds (though, as we shall see, that is not necessarily so). More important, the differences among the backward countries had become much smaller by 1960 than they had been in 1950. The relative variances of Table 1:1 provide one indication. According to Denison's estimates, the productivity indexes of five of the six north-west European Continental countries in 1960 fell within a range running from 56 to 61 per cent of the US level – under 10 per cent of their mean level. No one can suppose that differences so small are indicative of significant differences in growth potential. Moreover all the industrialised countries except Canada continued to gain on the USA. And the remaining broad differences among countries in relative productivity levels – as between Japan, Italy, north-west Europe, Canada – were accompanied by growth-rate differences which varied consistently and markedly in the inverse order as expected.[1]

The record of postwar growth, therefore, appears to be consistent with the view that relative backwardness, for countries with the proper apparatus of governmental and commercial institutions, with educated and skilled populations and advanced technological capabilities, is an important aspect of growth potential which shaped the postwar record. I have already argued, however,

[1] Since growth rates are calculated as rates of increase between standings at terminal dates, errors in the estimates of such standings will generate errors in the derivation growth rates. If errors at both terminal dates were random and if those at the end-year were independent of those at the initial year, the inverse correlations between initial-year standings and subsequent growth rates would be biased upward. The high coefficients we observe would be too high and the lower coefficient for 1960–70 might not be significant. But if errors at both dates were random and independent, there would on that account be no tendency for the variance of standings about the mean to decline between initial and end-year dates. The error bias would then run against the very marked decline in variance which we observe. I conclude, therefore, that there was, in fact, a strong, significant inverse correlation between initial year standings and subsequent growth rates.

the average productivity level in Table 1:1. If we did, the 1970 relative in Table 1:1 would have been 63·4 instead of 69·8.

TABLE 1:2 COEFFICIENTS OF RANK CORRELATIONS BETWEEN
THE LABOUR PRODUCTIVITY GROWTH RATES AND RELATIVE
PRODUCTIVITY LEVELS OF ELEVEN COUNTRIES

A *Growth rates 1950–70 and relative levels in 1950*	
1 Maddison-based levels, adjusted	–0·91
2 Maddison-based levels, unadjusted	–0·91
3 Denison levels	–0·89[a]
B *Growth rates 1950–60 and relative levels in 1950*	
1 Maddison-based levels, adjusted	–0·80
2 Maddison-based levels, unadjusted	–0·82
3 Denison levels	–0·80[a]
C *Growth rates 1960–70 and relative levels in 1960*	
1 Maddison-based levels, adjusted	–0·61
2 Maddison-based levels, unadjusted	–0·67
3 Denison levels	–0·65[a]

[a]Denison did not provide estimates of productivity levels for Japan and Canada. They were given arbitrary ranks of 1 (lowest) and 10 (next to the highest) respectively according to the showing of the Maddison-based data. There is no reason to think that direct estimates would have yielded any different result.

Source: The ranks of countries according to their productivity levels were obtained from the sources cited in Footnotes 1 and 2 on page 6 and further described in Footnote 3 on p. 6. See also note *a* to Table 1:2 of the text, above.

The ranks of countries according to their productivity growth rates are based on OECD data for output and employment with extensions as follows:

Output (gross domestic product) obtained by linking data for 1950 (or earliest available date) through 1968 from OECD, *National Accounts, 1950–68* to later data for 1968 through 1970 from OECD, *National Accounts, 1960–71.*

Employment: in general, data for 1957–8 from OECD, *Labor Force Statistics, 1957–68* were extrapolated forward to 1970 by the movement of data from OECD, *Labor Force Statistics, 1961–72* and backwards as far as possible by the movement of data from OECD, *Manpower Statistics, 1950–62.* In a few cases, other data were used, as follows:

France:	1955 OECD data extrapolated back to 1950 by data from Carré, Dubois and Malinvaud, *French Economic Growth* (Stanford: Stanford University Press, 1975) Appendix Table 4.
Italy:	1955 OECD data extrapolated back to 1950 by data from Fua (ed.), *Lo Sviluppo Economico in Italia,* vol. III, Table XII–2.4.
Switzerland:	1960 OECD figure was extrapolated directly to 1950 by data from OECD, *Labour Force Statistics, 1956–66.*
Canada:	The 1957 OECD was extrapolated to 1950 by data from Canadian Statistical Review, 1963 Supplement, *Historical Summary,* Table 14 augmented by members in the Armed Forces from Historical Statistics of Canada, Series C–48.

that it is only potential, a permissive not sufficient condition for rapid growth. The force of this distinction, is apparent when we consider the common observation that, if relative backwardness were by itself the governing determinant of growth, one would expect that the labour productivity growth rates of the follower countries would decline as the US lead was gradually reduced. But there is no evidence of a general marked retardation in postwar labour productivity growth before the 1970s.

The proximate cause of this is now apparent. As Christensen, Cummings and Jorgenson have now made clear, the 1960s saw a great investment boom in Europe and Japan in which growth rates of capital stock per worker rose above the high rates of the 1950s and in which the composition of capital shifted toward higher-yielding assets. The effect was to raise or sustain labour productivity growth in the fast-growing countries, a growth which would otherwise have declined markedly in the European countries, and risen by little in Japan, even if total productivity growth had been unaffected by slower capital accumulation.[1] I shall argue below, however, that the pace at which countries can exploit their potential for productivity advance is itself governed by investment and growth of capital. If the investment boom of the 1960s had been less pronounced, total factor productivity growth would also have been slower.

In addition to the speed-up in capital accumulation per worker, other developments took place in the course of the postwar period which helped to quicken the pace at which potential productivity could be realised. These emerge in Section II, below. I contend, therefore, that the retardation which one might otherwise expect to accompany catch-up was avoided during the 1960s by conditions which favoured capital investment and by these and other developments supporting more rapid exploitation of opportunities for modernisation.

II SOURCES AND PROCESSES

We can learn something more about backwardness as potential by considering the proximate sources from which the relative productivity gains of the poorer countries were obtained. This will also help us identify the processes through which catch-up and, indeed, contemporaneously generated progress operated and so enable us to go on to consider the factors which permitted those processes to run at a rapid pace.

---

[1] I depend on the following estimates for the growth of output per man and of the contributions of growing capital intensity and total factor productivity derived from L. R. Christensen, Dianne Cummings and D. W. Jorgenson, *Economic Growth, 1947–1973: An International Comparison,* Harvard Institute for Economic Research, Discussion Paper No. 521 (December 1976) Tables 11, 12, 13 and the various country tables in the Appendix. Quality of capital refers to an estimated change in capital service per unit due to shifts in the composition of capital stock between asset classes with characteristically different gross rental rates. Labour quality represents an allowance for the rise of labour service associated with longer schooling. Growth rates of labour and capital services are weighted by gross income shares (I have omitted figures for Korea, which the authors also estimate, because that country is not otherwise considered in the present paper. Its record is similar to that of the other fast-growing countries):

My point of departure is the calculation of 'sources of growth' carried out by Denison. His tables include three classes of contributions which are plausibly associated with backwardness itself. His 'improved allocation of resources' includes the effects of shifts of labour from agricultural to non-agricultural employment and from non-farm self-employment to dependent

CONTRIBUTIONS TO GROWTH OF REAL PRIVATE DOMESTIC PRODUCT PER WORKER (percentage points per annum)

	Product per worker	*Capital stock per worker*	*Quality of capital*	*Capital services per worker*	*Hours and quality of labour*	*Total factor productivity*
	(1)	*(2)*	*(3)*	*(4) = (2) + (3)*	*(5)*	*(6)*
Japan						
1952–60	4·1	−0·2	0·5	0·3	0·5	3·4
1960–73	8·2	2.4	1·2	3·6	−0·1	4·5
Change	4·1	2·6	0·8	3·4	−0·6	1·1
Italy						
1925–60	4·3	0·6	0·1	0·7	0·3	3·4
1969–73	4·0	1·6	0·2	1·8	−0·4	2·6
Change	−0·3	1·0	0·1	1·1	−0·7	−0·8
Germany						
1950–60	6·0	1·8	0·0	1·8	−0·6	4·7
1960–73	5·6	2·7	0·2	2·9	−0·4	3·0
Change	−0·4	0·9	0·2	1·1	0·2	−1·7
France						
1950–60	5·1	1·5	0·3	1·8	0·3	2·9
1960–73	5·3	1·9	0·5	2·4	−0·1	3·0
Change	0·2	0·4	0·2	0·6	−0·4	0·1
The Netherlands						
1951–60	4·1	1·0	0·4	1·4	0·4	2·3
1960–73	4·8	1·6	0·9	2·5	−0·3	2·6
Change	0·7	0·6	0·5	1·1	−0·7	0·3
UK						
1955–60	3·3	1·3	0·4	1·7	0·2	1·5
1960–73	4·0	1·7	0·2	1·9	0·2	2·1
Change	0·7	0·4	−0·2	0·2	0·0	0·6
Canada						
1947–60	4·0	1·6	0·7	2·3	0·0	1·7
1960–73	2·9	0·7	0·5	1·2	−0·1	1·8
Change	−1·1	−0·9	−0·2	−1·1	−0·1	0·1
USA						
1947–60	2·1	0·8	0·2	1·0	−0·3	1·1
1960–73	1·9	0·3	0·3	0·6	0·0	1·1
Change	−0·2	−0·5	0·1	−0·4	0·3	0·0

employment in larger factories and commercial establishments.[1] His 'economies of scale associated with income elasticities' measures one part of the gain from borrowing the more advanced technology of richer countries, a part which is supposedly dependent on the expansion of the market for consumer goods with income-elastic demand. His 'changes in the lag in application of knowledge, general efficiency and errors and omissions' includes the effects of non-scale-dependent modernisation either in the course of capital replacement and expansion or by the borrowing of technology not necessarily embodied in tangible capital. (This last is, for the countries behind the USA, Denison's ultimate residual.) These three sources together generally accounted for more than half,[2] and in France, Germany and Italy more than

---

[1] It also includes the effect of reduction of international trade barriers, but, in Denison's estimates, that is a tiny source.

[2]   SOURCES OF DIFFERENCES IN GROWTH RATES OF NATIONAL INCOME PER PERSON EMPLOYED BETWEEN USA 1948–69 AND JAPAN 1953–71 AND BETWEEN USA AND THREE EUROPEAN COUNTRIES,[a] 1950–62

Excess over USA *(in percentage points per annum)*	*3 European countries*[a] *1950–62*	*Japan* *1953–71*[b]
1 Standardised growth rate	2·18	4·79
2 Total Inputs	0·29	1·82
(a) Hours and age-sex composition	0·20	0·66
(b) Education	−0·15	−0·07
(c) Non-residential reproducible capital[c]	0·49	1·26
(d) Dwellings and other capital[d]	−0·24	−0·02
3 Improved allocation[e]	0·79	0·65
4 Total input and improved allocation	1·08	2·47
5 First residual [= line (1)−(4)]	1·09	2·32
(a) Economies of scale (A) (US prices)[f]	0·23	0·64
(b) Economies of scale (B) (associated with income elasticities)[g]	0·66	0·88
6 Second residual	0·17	0·80
(a) Advance of knowledge and n.e.c. in USA[h]	0	0

(b) Changes in the lag in the application
       of knowledge, general efficiency,
       errors and omissions, etc.
	0·17	0·80

7 Sum of 3 sources associated with catch- up [line 3 + line 5(b) + line 6(b)]	1·62	2·33
8 Standardised growth rate less line 5(a) [see text]	1·95	4·15
9 Ratio: line 7 ÷ line 8	0·83	0·56

three-quarters, of the excess of productivity growth in the poorer countries over that in the USA.

These figures are, in one sense, lower bounds on the contribution to fast productivity growth from catch-up-connected sources because they allow nothing for the support which opportunities for catch-up lent to rapid capital accumulation by supporting the rate of return to capital. If, say, half the excess contribution of growing capital per man in the poorer countries over that in the USA were so attributable, virtually the whole of the differential productivity growth rate would be accounted for. The figure for France, Germany and Italy together would be 95 per cent and that for Japan, 71 per cent.

The Denison figures suggest that there was not merely an empirical association between productivity levels and rates of growth, but that the proximate

---

[a]Average of France, Germany and Italy. Growth of national income and sources were combined by unweighed arithmetic averages.
[b]Compared with USA in 1948–69.
[c]Non-residential structures, equipment and inventories.
[d]Includes international assets and land.
[e]Includes contraction of agricultural inputs, non-agricultural self-employment and reduction in international trade barriers.
[f]Effects of expansion of national markets measured in US prices and independent growth of local markets.
[g]See text for explanation.
[h]Assumed to be the same in other countries as in USA.

Sources: 1950–62: From country tables in Denison, *Why Growth Rates Differ,* Chapter 21. German figures (or standardised growth rate adjusted downward to reflect Denison's estimates of the contribution in 1950–5 of 'capital balancing' and the difference between 1950–62 and 1955–60 in the change in the lag in application of knowledge, etc. Figures for the USA were adjusted to reflect Denison's later revisions. See his *Accounting for US Economic Growth,* Table S–2.
Japan, 1953–71: Denison and Chung, *How Japan's Economy Grew So Fast,* Table 5–1.
USA, 1948–69: Denison, *Accounting for US Economic Growth, 1929–69,* Table 9–7.

Note that the table above follows Denison in subtracting the extraordinary gains enjoyed by Germany between 1950 and 1955 due to 'balancing' its capital stock and because in that early period it was still overcoming inefficiencies connected with the aftermath of war. With these sources included, Germany's rate of catch-up would appear considerably more rapid and the average rate for the three countries somewhat more so.

sources of rapid growth are plausibly connected with relative backwardness. Viewed as a guide to the processes involved in exploiting productivity potential, however, Denison's sources also present certain difficulties.

To my mind, these centre in his ingenious estimates of 'economies of scale associated with income elasticities'. Denison's calculations[1] proceed from the well-established observations that shares of different kinds of products in the consumer expenditures of different countries are inversely related to their relative prices and that patterns of both prices and expenditures converge as the incomes of poorer countries rise relatively. Denison attributes the convergence of expenditure patterns to the similarities of income elasticities of demand and the convergence of price structures to the increasing ability of the faster-growing poorer countries to exploit the scale-dependent technologies earlier discovered and applied by the richer countries. As Denison's calculations of 'economies of scale associated with income elasticities' are constructed, this source contributes so much of the productivity growth of the pursuing countries that little remains in his ultimate residuals to be attributed to 'changes in the lag in the application of knowledge, general efficiency . . .' etc.

There is, however, another explanation for the convergence of price structures.[2] Consider the well-known difference between the prices of tradable and non-tradable goods in open economies with fixed exchange rates. Subject to the usual qualifications, the absolute prices of tradables are everywhere the same. Fixed exchange rates, however, ensure that average money wage rates are higher in the more productive countries, a difference which is necessarily reflected in the relative prices of labour-intensive, low productivity non-tradables. These tend to be relatively high in the high money-wage rich countries. Since such countries consume relatively more of the tradable durables than of the non-tradable, labour-intensive, low-productivity products, this helps account for the characteristic differences between price and expenditure structures and for the convergence of price structures as productivity levels converge.[3] The increasing ease of *scale-dependent* technological borrowing is no necessary part of this story.

I do not regard this hypothesis as an exclusive alternative to Denison's view, which I think carries part of the truth. The alternative does suggest, however, that Denison may have relied too much on his own interpretation of the convergence of price structures. If so, there is more room for a significantly large contribution from 'changes in the lag in the application of knowledge' — that is, for productivity growth connected with technological modernisation in the

[1] See Denison, *Why Growth Rates Differ,* pp. 239–45 for a description of his procedures.

[2] Denison himself considers but rejects still another, quite different alternative explanation based on a convergence in the supplies and prices of capital relative to labour as incomes *per capita* converge.

[3] Cf. Ronald I. McKinnon, 'Monetary Theory and Controlled Flexibility in the Foreign Exchanges', *Studies in International Finance,* Princeton (1971).

course of capital replacement and expansion without scale-constraint, as well as with other sorts of technical and organisational diffusion.

Denison's treatment of this subject may also be misleading in another way. His hypothesis makes economies of scale a function of the scale of consumer *expenditures*. The direct and true connection, however, is between efficiency and scale of *production*. Manifestly, there is a relation between patterns of consumer expenditure and of production. Changes in production structure, however, are responsive to more than the income elasticity of consumer demand. They also respond to the growing demand for capital goods in the course of development, to an increasing need for intermediate goods of industrial origin and, perhaps most important, to shifting comparative advantage which, by import substitution and export expansion, enables developing countries to move into those industrial sectors in which scale-dependent technology is important.[1] When, therefore, we consider what causes may have permitted the process of technological diffusion to proceed rapidly since the war, we should keep in mind these broader aspects of structural change.

We can, then, summarise the story to this point, by saying that the potentiality for rapid postwar productivity growth arose from rapid contemporaneous advance in knowledge and from enlarged initial gaps between actual and possible productivity. This potentiality was exploited through several channels:

(1) Substitution of more advanced for obsolescent methods in the course of capital turnover and expansion or, if improved capital goods are unimportant ingredients, simply in the course of reorganising production routines. The opportunity to apply both new and borrowed advanced techniques was, to some extent, scale-dependent. It arose in part, perhaps in substantial part, in connection with the establishment and growth of those industries in which the demand for products is income-elastic. The Denison hypothesis about 'scale economies associated with income elasticities' itself connects with Verdoorn's Law and with Kaldor's emphasis on scale-dependent technical progress associated with industrial growth.[2] The unbalanced growth which is basic to all these hypotheses, however, goes beyond that envisaged by Denison's theory about the high income elasticity of certain classes of consumer goods. It also comprehends the expansion of industries producing machinery and equipment and intermediate goods serving as industrial and agricultural raw materials. It also goes beyond the unbalanced industrial growth generated by the composition of domestic consumption and capital formation and extends to that which rests on import

[1] See Hollis B. Chenery, 'Patterns of Industrial Growth', *American Economic Review*, 50 (September 1960).
[2] Nicholas Kaldor, *Causes of the Slow Rate of Economic Growth of the United Kingdom* (Cambridge University Press, 1966).

substitution and export expansion. The process underlying the exploitation of available scale economies, therefore, involves the entire range of structural changes normally accompanying productivity growth which are described and rationalised by Kuznets[1] and adopted by Kaldor.

(2) Reallocation of labour, and presumably capital as well, from low productivity employment in agriculture and petty trade to more productive occupations in industry and larger-scale commercial establishments. This transfer is again associated with the process of structural change already mentioned.

(3) Capital accumulation, which entered the process in three ways. The first, which represents capital's own, so to speak independent contribution, consists in the increase of productivity associated with an increase of capital per man in an otherwise unchanging economy. Additional capital was also required, however, to permit the adoption of relatively capital-intensive techniques associated with large-scale production and with industrial compared with agricultural employment. Finally, the rate of capital accumulation influenced the pace of technical advance in so far as that rested on the replacement of capital goods, whether to modernise existing establishments or to reorganise production in larger or more specialised units or to establish or expand new lines of production.

III CONDITIONS CONTROLLING THE PACE OF DEVELOPMENT

I turn now to the behaviour of the economic agents which mediate between productivity potential and the pace of realisation. Having in mind the processes of growth just described, I take up three subjects, considering each in relation to this question: What conditions and developments supported the rapid, general and sustained exploitation of the postwar periods' large potential for productivity growth?

A Improved facilities for technological innovation, diffusion and adaptation

The practical application of existing technology demands, first awareness, then appraisal, then commercial acquisition, then adaptation from the form in which it may have been cast in the place of first application to one better suited to the resources, skills, scale of market and style of products of the firms and places to which it is to be spread. Having defined the problem in this way, one can see a number of developments which favoured more rapid diffusion and adaptation than had existed before the Second World War.[2]

[1] Simon Kuznets, *Modern Economic Growth Rate, Structure and Spread* (New Haven: Yale University Press, 1966) Chapter 3.

[2] My comments in this section are supported by evidence and appraisals from a variety of sources. See in particular, OECD, *Gaps in Technology, General Report* and

First, when the Second World War ended, the human capabilities for absorbing and using more advanced technology were better developed. General levels of education were higher, engineers and technicians were more numerous and their relative numbers kept rising during the postwar period itself. Further, as a reflection of the new importance of science-based industry, the need for highly trained engineers and scientists in industry became manifest, and they were more often drawn into leading positions. Longer experience with large-scale enterprise brought more systematic organisation of management. The increasing dependence on schools of business and engineering as training grounds for industrial administrators in America encouraged European countries and Japan to follow a similar practice.

The growing professionalisation of both administrative and technical leadership in business was matched by better facilities for the rapid diffusion of information. The technical and business press at the opening of the postwar period was already larger than it had been, and it expanded rapidly thereafter. The Marshall Plan, with its arrangements for the exchange of American and European productivity missions, was a rapid refresher course for both sides. Thereafter, the perfection of air travel sustained intense international communication.

The restoration of trade and capital movements to something like pre-1913 levels was also important. Revived trade provided practical demonstrations of new products and materials. Foreign competition, encouraged by the liberalisation of trade and payments, the opening of the Common Market and EFTA and the successive rounds of tariff reductions, was a spur to modernisation. When restrictions on capital and other payments had been reduced and when the potentialities of the European and Japanese markets had become clear, US industry became interested in obtaining a share of the business through patent licences, contracts for the transfer of technology, joint ventures and foreign subsidiaries. The Common Market encouraged the same sort of activity among European countries. By contrast with the portfolio investment which had dominated capital transfer to other industrialised countries before 1913, these methods were both carriers of technological knowledge and goads pressing domestic firms to modernise.

Finally, the increasingly scientific basis for industrial technology encouraged the establishment of research facilities by industrial concerns and associations, as well as by governments. These pioneered in the exploration of original advances and also worked to keep firms abreast of developments elsewhere and to adapt them to local circumstances. As time passed, moreover, firms

---

Analytical Reports (Paris, 1968); OECD, *The Conditions for Success in Technological Innovation* (Paris, 1971); L. Nabseth and G. F. Ray (eds), *The Diffusion of New Industrial Processes* (London: Cambridge University Press, 1974) Chapters 1, 2, 11 and *passim*; Carré, Dubois and Malinvaud, op. cit., pp. 208–21, Chapters 9, 14 and p. 495 ff.; Ohkawa and Rosovsky, op. cit., pp. 39–43; 204–16, and Chapter 9; Merton S. Peck and Shuji Tamura, 'Technology', in H. Patrick and H. Rosovsky (eds), *Asia's New Giant* (Washington, DC: Brookings Institution, 1976) Chapter 9.

became better aware of the problems involved in maintaining a proper connection between their R & D establishments and the commercial sides of their business, on the one hand, and the more basic engineering and scientific work of the universities on the other.

Besides helping to explain the generally rapid progress of the postwar years, these developments may provide another group of reasons why the high growth rates established by the mid-1950s should have been sustained for so long instead of suffering the retardation which catch-up is usually supposed to entail. Larger scale of markets and a relative cheapening of capital goods clearly favoured adoption of capital-using technological advances. But it was also true that conditions favoured a speed-up in the spread of information, in the transfer of know-how, and in the work of adapting it to local conditions, as well as increasing European and Japanese participation in original innovation.

B Conditions facilitating structural change

Transformation in the composition of output and employment holds a well-established place in the standard view of the development process. Kuznets has taught us that shifts between the broad sectors are founded on inter-sectoral differences in the income-elasticity of consumer demand; on the expanding roles of the industrial sector as producer of capital goods and of both the industrial and tertiary sectors as producers of intermediate goods and services; and on the advanced countries' growing comparative advantage in the production of industrial products. In these respects, structural change emerges as a necessary concomitant of productivity growth, if not for each country individually, at least for the industrialised countries as a group. In the earlier argument of this paper, however, it also appeared as a direct source of growth in two respects: by providing opportunities for transferring low productivity workers to more productive employments; and by furnishing relatively poor countries with a better chance to borrow technology as their production patterns converge towards those of richer countries in the course of catching up.

The process of structural change proceeds at a pace governed by both demand and supply conditions; and it seems that developments on both sides may have favoured easy and rapid adaptation to the structural requirements of development after the Second World War.

(1) Domestic markets for manufactured goods in Japan and the fast-growing European countries were especially strong and responsive to income growth. This was particularly true of those consumer and producer durables which typify the kinds of goods which had been used in quantity and which were relatively cheap in the USA and which, therefore, held out a particular promise of rapid, scale-dependent

productivity growth if produced in large quantities in the advancing countries. The special strength and responsiveness of these markets rested on several grounds. Stocks were badly depleted at the end of the Second World War. The widespread use of the new consumer durables – motor vehicles and household and other consumer equipment – had been developing in America since the First World War, but the economic and political disturbances from 1913 to 1950 had inhibited their spread to other countries. Once the more well-to-do countries of north-west Europe had regained and surpassed prewar income levels, households could afford to adopt the new durables. Finally, in Italy and Japan, the same process was favoured by the dual structure of these countries. Average incomes in both were, indeed, very low. Had earnings been more evenly distributed, the development of markets for the more durable and expensive types of consumer goods might have proceeded more slowly. Families with a member employed in the modern sectors, however, had incomes and consumption standards which soon approximated north-west European levels. So, in these countries too, the markets for complex consumer manufactures expanded rapidly. In some ways, the markets for producer durables were affected by similar influences, and I comment on that sector later.

(2) The establishment of domestic industries in all the industrialised countries to satisfy the demand for consumer and producer durables and more generally, for heavy industrial products had taken place well before the Second World War. In Europe the beginnings go back into the nineteenth century. There were, however, two noteworthy developments during the decades between 1913 and 1950 when, in an aggregate sense, the gap between Japan and Europe and the USA widened. In Japan, Italy and Germany, heavy industries were rapidly expanded as part of these countries' military programmes. In France, though output itself was restricted, technical preparation went forward.[1] The postwar period, therefore, opened with an industrial framework which required, indeed, to be fleshed out with modern equipment, but was otherwise better prepared to expand the output of durable goods and other heavy industrial products than had been true in the 1920s and earlier.

(3) In most of the industrialised countries, the modern non-agricultural industries had access to large supplies of cheap labour, flexibly responsive to additional demand. In some countries, these reserves of unemployed and of low productivity labour in agriculture and petty

---

[1] Carré *et. al.*, p. 501: 'The depression and the war probably interrupted growth in the relevant industry groups [i.e., the 'industries with a future']. But engineers and technicians continued to work on new techniques, and were ready to develop them rapidly after the war.'

trade were even larger in 1950 than they had been before the war.[1] In others, as in France, there had been a slowdown in rural-urban migration during the Depression and the Second World War which, having regard to the secular trend of population movement toward the city, must have built up the pool of potential migrants. That pool was also fed by the rapid postwar pace of labour-saving technology on the farms. Before the war, productivity growth rates on the farms were typically lower than in industry.[2] In the postwar period, they were much higher absolutely and in some countries matched or surpassed the high productivity growth rates in manufacturing. Finally, Germany, Switzerland, and, to a lesser extent, France and other countries

[1] Ratios of unemployed workers to the sum of non-agricultural wage and salary workers including the unemployed in 1950 were (in percentages):

Belgium	7·0	Netherlands	3·1
Denmark	6·7	Norway	1·0
France	2·6	Italy	17·6
Germany	11·1	UK	1·5

Source: Denison, *Why Growth Rates Differ,* Table 5–1A.

In Japan, the agricultural labour force was 14·3 million, or 44 per cent of the total number of workers in 1940. In 1950, the number was 17·3 million, or 48 per cent of the whole labour force. (Ohkawa and Rosovsky, op. cit., Basic Statistical Table 15.) Territorial change makes comparison difficult for Germany, but it seems likely, given the large inflow of refugees from East Germany and from Polish occupied territory to West Germany immediately after the war, that the West German farm population had also grown. On the slowdown of rural-urban migration in France from 1930 to 1950, see Carré *et al.,* op. cit., Chapter 3, Table 6.

The following illustrate the level of the reserves in 1950:

	France	Germany	Italy	Japan
1 Farm employment as per cent of total employment	29·3	24·8	42·8	48·3
2 Self-employed and unpaid family workers as per cent of civilian non-farm employment	21·4	15·7	31·3	–

Sources: France, Germany, Italy: Denison, op. cit., Table 16.4 and 16.5; Japan: Ohkawa and Rosovsky, op. cit., Basic Statistical Table 15.

[2] In France, the productivity growth rate in agriculture was 1·6 per cent per year from 1896 to 1929; in manufacturing, 2·7 per cent. From 1949 to 1963 the rates were 6·4 per cent and 5·0 per cent respectively. (Carré *et al.,* op. cit., Table 3.10). There was a similar development in Germany according to figures supplied by H. Gerfin, based on Hoffman and the reports of the Sachverstandigenrat. In Japan, the non-agricultural productivity growth rate rose from 2·1 per cent in 1917–37 to 10·1 per cent in 1956–62. The growth rate in agriculture went from 1·5 per cent to 5·4 per cent. (Ohkawa and Rosovsky, op. cit. Table 2.7)

Needless to say, measured productivity growth in agriculture reflected the rapid withdrawal of low-productivity farm workers to satisfy the growing demand for non-farm labour. But consolidation of holdings, mechanisation, fertilisers, chemical insect controls and better seeds were also driving up the productivity of the remaining farm workers.

enjoyed an augmented supply of labour from permanent or temporary immigration.[1]

Access to flexibly responsive labour supplies permitted the manufacturing and non-agricultural sectors generally to expand rapidly without provoking very large increases in wage rates. The increase in capital per worker associated with the relative growth of industry could more easily proceed without depressing the return to capital and checking the growth of profits. Wage restraint based on reserves of labour was also implicated in the process of structural change through its influence on international trade. Whether the increase in a country's domestic demand for durable manufactures is actually translated into expanded production must depend substantially on the course of change in the locus of its comparative advantage in trade. Given the rapid productivity growth associated with the expansion of industry, some shift of advantage towards industrial goods would be likely to occur. But the opportunity to combine productivity growth with additional cheap labour must have speeded up the process of industrial growth through import substitution and export expansion. This was further speeded for the faster-growing countries of Europe and for Japan, although not for the USA and the UK, because exchange rates were fixed before the rapid growth potentials of the former countries were perceived. And it was still further speeded up by the notable advances towards trade liberalisation made in the 1950s and early 1960s.

C Conditions encouraging and sustaining capital investment

Viewed from the standpoint of capital accumulation, the postwar period was an investment boom of unprecedented size both with respect to the rates of growth of stock and to the number of years these high rates were sustained. I have already emphasised the physical and technological opportunities for such a boom which were inherent in the depleted and obsolescent condition of capital at the end of the war. I now ask what postwar conditions facilitated the exploitation of these opportunities and helped to sustain the boom so long.

---

[1] Between 1945 and 1948, Japan received some 6·1 million persons (half-civilian, half-military), amounting to 7·6 per cent of the 1948 population and almost 18 per cent of the gainfully occupied. Between 1945 and 1950, West Germany received some 9 million refugees from the east (C. P. Kindleberger, *Europe's Postwar Growth: The Role of Labour Supply*, Cambridge, Massachusetts: Harvard University Press, 1967, p. 30). Between 1955 and 1961, about 150,000 workers per year came to West Germany from the east, accounting for 27 per cent of the labour force growth in that period (OECD Economic Survey of Germany, 1962). France repatriated 350,000 persons from Algeria in 1962 and had net immigration of 180,000 per year in 1964–8. (Carré *et al.*, op. cit., Chapter 2 and Appendix Tables III and IV). Germany, Switzerland and other northern countries enjoyed a large net immigration of foreign guest workers during the entire postwar period. The proportion of foreign workers in the German labour force rose from 1·3 per cent in 1960 to 10 per cent in 1971 (Statistiches Bundesamt, *Bevolkerung u. Wirtschaft*, 1872–1972, pp. 115, 116).

1 Conditions stemming from growth itself. Some of the more important of these conditions were created by the growth of output and productivity itself. On the side of demand for capital, they were an indirect reflection of the profits promised by investment when capital is in short supply and obsolescent and by other conditions which facilitated modernisation, structural change and capital investment itself. On the side of supply, high rates of household saving reflected the laggard adjustment of expenditures to fast-rising incomes and also the efforts of households to protect cash balances from being eroded by growth-induced inflation. The conservative projections of tax revenues in the fast-growing countries also made governments an unusual source of savings.

I am not in a position to measure the impact of these forces. They are repeatedly cited in analyses of postwar investment and saving,[1] and I do not doubt their importance. Moreover, the strength of some of these factors developed gradually. They may, therefore, have played a part in sustaining investment as some of the conditions which created a great initial demand for capital weakened. None the less, they are, as said, secondary effects of rapid growth itself. They would have played their part whenever growth for other reasons accelerated. I believe, therefore, that in a paper whose main concern is with the causes of rapid postwar growth, I ought to direct attention to other matters.

2 The initial financial condition of firms and households. Investment booms in the past typically took their start during recovery from serious depressions during which inventories were reduced, debts repaid and the financial structures of companies reorganised. As a result, the borrowing power of firms was strengthened. After the war, the financial environment also became immensely favourable to the development of a sustained investment boom. In all the industrialised countries, the real burden of debts had been substantially reduced compared with the value of physical assets, or even eliminated. In the Continental countries, and Japan, indeed, the wartime and postwar inflations essentially wiped out the financial indebtedness of firms and households. As soon as financial markets were reorganised, therefore, firms were willing and able to borrow with little concern for debt burden, and lenders were correspondingly willing to extend credit. In most countries, therefore, credit rationing, rather than concern for credit-worthiness, was the effective constraint on finance in the early postwar period. This initial freedom from debt served to support investment for many subsequent years. It was an underpinning for an investment boom clearly analogous in a qualitative sense to that afforded by the post-Depression origins of earlier booms, but it was quantitatively of a higher order of magnitude.[2]

It is harder to generalise about later experience. Certainly, after an initial

---

[1] See Ohkawa and Rosovsky, op. cit., Chapters 6 and 8; Henry C. Wallich and Mabel Wallich, 'Banking and Finance', in Patrick and Rosovsky (eds), op. cit., pp. 256–64; Carré *et al.,* op. cit., Chapter 9.

[2] Carré *et al.,* op. cit., pp. 313 and 501.

period of high profits and reliance on retained earnings, the debt ratios of corporations began to rise and, in some countries — France, for example — dependence on short-term borrowing increased. The significance of this change is, however, hard to gauge. As Carré and his collaborators say, 'it may be that the development observed is a return to a "normal" situation rather than the gradual establishment of an unfavourable economic condition.'[1]

There is no basis for comparing the postwar financial development systematically with that in earlier investment booms. There is some presumption, however, that the cumulation of debt which normally takes place during a period of heavy investment and serves, after a time, to check expansion, did not reach serious levels in the postwar period.

3 Government support for investment. In all the industrialised market economies, private business firms were the dominant agents of capital formation, but governments participated in different ways and to varying degrees. In Germany, the government's role does not appear to have been very different after the war from what it had been before the advent of the Nazis, possibly because large-scale industry in Germany was already better established than in other countries except for the USA. Moreover, German industry had enjoyed a relatively recent period of profitable expansion during the 1930s and during much of the war under the stimulus of Nazi military preparation and war production. Elsewhere, however, large-scale industry was less developed. France and, to a lesser degree, Italy had suffered longer periods of stagnation more recently. Those countries, and still more Japan, had traditions of regulation and protection which gave governments postwar roles of particular importance.

To appreciate that influence, one must recall that, at the outset, expectations of rapid growth were not common. Few people in Japan or in the Continental countries appreciated the growth potentials of their economies.[2] In the initial atmosphere of uncertainty and indecision, governments acted to provide a necessary impetus to investment. Schumpeter stressed the role of New Men as the entrepreneurial galvanisers of his classic investment booms before the First World War. After the Second World War, there were again New Men, who got their chance in the train of war and defeat and who operated in and through government. France is the type case. Spurred by Jean Monnet and the group who established the Plan, the government committed itself to unprecedentedly large programmes to expand and modernise transport, power and heavy industry generally. Its ability to carry through this programme was strengthened because the scope of state-owned industry had been enlarged by the postwar nationalisations and because it had sufficient control over finance and trade to give effective priority to other heavy industry not directly owned.[3] In Italy, there had also been an enlargement of the public sector because of

[1] Ibid., pp. 320–1, and Chapter 10, *passim.*
[2] Ibid., pp. 278–9, 471; Ohkawa and Rosovsky, op. cit., p. 232.
[3] Carré *et al.,* op. cit., p. 477; also pp. 274–6. The more general influence of the Plan and of French planning is described and appraised in Chapter 14.

the government takeover of industrial facilities both under fascism and after the war. Grouped in ENI and IRI and led by forceful and energetic new personalities, these government-directed corporations also took the lead in supporting the early enlargement of capital investment.

In Japan, the government made itself felt chiefly through the Ministry of International Trade and Industry. The Ministry's purpose and effect appear to have been to provide guidance and to reduce the risks of innovation and investment faced by Japanese business in venturing into so many new lines on such a large scale. It operated by selecting sectors for development, by supporting tariff protection, by choosing firms as instruments for the importation and exploitation of foreign technology and by helping to arrange the industrial combinations needed to ensure a proper scale of operation. Together with other government agencies, its activities served to raise the sights of private business.[1]

These considerations explain something about the otherwise puzzling disjunction between catch-up and sustained rapid growth. Private-sector investment went forward boldly only as the growth potential of the postwar economies became clearly revealed. Governments, therefore, played a crucial role in providing early impetus, which was carried forward later by the rising confidence of private business. Partly for this reason, the investment of the earlier years was somewhat more heavily concentrated in the sectors under government ownership and special influence: that is, transport, power and heavy industry generally. These demanded heavy forward-looking investment which yielded its returns relatively slowly. The private investment of subsequent years could be more largely applied to equipment which both raised the utilisation rate of basic capacity and yielded more immediate returns.

4 Flexible labour supplies again. I have already indicated how access to cheap labour acted to facilitate structural change. I must add some brief comments concerning the influence of flexible labour supplies on the level, the sustained duration and the international diffusion of the investment boom.

Movement of workers from the farms, from petty trade and from less developed countries in Europe and Africa provided very large fractions of the growth of employment in the more advanced non-farm sectors of the industrialized countries.[2] The availability of this supply of cheap labour must have inhibited the rise in non-farm wages and so sustained the rate of return to investment in the face of large expansions of capital stock. By permitting large productivity gains to be achieved in the industrial sector without provoking an unduly rapid rise in wages, it also encouraged the expansion of industry through import substitution and export growth and, in this way, enlarged the

[1] Ohkawa and Rosovsky, op. cit., Chapter 9.
[2] I have already cited evidence about the importance of inflows of workers from abroad. See Footnote 3, p. 23.
   I have estimated that migration of workers from farms accounted for the following percentage rises in non-farm employment:

scope for capital investment. On both counts, therefore, the level of investment must have been raised and the boom protracted instead of being cut short by the need to intensify capital-labour substitution.

That need, of course, could not be avoided for ever. Reserve labour pools were being drained during the 1960s, and resistance to foreign workers was growing. I have already indicated how the sustained increase of productivity in that decade came to depend on an accelerated rate of rise of capital-labour ratios. Such dependence, however, has its limits, and if the investment boom had not been cut short by other causes – as it was – a tightening labour market might soon have imposed a slowdown.

There was a noteworthy difference between the pattern of international migration in the postwar period and that before 1914 when such movements last were large. Before the First World War, the movement was from Europe to the USA, Canada and other countries of recent settlement. One may, therefore, say that the non-farm sectors in both Europe and overseas countries formerly were fed in part from a common reserve pool of labour on the European farms. Sustained investment booms in the USA and other overseas areas were marked by heavy emigration from Europe and, in part for this reason, they were associated with less active home investment in the UK, Scandinavia and, to a lesser degree, Germany. Growth in the industrialising west, therefore, moved in a seesaw pattern. Decades of rapid development overseas alternated with decades of rapid development in the UK and Europe. In the postwar period, however, immigration restriction in the USA, Canada and elsewhere made these countries only limited rivals for the supply of

Countries	1950–60	1960–70
USA	28	20
UK	17	52
Germany	41	62
France	95	60
Italy	53	148
Japan	58	59

The underlying data are derived from OECD *Manpower Statistics, 1950–62*, Tables II and III and OECD *Labour Force Statistics, 1960–71*, Tables 3 and 6. To estimate farm-worker migration, I assumed that in the absence of migration, farm employment would have increased in the same proportion as total employment. An estimate of worker migration from farms was, therefore, obtained by subtracting actual end-of-decade farm employment from the hypothetical figure obtained by applying the percentage increase in total employment to the beginning-of-decade farm figure. The estimate understates the contribution of farm migration to domestic non-farm employment to the extent that natural increase on the farms exceeds that in the towns. It overstates such migration to the extent that immigration was included in total employment increase and if migrants from farms went abroad. The latter bias was important for Italy and helps account for the fact that estimated farm worker migration exceeded the rise in Italian non-farm employment from 1960 to 1970.

European reserve labour. Instead, the overseas countries, aided by large increases in agricultural productivity, drew heavily on their own farm populations. At the same time, European industry gained labour by immigration from the less developed countries bordering the Mediterranean. The obstacle which population flows among the industrialised countries posed to simultaneous expansion on both sides of the Atlantic was, therefore, largely removed. Since, as I shall next argue, another obstacle which used to be raised by international flows of capital and monetary reserves was also lowered, a vigorous and sustained investment boom in the USA and Canada could be accompanied by a still more vigorous investment boom in Europe.

5 International accounts and supplies of money. The considerations already discussed bear on the investment boom from the real side. The boom also had a monetary side.

It is a necessary element in a sustained investment boom that real money stock should grow roughly in proportion to the accompanying growth of aggregate real output. In principle, of course, any growth rate of nominal money stock could satisfy this requirement if the rate of price-change were sufficiently accommodating. A long-term decline in prices, however, was neither practical economics nor practical politics in the postwar years. In the USA, for example, the release of suppressed wartime inflation made a large postwar price-rise inevitable, and the Korean War caused renewed inflation. Considering the price expectations so generated, it was something of a triumph of monetary management that the subsequent rate of increase of US consumer prices was no more than 1·3 per cent a year from 1952 to 1965 and the rate of increase in wholesale prices no more than 0·5 per cent.

One may, I believe, take this to be about the slowest rate of increase consistent with avoiding protracted stagnation in the USA. If so, the money stock growth needed in the industrialised world at large must have been considerably faster than real output growth itself. The reason is that in a fixed exchange rate system, the process of balance of payments adjustment forces up money wages faster in countries whose productivity growth is relatively rapid than in countries where it is slower. Further, since differences in productivity growth are concentrated in the production of traded goods whose product prices move in a similar way everywhere, the relatively fast rise of money wages means relatively fast rise of prices of non-tradables and, therefore, of general price indexes in countries with rapid productivity growth.[1] It follows, then, that even when US prices were stable, prices in the more progressive remainder of the industrialised world had to be rising. The necessary growth rate of nominal income was, therefore, even faster than that of real output. And, while it might have been possible for a rise in velocity to have substituted for growth of money stock, that, in fact, did not occur (except, to some degree, in the USA itself).

[1] McKinnon, op. cit., explains this process more fully and shows that differences in national price trends were consistent with these views.

The necessary growth of money stock demanded a rapid, but by no means equal, growth of monetary reserves and, considering the exigencies of fixed exchange rates, a large part of these reserves had to have international currency. And since the world stock of monetary gold was itself expanding only slowly, that need could only be satisfied by redistribution of the initial US gold holdings and, still more, by the adoption of some internationally acceptable supplementary reserve asset. The Bretton Woods scheme and the economic strength of the USA made that asset short-term claims on dollars.

Monetary growth, therefore, came to depend on an arrangement of considerable delicacy. Successful operation over a protracted period demanded simultaneous fulfilment of two basically contradictory conditions: first, a chronic US deficit and, therefore, the cumulative deterioration of the US reserve position; second, continued faith in the ability of the USA to maintain convertibility and the par of exchange, thereby avoiding both a flight from the dollar and a US monetary policy tight enough to produce serious constriction in the USA and secondarily in the rest of the industrialised countries.

Needless to say, it did not prove hard to maintain a chronic deficit. The system, indeed, worked as designed. By 1970, the USA had lost $13·5 billion in gold, $2 billion in other international reserves and accepted some $41 billion of additional short-term liabilities. Meanwhile, the international reserves of other countries had risen by some $52 billion and those of developed countries alone by $42 billions – a rough quadrupling of their 1949 holdings.[1]

This process, by which the monetary side of the European and Japanese investment booms was supported for over two decades by US balance of payments deficits and by cumulative gold losses and deterioration of her international reserve position, constitutes a basic difference between the postwar and earlier periods. In earlier times, when investment booms and growth spurts overseas led to a deterioration of Britain's reserve position, losses even a fraction as large as those of the USA in the postwar period would have caused the Bank of England to impose severe checks on monetary expansion and capital exports. The dollar basis of the postwar boom proved as durable as it did because of several peculiarities of the postwar economy:

(1) The dollar was initially extremely strong. The USA had at first an enormous stock of gold and other international reserves and few liquid liabilities. There was then an excess demand for dollars. The actual deficit was discretionary – not only planned, but perceived to be planned.

(2) Although short-term claims on dollars cumulated, some part of them were willingly held as working balances to support a growing trade in which debts and credits were denominated and settled in dollars.

[1] US gold and US and other country international reserves from *Economic Report of the President* (February 1971) Tables C–91 and 92, Short-term liabilities of the US from US Bureau of the Census, *Historical Statistics of the US, Colonial Times to 1970,* Bicentennial Edition, Part 2, Table U–37.

(3) The USA proved politically capable of exercising monetary and fiscal restraint for some dozen years after the end of the Korean War. By accepting a certain degree of underemployment, it limited the size of its deficits. As indicated, it reduced its own rate of inflation to a practical minimum and, by the same token, limited the rate of inflation in the rest of the world.

(4) When, finally, the US international position came to be viewed unfavourably, other countries were faced with a dilemma: whether to continue to accumulate dollar claims and to accept an increasing risk that these would eventually be devalued, or, by demanding gold at once, to precipitate an immediate devaluation and, perhaps, the demonetisation of gold as well. The two dangers being equally unacceptable, countries chose to postpone rather than to hasten the event. By continuing to accumulate dollar claims, the life of the system was extended for some years.

The pressures of two political developments then joined to bring the process to a halt. First, the politics of the Vietnam War ultimately imposed on the US government a policy of inflationary war finance. The rate of US inflation rose. The size of the US balance of payments deficit increased both on that account and because of speculation against the dollar. In so far as European and Japanese authorities monetised the claims arising from the mounting US deficit, the US inflation was duly exported. In so far as they tried to sterilise the claims, they discovered that the process was costly, since it involved deflationary fiscal or monetary policy. And in so far as such sterilisation succeeded in curbing inflation, it was hard to maintain. For then dollar claims of dubious future value mounted all the faster. Dollar devaluation and the realignment of exchange rates followed. Finally, the formation of OPEC and the rise in the price of oil completed the downfall of the postwar system of monetary growth and, at least for a time, brought to a halt the generalised investment boom which that monetary growth had supported.

Discussion of Professor Abramovitz's Paper*

Professor Okhawa, the first speaker, said that Professor Abramovitz's paper was interesting and illuminating. The analysis was confined to an aspect of productivity as measured by output per worker. The forces determining productivity growth rate were thought to consist of two classes: those governing the potential for productivity growth and those controlling the pace at which that potential was exploited.

In applying this conceptual frame to the postwar experience, Professor Abramovitz had specified the potential in terms, first, of enlargement of technological-organisational knowledge in general, and second, in particular for countries which had an advanced state of institutions (administrative, commercial and financial) and a high degree of technical competence, in terms of their achieved productivity level behind the industrial leader. The degree of postwar initial backwardness in productivity level of those countries was thus regarded as the rough measure of the gap between existing and potential productivity.

On the one hand, he said, Professor Abramovitz argued that this gap had been the major source of potentially rapid postwar growth. On the other hand, however, he found a crucial problem in applying this hypothesis to the 1960s onwards (before the oil shock) because productivity growth had continued to be high, without showing the retardation one would expect due to the narrowed backwardness of productivity level of those countries. Professor Abramovitz's answer to this problem was to attribute it to the forces of exploiting the potential: the pace at which those countries could exploit their potential for productivity advance was itself governed by investment and growth of capital. Detailed explanations were given for the factors and circumstances which actually favoured capital investment in a period in the latter part of Professor Abramovitz's paper.

The relative backwardness of less advanced countries (LACs), as measured taking the USA as the standard for 1950, was far greater than that for 1913, which was reached so late as between 1965 and 1970 despite postwar rapid growth rate (Table 1:1). Professor Abramovitz's observation that 'the record of postwar growth appears to be consistent with the view that relative backwardness . . . is an important aspect of growth potential which shaped the postwar record' (p. 11) seemed acceptable. However, to be able to share his view, said Professor Okhawa, more clarification would be needed with respect to the specific nature of the postwar initial backwardness, as distinct from relative backwardness in general. Otherwise, we could not apply Professor Abramovitz's hypothesis to the period after 'normalisation'.

Professor Okhawa said that Professor Abramovitz distinguished specific causes for such a big gap: 'The Second World War itself . . . and frustration of normal growth caused by war, political upheaval and depression during the longer period beginning 1914' (p. 2). As a number of writers had pointed out before, the preceding period of lower-than-average growth rate (Kuznets) was the cause of the postwar initial backwardness for most, not all, of LACs, as measured by the level of the USA, the growth rate of which had almost

---

*The numbered footnotes within the discussion section that follows are the speakers' own.

remained unchanged during that particular period. A process of recovery to normal growth thus heavily involved in applying the author's hypothesis to the postwar growth analysis. If this understanding was valid, was it legitimate to apply Professor Abramovitz's hypothesis to the subsequent period after normalisation?

Professor Abramovitz had carefully defined potentiality for productivity growth of LACs in terms of factors which seemed very close to his own concept of social capability, said Professor Okhawa;[1] he applied it 'for countries with the proper apparatus of governmental and commercial institutions, with educated and skilled populations and advanced technological capabilities' (p. 11). These capabilities could not actually be so uniform for all the LACs and the statement might be a simplification. However, one might get the impression that these capabilities were treated conceptually as if they were 'unchanged or given' during the long period under consideration. In the light of his own research experience of Japan with Henry Rosovsky, said Professor Okhawa, their change as a function of time was, he believed, an indispensable factor in interpreting the long-term growth pattern of a country.

This point of view was, he thought, relevant to a gap between potentiality for and realisation of productivity growth. The potentiality itself would not be given for a country of economic backwardness, because, since its social capability would be greater, the amount and level of borrowable technological knowledge from advanced countries would be enlarged and/or raised. Though his knowledge of LACs other than Japan was limited, this might be applicable to other countries as well. Hence an alternative hypothesis might be worth discussing. As relative backwardness was narrowed, the productivity growth potential of LACs would be increased and its rate could even be accelerated. Why should continued rapid productivity growth after normalisation be considered only from the forces of realisation?

Professor Okhawa said that he would like to put forward these questions for discussion. Even a rough empirical test of the alternative hypothesis was beyond his competence at present. However, it might be convenient for the session participants to present some of the relevant data.

In order to do so, beyond the short-term process of catch-up peculiar to the postwar years, we would have to know more about a 'normal growth path'. Over-time changes in the relevance of borrowable stock of unexploited technological knowledge, due to a process of increase in the social capability of LACs, could not legitimately be identified in a short-term observation. For these two reasons, long-term data were set out for comparison with the postwar data in Table 1:3. These were all in terms of the rate of growth in *per capita* product. An exact comparison with that of product per worker was not intended. This series had its own meaning and broadly, the pattern of the former might not differ much from that of the latter, although trends of the ratio of labour force to the total population were not uniform among the

[1] Kazushi Ohkawa and Henry Rosovsky, *Japanese Economic Growth: Trend Acceleration in the Twentieth Century* (Stanford University Press, 1973). This is close to Kuznets's concept of *relevance* of the existing stock of unexploited technology to less advanced countries. See Simon Kuznets, 'Notes on Japan's Economic Growth', in L. Klein and K. Ohkawa (eds), *Economic Growth: The Japanese Experience Since the Meiji Era* (Economic Growth Center, Yale University, 1968) Chapter 13.

TABLE 1:3 ANNUAL RATES OF GROWTH OF *PER CAPITA* PRODUCT (%)

		(1)	(2)	(3)	(4)	(5)	(6)
1	Japan	1·6	1·4	8·4	3·6	9·5	9·9
2	Germany—West Germany	0·7	1·2	5·0	2·5	3·6	3·5
3	Italy	1·6	1·3	4·8	2·5	4·6	3·8
4	France	1·5	1·0	3·7	1·9	4·7	4·9
5	Sweden	2·0	3·2	3·5	3·3	3·2	2·5
6	Denmark	1·2	1·3	3·4	2·0	4·0	3·8
7	Netherland	1·5	0·3	3·3	1·3	4·2	4·3
8	Norway	2·5	2·6	3·2	2·8	4·0	3·9
9	Belgium	1·2	0·6	3·0	1·9	4·2	4·3
10	UK	0·5	1·1	2·5	1·5	2·0	1·9
11	Australia	0·4	1·8	2·2	1·6	3·3	3·2
12	Canada	0·8	1·9	1·9	1·9	3·7	3·5
13	USA	1·5	1·3	1·9	1·8	3·1	2·3

Source: (1), (2), (3), (4) from Simon Kuznets, *Economic Growth of Nations* (Harvard University Press, 1972) (Tables 4, pp. 38–40, except Japan, which is from K. Ohkawa *et al., Kokumin shotoku* (National Income), LTES, vol. 1 (Toyokeizai Shinposha, 1974) Table 32, pp. 237 and Table 1–2, p. 17; (5) and (6) are from United Nations, *Statistical Yearbook* (1974).
Remarks: (a) Columns (1) to (6) represent the following periods:
   (1) Beginning of the twentieth century to 1925–9.
   (2) 1925–9 to 1950–4.
   (3) 1950–4 to 1963–7.
   (4) 1925–9 to 1963–7.
   (5) 1960–71 or –72.
   (6) 1965–71.
Dates differ slightly among countries.
(b) Annual rates of growth are derived from Kuznets decade rate approximately to be comparable with other data.

countries at issue. The following points were, in his view, worth noting:

   (1) In comparison with the figures in other columns, the figures in Column (2) really showed lower-than-average rates for many countries. However, it was also important to note that several countries' performance did not belong to this category (Sweden, Norway, Canada as well as the USA). The short-term catch-up process could not be applied to those nations. It was important to note that Sweden and Norway, in particular, showed a trend acceleration of their growth rate through periods (1), (2) and (3).
   (2) A long-term average comparison between periods (1) and (4) revealed a general tendency of growth-rate increase with only a slight exception in the case of The Netherlands. Although this must contain various shorter-term fluctuations, a broadly sustained trend acceleration was suggested to work in the twentieth century. The growth rate of the USA had increased only slightly, so that by taking it as the potentiality, we could say that most of the LACs had had a process of long-term catch-up. If this was accepted, a further suggestion could be made:

namely, that there was no reason for ignoring the possibility of sustained operation of this trend of accelerating process of catch-up during
the entire postwar period, including the subsequent years towards the
beginning of the 1970s.
(3) Nevertheless, the sizable differences between the figures in Column (4)
and those of Columns (5) and (6) were still a challenge for us. We had
to consider other forces peculiar to period (6) in particular. Of course
such a long-term observation could not provide the answer to a problem
of such a short-term nature. In this respect, the explanation put forward
by Professor Abramovitz of a capital investment boom was acceptable.
What was suggested here was an additional explanation, emphasising
the significance of a postwar trend of decreasing relative variance of
productivity among LACs which Professor Abramovitz had found in
Table 1:1 in the paper. Some nations such as The Netherlands and
Belgium, for example, showed a high growth rate close to those of other
nations in periods (5) and (6), although their growth rate was even
lower than that of the USA in period (4). On the other hand, relatively
rapidly growing nations such as West Germany and Italy, for example,
did not accelerate their pace of growth, even with a sign of slowdown.
Thus, for the nine European nations in the table taken as a whole, the
relative variance of growth rates had rapidly become smaller. It had
increased from 2·2 per cent in period (1) to 2·6 per cent in period (3),
but decreased drastically to 1·2 per cent in period (6).

A trend of increasing uniformity in creating favourable environments for
capital investment might be one of the explanations. In this respect, said
Professor Okhawa, we had additional evidence that a worldwide increase
occurred in the rate of growth of trade in technology from the latter part of
the 1960s.[1] However, from the aspect of social capability of an administrative,
commercial and financial nature, it might be suggested that the achievement
of a similar trend towards increasing uniformity might also be possible. Such a
trend would contribute to sustaining the catch-up process of European
countries as a whole and this could be said to be a new factor that had
emerged as a result of recent experience.

*

Professor Richard Stone spoke next. He said that seeking a well-tested
explanation for the remarkable growth of industrialised market economies
since the Second World War, Professor Abramovitz had chosen a difficult
subject of great interest at the present time. The topic was a large one and
Professor Abramovitz had concentrated on the experience of industrialised
market economies as a group and confined his attention to one aspect of
growth, namely output per worker, dividing the forces determining the
rapidity of its growth into (a) those governing the potential for such growth
and (b) those governing the pace of its realisation. Professor Abramovitz
believed that, for largely transient reasons, the potential under (a) and the
pace under (b) were unusually high in the postwar period. The potential was

[1] Merton J. Peck with the collaboration of Shuji Tamura, 'Technology', in Hugh
Patrick and Henry Rosovsky (eds), *Asia's New Giant* (Brookings Institution, 1976).

EEC	3·7	1,200·16	257,740	4,656
Belgium	4·5	55·43	9,770	5,670
France	4·4	285·78	52,510	5,440
Italy	4·2	156·51	55,410	2,820
Netherlands	4·0	71·12	13,540	5,250
Denmark	3·8	32·47	5,050	6,430
Germany, Fed. Rep.	3·7	388·67	62,040	6,260
Ireland	3·6	7·17	3,090	2,320
United Kingdom	2·3	200·83	55,970	3,590
Asia	3·6	1,054·04	2,200,317	479
East Asia	5·7	733·13	989,448	741
Japan	8·8	446·03	109,670	4,070
South Korea	7·3	15·98	33,459	480
Hong Kong	6·6	6·85	4,249	1,610
China, Taiwan	6·5	12·71	15,710	810
China, Mainland	5·2	244·64	809,251	300
North Korea	4·4	5·98	15,443	390
Mongolia	0·8	0·86	1,396	610
Middle East	5·1	146·57	118,585	1,236
Saudi Arabia	8·4	22·67	8,008	2,830
Iran	6·7	41·44	33,100	1,250
Israel	5·3	11·63	3,359	3,460
Iraq	4·0	12·00	10,770	1,110
Syrian Arab Rep.	4·0	3·99	7,177	560
Turkey	3·9	29·46	39,167	750
Lebanon	3·1	3·29	3,065	1,070
Jordan	0·9	1·12	2,620	430
Yemen, Arab. Rep.	—	1·16	6,379	180
Yemen, People's Dem. Rep.	—	0·36	1,632	220
South-East Asia	2·3	72·28	309,995	233
Singapore	7·6	4·97	2,219	2,240
Thailand	4·6	12·67	40,780	310
Malaysia	3·9	7·91	11,702	680

TABLE 1:4 continued

Region	Average annual growth rate of GNP per head 1960–74 (%)		GNP in 1974 10⁹ $US 1974		Population in 1974 10³		GNP per head in 1974 $US 1974	
	(1)	(2)	(3)	(4)	(5)	(6)	(7)	(8)
Asia – South-East Asia – continued								
Indonesia		2·4		21·78		128,400		170
Philippines		2·4		13·65		41,433		330
Laos People's Dem. Rep.		1·8		0·22		3,260		70
Burma		0·7		2·91		29,521		100
Viet Nam Soc. Rep.		0·3		6·51		44,155		150
Cambodia (Khmer Rep.)		−2·7		0·57		7,725		70
South Asia	1·1		102·06		782,289		130	
Pakistan		3·4		8·76		67,213		130
Sri Lanka		2·1		1·76		13,393		130
India		1·1		80·41		595,586		140
Afghanistan		0·5		1·88		16,311		110
Nepal		0·4		1·25		12,320		100
Bangladesh		−0·5		7·91		76,200		100
Oceania	3·1		87·52		20,677		4,233	
Papua New Guinea		4·2		1·25		2,650		470
Australia		3·2		71·08		13,340		5,330
New Zealand		2·1		13·07		3,030		4,310
America	3·0		1,848·60		543,999		3,398	
South America	3·2		197·87		207,641		953	
Brazil		4·0		95·92		103,981		920
Argentina		2·8		37·38		24,646		1,520
Colombia		2·6		11·64		23,125		500

Bolivia	2·5		1·55			5,470		280
Venezuela	2·4		22·78			11,632		1,960
Ecuador	2·4		3·31			6,952		480
Peru	2·0		11·11			14,953		740
Paraguay	2·0		1·27			2,484		510
Chile	1·7		8·68			10,408		830
Uruguay	0·5		3·29			2,754		1,190
Central America		3·2		73·53	75,637		972	
Panama	4·1		1·61			1,618		1,000
Mexico	3·3		63·05			57,899		1,090
Guatemala	3·3		3·06			5,284		580
Nicaragua	3·0		1·36			2,041		670
Costa Rica	2·9		1·61			1,921		840
El Salvador	1·8		1·59			3,887		410
Honduras	1·6		0·95			2,806		340
North America		2·9		1,553·23	234,474		6,624	
Canada	3·7		139·26			22,480		6,190
United States	2·9		1,413·53			211,890		6,670
The Caribbean		1·4		23·97	26,247		913	
Puerto Rico	5·3		6·77			3,030		2,230
Jamaica	3·6		2·39			2,008		1,190
Dominican Rep.	3·1		2·96			4,562		650
Trinidad and Tobago	2·1		1·81			1,070		1,700
Haiti	-0·1		0·75			4,514		170
Cuba	-0·9		6·48			9,090		710
Africa		2·2		147·62	403,344		366	
Southern Africa		3·0		31·42	28,123		1,117	
South Africa	2·9		30·18			24,940		1,210
Central Africa		2·5		12·13	45,166		269	
Cameroon	3·9		1·76			7,120		250
Angola	3·7		4·29			6,050		710
Congo, People's Rep.	2·8		0·61			1,300		470
Congo, Dem. Rep. (Zaire)	2·6		3·53			24,071		150

TABLE 1:4 *continued*

Region	Average annual growth rate of GNP per head 1960–74 (%)		GNP in 1974 10⁹ $ US 1974		Population in 1974 10³		GNP per head in 1974 $ US 1974	
	(1)	(2)	(3)	(4)	(5)	(6)	(7)	(8)
Africa – Central Africa – continued								
Central African Rep. (Empire)		0·4		0·37		1,748		210
Chad		−1·2		0·41		3,952		100
East Africa	2·1		23·69		111,714		212	
Malawi		3·9		0·66		4,958		130
Kenya		3·2		2·61		12,910		200
Mozambique		2·8		3·03		9,030		340
Tanzania		2·6		2·32		14,351		160
Zambia		2·3		2·47		4,781		520
Ethiopia		2·2		2·66		27,240		100
Rhodesia		1·9		3·20		6,100		520
Uganda		1·8		2·70		11,186		240
Burundi		1·3		0·33		3,655		90
Madagascar (Malagasy Rep.)		0·1		1·57		8,560		180
Rwanda		−0·2		0·31		4,058		80
Somalia		−0·3		0·29		3,100		90
West Africa	2·0		34·46		127,320		271	
Togo		4·4		0·55		2,176		250
Mauritania		3·8		0·38		1,290		290
Ivory Coast		3·5		2·93		6,387		460
Nigeria		2·9		20·81		73,044		280
Liberia		2·2		0·58		1,500		390
Sierra Leone		1·6		0·54		2,911		190
Mali		0·9		0·45		5,560		80

Dahomey (Benin People's Rep.)	0·7	0·37	3,027	120
Guinea	0·0	0·63	5,390	120
Upper Volta	−0·1	0·52	5,760	90
Ghana	−0·2	4·13	9,610	430
Senegal	−1·1	1·59	4,869	330
Niger	−1·8	0·54	4,480	120
North Africa	2·0	45·92	91,021	504
Libyan Arab Rep.	12·5	10·43	2,352	4,440
Tunisia	3·9	3·56	5,460	650
Morocco	1·9	7·07	16,291	430
Sudan	1·7	3·46	15,227	230
Egypt Arab Rep.	1·5	10·21	36,350	280
Algeria	1·3	11·10	15,215	730

cent; but even this might not seem so very remarkable when compared with the world average.

Since in many countries the rate of economic growth was not nearly as high as the world average, there must be countries and even regions above this average. Outside Europe, the only major regions above the world average were in Asia: East Asia with 5·7 per cent and the Middle East with 5·1 per cent. But apart from the existence of fast-growing regions, individual countries in all regions showed a wide variety of growth rates and however poor or slow-growing a region might be it always contained one or more countries which grew at the world average or above. Thus we could see that being poor was not necessarily a bar to growth, though it might make growth difficult to achieve. We could also see, though it was not strictly relevant to the present argument, that smallness, as measured by population, was not necessarily a bar to either a high growth rate or a high level of product per head.

Professor Stone felt that he should perhaps emphasise at this point that the estimates of total product and its rate of growth given for the communist countries were based, as the table indicated, on attempts to measure the GNP of those countries: they did not relate to the NMP, which would show higher, in some cases much higher, growth rates. The means used to construct these estimates were briefly referred to in the *World Bank Atlas* (1976). Alternative estimates, obtained by more direct methods, were given in documents submitted to the Joint Economic Committee of Congress, such as USJEC (1974, 1975, 1976). The results were in general similar: for instance, 3·8 for the USSR, exactly the same as the World Bank's figure, and 4·5, as against the World Bank's 5·2, for mainland China.

In looking at these growth-rate averages it should of course be borne in mind that an exponential trend coefficient was not for all purposes a substitute for a diagram showing the underlying annual series: many factors, such as the exploitation of new resources or the occurrence of wars and revolutions, could destroy temporarily or permanently any smooth progression that might have preceded them. Still, so long as the underlying series was not too disturbed, exponential trend coefficients provided useful information and he would continue to use them in his argument.

As the World Bank recognised, said Professor Stone, the data shown in the *Atlas* 'provide only an approximate measure of economic conditions and trends'. Still, for recent years the picture, such as it was, was almost complete, covering as it did 187 countries and territories. But this comprehensive picture could not easily be carried back in time, not so much because of the scarcity of data as because of their spottiness. Fortunately, thanks to the energy both of individual workers and of international organisations, more and more information was being resurrected and more and more gaps filled. In the last few months he had been collecting historical statistics from all over the place, with the aim of producing a comparative study of economic behaviour in the last 100 or so years throughout the world. Although he could not yet say how far his researches would carry him, he could summarise some of his findings to date.

For many of the more developed countries it was a simple matter to carry the 1950 estimates of total product per head (not always measured by GNP) back to 1950 and to compare the trends over the period 1950–74 with the more limited experience of 1960—74. All possible patterns emerged from this comparison. For instance, in Austria, East and West Germany, and Italy the average growth rate was higher over the longer period than over the shorter one, indicating a tendency for the pace to slacken. In Britain, Denmark, Sweden and the USSR the two averages were virtually the same. And in Argentina, Australia, Belgium, China, France, Greece and the United States the average growth rate was lower over the longer period than over the shorter one, indicating a tendency for the pace to accelerate. Professor Stone's impression was that there was more evidence of acceleration than of slackening, so that we could not conclude that the rapid growth of the postwar decades was coming to an end. It was true that some countries, such as Britain, Japan, Switzerland and the USA, showed a peak in 1973 and that in Western Europe (with the exception of Norway) the downturn became fairly general in 1974; but this pattern was less in evidence in other parts of the world.

If we tried to go back beyond the Second World War, we came first to the interwar period, which was a pretty disturbed time for most European countries and many extra-European ones; so disturbed, in fact, that Professor Stone did not feel that it could be discussed meaningfully in terms of average growth rates. For this reason he would skip it and go straight to the period preceding the First World War. His impression was that as we went back into the nineteenth century we rarely found growth rates higher than those achieved over the period 1950—74. It was true that in the USA we found 2·2 per cent for the years 1889—1913 compared with 2·1 per cent for 1950—74. However, in Denmark and Sweden we found respectively 2·2 and 2·4 per cent for 1880—1914 compared with 3·5 and 3·2 per cent; in Germany we found 1·7 per cent for 1880—1913 compared with 4·5 per cent (in the Federal Republic); in Italy we found 0·1 per cent for 1861—99 and 1·5 per cent for 1900—14 compared with 4·6 per cent; and in Britain we found 1·5 per cent for 1830—70 and 1·0 per cent for 1871—1913 compared with 2·3 per cent. Other countries where growth rates before the First World War (inevitably for different time-spans) seem to have been notably less fast than after the Second are Argentina, Australia, Belgium, France, the Netherlands and Norway. The picture which some of us might have in mind, of the industrialised countries gradually slowing down since the nineteenth century does not seem to be borne out by observation.

As regards the non-industrialised extra-European countries, historical data for these are pretty scarce, in most cases non-existent. But we could call logic to our assistance, as follows. If we expressed our European estimates in 1974 $ US and carried them back to the middle of the nineteenth century, we reached in many cases very low figures; for instance, about $500 per head in Italy and Sweden. Since countries such as these, which were certainly not of the poorest, appeared to have been growing relatively slowly for the half-century before the First World War, it was hard to believe that the really poor countries, the 'underdeveloped' of our day, could have been growing at all fast: if they had, their starting point would have been below any imaginable subsistence level; especially as they had also had to contend with the problem of population growth brought about by medical progress. Thus it would seem that the postwar acceleration in growth rates was a fairly general phenomenon, not confined to the industrialised market economies.

If he was right in supposing that rapid economic growth, though not to be found everywhere, was more widespread than it used to be, there remained the question of why this should be so, said Professor Stone. The reasons advanced by Professor Abramovitz had no doubt played their part in the countries he considered but Professor Stone thought that we should expect to find still more general factors at work. Those he had in mind arise from a change in attitudes towards economic performance. This change could be summed up as the belief that it was both possible and desirable to improve the material conditions of human existence. And the forging of tools designed to carry this out, the training of people capable of using the tools and, ultimately, the practical application of the tools by the International Monetary Fund or any other agency, were merely the consequences of this belief. In other words it seemed to him that the phenomenon to which Professor Abramovitz had drawn attention was part of a worldwide movement which could be regarded as new and likely to continue, rather than an occurrence affecting a limited range of countries and destined to be no more than a flash in the pan of history.

On the other hand it was obvious that exponential growth in both population and product per head could not go on indefinitely. A choice would have to be made, a balance struck between quality and quantity of life. Would improvements not just in technology but in human understanding enable us to strike the right balance? Would the pressure on resources brought about by continuing growth help to strengthen the forces of moderation or simply add fuel to the fires of conflict which seemed to be smouldering on so many fronts?

He could not pretend to know the answers to these questions, said Professor Stone, and Professor Abramovitz might feel with some justice that he had exceeded his brief. But he had thought that the discussion would be more interesting if set in the context of contemporary economic growth the world over. Unfortunately, circumstances beyond his control had prevented me from doing any more than sketch out the scenario and he would have to leave the detailed discussion to others.[1]

*

In the discussion from the floor *Christian Sautter* said that he would like to make three comments on Professor Abramovitz's paper, in an attempt to brighten what Professor Abramovitz himself had called the somewhat gloomy implications of his analysis for the long-term prospects of growth.

Professor Abramovitz had first shown that in the European countries and in Japan the potential for productivity growth remains high. In 1970, their mean productivity was still only 70 per cent of the US level, and in the leader

---

[1] The works cited are: US Joint Economic Committee, *Reorientation and Commercial Relations of the Economics of Eastern Europe* (Washington DC: US Government Printing Office, 1974); US Joint Economic Committee, *China: a Reassessment of the Economy* (Washington DC: US Government Printing Office, 1975); US Joint Economic Committee, *Soviet Economy in a New Perspective* (Washington DC: US Government Printing Office, 1976); World Bank, *World Bank Atlas,* Eleventh Edition (Washington DC, World Bank, 1976).

country, the USA, productivity suffered no marked decline during the 1960s, in terms either of product per worker or of total productivity (the footnote on pp. 12–13).

The report thus clearly confuted the views of the prophets of stagnation, who maintained that the possibilities of technical progress were all but exhausted.

If the potential of productivity growth was still so large, was perhaps the speed of the catch-up process in question?

Second, Professor Abramovitz had rightly stressed the key importance of capital accumulation in the processes of productivity growth and catch-up. At present all the evidence pointed to an investment crisis in the developed capitalist economies. But this did not automatically imply a crisis of growth in the long-term.

As Ohkawa and Rosovsky had shown in their study of long-term growth in Japan, capital accumulation was not a continuous process, but happened via a succession of forward leaps interrupted by pauses. Even in France, where postwar growth was remarkably steady, this pattern was evident in manufacturing industry, the mainspring of capital accumulation and growth.

The question was whether the present pause was one of the ordinary, recurrent ones, or an accidental pause (due to the fourfold rise in the price of oil), or an irreversible pause.

Third, although the timing of the investment pause happened to coincide in so many countries, its causes differed somewhat from case to case. In France, it was possible to distinguish long-term causes, which were among those listed by Professor Abramovitz, and medium-term causes which, in his view, were more constraining.

The system we might call 'Fordism' after the American motor car manufacturer, was more and more falling into disrepute, he said. This system might be described as a balanced combination of (a) high-efficiency, conveyor-belt production of standardised goods, and (b) mass consumption of durables. Today, conveyor-belt methods were increasingly becoming unacceptable to workers, whose level of education was much higher than it used to be, and demand was shifting from durable goods to tradable and non-tradable services, which were produced in conditions of low efficiency.

But it seems to him, said Mr Sautter, that the decline of 'Fordism' was fairly slow and that there was nothing to prevent us replacing that system gradually by less alienating and equally efficient production methods for services in increasing demand, such as those in the field of health, education and the quality of life generally.

The medium-term causes were more serious for the immediate future, but were not unsurmountable. He would like to mention four of them: (a) mounting social unrest in the late 1960s in connection with the distribution of the national income; (b) the related rise in the debt burden of firms; (c) the demise of the international monetary order; and (d) the 'oil shock', as the Japanese called it.

Today conflict was the rule in trying to solve both national and international problems, with everyone intent on shifting on to others the whole weight of necessary sacrifices. If this conflict-laden situation lasted, it might well be that irreversible decisions would be taken which would preclude every further

chance of rapid growth. This was the only point on which he was inclined to
share Professor Abramovitz's 'somewhat gloomy' view.

Mr Sautter ended by quoting some figures on the French economy, to
illustrate what he had said. The latest calculations by Carré, Dubois and
Malinvaud showed that potential growth had declined slightly at the end of
the 1960s, from 5·5 to 5 per cent annually; but, at 3·5 to 4 per cent annually
for the years 1973 to 1980, actual growth was expected to fall well short of
potential growth. The reason for this lay in the difficulties of controlling
domestic inflation in an international environment where, too, growth had
slowed down and where the new rules − or rather, absence of rules − made
exchange rate adjustments ineffective, if not dangerous. This divergence
between potential and foreseeable growth naturally created problems of
unemployment.

Professor John Kendrick intervened to say that, as noted by Professor
Abramovitz (in Footnote 1, p. 4, of his paper), his own estimates regarding
the acceleration of productivity growth in the US economy in the latter
nineteenth century, and again after the First World War, and for the two
decades following the Second World War (especially with respect to labour
productivity as distinguished from total factor productivity) confirmed those
of Professor Abramovitz. But he would like first to emphasise more sharply
than Professor Abramovitz had done the slow-down in US productivity growth
since 1966, which had amounted to about one-third, from 3·3 per cent to
2·2 per cent a year in real product per hour, and from 2·3 per cent to 1·7 per
cent in total factor productivity, at average annual rates.

In part, the slow-down was due to natural or non-policy forces such as the
declining average quality of natural resources, and changes in the composition
of the labour force. In part, it reflected policies which resulted in a decline in
the ratio of R & D to GNP, a reduction of profit margins (due to macro-
policies designed to combat inflation) which slowed the growth of capital per
worker, and social programmes to protect the environment and the worker
which increased real costs but not real product as measured. And, partly, it
might have reflected social tendencies such as a decline in the work-ethic.

In the decade ahead, changes in labour-force mix would become more
favourable to productivity growth. But the programme for greater energy
independence would accentuate diminishing returns to domestic natural
resources. It was feasible, however, for proper policy measures to restore the
1946−66 trend in productivity − especially policies to promote tangible and
intangible investments, particularly in R & D. He was inclined to agree with
Professor Abramovitz that the policy measures might not be strong enough to
restore the relatively high productivity growth of the two post-war decades
1946−66, although he expected that we would do better than in the decade
1966−76. He would appreciate it if Professor Abramovitz would elaborate
more specifically on his view of the productivity outlook for the next decade
or two.

*

Replying to the discussion, *Professor Abramovitz* said that Professor Ohkawa's
central question had to do with his treatment of that part of the potential for
productivity growth which was enjoyed especially by the less advanced

industrialised countries. As Professor Ohkawa had said, he held that there was a special opportunity for growth 'When a country, relatively advanced in the state of its political, commercial and financial institutions and in its degree of technical competence, nevertheless finds itself behind the industrial leader in the level of achieved productivity'. In that case, his view was that 'the country's degree of initial backwardness [in productivity] can be regarded as a rough measure of a gap between existing and potential productivity, and, therefore, of the advance potentially open to it'. This view, together with observable features of economic history, generated certain expectations:

(1) One could observe that the productivity gaps between the USA and most other industrialised countries, in particular between the USA and the other major industrialised countries, widened between 1914 and 1950. This was an expression of the differential impact of the military, political and economic disturbances of that era. On balance, these fell more heavily on the less advanced countries than on the USA. Granted that the industrialised countries generally had the requisite institutional apparatus and skills to absorb and apply the technology already exhibited in US practice, one could infer that their potential for growth had become stronger and, *ceteris paribus*, one could expect to see generally faster rates of growth in the postwar era than in earlier decades.

(2) The initial productivity gaps in 1950 differed widely among countries. One could, therefore, expect to find an inverse correlation between countries' initial levels of productivity and subsequent growth rates, and to see a decline over time in the variance among countries in productivity levels.

Since actual experience conformed to these expectations, one might well think that the view he had expressed regarding this aspect of growth potential – it was not, of course, a view original to him – could take us a considerable distance in understanding postwar experience.

It seems to him, said Professor Abramovitz, that Professor Okhawa was in general agreement with this view. Yet he had had two objections to his treatment. First, Professor Ohkawa had argued that his (Professor Abramovitz's) expectations rested on an assumption that the technical and other capabilities of the industrialised countries were uniform, and Professor Ohkawa held that such a view constituted a simplification. Professor Abramovitz agreed. He believed that it was a justifiable simplification for the purposes of a very broad overview of a very large subject. Moreover, the required assumption was weaker than Professor Ohkawa suggested. We required not uniformity in capabilities, but only that the differences among countries in levels of capability be not so large as to overcome and smother differences in levels of achieved productivity. Professor Abramovitz believed that to be the case, and had tried to offer some evidence by reference to the relatively small gaps between the USA and other industrialised countries in levels of education compared with those in levels of tangible capital and output per man. Nevertheless, both he and Professor Ohkawa, and, indeed, everyone else who believed that the relative backwardness of the less advanced industrialised countries gave them a growth-rate advantage, faced a common difficulty. They could not yet provide a satisfactory operational definition of the institutional, educational and technological capabilities of countries – what Professor Ohkawa referred to, more concisely, as their 'social capabilities'. Granting this, the only way, for the time being, to make use of the hypothesis that growth rates were influenced by relative backwardness was on the assumption that, for some selected group of countries, social capabilities were *relatively* similar. At the same time, the further refinement and elaboration of the hypothesis clearly required that we should now try to give up our dependence on that simplifying assumption by defining the elements of social capability in an operational way and by testing the connection between growth rates and the measurable elements of capability.

Professor Ohkawa's second difficulty was that people might gain the impression from the paper that social capabilities were 'unchanged or given' over time. Professor Abramovitz did not, in fact, regard them as unchanging and had not intended to leave that impression. In any event, Professor Ohkawa believed that such a view of constancy in social capabilities might have misled Professor Abramovitz in two ways.

First, that by neglecting the growth of social capabilities during the long era before the war he might have missed one important reason why the follower countries were able to achieve growth rates so much higher than the USA itself in the postwar period. Professor Abramovitz believed that there was something to this point, perhaps a great deal. We could not say until we had solved the problems of defining and measuring the elements of social capability something we could not yet do. Yet he had not neglected the matter entirely, he had pointed to changes between 1913 and 1950 in levels of education, in the supplies of engineering talent, in the experience of business managers, in the development of heavy and other large-scale industry, in facilities for international communication and diffusion of technical and managerial knowledge and in governmental competence in the areas of economic policy and organisation. Indeed, the whole matter of social capability tended to merge with that of the 'forces controlling the pace of exploitation of potential productivity', a subject to which, of course, his paper gave a great deal of attention. Professor Ohkawa's discussion, therefore, pointed to the need for clearer distinctions and, as had already been said, operational definitions.

Second, Professor Ohkawa believed that failure to pay enough attention to the possible growth in social capabilities during the postwar period itself might have misled Professor Abramovitz and might mislead others in another way. Was it not possible, he asked, that '[as] relative backwardness is narrowed, the productivity growth potential of LACs will be increased', presumably because of an accompanying rise in social capabilities which enlarges the amount and level of technological knowledge borrowable from advanced countries? By neglecting this possibility, one is led to entertain an inappropriate expectation and to grapple with an unnecessary difficulty. A simple view of the catch-up hypothesis, which neglects a possible accompanying rise in capabilities, leads to the expectation that growth rates should decline as the measured productivity gap narrows. Postwar experience displayed no general, marked retardation in growth rates and, in this respect, was inconsistent with the simple hypothesis. But, on the assumption that capabilities rose as the gap narrowed, there was no clear expectation of retardation and no inconsistency with experience.

Clearly, said Professor Abramovitz, Professor Ohkawa's point had not escaped him, and though he did not give the matter the central role which Professor Ohkawa believed it deserved, and which it might indeed deserve, he had directed attention to such possibilities at several points. With particular reference to an explanation for the absence of retardation in the face of narrowing productivity gaps, he had referred to the continuing postwar rise in levels of education, to the growing numbers of highly trained engineers and scientists, to the enlarged facilities for R & D, to the accumulation of managerial competence in administering large firms, to the liberalisation of trade and payments and to the expansion of direct foreign investment as agencies for technological diffusion. In the same connection, he had given special attention to the implications of Denison's hypothesis which holds that follower countries gain increasing access to the scale-dependent technologies already developed by more advanced countries because their production structures converge on that of the leader as the productivity gaps close.

However, said Professor Abramovitz, having defended himself so far, he must say again that his main reaction to Professor Ohkawa's comments was a desire to join him in stressing the need to work out the operational content of social capability so that we should at some time be able to measure differences among countries and over time. It would be an invaluable advance if we could learn to treat that important component of growth quantitatively and, therefore, give it the weight it deserves.

Turning to Professor Stone's points, Professor Abramovitz said that Professor Stone had proceeded from the premise that, in considering the causes of economic growth, we ought to take into account the widest range of experience which historical and international comparison permits. It was, therefore, a weakness of his (Professor Abramovitz's) paper that he formed his views about the postwar growth of the industrialised capitalist countries — admittedly very rapid by historical standards — without regard for the similarly rapid growth of the LDCs and of the collectivist economies of the USSR and eastern Europe.

As a general proposition, he readily conceded and supported Professor Stone's position. He was less convinced, however, by Professor Stone's suggestion that, because we find rapid growth in many groups of countries in the postwar period, we ought to adopt the hypothesis that some generally applicable, world-wide condition was the main basis for rapid growth everywhere. In Professor Stone's view, this generally applicable condition was the emergence of the belief

> that it is both possible and desirable to improve the material conditions of human existence. And the forging of tools to carry this out, the training of people capable of using the tools and, ultimately, the practical application of the tools by the International Monetary Fund or what you will, are merely the consequences of this belief.

Professor Abramovitz said that he agreed that some such belief had emerged and had been important. On the other hand, the appearance of such a belief, at least in western Europe, North America and Japan clearly antedated the

postwar era by many decades. The belief and its sequelae by themselves, therefore, could hardly account for the acceleration in growth in the regions of the
world with which he was specially concerned. Moreover, he was not sure how
far the appearance of a belief in the possibility of promoting economic advance
could take us in accounting for the revolutionary changes which produced the
socialist planned economies of the USSR and eastern Europe or the substitution
of independent national governments for colonial regimes – by contrast with
the variety of activist governments in Europe and Japan. The belief in progress
was a concomitant of these revolutionary changes, but their occurrence surely
stemmed from a wider array of causes than the belief itself. The new regimes,
moreover, different in themselves, faced the problems of economic development
in radically different circumstances. Could it then have been just the shared
belief in progress which produced fairly similar growth rates in such drastically
disparate conditions? It was, indeed, because the general social conditions
and circumstances of eastern Europe, the LDCs and the industrialised capitalist
countries were so different from one another that it made sense to consider
them separately, at least as a first step. By singling out the growth acceleration
of the industrialised capitalist countries for special attention, he did not mean,
as Professor Stone suggested, that acceleration was an occurrence affecting a
limited range of countries. It did mean that the bases for that experience were
sufficiently special for the members of the advanced capitalist group to justify
treating them separately, at least provisionally.

Finally, when he had suggested that many of the bases on which the postwar progress of the capitalist countries depended had weakened or disappeared,
he had not meant that capitalist growth itself was likely to cease. He had
meant only that it is doubtful whether it would continue during the next
decade or two at the same exceptionally rapid pace. As to that, a formidable
list of factors could be assembled which pointed to slower growth for the
industrialised countries during the decades immediately ahead. As he had said,
however, 'There are other forces – an expanding technological frontier, rising
education, growing managerial competence – which continue to work steadily
for material progress'. His qualified, and in his view somewhat moderate, vision
of a slowdown was, therefore, quite consistent with growth during the next
decades which was fast by prewar standards, while significantly slower than
that in the postwar period itself.

Professor Abramovitz then addressed himself to the points made by
M. Sautter and Professor Kendrick. Their comments, he said, were both
directed to his very brief remarks concerning the outlook for growth in the
capitalist countries during the next decades. M. Sautter was inclined to be
more optimistic than he was, while Professor Kendrick appeared to share his
view that growth was now likely to proceed at a slower pace than during the
1950s and 1960s. Since space did not permit him to elaborate the basis for
his views, he could not reply adequately. In briefest outline, however, his
conclusion stemmed from a judgement that the potential for growth (looking
beyond recovery from the present contraction) was weaker and that the
conditions for rapid realisation of potential were less favourable. The potential
was weaker mainly because the countries of western Europe and Japan had
already gone a long distance in reducing the gaps between their own levels of
productivity and that in the USA. The conditions for rapid realisation were

less favourable on a number of counts:

(1) labour supply would be less flexibly responsive to rapid increase in demand for additional workers in the non-farm sector because natural increase was slowing down, because reserves of low productivity labour on farms and in petty trade had been substantially reduced and because of resistance to continued immigration of workers from the Mediterranean countries;

(2) new barriers to international trade, now in course of erection because of foreign threats to basic industries in many countries, would dampen the rapid expansion of those manufacturing industries where productivity might grow rapidly;

(3) the income elasticity of demands at levels of income now achieved would also retard the growth of manufacturers in favour of expansion in the tertiary sector;

(4) investment was discouraged because of a persistent threat of serious inflation, because the drive for environmental protection was raising the cost of providing additional productive capacity and because the high price of energy had raised the cost of an important input complementary with capital;

(5) the uncertain future of exchange rates, reflecting unresolved imbalances in countries' foreign accounts, was likely to discourage international flows of capital and other long-term foreign commitments, with consequent retardation in the rate of diffusion of new technology.

This seemed to him to be a formidable list. None the less, he did not conclude that growth would now cease, but only that it was unlikely to proceed at the same rapid pace as it had in the quarter-century following the war. As he had said in his paper, 'there are other forces — an expanding technological frontier, rising education, growing managerial competence — which continue to work steadily for material progress'. Moreover, there were great uncertainties, some favourable to growth, some unfavourable, which clouded any view of the next decade or two. What directions would political developments and changes in social attitudes take? How successful would domestic policy and international co-operation be in re-establishing stable monetary regimes, in avoiding protectionism, in providing a favourable environment for domestic and international investment, in stimulating research and development? Would the industrialised countries finally find effective ways of helping the LDCs, and how much would the development of trade and capital movement between the richer and poorer countries do to sustain the rate of progress in both groups? Although he believed that, on net balance, the outlook was for slower growth, any such judgement was highly speculative. Perhaps we would be as happily surprised by the progress of the next quarter-century as we had been by that of the last.

2 The Kuznets Curve and Beyond: Growth and Changes in Inequalities[1]

Edmar L. Bacha

UNIVERSITY OF BRASILIA, BRAZIL

I INTRODUCTION

The Kuznets curve — an inverse-U shaped relation between income inequality and GNP *per capita* — plays in development economics a role similar to that of the Phillips curve in modern macroeconomics. Both are 'measurements without a theory' which have forced a reconsideration of entrenched analytical schemes. Their strength lies in bringing neglected variables of critical importance for economic policy-making into sharper focus. The Phillips curve challenges the IS—LM framework, and places the inflation rate at the centre of the macroeconomic stage. The Kuznets curve concerns the size distribution of income and questions the emphasis of formal growth models on factor shares and modern sector output growth.

The debate on the Kuznets relation is used in this paper as an organising device to survey a recent but rapidly expanding literature on the interaction between economic growth and income distribution.

The Kuznets curve relates to longitudinal phenomena, but the available evidence on growth patterns is mostly cross-sectional (see Section II). Many commentators find that cross-section regressions are inappropriate to study historical relations. Some of them maintain that distributional experiences vary according to chosen development paths and corresponding country-specific development policies (see Section V). The 'structuralist' view is more pessimistic with respect to the options actually available to policy makers. Governments are seen as the slaves rather than masters of the historic-structural conditions which determine the contours of the growth-distribution relationship. This approach emphasises the 'structural heterogeneity' inherent in import substitution industrialisation, and the 'dependencia-marginalidad' syndrome of Periphery growth (see Section III).

Human capital theory disregards market imperfections and focuses attention

[1] This paper was written in 1976/77 while the author was a Visiting Fellow of the Harvard Institute for International Development. Comments from Juan-Carlos Lerda, Joseph Stern, Edward Strasser, and participants of the World Bank-sponsored Workshop on Analysis of Distributional Issues in Development Planning, Bellagio, Italy, April 1977, and of the Seminario sobre Distribución del Ingreso, jointly sponsored by CIEPLAN, CLACSO and UN-ECLA, Santiago, Chile, June 1977, are gratefully acknowledged. The author is also indebted to CAPES/Brazil for research support.

on the educational determinants of earnings inequality. Growth associated changes in income distribution patterns can be predicted from the earnings function (see Section IV). For the remaining group of authors, it is the socio-political forces which prevail over strict economic phenomena in moulding income distributions; violence, in the form of external wars or internal revolutions, is viewed as the single most important determinant of distributional changes (see Section VI).

II KUZNETS PARABOLA

The inverted-U relation between income inequality and GNP *per capita* was first conjectured in Kuznets (1955), but it is only in Kuznets (1963) that it is given empirical support and an explicit formulation:

> In the process of growth, the earlier periods are characterized by a balance of counteracting forces that may have widened the inequality in the size distribution of total income for a while, because of the rapid growth of the non-agricultural sector and wider inequality within it. It is even more plausible to argue that the recent narrowing of income inequality observed in the developed countries was due to a combination of the narrowing inter-sectoral inequalities in product per worker, the decline in the share of property income in total income of households, and the institutional changes that reflect decisions concerning social security and full employment [Kuznets, (1963), p. 67].

Statistical tests have tended to short-cut the inter-sectoral differentials stage (which is dealt with in Section III), and proceeded to relate inequality measures of size income distribution directly to GDP *per capita*.

The first large-scale econometric test was performed by Adelman and Morris (1973, Appendix C), using 1960 referenced income decile shares for forty-four countries. Their work has been criticised, particularly for the poor quality of the data,[1] but it has set a pattern for further studies. These involve the income shares of selected deciles as dependent variables, and transforms of GDP *per capita* as independent variables. Other 'available' exogenous variables are generally added to the right-hand side for good measure.

Papanek (1975) complained that the inverted-U shape obtained by Adelman and Morris depended on the inclusion of 'strongly dualistic' intermediate income countries (namely, South Africa, Rhodesia, Libya, Trinidad, Iraq, Peru, and Gabon), which, according to him, are rather unrepresentative of the likely growth paths of most developing economies. David Felix (1974) added that the relationship was not valid because of the inclusion of highly developed

[1] Little (1976) wonders about the 'sense of economic magnitudes' displayed by the authors in their retention in the sample of Libyan data showing an income share of 0·5 per cent for the lowest 40 per cent of the population. Similarly, Paukert (1973) found it necessary to replace 16 of Adelman-Morris's 44 observations before performing his own tests.

economies in the sample. These hardly present an image of the likely future of present underdeveloped countries according to this author (more on this in Section III). The circle is closed by Paukert (1973, Appendix 2), who rejects as unreliable most of the income distribution data for the poorest countries in the Adelman-Morris sample.

Paukert himself found it advisable not to run any regressions.[1] Instead, he performed a graphical analysis of grouped data which tended to confirm Kuznets's hypothesis for his sample of fifty-six countries.

Using the log of *per capita* GDP (and of its squared value), both Chenery and Syrquin (1975, Chapter 4) and Ahluwalia (1974) were able to establish empirically the inverted-U relationship between inequality and growth. But the most elaborate confirmation of Kuznets's hypothesis using World Bank data is by Ahluwalia (1976). He estimates cross-section regressions using data for 60 countries, from the mid-1950s to the early-1970s. In his sample, 40 countries are LDCs and 6 are socialist. The estimated equations test for a quadratic relationship with the log of *per capita* GNP (in 1970 $ US), using as dependent variables the income shares of five different percentile groups (the top 20 per cent, the next 40 per cent, the lowest 60 per cent, the lowest 40 per cent, and the lowest 20 per cent). In all cases, both terms of the quadratic are significant and the coefficients have the appropriate opposite signs to generate the U-shaped pattern hypothesised by Kuznets. Interestingly enough, the 'turning point' of income shares shifts systematically as one goes down the percentile groups, with the lowest 20 per cent having to wait until *per capita* GNP levels of about $600 are reached. 'It is as if the "trickle down" took longer to reach the bottom', Ahluwalia observes.

Papanek's objections apparently are put to rest here, since Ahluwalia does not include South Africa, Rhodesia, Libya or Trinidad in his sample. A 'Latin American' dummy variable is also tried as a possible *regional* explanation of the U-shape, with negative results. This is really beside the point, since economists acquainted with the region would hardly want to place the 'newly settled regions' of Argentina, Chile, and Costa Rica (besides Puerto Rico, for different reasons) in the same distribution bag as the 'old colonial states' of Brazil, Colombia, Mexico, Peru, Venezuela and other Central American countries.

David Felix's objection is also tested in regressions excluding the high income countries. R^2's drop substantially as a result, from 0·6 to 0·2 in the regressions for the income share of the lowest 40 per cent, but the F-test remains significant. Contrary to Felix's expectations, a much more pronounced U-shaped curve is uncovered in the regression including only LDCs. This is illustrated in Figure 2:1, adapted from Ahluwalia. For national income levels ranging from 110 to 570 dollars *per capita*, the share of the poorest 40 per cent is lower in the LDC sample than in the full sample. Moreover, this share

---

[1] A possible reason, according to Fishlow (1973), is that there is no significant regression of inequality measures on GDP *per capita* in Paukert's original data set.

starts increasing at a lower income level, $371 compared with $468 for the full sample.

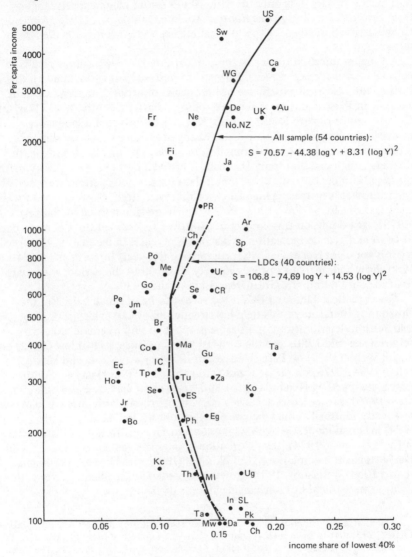

Fig. 2:1 Ahluwalia's Kuznets curves for market economies, 1960s

Ahluwalia's regressions do not support the Adelman and Morris (1973) contention that growth at low income levels leads to worsening absolute incomes for the poor. Starting from national income levels of 75 dollars *per capita* (the lowest observed value in his sample), absolute incomes of the poorest 60, 40 and 20 per cent of the population increase steadily with income *per capita*. As a matter of fact, it is only for national *per capita* income levels ranging from zero to 25 dollars *per capita* that Adelman and Morris (1973, Appendix C) own regression equations yield declining absolute incomes for the lowest 40 per cent.[1]

A tougher question relates to the applicability of cross-country results to particular country experiences. Kuznets' hypothesis was formulated on the basis of the historical experience of European countries. The trend towards equality in these countries is generally observed after the First World War. Of the few countries with longer records, Kuznets (1963) found inequality increasing in Prussia and Saxony, decreasing in Denmark, and remaining roughly constant in the UK during the second half of the nineteenth century. Kuznets concluded that 'only Denmark' showed a narrowing inequality before the twentieth century, implying that if data for previous periods were available a trend towards increasing inequality would reveal itself. However, historical investigations by Soltow (1965, 1968), which are summarised by Paukert (1973), cast doubt on this conjecture. Soltow's records for the UK reach back to 1436 and give no indication of sustained increases in inequality. Historical records for eight Norwegian cities comprising ten-years intervals from 1840 to 1960 show a clear trend towards equality throughout the period, with sharp reversals only during the Great Depression of the 1930s.

The statistical data for LDCs is too recent to be of much help. But the blossoming literature in this field has already uncovered evidence of income distribution deterioration for a sizable number of 'intermediate' countries, between the mid-1950s and the early 1970s. This includes Fishlow (1972) on Brazil, Webb (1977) on Peru, Weisskopf (1970) on Argentina and Mexico, Felix (1974, 1976) on Mexico, and Snodgrass (1975) on Malaysia. South Korea, surveyed by Renaud (1976), and Taiwan, studied by Fei, Ranis and Kuo (1976), succeeded in achieving impressive growth with improvements on an already unusually equal income distribution. Sri Lanka (Jayawardena, 1974) attained modest growth with a substantial equalisation of distribution. In India (Kumar, 1974), the distribution apparently remained invariant with nearly stagnant income levels. In Colombia (Berry and Urrutia, 1976) and Puerto Rico (Weisskopf, 1970) growth proceeded at satisfactory rates with highly concentrated but unchanging income distributions.

---

[1] The alternative evidence for absolute impoverishment presented by Adelman and Morris (1973) derives from their assumption that when growth starts, the incomes of the poor immediately fall off, and that it takes 'a generation' to recover this loss. The logic of their assertions was assailed by Cline (1975). In Adelman and Morris (1975), these authors are adamant in maintaining the correctness of their assertion. This has disturbed further commentators, with the unfortunate result that expressions like 'breathtaking logic', 'neo-Marxian nonsense', and 'far-fetched fantasy' found their way into one of the few corners of the income distribution literature where debates were producing more light than heat (Lal, 1976; Little, 1976).

For the industrial market economies, the post-Second World War picture is clearer. Roberti's (1974) statistical investigation covers Finland, Netherlands, Norway, Sweden, the UK and the USA. He concludes that everywhere the income share of the highest decile has fallen; whereas all other deciles above the fifth have increased their share. No clear, general pattern is detected for the income share of the deciles below the fifth. In the first broadly based effort at deriving reasonably comparable income distributions at the international level, Sawyer (1976) surveys the statistical evidence for the OECD countries. Excepting those few countries where the gains of the 1950s were partially eroded in the 1960s, he concluded that there was a clear postwar trend towards greater equality.

Table 2:1 and Figure 2:2 summarise the available information for thirty countries in the 1960s in a regression format. In an attempt to measure directly the time-derivative of the Kuznets relations, the ratio to the average growth rate of GNP *per capita* of the changes in the income shares of the lowest 40 per cent of households are regressed on GNP *per capita*.[1] Jain (1975) is the data source for income shares, except for some OECD countries, Mexico and Malaysia. Income *per capita* for the mid-1960s and its yearly growth rate in the 1960s are calculated from the 1975 *World Bank Atlas*, the former at 1973 dollar prices. The changes in the income share of the lowest 40 per cent of the population tend to be negative for low income *per capita* levels and are positively correlated with GNP *per capita*, as predicted by Kuznets. But the turning point towards equality is found at higher income levels than anticipated by Ahluwalia's regressions. Positive changes in the income shares of the lowest 40 per cent are predicted only for national income levels over 900 dollars *per capita*.

Regression results for the absolute change during the 1960s of the income share of the lowest 40 per cent are as follows (standard errors in parentheses):

$$\begin{matrix} \text{absolute change in} \\ \text{income share of lowest} \\ \text{40 per cent divided by} \\ \text{yearly growth rate of} \\ per\ capita\ \text{GNP} \end{matrix} = \underset{(0\cdot098)}{0\cdot314}\ \text{Ln}\ \underset{\text{in mid-1960s}}{(per\text{-}capita\ \text{GNP}} - \underset{(0\cdot70)}{2\cdot13}$$

$$R^2 = 0\cdot27;\ DW = 2\cdot13;\ SE = 0\cdot55$$

(Countries are ordered according to increasing GNP *per capita*).

According to this equation, the 'turning point' occurs at income levels of $902 *per capita*. According to a second equation (not shown here), where the independent variable is the ratio to GNP growth of the *proportional* change in the income share of the lowest 40 per cent, the turning point is at $991 *per capita*.

[1] The Ahluwalia-Kuznets relation can be written: $S(t) = a - b \ln Y(t) + c(\ln Y(t))^2$, where S is the income share of the lowest 40 per cent, Y is income *per capita* and t is time. The time derivative of this expression is: $dS/dt = (-b + 2c \ln Y)dY/dt/Y$.

TABLE 2:1 CHANGES IN INCOME SHARES OF LOWEST 40 PER CENT OF
HOUSEHOLDS: [a]30 COUNTRIES, 1960s

Country	Years 1st	2nd	Mid-point GNP per capita (1973 $ US)	Income share 1st year	Change in income share (2nd – 1st)	Annual per capita income growth
India	1960	1967/8	107	13·6	−0·5	1·3
Philippines	1961	1971	233	12·7	−0·8	2·3
Korea	1966	1970	259	18·4	−0·7	7·1
Colombia	1962	1970	354	11·4	−1·4	2·4
Malaysia	1957/8	1970	409	15·9	−4·6	3·9
Iran	1959	1968	431	11·8	0·9	6·4
Taiwan	1964	1972	458	20·3	2·0	6·9
Brazil	1960	1970	470	10·3	−2·2	3·6
Peru	1961	1970/1	547	8·1	−0·8	2·1
Costa Rica	1961	1971	556	13·0	1·6	2·7
Mexico	1957	1969	640	15·5	−4·7	3·3
Panama	1960	1970	642	13·4	0·4	4·4
Yugoslavia	1963	1968	721	19·0	−0·6	4·3
Bulgaria	1957	1962	863	24·3	2·3	4·7
Poland	1956	1964	1259	23·2	0·2	3·9
Hungary	1958	1964	1260	26·7	−0·1	3·2
Israel	1963/4	1968/9	1883	18·6	−2·4	5·6
Italy	1967	1972	2115	15·8	0·5	4·3
Czechoslovakia	1959	1964	2178	26·4	1·0	2·4
Japan	1963	1971	2246	20·4	1·9	9·4
UK	1959	1972/3	2605	15·6	0·9	2·4
Norway	1957	1963	2770	16·0	1·1	4·0
Netherlands	1959	1967	2874	16·7	7·8	4·1
France	1962	1970	3199	9·5	4·3	4·7
Denmark	1955	1966	3240	15·4	1·5	3·9
New Zealand	1967/8	1971/2	3397	15·3	2·5	2·2
Canada	1959	1965	3708	16·8	−0·1	3·7
Germany, FR	1960	1973	4102	16·7	0·1	3·7
Sweden	1963	1970	5059	15·1	1·1	3·0
USA	1964	1971	5404	14·7	0·4	3·1

Sources: Canada, France, Germany FR, Italy, Netherlands, the UK and the USA: Sawyer
(1976, pre-tax data); Malaysia: Snodgrass (1974); Mexico: Felix (1974); all other
countries: Jain (1975). GNP estimated from 1975 *World Bank Atlas* income data.

[a]Brazil, Colombia, Denmark: Income recipients; New Zealand, Norway, Panama, Peru,
Sweden: Individuals; Bulgaria, Czechoslovakia, Hungary, Poland: Workers; Iran, Israel:
Urban households; Canada: Non-farm households. Incomes do not necessarily include
income in kind and generally are estimated before taxes and transfers.

These results are not very robust. Sri Lanka and Pakistan were excluded
from the sample because their income distribution data seemed particularly
unreliable. If these two countries are included and alternative estimates for
the UK and the USA are adopted (showing declining income shares for the
lowest 40 per cent) no significant results can be obtained. Shifts in income

shares in the 1960s appear as purely random. It is as if the 'turning point' were at infinity (or zero)!

An outward shift of the Kuznets curve suggests itself when this statistical evidence is joined to our discussion of the historical trends in the income distribution of the industrial market economies: whereas the industrialisation pioneers soon overcame the increasing inequality phase, the latecomers have to wait much longer to reach the point where inequality starts to decline with economic growth. The Section that follows surveys some explanations that have been offered for this phenomenon.

III HISTORICAL TWISTS

The intuitive perception of a shifting Kuznets curve may underlie the renewed interest on distributional questions in the development literature. The historical specificity of the Kuznets relation also tends to support the contention of Felix (1974) and the Latin American structuralist school that growth experiences are not replicable, and that twentieth-century industrialisation is inherently more unequalising than the eighteenth- and nineteenth-century experiences of present-day industrial economies.

Furtado (1973a, 1973b) and Pinto (1965, 1970, 1976) are representatives of Latin American structuralist thought on distributional questions. For them the organising concept is the Centre-Periphery relationship, first proposed in Prebisch's seminal 1949 paper, 'El desarrollo económico de América Latina y sus principales problemas' (for an English version, see Prebisch, 1962). Furtado's historical scenario can be sketched briefly. The productivity increases resulting from the exports of raw materials caused an expansion and diversification of consumption of the well-off minority in the Periphery. The export-oriented 'Hong Kong' model apart, further growth through industrialisation occurred only when compatibility existed between the market created by the modernising minority and the techniques required for local production of the diversified basket of consumer goods. The ability of the central countries to control these techniques and to impose consumption patterns became the decisive factor in the structure of the productive apparatus of the Periphery, which as a consequence, became *dependent.* Thus growth in the Periphery, on the one hand, relies on the ability of the ruling class to keep income concentrated to generate a demand profile that replicates in a smaller scale that obtaining in the Centre. On the other hand, it presupposes access to technical innovations which are increasingly under the control of transnational corporations. These provide the new products for the expansion of consumption of the modernising minority, and hence play the role of an engine of growth which further tightens the links of dependence. This process implies a widening gap between the consumption level of the modernising minorities and the mass of the population, who remain *marginalised* from the benefits of dependent growth.

Attempts at formalising this historical vision of Belidian (Belgium + India) growth have barely started. Taylor and Bacha (1976) provide a theoretical mechanism for the 'unequalising spiral' which, as shown by Lluch (1977), is heavily dependent on the sizes of capital and labour input coefficients; but these are conspicuously absent from Furtado's demand-oriented interpretation. Moreover, empirical investigations of demand patterns by income classes in Brazil (Fishlow, 1974; Wells, 1976) cast doubt on the existence of the sharp *discontinuities in demand* (workers consume necessities; managers and capitalists consume luxuries) which are an important ingredient of Furtado's model.

Anibal Pinto's analysis emphasises the *structural heterogeneity* provoked by import substitution industrialisation in the economies of Latin America. The simple 'dualism' of the primary export growth phase is replaced by a more complex structure characterised by extreme inter- and intra-sectoral differentials in productivity. These tend to be larger than those that Kuznets (1957) detected in the historical evolution of the central countries. The first reason is that the structural transformation of the Centre was continuous and gradual, whereas in Latin America the industrial revolution occurred in a much shorter time-span, and was not preceded by agricultural modernisation. A second reason is that technology was generated endogenously in the industrialisation process of the centre. This was characterised more by organisational changes (artisan shops, the putting-out system, factory operations) than by the introduction of labour-saving devices. Industrial technologies in Latin America, on the other hand, are imported from more advanced countries and, hence, tend to generate substantial localised increases in labour productivity.[1]

The papers by A. Pinto provide ample evidence of 'structural heterogeneity' in Latin America, but fail to substantiate his case with detailed historical-comparative studies. Nor are the conditions under which intersectoral productivity differentials lead to concentration of personal income distribution spelled out. The latter can be provided without much effort. *Ceteris paribus*, larger intersectoral differentials in labour productivity will result in more income concentration if intersectoral labour and capital flows adjust slowly to market signals. It is intuitively appealing and it can be shown analytically that intersectoral wage differentials in a growing economy should be positively related to intersectoral productivity differentials and to their relative rates of growth. Wage differentials also should be negatively related to the speed of adjustment of intersectoral migration. As long as these speeds of adjustment do not vary very much internationally, the earnings distribution should be more concentrated in those countries where intersectoral productivity differentials are larger and growing faster.[2]

---

[1] An additional factor of obvious importance, not included in Pinto's analysis, is the much higher growth rate of population in Latin America since 1930 than in the industrial countries in the nineteenth century.

[2] True believers in market clearing forces may want to substitute minimum wages clauses and labour union pressures for the above explanation. However, they will have to contend with the evidence amassed by Watanable (1976) to the effect that minimum wage legislation in LDCs is largely ineffective.

Kuznets (1957) again was the first to point out that intersectoral productivity differentials are larger in LDCs than in industrial countries. Baster (1970) relates Kuznets's inequality index or 'total structural differential in productivity' (equal to the sum of the absolute values of the differences between the labour share and the GNP share of agriculture, industry and 'others') to *per capita* GNP and to the percentage of male workers in agriculture. She finds clearly negative associations between the first variable and these two indicators of levels of development. Her linear relationships disappear below the level of $500 *per capita* GNP or when more than 50 per cent of male workers are in agriculture. No regressions results are reported but the scatter diagrams (Baster, 1970, pp. 71—2) are highly suggestive of a parabolic relation.

Using labour productivity in primary production relative to average national productivity as an index of intersectoral differentials, Chenery and Syrquin (1975, pp. 48—53) find an inverse U-shaped relation between this indicator and *per capita* GNP. They explicitly note that the productivity gap between primary production and industry plus services is greatest in the middle income range ($200 to $500), which is also the range of greatest inequality of income in their sample. Chenery and Syrquin keep GNP *per capita* as the fundamental exogenous variable explaining both relations. Latin American structuralists would rather see the causation running from growth 'models' to intersectoral productivity differentials and then to income distribution, with GNP *per capita* appearing only as an intervening variable. It would hardly settle this particular controversy, but it might be interesting to see the results of the introduction of a 'structural heterogeneity' variable in Ahluwalia's (1976) regressions. Chenery-Syrquin's relative productivity index would do for these purposes, as long as it is calculated with fixed weights: i.e., same shares of labour force in the different sectors in all countries.[1] The *structuralist* thesis would receive a boost if the coefficient of the term in squared GNP *per capita* yielded its statistical significance to the newly introduced 'structural heterogeneity' variable.

The cross-section results of Adelman and Morris (1973) might be interpreted as evidence for the structuralist hypothesis. They find that the dominating influence on income concentration is the 'degree of dualism' of the country concerned. *Per capita* income does not appear as a major explanatory variable. Unfortunately, their criterion for 'dualism' is not only ordinal but also subjective, constructed by 'reading unamed books and consulting unamed experts . . . . Even if dualism and inequality are conceptually quite distinct, would not the books and experts tend to mingle them?' (Little, 1976, p. 100). Moreover, in the Adelman and Morris binary analysis of variance, low- and high-income countries should be in one group and middle-income countries in the other one, if the relation between *per capita* GNP and

---

[1] The original Chenery-Syrquin index cannot be used in this exercise because it declines in value as people move out of the low productivity agricultural sector even as relative intersectoral productivities remain constant.

inequality is as postulated by Kuznets. But Adelman and Morris (1973, p. 147) only let the computer scan sample partitions with successive values of the independent variables in each group. This effectively precludes them from capturing a non-linear Kuznets relationship.

IV HUMAN CAPITAL

An alternative view of earnings differentials and of its changes with economic growth is developed by Chiswick (1971). Homogeneous labour is assumed to receive the same expected wage everywhere, observed systematic wage differentials being related to the 'human capital' content of different labourers. From the well-known earnings function: $\ln y_i = \ln y_o + v_i r_i$ (where y_i are the earnings of the ith individual; y_o, the earnings of raw labour; v_i, the amount of investment in human capital by the ith individual; and r_i, the average rate of return on human capital of individual i), the log variance expression is immediately derived: $\text{var}(\ln y) = \text{var}(v \cdot r)$. This can be expanded as: $\text{var}(\ln y) = {}^*v^2 \cdot \text{var } r + {}^*r^2 \cdot \text{var } v + \text{var } v \cdot \text{var } r$, where $^*v$ is the overall average of investment in human capital, and $^*r$ its overall average rate of return.

This equation shows that the log variance of earnings, a widely used index of inequality, is positively related to the means and the variances of investment levels and rates of return on human capital. *A priori*, the average level of investment is positively correlated with the level of *per capita* income, and the sign of the correlation between the (equilibrium) average rate of return and GNP *per capita* is indeterminate.[1] Empirically, the variance of rates of return is negatively correlated with GNP *per capita* 'because of more imperfection in capital markets in LDCs'. Inequality of investment in human capital is positively correlated with the concentration of private wealth and, hence, empirically, negatively associated with levels of development.

In view of these conflicting influences, the sign of the relationship between income *per capita* and income inequality is indeterminate. Using very meagre evidence for ten countries, Chiswick finds that earnings inequality and GNP *per capita* are negatively correlated. But this correlation becomes statistically non-significant when the rate of output growth and schooling inequality are held constant. Chiswick does not consider the possibility that a parabolic relationship between earnings inequality and GNP *per capita* may explain his negative linear regression results. The parabolic relation can be made consistent with the human capital view on the plausible assumptions that in the early periods of growth the average level of investment in human capital increases while its variance remains constant at first and decreases only at later stages (say, through a better distribution of material wealth).

[1] The demand curve shifts up with income but the supply curve shifts down because of the higher average levels of material wealth and the less imperfect capital markets that accompany growth. The results are higher levels of investment in human capital and an indeterminate sign on rates of return.

Chiswick also finds earnings inequality to be positively related to schooling inequality, and this result is confirmed for larger samples by both Adelman and Morris (1974) and Ahluwalia (1976). The most interesting of Chiswick's findings is an analytical one: with variances constant, economic growth leading to more education results in more inequality. The opposite empirical result for GDPs *per capita* beyond the Kuznets turning point must then be imputed to the operation of factors outside the realm of human capital theory, such as decreasing inequality of material wealth and/or more democratic educational policies in the developed countries.

V DEVELOPMENT POLICIES

'Transition growth' is a phenomenon associated with US development economists. When writing in a positive vein, a deterministic view of growth paths is implied, with *per capita* GDP the all-important determinant of distribution patterns (Kuznets, 1966; Chenery and Syrquin, 1975). As the transition from Cambridge (New Haven, Baltimore, Berkeley) scholar to Washington DC policymaker takes place, a more choice-laden view wins over, and the distributional consequences of *development policies* start to matter very much (Fishlow, 1972, 1973; Adelman and Morris, 1973; Chenery *et al.*, 1974; Ranis, Fei and Kuo, 1976). The relevant problem is the reconciliation of GNP growth with improved income distribution. As a consequence, the experience of Brazil, Mexico, South Korea and Taiwan, four countries with impressive growth records but widely distinct distributional trends, has attracted an unusual amount of attention.

Ranis, Fei and Kuo (1976) is an attempt to assess with methodological rigour the successful postwar growth and distribution experience of Taiwan. They conclude that the Kuznets-path is far from inevitable. According to them, in the early 1950s income distribution in Taiwan was as highly concentrated as in Mexico and Brazil today (but this assertion is highly questionable, as they are ready to admit). During the last twenty-five years, the country's growth rate averaged 6·5 per cent a year. At present, Taiwan's income distribution compares favourably with any other non-socialist country in the world. Ranis, Fei and Kuo attribute the success of the Taiwanese distribution experience basically to two factors: first, the emphasis on agricultural modernisation and on the development of rural industries; second, the adoption of labour-intensive processes in urban industrial growth.

Unfortunately, the available data are insufficient for hypothesis testing. Ranis–Fei–Kuo's assertions have to rely mostly on *a priori* considerations, and on the simultaneous observation of policy measures, on the one hand, and distributional trends, on the other. Alternatively, one might want to emphasise the redistributional impacts of the war, the mainland migration and the agarian reforms as the fundamental factors explaining Taiwan's low income inequality (these factors are stressed in Ranis, 1974 and 1976). Better distributional data for the early 1950s are essential to establish some distinction between these two interpretations. Even if further research reveals that income distribution in Taiwan in the early 1950s was much more equal than Ranis–Fei–Kuo imply, their finding of mildly declining inequality in a process of very fast growth during the 1960s will remain as a reminder of the possibility

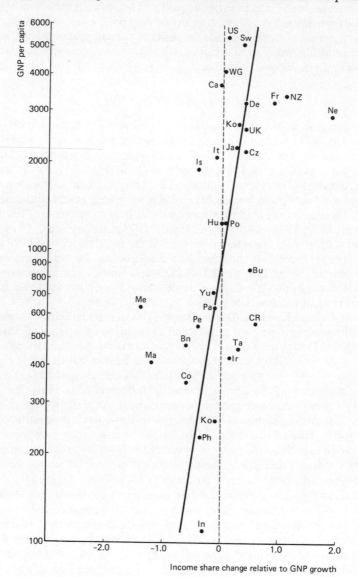

Fig. 2:2 Changes in income share of lowest 40% of households: 30 countries, 1960s

of avoiding the increasing inequality growth phase even under the structural conditions of the late-twentieth-century industrialisation. A pattern similar to Taiwan's is revealed and identical questions are raised by the growth-cum-redistribution postwar history of South Korea (Adelman, 1974; Renaud, 1976).

The experience of Brazil (Fishlow, 1972, 1973; Bacha and Taylor, 1978) and Mexico (Felix, 1974; 1976) between the 1950s and the 1970s on the other hand, are a reminder that 'tinkering with the price system' may do wonders for growth but offers little comfort on the distribution front. Following Korea and Taiwan as much as their large sizes would allow, Brazil and Mexico shifted from import substitution to export promotion. Both developed sophisticated capital markets and adopted liberal interest rate policies. High minimum wage policies were discontinued and labour unions demands were tightly controlled. Favourable legislation facilitated large inflows of foreign capital and technology.[1] Brazil and Mexico achieved, as did Korea and Taiwan, rapid GNP growth and export expansion. But income distribution, which already was highly inequitable, worsened considerably.

Two lessons can be drawn from these examples:

(1) there is a high pay-off for future historical comparative studies of country experiences using a common methodological framework; only these can reveal the full diversity of distributional histories, allowing an empirical evaluation of different policy interventions under changing structural conditions;

(2) as a working hypothesis, the experiences of Korea—Taiwan and Brazil—Mexico suggest that market allocations and removal of price distortions are a good thing for GNP growth. Under conditions of reasonably equal 'original' distribution of the factor endowments, these policies are not detrimental to income equalisation. However, if the starting point is one of very unequal distributions of land endowments and physical and human capital, then policies directed at getting the prices 'right' will tend to concentrate the personal income distribution even further than before, at least in the short- and medium-runs.

VI SOCIO-POLITICAL ORDINANCES

Ahluwalia's (1976) empirical investigation of distribution patterns uncovers the following relationship as determinant of the income share of the lowest 40 per cent of the population:

$$\text{Income share of lowest 40 per cent} = \begin{array}{l} 85 \cdot 66 - 51 \cdot 44 \ (\log \text{GNPpc}) + 8 \cdot 41 \ (\log \text{GNPpc})^2 + \\ + \ 0 \cdot 057 \ (\text{share of urban population}) + 0 \cdot 056 \ (\text{literacy rate}) - \\ - \ 1 \cdot 155 \ (\text{population growth rate}) + 9 \cdot 184 \ (\text{socialist dummy}) \end{array}$$

[1] Other characteristics common to the four countries are authoritarian governments with a modernising outlook and reasonable well-administered public enterprise systems (Baer, Kerstenetzky and Villella, 1973; Jones, 1975; and Vernon, 1963).

According to this result, increasing *per capita* income from $250 to $500 leads to a reduction of 2 percentage points in the income share of the lowest 40 per cent of the population (the share might be around 12 per cent to start with). A progressive government could contemplate the following compensatory policies: (i) raising the literacy rate from 40 to 100 per cent; (ii) reducing population growth rates from 3 to 1·5 per cent a year; (iii) opening up new modern sector employment opportunities which lead to an increase in the share of urban population of from 30 to 50 per cent. These measures lead to gains in the share of the lowest 40 per cent of 3·4, 1·7 and 1·1 percentage points, respectively, adding up to 6·2 percentage points. The distribution gains of *reformist* policies seem substantial, but they are overshadowed by the benefits of becoming socialist. In this case, the equation predicts an addition of 9·2 percentage points to the income share of the lowest 40 per cent.

Regression results aside, looking back at a number of country experiences, development economists have come to express increasing doubts about the feasibility of *reform* as a means of dealing with the inequality problem in LDCs. Bhardan (1974: 261) summarises well a widely held view that the issue is one of power relations not economics:

> the problem of poverty in India remains intractable, not because re-distribution objectives were inadequately considered in the planning models, nor because redistributive policies . . . were not attempted . . . . The major constraint is rooted in the power realities of a political system dominated by a complex coalition of forces representing rich farmers, big business, and the so-called petite bourgeoisie, including the unionized workers of the organized sector.

The undoing from 1920 through to 1970 of the redistributional achievements of the Mexican Revolution of 1910 (Felix, 1974, 1976) is an even more telling testimonial to the extraordinary resilience of powerful minorities.

Populism seems to be the inevitable political course of reformist governments lacking military muscle. The dead-end in economic policy-making in Chile before the 1973 military takeover is surveyed by Foxley and Muñoz (1976). India is the embodiment of the dilemma of 'soft' reformist regimes:

> with low rates of profit in public enterprises, huge subsidies in supporting prices paid to big farmers, and wages and salaries increases paid to white-collar workers, there is little surplus left to help the poor . . . .. It is the paucity of the surplus and the consequent fall in the rate of public investment which largely explain why in recent years India has had a miserable performance in overall growth as well as in mitigation of poverty [Bardhan, 1974: p. 261].

The contrast between the stagnation-cum-maldistribution of India and the growth-cum-redistribution of Korea and Taiwan strengthens the arguments of

Ranis (1976), Little (1976) and Lal (1976) against the 'interventionist' stance of Adelman and Morris (1974) and Chenery *et al.* (1974). Ranis goes so far as to assert that 'every time a mixed economy government intervenes on behalf of the poor, the poor find themselves worse off'. The implication is that 'trickle down' is still the best strategy to follow both for growth and poverty alleviation purposes.[1] 'Increasing the demand for the unskilled labour is the best way to help the poor in most countries', says Little (1976, p. 104). In a similar vein, Lal (1976, p. 737) adds that:

> the incessant search for 'new strategies of development' may perhaps do indirect damage to the prospects of the poor by not emphasizing enough that efficient growth which raises the demand for labor is probably the single most important measure available for alleviating poverty in the Third World.

Chenery and Ahluwalia's (1974) attempt at escaping the evils of populism by stressing an incremental asset redistribution strategy is also attacked by Lal (1976) and Little (1976). The former authors single out education as their main redistributional weapon. This is consistent with Ahluwalia's (1976) empirical findings but, more important, it may be the only reformist course of action that conforms to the power realities of mixed-economy LDCs. Lal's and Little's counterpoints are familiar from the debate on the impact of education on income distribution in the USA (Mincer, 1974; Thurow, 1975; Bowles and Gintis, 1976; Levine and Bane, 1975) and no new insights are provided. However, the interesting empirical denials of the importance of education as determinant of income distribution patterns by Bhagwati (1973), on India, and Fishlow (1973), on Brazil, should be noted.[2]

Since middle-of-the-road reformist policies appear to hold little promise, two radically opposed groups of alternatives present themselves. One is illustrated by Ranis, Little and Lal (and may well reflect the inner feelings of most of the development economics profession in the USA). It can be characterised as a return to 'trickle down' with an emphasis on 'getting the prices right' to maximise employment growth. The other one is revolution.

There are two strands of pro-revolution argument. A more limited one does not argue with the Kuznets hypothesis that the 'trickle down' worked well in western Europe and North America. According to this view, the Kuznets curve has shifted: present-day LDCs face a much steeper and longer inequality increasing phase than that experienced by the central countries (see

---

[1] These authors also believe that equality is a 'luxury' which only rich countries can afford. Sen (1963) suggests that exactly the opposite is true, for the simple ethical reason that at 'low income levels the inequality measures should take much sharper note of the same degree of relative variation on the ground that inequality pinches most when people are closer to starvation' (Sen, 1963, p. 70).

[2] As a curiosum, we may also register the generalised hostility bestowed on the 'human capital' school by the development economics profession. This is illustrated in the papers edited by Atkinson (1976) as well as in the cold reception accorded to Tingergen's (1975) inequality model based on the supply and demand of personal attributes.

Section III). It follows that the poor of mixed-economy developing countries have no reasons to wait, particularly in view of the high pay-offs for them of a socialist revolution (more on this below). A more radical line of reasoning denies historical validity to the hypothesis of a peaceful transition to the decreasing inequality phase even in central countries. The sociological pro-position is hard to test empirically, but it maintains that nothing short of a cataclysm is required to effect significant distributional changes. In this view, the First and Second World Wars substituted for a socialist revolution in the industrialised west. There is no denying that capital losses, rationing and stiff price and wage controls during the two wars reduced both the property share in national income and the earnings inequality. The surprising fact is that pre-war patterns were not re-established after the wars were over. Runciman's (1966) theory of relative deprivation explains only the supply side of the labour market: workers were simply unwilling to return to their previous relative position after sharing the costs and triumphs of the war. Thurow (1975) ventures the hypothesis that the demand side is inconsequential; wage differentials are purely conventional. Once the reduced differentials were embedded in the labour market they became the new standards of relative deprivation and were regarded as 'just' by all parties concerned, even after the egalitarian pressures of the war had disappeared.

Wiles (1974) maintains that the history of Britain confirms the necessity of violence to effect significant distributional changes. According to him, nothing was taken from anyone other than the landed aristocracy, except during the two world wars. The wartime measures achieved a pre-tax redistribution which has since remained. At least until 1969, mere taxation has had little further equalising effect. Even Kuznets (1963, p. 66), after listing the 'statistical determinants' of decreasing inequality with growth, grudgingly admits that 'the trends towards income equality received a strong push during and immediately after the two world wars'.

Revolutions are obviously equalising, since they imply confiscation of property. But the accompanying violence may well lead to both a reduction of current output and a decrease in the growth rate of GNP. Costs may be large and, in the end, the poor may find themselves worse off than under some capitalist alternative. In the absence of hard facts, economists have proceeded to simulate policy alternatives in simple growth models. Predictably, results depend on assumptions and numbers. Chenery and Ahluwalia (1974) favour an investment redistribution path over two alternative non-revolutionary strategies. Wiles (1974) prefers a *Polish* alternative where the revolutionaries sack the rich but play safe with peasants and artisans. Enos' (1976) model is technically more satisfactory, and explicitly allows for the destruction of capital stock and a period of upheaval following the revolution. He concludes that it takes sixteen years for the social utility generated by 'Expropriation and Assimilation' to overtake an 'Impoverishment with Growth' capitalist strategy. For an 'Expropriation and Exile' alternative the overtaking period is eighteen years.

Potential revolutionaries, interested in serving the interests of the poor, have to consider the economic costs of past revolutions, as Lal (1976) concludes. Wiles (1974, p. 96) pointedly argues that a non-negligible portion of these costs derived from economic policy blunders committed by economically unsophisticated revolutionary regimes. With the rebirth of interest in distributional questions, perhaps economists will be willing to give more of a helping hand than in the past. For it is only by immersing themselves in processes of radical social change that economists may hope to minimise the costs of structural transformations and thus disprove in practice the socially unacceptable Kuznets curve proposition that the rich must be made richer before the poor can hope to become better off.

REFERENCES

I. Adelman (1974), 'South Korea', in H. Chenery *et. al.* (1974), pp. 280–5.

I. Adelman and C. Morris (1973), *Economic Growth and Social Equity in Developing Countries* (Stanford, California: Stanford University Press).

I. Adelman and C. Morris (1975), 'Distribution and Development: A Comment', *Journal of Development Economics,* 1(4) (February) pp. 401–2.

M. Ahluwalia (1974), 'Income Inequality: Some Dimensions of the Problem', in H. Chenery *et. al.* (1974), pp. 3–37.

M. Ahluwalia (1976), 'Inequality, Poverty and Development', *Journal of Development Economics,* 3(4) (December) pp. 307–42.

M. Ahluwalia and H. Chenery, 'A Model of Distribution and Growth', in H. Chenery *et. al.* (1974), pp. 209–35.

A. Atkinson (ed.) (1976), The Personal Distribution of Income (Boulder, Colorado: Westview Press).

W. Baer, I. Kerstenetzky and A. Villella (1973), 'The Changing Role of the State in the Brazilian Economy', *World Development,* 1(11) pp. 23–34.

E. Bacha and L. Taylor (1978), 'Brazilian Income Distribution in the 1960s: "Facts", Model Results and the Controversy', *Journal of Development Studies,* forthcoming.

N. Baster (1970), *Distribution of Income and Economic Growth: Concepts and Issues* (Geneva: United Nations, Research Institute for Social Development).

A. Berry and M. Urrutia (1976), *Income Distribution in Colombia* (New Haven: Yale University Press).

J. Bhagwati, 'Education, Class Structure and Income Inequality'. *World Development,* 1(5) (May) pp. 21–36.

P. Bhardan (1974), 'India', in H. Chenery *et al.* (1974), pp. 225–62.

S. Bowles and H. Gintis (1976), *Schooling in Capitalist America: Educational Reform and the Contradictions of Economic Life* (New York: Basic Books).

H. Chenery *et al.* (1974), *Redistribution with Growth* (London: Oxford University Press).

H. Chenery and M. Syrquin (1975), *Patterns of Development, 1950–1970* (London: Oxford University Press).

B. Chiswick (1971), 'Earnings Inequality and Economic Development', *Quarterly Journal of Economics,* 85(1) (February) pp. 21–39.

W. Cline (1975), 'Distribution and Development: A Survey of the Literature', *Journal of Development Economics,* 1(4) (February).

J. L. Enos (1976), 'Thoughts Upon Reading Redistribution With Growth' (Oxford: Magdalen College, February, mimeo) 20 pp.

J. Fei, G. Ranis and S. Kuo (1976), *Equity With Growth: The Taiwan Case* (New Haven: mimeo).

D. Felix (1974), 'Trickling Down in Mexico and the Debate Over Long Term Growth-Equity Relationships in the LDCs' (St. Louis: Washington University, mimeo) 39 + 5 pp.

D. Felix (1976), 'Economic Growth and Income Distribution in Mexico' (St Louis: Washington University, mimeo) 17 pp. (Forthcoming in *Current History*).

A. Fishlow (1972), 'Brazilian Size Distribution of Income', *American Economic Review*, 62(2), pp. 391–402.

A. Fishlow (1973), 'Brazilian Income Size Distribution – Another Look' (Berkeley: University of California, mimeo) 112 pp. (Portuguese version in *Dados*, 11, pp. 10–80).

A. Foxley (ed.) (1976), *Income Distribution in Latin America* (Cambridge: Cambridge University Press).

A. Foxley and O. Muñoz (1976), 'Income Redistribution, Economic Growth and Social Structure: The Case of Chile', in A. Foxley (1976).

C. Furtado (1973a), 'The Concept of External Dependence in the Study of Under-development', in C. Wilber (ed.), *The Political Economy of Development and Underdevelopment* (New York: Random House).

C. Furtado (1973b), 'The Post-1964 Brazilian "Model" of Development', *Studies in Comparative International Development*, 8(2).

S. Jain (1975), *Size Distribution of Income – A Compilation of Data* (Washington, DC: The World Bank).

L. Jayawardena (1974), 'Sri Lanka', in H. Chenery *et al.* (1974), pp. 273–80.

L. Jones (1975), *Public Enterprise and Economic Development: The Korean Case* (Seoul: Korea Development Institute).

D. Kumar (1974), 'Changes in Income Distribution and Poverty in India: A Review of the Literature', *World Development*, 2(1) (January) pp. 31–41.

S. Kuznets (1955), 'Economic Growth and Income Inequality', *American Economic Review*, 45(1), pp. 1–28.

S. Kuznets (1957), 'Quantitative Aspects of the Economic Growth of Nations: II. Industrial Distribution of National Product and Labor Force', *Economic Development and Cultural Change*, 5(Supplement) (July).

S. Kuznets (1963), 'Quantitative Aspects of the Economic Growth of Nations: VIII, Distribution of Income by Size', *Economic Development and Cultural Change*, 11(2), 1–80.

S. Kuznets (1966), *Modern Economic Growth* (New Haven: Yale University Press).

D. Lal (1976), 'Distribution and Development: A Review Article', *World Development*, 4(9), pp. 725–38.

D. Levine and M. Bane (eds) (1975), *The 'Inequality' Controversy: Schooling and Distributive Justice* (New York: Basic Books).

I. Little (1976), book review of Adelman and Morris (1973) and H. Chenery *et. al.* (1974), *Journal of Development Economics*, 3, pp. 99–116.

C. Lluch (1977), 'Theory of Development in Dual Economies: A Survey' (Washington, DC: World Bank Development Research Center, mimeo).

J. Mincer (1974), *Schooling, Experience, and Earnings*, National Bureau of Economic Research (New York: Columbia University Press).

G. Papanek (1975), 'Growth, Income Distribution and Politics in Less Developed Countries', in Y. Ramati (ed), *Economic Growth in Developing Countries* (New York: Praeger).

F. Paukert (1973), 'Income Distribution at Different Levels of Development: A Survey of Evidence', *International Labour Review*, 108, pp. 97–125.

A. Pinto (1965), 'Concentración del Progreso Técnico y de Sus Frutos en el Desarrollo Latino-Americano', *El Trimestre Económico*, 32(1), pp. 3–69.

A. Pinto (1970), 'Naturaleza e Implicaciones de la "Heterogeneidad Estructural" de la América Latina', *El Trimestre Económico*, 37, no. 145, pp. 83–100.

A. Pinto and A. Filippo (1976), 'Notes on Income Distribution and Redistribution

Strategy in Latin America', in A. Foxley (1976).
R. Prebisch (1962), 'Latin American Economic Development and Its Main Problems', *Economic Bulletin for Latin America,* United Nations Economic Commission for Latin America.
G. Ranis (1974), 'Taiwan', in H. Chenery *et al.* (1974), pp. 285–90.
G. Ranis (1976), 'Growth and Redistribution: Trade-offs or Complements' (New Haven: Yale University Economic Growth Center Discussion Paper no. 245, May) 24 pp.
B. Renaud (1976), 'Economic Growth and Income Inequality in Korea', (Washington, DC: World Bank Staff Working Paper no. 240, February) 45 pp.
P. Roberti (1974), 'Income Distribution: A Time-Series and a Cross-Section Study', *Economic Journal,* 84(335) (September) pp. 629–38.
W. Runciman (1966), *Relative Deprivation and Social Justice* (Berkeley: University of California Press).
M. Sawyer (1976), 'Income Distribution in OECD Countries', *OECD Economic Outlook,* Occasional Studies (July) pp. 3–36.
A. Sen (1973), *On Economic Inequality* (Oxford: Clarendon Press).
D. Snodgrass (1975), 'Trends and Patterns in Malaysian Income Distribution, 1957–70', in David Lim (ed.), *Readings on Malaysian Economic Development* (London: Oxford University Press).
L. Soltow (1968), 'Long-Run Changes in British Income Inequality', *Economic History Review* (April) pp. 17–29.
L. Soltow (1965), *Toward Income Equality in Norway* (Madison: University of Wisconsin Press).
L. Taylor (ed.) (1977), *Models of Growth and Distribution in Brazil.* (Cambridge, Massachusetts: mimeo).
L. Taylor and E. Bacha (1976), 'The Unequalising Spiral: A First Growth Model for Belindia', *Quarterly Journal of Economics,* 90(2) (May) pp. 197–218.
L. Thurow (1975), *Generating Inequality* (New York: Basic Books).
J. Tingergen (1975), *Income Distribution: Analysis and Policies* (Amsterdam: North-Holland).
R. Vernon (1963), *The Dilemma of Mexico's Development* (Cambridge, Massachusetts: Harvard University Press).
S. Watanable (1976), 'Minimum Wages in Developing Countries: Myth and Reality', *International Labour Review,* 113(3) (May–June) pp. 345–58.
R. Webb (1977), *Government Policy and the Distribution of Income in Peru, 1963–73* (Cambridge, Massachusetts: Harvard University Press).
R. Weisskoff (1970), 'Income Distribution and Economic Growth in Puerto Rico, Argentina and Mexico', *Review of Income and Wealth,* 16 (December) pp. 303–332; reproduced in A. Foxley (1976).
J. Wells (1976), 'Underconsumption, Market Size and Expenditure Patterns in Brazil', *Bulletin of the Society for Latin American Studies* (University of Liverpool), no. 4, pp. 23–58.
P. Wiles (1974), *Distribution of Income: East and West* (Amsterdam: North-Holland).

Appendix

KEY FOR FIGURE 2:1

Acronym	Country	Per capita income	Income share of lowest 40%
Ch	Chad	79·5	18·0
Mw	Malawi	80·0	14·9
Da	Dahomey	91·3	15·5
Pk	Pakistan	93·7	17·5
Ta	Tanzania	103·8	14·0
SL	Sri Lanka	108·6	17·0
In	India	110·3	16·0
Ml	Malagasy	138·7	13·5
Th	Thailand	142·8	12·9
Ug	Uganda	144·3	17·1
Ke	Kenya	153·2	10·0
Bo	Botswana	216·6	6·9
Ph	Philippines	224·4	11·8
Eg	Egypt	232·8	14·0
Ir	Iraq	235·5	6·8
ES	El Salvador	267·4	12·0
Ko	Korea	269·2	18·0
Se	Senegal	281·8	10·0
Ho	Honduras	301·0	6·4
Tu	Tunisia	306·1	11·4
Za	Zambia	308·2	14·6
Ec	Ecuador	313·6	6·4
Tr	Turkey	322·2	9·5
IC	Ivory Coast	328·7	10·1
Gu	Guyana	350·8	14·0
Ta	Taiwan	366·1	20·0
Co	Colombia	388·2	9·4
Ma	Malaysia	401·4	11·4
Br	Brazil	456·5	10·0
Jm	Jamaica	515·6	8·2
Pe	Peru	546·1	6·5
Le	Lebanon	588·3	13·0
Ga	Gabon	608·1	8·8
CR	Costa Rica	617·1	14·7
Me	Mexico	696·9	10·5
Ur	Uruguay	720·8	14·3
Pa	Panama	773·4	9·4
Sp	Spain	852·1	17·0
Ch	Chile	903·5	13·0
Ar	Argentine	1004·6	17·3
PR	Puerto Rico	1217·4	13·7
Ja	Japan	1712·8	15·9
Fi	Finland	1839·8	11·1
Ne	Netherlands	2297·0	13·6
Fr	France	2303·1	9·5
No	Norway	2361·9	16·6
UK	UK	2414·3	18·8
NZ	New Zealand	2501·5	16·9

De	Denmark	2563·9	15·8
Au	Australia	2632·4	20·1
WG	West Germany	3208·6	16·3
Ca	Canada	3509·6	20·0
Sw	Sweden	4452·2	15·3
US	USA	5244·1	19·7

Source: Ahluwalia (1976), pp. 340–1.

KEY FOR FIGURE 2:2

Acronym	Country
In	India
Ph	Philippines
Ko	Korea
Co	Colombia
Ma	Malaysia
Ir	Iran
Ta	Taiwan
Br	Brazil
Pe	Peru
CR	Costa Rica
Me	Mexico
Pa	Panama
Yu	Yugoslavia
Bu	Bulgaria
Po	Poland
Hu	Hungary
Is	Israel
It	Italy
Cz	Czechoslovakia
Ja	Japan
UK	UK
No	Norway
Ne	Netherlands
Fr	France
De	Denmark
NZ	New Zealand
Ca	Canada
WG	West Germany
SW	Sweden
US	USA

Source: Bacha, Table 1, p. 11.

Discussion of Professor Bacha's Paper*

Dr Odd Aukrust was the first to comment. He said that Professor Bacha's
paper was a survey of the large literature from the last decade or so on
'income distribution under economic growth'. Professor Bacha had searched
this literature for answers to three groups of questions:

(1) The first group concerned *facts*: What happens to income distribution
when an economy grows? Do statistics reveal any regularities in the
way in which inequality of income distribution changes as economies
pass through successive stages of development? If a relationship
between income distribution and development does exist, what is the
form of this relationship?

(2) The second group of questions concerned *theory*: What are the forces —
economical, or political, or both — which cause income distribution to
change during the process of development? If there is a fixed relationship between inequality and growth, how do we explain this fact? How
do we choose between competing explanations?

(3) The third and last group of questions concerned *policy*: Granted the
facts and our understanding of them, is there anything man can do
to influence the distribution of incomes at various stages of development? Through which instruments can this be done? If we have a
choice between equality and growth, what is the trade-off between the
two?

Since Professor Bacha had mainly reported the views of others, Dr Aukrust
said there was not much in his presentation which was controversial and
asked for comment, and he would use the time instead to sum up what he
had personally got out of the paper in the way of answers to the questions
asked. In the interest of discussion he would deliberately state his views rather
provocatively.

First, however, he wanted to pay Professor Bacha a sincere compliment for
having presented a very fine survey paper. He has succeeded admirably in
putting forward a tightly composed guide to a vast literature, and everyone
was grateful to him for providing such an excellent starting-point for a
discussion of what was a controversial and politically rather 'hot' subject.

Outlining the facts, Dr Aukrust said that the basic hypothesis had been
formulated by Kuznets more than twenty years ago. Whereas economists
before Kuznets tended to believe, with Pareto, that the distribution of incomes
remained in all places and at all times more or less the same, Kuznets speculated
that, as an economy grows, the distribution of incomes would *not* remain
stable but would change everywhere according to a characteristic pattern.
According to Kuznets, income inequalities would increase during the early
stages of development, then become stable, and later narrow again.

Did the statistical facts support the Kuznets view? To him, said Dr Aukrust,
this was not obvious. Or, to be more precise, the evidence did not seem to him
to be in any way conclusive.

On the history of individual countries, two sets of statistics were available.
One (summarised by Professor Bacha on pp. 56–7) related to the records of

*The numbered footnotes within the discussion section that follows are the speakers'
own.

a small number of European countries. These statistics showed a rather strong and uniform trend towards equality starting at about the time of the First World War. However, we were certainly not justified in concluding that those trends — observed during one single historical epoch for a small number of homogeneous economies — would repeat themselves under different circumstances in countries with different economic and social structures. Indeed, scattered data for a few countries *before* the First World War showed no such regularity.

The second set of historical statistics bearing on the subject had been brought together by Professor Bacha in Table 2:1 and Figure 2:2. This material was interesting and deserved close examination. The statistics showed changes in income shares of the lowest 40 per cent of households in thirty countries during (roughly) the 1960s. The data apparently behaved as, according to Kuznets, they should: they showed that inequalities had increased in a majority of the low-income countries and decreased in most high-income countries. However, Figure 2:2 showed clearly that the slope of the regression line depended heavily on observations for a small number of countries (France, New Zealand, and The Netherlands at one end, Mexico, Malaysia and Brazil at the other). As Professor Bacha himself had commented: 'These results are not very robust . . .. If Sri Lanka and Pakistan are included in the sample and alternative estimates for the UK and US are adopted . . . no significant results can be obtained. Shifts in income shares in the 1960s appear as purely random.' So much for historical data.

On the other hand, it must be admitted that studies of cross-section data seemed to prove that a U-shaped Kuznets curve did exist in such data. A fairly large number of such studies had been undertaken in recent years. They were exemplified in Professor Bacha's paper by his Figure 2:1, which reproduced Ahluwalia's data for fifty-four market economies.

Many question marks could be put against the value of such studies. First, the figures used were of doubtful quality. Kuznets had once commented on them as follows:

> It may not be an exaggeration to say that we deal here not with *data* on the distribution of income by size but with estimates or judgements by courageous and ingenious scholars relating to size distribution of income in the country of their concern.

Second, we had the fundamental question of whether conclusions about *causal* historical relationships could be drawn from *associational* relationships shown to exist in cross-section data. Third, the significance of the cross-section studies had been questioned. It had been argued, for instance, that a U-shaped curve was revealed by the data only because the sample of countries included a number of non-typical countries with a mixed white—non-white population (South Africa, Rhodesia, Brazil, Venezuela and others) which happened to be at a medium level of *per capita* income while portraying at the same time an extremely unequal income distribution.

In his opinion, said Dr Aukrust, the cross-section data seemed to suggest the following generalisations:

(1) As far as one could tell, cross-section data were in a broad sense consistent with the Kuznets hypothesis: they did show inequalities

of income to be low in poor countries, to be at a maximum in countries with a higher income level, and to be lower again in the high-income countries.
(2) However, it was equally evident that this was a rule with many exceptions, as was seen by the spread of countries around the regression lines in Figure 2:1.

He concluded from this that the relationship between inequality and development was certainly not a simple one. We might speculate that there could be mechanisms associated with growth which operate universally to cause the regularities observed in the data. However, it was equally obvious that there were forces which were peculiar to individual countries and which, together with development, determined the actual distribution of incomes in any individual country at any point of time. This being the case, it was doubtful how far a general theory of inequality and growth could be developed.

Most theories of inequalities and growth had in common that they stressed the importance of income differentials between sectors and the effects of transfers of population from one sector to another. The explanatory power of this idea was illustrated in a particularly simple way by means of a two-sector model in an unpublished paper by Harold Lydall. Mr Aukrust said that he would permit himself to quote from that paper. Professor Lydall had written:

> Suppose that everyone in sector A receives an income of $100 and everyone in sector B receives an income of $200, and that there are 100 persons in the population, all of whom initially are in sector A. Now, if one person shifts from A to B, this has the following effects: (1) aggregate income increases by $100 to $10,100; (2) the income of the top 20 persons increases from $2000 to $2100, and their share of total income rises from 20 per cent to 20·8 per cent; (3) the income of the bottom 20 persons is unchanged at $2000, but their *share* of total income falls from 20 per cent to 19·8 per cent. Clearly, the tendency for the share of the top 20 persons to increase will continue until all of them are in sector B. At this point aggregate income will be $12,000, the income of the top 20 persons will be $4000, and their share of the total will be 33·3 per cent. Meanwhile, the share of the bottom 20 persons will have fallen to 16·7 per cent.
>
> Now assume that the transfer of population from A to B continues further. When an additional 20 persons have moved to B, aggregate income will be $14,000, the share of the top 20 persons will have *fallen* from 33·3 per cent to 28·6 per cent, the share of the second group of 20 persons will have risen from 16·7 per cent to 28·6 per cent, and the share of the bottom 20 persons will have fallen from 16·7 per cent to 14·3 per cent. It is clear that the share of the bottom group will go on falling until 80 persons have moved to B, and that their share will start rising only when it is their own turn to move to B. Thus, in this example, the share of the top 20 persons grows until 20 per cent of the population have moved to B and falls continuously thereafter, while the share of the bottom 20 persons falls continuously until 80 per cent of the population have moved to B, and only then begins to recover.

We could probably agree with Professor Lydall that the explanatory power of this simple model was surprisingly high. Of course, other elements had to be added if the model was to be realistic. For instance, we should certainly allow for some dispersion of incomes *within* each sector. We might specify how intersectoral and intrasectoral income differentials were supposed to change over time. We should definitely distinguish more sectors than just two. Such modifications would certainly affect the numerical results to be computed by the model without necessarily changing them in any fundamental way. It seemed to him, therefore, that we had available the *framework* of a model of inequalities and growth on which economists might agree.

However, when it came to filling this frame with empirical content the situation was much less satisfactory. This was the impression the middle sections of Professor Bacha's paper had left him with. For instance, authors were seen to differ considerably with respect to the industries selected to represent low- and high-income sectors respectively. Thus, *Kuznets'* fundamental distinction was between the agricultural and the non-agricultural sectors. *Furtado*, on the other hand, according to Professor Bacha, stressed the productivity increases and high incomes resulting from exports of raw materials. *Pinto*, still according to Professor Bacha, might not disagree with Furtado but emphasised at the same time the 'structural heterogeneity' provoked by import substitution – which pointed in the direction of a many-sector model. At the same time, there were important differences in what different authors had to say about the reasons for income differentials *within* sectors. Some stressed inequalities in the distribution of property rights and wealth, others inequalities in education, and others the effect of the types of policies pursued in different countries.

The lack of agreed knowledge was probably even greater when it came to quantification and actual measurement of key variables. Too little was known empirically about, for instance, the actual magnitude of income differentials between industries and changes in such differentials over time. We also knew too little about the speed by which income differentials lead to the transfer of people and capital from one industry to another. Finally, we did not know enough empirically about how intersectoral income differentials came to be generated.

On the last point one comment might be in order, said Mr Aukrust. It was sometimes argued that intersectoral income differentials were simply a reflection of relative productivities. This was clearly wrong: Intersector income differentials did not depend on physical productivities only, but just as much on relative prices. We knew that prices, in the case of traded commodities, were determined largely on the world market. Two things followed: First, the distribution of incomes prevailing at any one time in any one country was determined to some extent by forces operating entirely outside that country's control; these forces would include existing productivities of other countries. Second, since countries embarking on industrialisation today were faced with relative prices very different from those which confronted the industrial pioneers decades ago, the experiences of the newcomers with respect to growth and equalities were also likely to be different.

In Dr Aukrust's opinion, economists were still very far from understanding fully the interrelationship between development and inequalities. It appeared to him from the research he had undertaken so far that the mechanisms at work were complex, and that they showed great variability over time and amongst countries. However, our empirical knowledge about this was extremely meagre. He wholeheartedly agreed with Professor Bacha's conclusion at the end of Section V: 'There is a high pay-off for future historical comparative studies of country experiences using a common methodological framework . . . '

Finally Dr Aukrust wanted to say a few words about policy. A cynic might conclude from what he had said that not only do economists not know for certain what the historical facts are, but they also don't know much about how supposed 'facts' are to be explained. If so (it might be claimed), economists are not really well placed to give authorative advice on policies for greater equality. He would not disagree fundamentally with such a view.

It seemed to him that what did emerge from the literature on equality and growth was little more than some consensus that the distribution of incomes in an economy was largely the result of two groups of influences: first, the usual laws of supply and demand which implied that incomes would reflect the relative scarcity of various types of factor services, given the existing technology; and, second, the social and political environment, which *might* influence the actual choice of technologies as well as the demand for and supply of factor services, and which certainly influences the distribution of ownership of the factors. But these were general statements from which no definite action programme for increased equality could be deduced.

Laws of supply and demand were not easy to control. The scope for policies to reduce inequality, therefore, would seem to lie primarily in the second area — that of the social and political environment. Professor Bacha had shown in the last sections of his paper that economists had offered a long and varied menu of policy measures which, they claimed, would lead to a more even distribution of incomes. The list ranged from recommendations for the choice of particular technologies for the expanding industries, on the one hand, to proposals for improvements in the educational system, or land reforms, or nationalisation of industries on the other. The trouble was that they had very little to say either on the exact income effects of each of these measures, or about their possible side-effects on total output.

Since this was the case, the advice which economists could give to policy-makers at present on the important issue of growth and inequality did not seem to be of much practical value. This, to him, he said, was perhaps the most important conclusion to emerge from Professor Bacha's survey paper.

*

Professor Bogomolov, as the second discussant, said that the relation between economic growth and income distribution dealt with by Professor Bacha in his paper was a problem that was not only scientifically meaningful but socially very important. The author had brought together a large array of interesting data on the differentiation, size and dynamics of incomes in various countries of the world.

Professor Bacha had made a profound study of the writings on this subject published in the USA and other western countries. His paper drew attention to many important aspects of the income inequality problem and showed its specifics in the various types of country. The author was aware that under the market economy in the capitalist countries, and especially in the developing countries, it was very hard to achieve a fair distribution of material and spiritual values between members of society, and considered some ways of overcoming the extreme inequality in incomes.

In the course of economic growth there was, of course, a growth in the national income and the volume of goods per head of the population, but this did not necessarily lead to a more equitable and fair distribution of incomes. The differentiation of income depended on social relations and was determined primarily by the principle of distribution which prevailed in a society. Regrettably this relation had been given undeservedly little attention in economic and social writings in the west, and Dr Bogolov felt that this also applied to the paper presented by Professor Bacha.

The main part of the paper dealt with an analysis of the Kuznets curve and the various efforts to verify it on the strength of concrete statistical data relating not only to industrial, but also to developing countries. One table which he had found highly interesting was that dealing with the changes in income shares of the lowest 40 per cent of households in thirty countries in the 1960s (Table 2:1), which suggested that the share tended to diminish in countries with a GNP *per capita* of under $800, and to increase in countries with a GNP *per capita* of over $800, which could signal a reduction in the unevenness of income distribution.

In order to reduce the inequality, there was a need, in the light of the Kuznets curve, to reach a sufficiently high level of production of the national income *per capita*, so that, starting from this critical level, subsequent economic growth would appear to result in a reduction of the inequality almost automatically. Professor Bacha accepted this general conclusion as self-evident. But he dealt specifically with the possibilities of reducing the income inequality at the stages before the breaking point had been reached. These possibilities were offered by a higher literacy rate, lower population growth rate, and more employment opportunities for the urban population. But, as Professor Bacha had said, 'the distribution gains of reformist policies seem substantial, but they are overshadowed by the benefits of becoming socialist'. As the data on his p. 58 showed, the socialist system helped sharply to increase the income share of the lowest 40 per cent of households.

However, Professor Bacha did not believe that the socialist way of achieving a fairer income distribution was a promising one. He had said:

> Revolutions are obviously equalising, since they imply confiscation of property. But the accompanying violence may well lead to both a reduction of current output and a decrease in the growth rate of GNP. Costs may be large and, in the end, the poor may find themselves worse off than under some capitalist alternative [p. 68].

Unfortunately, Professor Bacha had not mustered any convincing evidence to back up his conclusion, which carried important political overtones. What is more, said Dr Bogomolov, he had found Professor Bacha's conclusion rather unexpected, for, having concentrated on establishing the parabolic relation between income inequality and GNP *per capita*, Professor Bacha had shown virtually no interest in how a social system bears on economic growth rate and the rise in living standards, and also on the elimination of inequality, although, to his mind, that was the whole point.

If one were to examine the Kuznets curve from this angle, one would find that it amounted to no more than a curious econometric construction, and not in any sense to evidence that income inequality is overcome in the course of economic growth. Indeed, there were far too many facts that could not be squared with this, and that could be explained correctly only through an analysis of the social elements in distributive relationships.

Thus, the USA led the world in national income *per capita*, but in 1975 33 million persons had a family income which came to 60 per cent of the figure accepted as the official poverty line, and from 1972 to 1975 the number of poor increased from 11·9 per cent to 17·3 per cent of the population.[1]

According to OECD studies, average figures for the ten most developed capitalist countries (Australia, Canada, France, FRG, Netherlands, Norway, Sweden, the UK, the USA and Japan) in the early 1970s were as follows: the lowest 40 per cent of households accounted for 23·1 per cent of the aggregate personal family income, and the top 10 per cent for 27·3 per cent of the income, while the poorest 10 per cent of the households had only 2·0 per cent of the total.[2]

A study of statistical data very frequently made it impossible to establish any direct relation between economic growth rate and income distribution. Thus, in Canada, while national income from 1951 to 1972 increased by 160 per cent, and national income *per capita* by 70 per cent, the share of the lowest 40 per cent of households dropped from 16·6 per cent in 1951 to 14·4 per cent in 1972; in the USA, while the national income increased from 1950 to 1972 by 100 per cent, and national income *per capita* by 50 per cent, the share of that group dropped from 14·7 per cent to 12·8 per cent. In the FRG, which developed more dynamically than the USA or Canada, there was no decline in the share, but then there was no marked increase either. There, from 1950 to 1973, the national income went up by 290 per cent, *per capita* national income by 210 per cent, and the share of the lowest 40 per cent changed from 16·2 per cent in 1950 to 16·8 per cent in 1973.[3]

According to a study made by two FRG economists, Hauser and Lörcher, to determine the relation between the growth of social production and living standards (taking account of 35 standard-of-living indicators, ranging from consumption of protein per head of the population and the relative number of students, to the number of accidents and amount of green area per head), from 1955 to 1966, a 10 per cent increase in the gross social product in the FRG yielded a 7·4 per cent rise in living standards, from 1960 to 1965 a 5·8 per cent rise, and from 1965 to 1970 only a 4·7 per cent rise.[4] This kind of

[1] *The Working Class and the Modern World,* no. 6 (1976) pp. 51–2.

[2] Malcolm Sawyer, *Income Distribution in OECD Countries,* OECD Economic Outlook Occasional Studies (July 1976) p. 14.

[3] Idem, pp. 26–9. The data on national income growth rate in Canada, the USA and the FRG are taken from the statistical annuals of the USSR's Central Statistical Administration, the USSR economy for the corresponding years.

[4] E. Eppler, *Iné Beiträge zur Theoriediskussion,* Hrg. von Lührs, B.e.a. (1974) S, pp. 71–86.

regression hardly helped to even out income among various groups of the
population.

In the past few years, the operation of factors in the capitalist countries
which tended to worsen the condition of broad masses of people and to
depress the level of their income — unemployment, inflation and higher taxes —
had increased. At the end of 1976, the number of fully unemployed in the
developed capitalist countries was more than 15 million. On the whole, the
cost of living in the developed capitalist countries rose by 8·2 per cent a year
from 1971 to 1975, and by 8·5 per cent in 1976.[1] Far from all the groups of
the population managed to increase their incomes to compensate the losses
incurred through the rising cost of living.

The experience of the socialist countries showed that the only reliable way
of accelerating economic growth, rapidly raising the people's material well-
being and combating poverty and growing inequality in income distribution
was to organise economic life on socialist lines and to adopt the principle of
distribution according to labour.

Under socialism, said Dr Bogomolov, the principle of distribution of the
social product and the formation of the working people's income tended
radically to change. The whole of the national income was placed at the
disposal of society and was distributed only among the working people and
members of their families. The experience of socialist construction had borne
out Marx's prediction that under socialism the working people's share of the
product would be free of capitalist limitations and would be enlarged to the
proportions which were, on the one hand, allowed by society's available
productive forces, and on the other, were required for the fuller development
of the individual.

Under socialism, there was an objective and stable connection between
economic development and the growth of the people's incomes, as could be
seen from the comparison of national income and real income per head in
Table 2:2. This showed that with the rise in the level of economic development
of the countries listed there was an ever more pronounced tendency for an
approximation between the rate of growth of the national income and real
income per head.

However, proportions in the distribution of the national income and the
level of personal income among various sections of the population under
socialism were not only a function of economic growth, but were shaped on
the basis of the socialist principle of distribution. The various goods were
distributed among the members of socialist society, first in proportion to the
individuals' inputs of labour for the benefit of society, and second through
the system of social consumption funds, from which the socialist state provided
free medical assistance, free education and social security for those who are
unable to work, thereby creating for all members of socialist society equal
conditions for satisfying their basic social and spiritual requirements.

In the socialist countries, the great gap which had existed in the level of
incomes which went to the various sections of the population before the
socialist revolution, a gap which still existed in the capitalist countries, had
been eliminated.

[1] *World Economics and International Relations*, no. 3 (1977) pp. 50—1.

TABLE 2:2 ANNUAL AVERAGE RATE OF GROWTH (%)

	National income per head			Real income per head		
	1961–5	*1966–70*	*1971–5*	*1961–5*	*1966–70*	*1971–5*
Bulgaria	6·0	8·0	7·3	4·6	5·9	5·7
Hungary	3·8	6·5	5·7	3·4	6·2	4·6
GDR	3·8	5·1	5·7	2·5	4·3	5·6
Poland	4·8	5·4	8·8	4·3	3·7	8·8
Rumania	8·3	6·5	10·3	–	–	7·2
USSR	4·8	6·8	4·8	3·7	5·9	4·4
Czechoslovakia	1·0	6·8	4·9	2·2	5·2	4·2

Sources: National income: Statistical Annual of the CMEA Countries (1976) p. 42.
Real income:
 Statistical Annual of Bulgaria (1975) p. 71.
 Statistical Annual (1975) Central Statistical Administration of Hungary, p. 351.
 Statistisches Jahrbuch der DDR (1976) S.310.
 Rocznik statystyczny (Warsaw, 1976) s.80.
 USSR Economy in 1975, p. 56.
 Statisticka Rocenks CSSR (1976) s.22.
For Czechoslovakia, the indicator is for personal consumption per head of the population, whose dynamic is a reflection of the real income dynamic).

This was also borne out by the figures presented by Professor Bacha on p. 58 of his paper. While the socialist countries had a lower GNP *per capita* than the developed capitalist countries, the share of the lowest 40 per cent of households was much higher (roughly 25 per cent, as compared with 15 per cent for the USA, 10 per cent for Brazil, and 9 per cent for France). A point to note here was that socialist construction in those countries started when they were at a much lower level of economic development than most of the developed capitalist countries. Despite the different GNP *per capita* in the socialist countries (according to the paper, from $863 for Bulgaria, to $2178 for Czechoslovakia) the shares of the lowest 40 per cent of households were very much alike. This meant that this share was a function not only of economic growth, but also of the purposeful socio-economic policy which was basically similar in all the socialist countries.

National statistical data for the socialist countries showed that the rapid growth of the incomes of their populations has gone hand-in-hand with an even more rapid decline in the proportion of households at the lowest income level. Thus, in the ten years from 1965 to 1975 in Bulgaria, the proportion of households with an income of under 450 levs a year per family member dropped from 19·6 per cent to 0·4 per cent, and with incomes of over 1250 levs a year increased from 3 per cent to 49·4 per cent.[1] In Hungary, from 1962 to 1969, the proportion of persons with a monthly income of under 600 forints dropped from 31·3 per cent to 6·3 per cent, while the share of those earning over 1800 forints a month went up from 2·5 per cent to 15·6 per cent.[2]

[1] *Statistical Annual for Bulgaria* (1976) p. 91.
[2] *Kögazdasagi szemle* (1971) no. 2, pp. 318–19 old.

The reduction of the differences in the remuneration of labour as between various categories of working people came from the uniformity underlying the development of the socialist economy, and sprang from the steady rise in the educational and skill standards of the working people, the mechanisation and automation of labour, and also the socialist state's policy of raising minimum wages and earnings for the middle and lower brackets. Thus, over the past twenty years, minimum wages in the USSR had been increased by 200 per cent and average wages by roughly 100 per cent.[1] In the early 1970s, the decile coefficient of wage differentials among industrial and office workers (the relation between wage levels above and below which wages are received by 10 per cent of persons) came to 2·5 in Bulgaria and Czechoslovakia, 2·8 in Hungary, 2·3 in the GDR, and 3·2 in Poland and the USSR.[2]

Social consumption funds helped to reduce the household income differentials along two lines. First, free services and benefits in education, public health, and rest, leisure and cultural facilities helped to provide balanced satisfaction of the spiritual and social requirements of working people's families, regardless of income levels. It should also be noted, said Mr Bogomolov, that more benefits of every kind went to the lower-income families, which helped to even out the family incomes among various sections of the population. Second, the same purpose was served by the extensive system of cash payments by the state to members of families who were unable to earn and who were fully or partially dependent on those who were working (pensions, scholarships, aids to mothers and children). Thus, the size of allowances for children was differentiated in some socialist countries, depending on the level of the households' income. The state allowed large subsidies for the maintenance of child welfare establishments, and this helped to reduce income differentials, depending on the size of family.

In the light of the data and considerations he had set forth he felt that some of the key propositions in Professor Bacha's paper needed to be clarified and supplemented. For a start, scientific objectivity required a statement about the crucial influence of the social system in overcoming social inequality and securing a fair distribution of incomes in society.

*

Dr Constantino Lluch spoke next, pointing out first that the views he would be expressing would be his own and did not necessarily reflect those of the World Bank. He said that the concern with distributional issues in economics was as old as the discipline itself. In recent years, it had been reactivated among growth-oriented development economists. Why, was beside the point here. How, was partly the object of Professor Bacha's survey. In addition, Professor Bacha had related the recent concern to long-standing views on inequality. He himself would try to summarise Professor Bacha's argument and venture opinions on useful directions of work.

The problem was that of the relationship between growth and equity and how, in market economies, they are enemies before they become friends,

[1] *Statistical Annual of the CMEA Countries* (1976) p. 423; *USSR Economy, 1922–1972*, p. 350; 'Labour and Wages in the USSR', *Ekonomika* (1974) p. 354.
[2] *Planovane hospodarstvi* (1976) no. 8, s.87.

according to an original hypothesis by Kuznets and recent cross-country estimates of the Kuznets curve. Of course, much had already crept into those estimates: levels of development were measured by average income in $ USA; levels of equity, by a single characteristic of the income distribution around that average; and, most importantly, whole countries were the chosen units of observation. Without adjusting for any population attribute other than current income, data for fifty-six market economies during the 1960s showed that their poorest 40 per cent got anywhere between 7 per cent and 20 per cent of total income. This broad interval was not independent of income levels: the lowest shares tended to be associated with middle incomes. Thus, a twisted band (the Kuznets curve and some confidence region for it) described the empirical regularity between the level of development and the level of equity.

Dr Lluch said that levels were only half the story. How countries moved away from them was the other, and more interesting, half. Professor Bacha had something new and important to say about that. His estimates of the time differential of the Kuznets curve for a sample of thrity countries suggested that the middle income at which growth and equity moved in the same direction shifts upwards over time and might double over a ten-year period. This would mean that market economies would have to grow at 7 per cent to stand still from the point of view of equity. Obviously, not a comforting thought; unfortunately, not easy to verify with additional evidence. The individual country experiences over time for LDCs were not well documented yet, and it appeared that quite different combinations of growth and changes in distribution were being recorded.

Then, if the empirical regularity on the twisted band was not very strong, the band itself changed over time, and the country experiences were too varied to support generalisations, where did we go from there? One might look under the Kuznets curve, and consider broad characteristics of development processes, besides income, such as urbanisation, literacy or population growth. At 1970 $250 and with a 12 per cent income share for the poorest 40 per cent of the people, their combined effect on inequality was given by an elasticity of about 1/2: a 10 per cent reduction in a rate of population growth of 3 per cent, and 10 per cent increases in urbanisation and literacy indices of 30 per cent and 40 per cent, would change the share to 12·6 per cent. This compared with an income elasticity of −1/6. Thus, shifts in the curve were found — but, alas, we did not know what these elasticities meant in the context of projections or policy.

Alternatively, said Dr Lluch, one might want to look beyond the Kuznets curve and let the unit of observation be larger (or smaller) than a country. If transition growth was not a historical necessity, there might be conditions that produced, perpetuated and perhaps increased inequality. Across countries, one might want to ask why some market economies had industrialised; others had not, and would not in the foreseeable future; and others were somewhere in between. Within countries, one might want to know the income share of the poorest x per cent of the population and who they were; why they were there and for how long they would be there before someone else took their place; and how badly off were they in some absolute, rather than relative, sense. All these were weighty and interrelated questions. The answers were bound to be speculative and to generate considerable heat.

Recently, said Dr Lluch, Arthur Lewis[1] had admirably analysed how the present international economic order came to be and how it was changing. His views were very illuminating, especially from the 'structuralist' and 'dependence' perspective of Latin American political economists, presented by Bacha as the first group of contributors looking beyond the Kuznets curve.

Before the great Depression, the world market economy grew as a peculiar system with foodgrain land productivity, industrial technology, massive worldwide migrations and climate as its main ingredients. It all began with successful revolutions in agriculture and social institutions in England: given high foodgrain land productivity (in 1900, 1600 lbs per acre) and a distribution of social power favouring industrial interests, industrial technical progress took hold. The rest of the world had to react by adopting the new technology or by trading. Where agricultural productivity was high, colonial constraints low and landed aristocracies weak, technological diffusion and industrialisation took place. Everywhere else, exports of primary products and imports of manufactures became the backbone of economic activity. Relative income and the composition of output in the primary export countries were determined by unlimited labour supplies from different parts of the world at very different subsistence wages: 50 million Europeans improved their lot by moving to temperate zones – their standard of comparison was based on the 1600 lbs per acre of foodgrain to be had at home; 50 million Asians improved their lot by moving temporarily to tropical zones – their standard of comparison was based on the 700 lbs of foodgrain per acre to be had at home. Thus, differential foodgrain land productivities determined relative income in terms of food in temperate and tropical zones. Everyone was self-sufficient in food, and relative productivity in other primary exports determined the geographical composition of output. Trade expansion benefited more the temperate settlements: they could use trade to develop faster. Tropical settlements, hampered by low food productivity, foreign influence on the external sector and a strong political voice of landed interests could not use trade to the same extent.

After the great Depression and its drastic changes in the terms of trade between primary products and manufactures, import substitution began, without important changes in food productivity. Limited therefore by the smallness of the internal market, continued industrialisation called for exporting manufactures. Industrial countries began importing them. Their labour markets, broken into protected and low-wage segments, experienced shrinkages in the latter due to fast technical progress and low population growth. Thus, imports of low-wage manufactures was, for them, an alternative to immigrations. At the same time, high population growth, urbanisation and low food productivity in LDCs made them increasingly dependent on food imports from the industrial world.

Lewis's view of the world market economy and its evolving turnabout in trade regimes provided, Dr Lluch thought, a very useful background on which to pose growth and equity questions. It was also the source of working hypotheses about them, both across and within countries. The link between relative food productivities and relative wages served to anchor down an

[1] Arthur W. Lewis, 'The Evolution of the International Economic Order', Discussion Paper 74, Research Program in Development Studies (Princeton University, March 1977).

important component of world inequality, at least at the beginning of the process of development in the world market economy. And, within countries, the political economy of structuralism and dependence fitted quite naturally into the import substitution phase of the overall view by Lewis. Usually, the focus was on the 'modern' sector: how it imported technology through the transnational corporation and became a separate sub-economy imitating the demand patterns of the centre. Left behind, except to mention its existence as a reservoir of labour, was the mass of the population. But this was mainly the food-producing mass! The distinction between urban and rural peoples was (together with class breakdowns) basic to getting a handle on the economic mechanisms that produced wide income differences.

According to Lewis, said Dr Lluch, the basic tenet of orderly (rather than unequalising) development was the increase in food productivity: the agricultural revolution must go hand in hand with the industrial revolution. History showed that this was easy to say and difficult to do. Were there forms of internal trade that made it particularly difficult? Was there anything inherent in the production and distribution of food that put food producers at a disadvantage in exchange? If food producers were many and food buyers (the traders taking the food to urban markets) were few, monopsony could be blamed for the disadvantage, and, by the same token, the remedies would be at hand. The problem was probably deeper and lay in the preferences and opportunities of rural and urban population groups. The extreme case was best seen by applying to both groups the formal structure of a model of trade under specialisation in production and specific factor endowments in the short-run. This structure would help to focus attention on demand forces. With supplies of food and urban output given, their relative price (the commodity terms of trade) would be determined by demand only, and relative income would be the product of the terms of trade and relative supplies. In turn, how sectoral incomes are distributed to the specific factors might be crucial to characterise within-sector inequalities and to determine the behaviour of productive agents over time (labour migration and the use of profits and land rents). But demand and terms of trade would occupy centre stage in the generation of the personal distribution of incomes for the economy as a whole.

The evolution of such exchange system over time depended on accumulation, technical progress and differential rates of population growth. Thus, many outcomes were possible. But it was important to emphasise that Engel's Law eliminates any automatic tendency of markets to produce rural growth if only rural producers save enough. And if this is so, the study of how to characterise (and how to change) initial conditions in the growth process became a central concern for distribution-oriented development economists. The concern was not new (as exemplified by the abundant viability conditions in dual development models and the notions of a 'minimal critical effort'), but was far from being translated into testable hypothesis that could guide empirical work.

He would end his discussion of Professor Bacha's survey with a few observations on his treatment of human capital and revolution, said Mr Lluch. Professor Bacha had chosen to identify the human capital approach to inequality with the empirical literature on schooling and earning functions. This

particular choice seemed too easy a target for criticism. Wage earnings from
regular employment contracts did not account for much of income in LDCs.
And the issues of how productivity related to investment in humans (nutrition,
health, education) and the value of human time were touched only in part.
For some people, the human capital issue could be roughly put as 'the trans-
planted Iowa farmer': how well would he do in the tropics? Dr Lluch said that
he did not know whether such conceptual experiment was of any use, i.e.,
how to separate the farmer from his good land, his cheap energy or his
benevolent government. But it was probably worth a try.

Throughout the discussion, the term 'market economy' had been profusely
used. Many forms of political and economic organisation fell under that
heading. So much so, that the term was more simply defined by exclusion: a
market economy was whatever was not a centrally planned one without
private ownership of factors of production. Revolution, then, was to leave the
market economy bag. The decision between socialism and capitalism was
momentous, to say the least, for any political community. Socialism was
probably quite important for distribution, as the cross-country data indicated
– but he doubted whether it was any easier than improvements in food
productivity.

*

Discussion from the floor then followed. *Professor Wilfred Beckerman's* view
was that if one read him carefully it was clear that Kuznets was not putting
forward any firm hypothesis concerning the relationship between economic
growth and income distribution in general, or the U-shape of this relationship
in particular. He was always very careful to emphasise that economic growth
affected income distribution in numerous and complex ways, some of which
led to greater equality and others to less equality, so that the final net effect
depended largely on the chance balance of these different forces.

It was not at all clear what precise causal hypothesis was being tested by
the statistical measurements of the so-called 'Kuznets' hypothesis. For
example, was the hypothesis that, beyond a point, economic growth was a
necessary condition for greater equality or that greater equality was a necessary condition for growth? And, before the turning point, was it being
suggested that greater inequality was a necessary condition for the initial
stages of growth? The alternative interpretations of the results were, of course,
very important for policy purposes – or at least they would be if the results
were most significant statistically.

The statistical basis for the various results tending to confirm the Kuznets
hypothesis were very shaky, for various reasons:

(1) below the turning point there was only a small sample of countries,
     (for whom the data were anyway particularly suspect), and his own
     recent calculations based only on countries below the turning point
     (forthcoming in the July issue of *World Development*), yielded far
     lower correlation coefficients than those obtained in other studies
     with the aid of quadratic equations that boost the correlation co-
     efficients on account of the inclusion of the results for many richer
     countries above the turning point;

(2) there was a bias in the results arising out of the fact that family size tended to decrease in the course of development and this had a major impact on measures of equality that do not allow for family size;

(3) another bias arose from the fact that cross-country comparisons of income shares related only to shares in *money* income, not real incomes, and there was reason to believe that the relative prices of basic necessities (chiefly food) changed in the course of economic development in a manner that would tend to bias the results in favour of the so-called Kuznets hypothesis, a point which he would also be discussing in more detail in his *World Development* article.

Dr Nicholas Bruck said that his comments related to the interesting observations presented by Professor Bacha on the substantial difference in the impact of individual sector activity on income distribution. They might also be pertinent to the model quoted by Professor Aukrust, illustrating the income effects of the shift of human resources from the agricultural to the industrial sector.

He wished to call attention to the important role that the public sector might play in relation to income distribution. Income distribution patterns might be affected by income equalisation policies and measures built into and operating through the public sector. These might include:

(1) the system of taxation, through the use of a progressive rate structure of direct taxes;

(2) the provision of public services, such as education, health services, public transportation and other social infrastructure; and

(3) the provision of direct subsidies for income maintenance, housing, and for other social and welfare purposes.

He would suggest that the above-mentioned factors could substantially contribute to modifying income distribution patterns, which, in the absence of such policies, might be determined primarily by the level of development; and recommended, therefore, that an analysis of the role of the public sector specifically should be included in this type of research.

3 The Long-run Movement of the Prices of Exhaustible Resources[1]

Geoffrey Heal
UNIVERSITY OF SUSSEX, UK

I INTRODUCTION

Obviously the long-run behaviour of resource prices is a matter of great import-ance to many countries. The chances that some of the world's poorest people have of improving their lot, must depend very much on the movement of these prices, as must the payments positions of many of the more affluent states, and the stocks of resources that our successors inherit from us.

An expectation to the effect that, in the long-run, resource prices will be very high in real terms, will obviously induce resource owners to hold stocks off the market and increase future supplies at the expense of present supplies. At the same time, such expectations must induce users to invent substitutes and find alternative sources. These reactions to the expectations of high long-run prices will of course tend to increase future supply and reduce future demand, thus possibly invalidating the expectations on which they were based. Clearly a similar story can be told if in the long-run prices are expected to be low in real terms: present sales will be substituted for future sales (reducing future supply) while users will have no incentive to make corresponding reductions in demand and the future may bring lean years, rather than the expected glut.

Elementary though they are, these observations indicate that our subject matter is both important and complex. They also hint at the factors we shall have to consider in analysing the determinants of long-run price movements. Amongst these are the owner's decision to hold or supply, the substitution possibilities available to the user, and the chances of discovering alternative sources. In the next two Sections we shall consider, at a theoretical level, the ways in which these and other factors influence price movements. In the remaining Section, we shall turn briefly to several empirical studies, to see whether they seem to confirm the theory.

II RESOURCE PRICES IN COMPETITIVE MARKETS

Suppose that a resource can be extracted at a marginal and average extraction

[1] Much of this paper is the product of joint work conducted with Partha Dasgupta of the London School of Economics.

cost of C(t) at date t. Then if r(t) is the going rate of interest on capital assets, and there is perfect competition and complete certainty, the resource price p(t) must satisfy the equation

$$\frac{\dot{p}(t) - \dot{C}(t)}{p(t) - C(t)} = r(t) \tag{1}$$

The reasoning that produces this is simple: if the sale of one unit were delayed from t by Δt, the profit then realised would be

$$(p(t) + \dot{p}(t)\Delta t) - (C(t) + \dot{C}(t)\Delta t),$$

whereas if the sale were carried out at t and the proceeds invested, the result at time t + Δt would be worth

$$(p(t) - C(t))(1 + r(t)\Delta t)$$

In equilibrium these two alternatives must be equally profitable — hence (1). If costs are negligible relative to price (perhaps an acceptable approximation for Middle Eastern oil) and the interest rate is constant, (1) reduces to

$$\frac{\dot{p}(t)}{p(t)} = r \quad \text{or} \quad p(t) = p(0)e^{rt} \tag{2}$$

and the price rises at the rate of interest.

(1) can of course be interpreted as saying that the royalty rises at the interest rate, which gives it an obvious interpretation as an asset market equilibrium condition. This is that the resource is an asset which a net market value of $p(t) - C(t)$, and a rate of return identical to the rate of increase of this net value. (1) is then seen as an equilibrium condition for a market containing two assets, and one might expect this equality to be established by arbitrage between these assets. In Section 4 we shall investigate the nature and influence of such arbitrage. In the meantime it is important to bear in mind the dual interpretations of (1) both as an equilibrium condition in a market for flows and also as such a condition in a market for stocks.[1] An interesting reformulation of (1) is

$$\frac{\dot{p}(t)}{p(t)} = r(t)\frac{(p(t) - C(t))}{p(t)} + \frac{\dot{C}(t)}{C(t)}\frac{C(t)}{p(t)} \tag{1'}$$

which shows that the rate of change of price is a weighted average of the interest rate and the rate of change of costs, the weights being respectively the fraction of the selling price made up of rent (i.e. $p(t) - C(t)$) and of costs. Thus royalties grow at the interest rate, and prices at a weighted average of the growth rates of royalties and costs.[2]

[1] These interpretations are set out in detail in Dasgupta and Heal (1977) and Solow (1973). They were first noted by Hotelling (1931) in a seminal forerunner of much modern work in the area.

[2] A derivation of this result under more general assumptions about costs can be found in Heal (1976).

As extraction costs C(t) cannot fall without bound, equation (1) implies that in the long-run resource prices will rise, and indeed will rise asymptotically at the interest rate and eventually exceed any pre-assigned positive number. This is a rather implausible, and indeed for buyers unpalatable, conclusion. But what economic forces could counter the simple logic on which it rests? The answer must be obvious – the possibility of substitution out of the resource concerned. To investigate this a little further, we consider a case where a perfect substitute for the resource is available at a price $\bar{p} > 0$:[1] the extraction cost of the resource is constant at C, and $C < \bar{p}$. In this case $\dot{C}(t) = 0$ and equation (1) integrates to

$$p(t) = qe^{rt} + C \tag{3}$$

where q is a constant of integration: price thus draws exponentially away from the constant cost C. Now, it is clear that under competitive conditions the price of the resource will never exceed $\bar{p}$: however, the reasoning leading to (1) continues to be valid. One can therefore establish[2] that, in a competitive market with perfect foresight, the price will rise from an initial level p(0) according to (3) (or, more generally, (1)) until it reaches the level $\bar{p}$: furthermore, the initial price p(0) will be so chosen that the total stock of the resource is just exhausted as the price $\bar{p}$ is reached. This condition that the stock should just be exhausted as $\bar{p}$ is reached, so that the economy then switches smoothly from the low- to the high-cost source, provides a link between the initial price p(0) and the substitute price $\bar{p}$: an increase in the latter leads to an increase in the former. One can therefore say that the general shape of the price path is determined by the equilibrium conditions underlying (1), while the level of this path is determined by the price $\bar{p}$ of the substitute. Obviously this gives the price of substitutes a crucial role in determining the long-run movement of resource prices. In many cases, these prices are as yet unknown, and will depend on the success of research and development currently being conducted. For example, fusion and breeder reactors provide a substitute for oil in its most important applications: the long-run price of oil must therefore depend on the sucess of the associated research programmes, and indeed on the success of programmes for developing solar energy sources and shale and tar sand deposits.

III RESOURCE PRICES IN IMPERFECTLY COMPETITIVE MARKETS

3:1 Monopoly

Suppose now that a monopolist owns the entire stock S_0 of an exhaustible resource, and faces a demand curve p(R(t)), where R(t) is the rate at which the resource is supplied to the market at date t. Then, neglecting extraction

---

[1] Nordhaus (1973) has termed this a *backstop technology*.
[2] Details are in Dasgupta and Heal (1977), Chapter 6.

costs, he will wish to choose a supply profile $R(t)$ so as to maximise

$$\int_0^\infty R(t)p(R(t))e^{-rt}\, dt$$

subject of course to the constraint that

$$\int_0^\infty R(t)\, dt = S_0$$

Letting $M(t)$ stand for marginal revenue,

$$M(t) = \frac{\partial(R(t)p(R(t)))}{(\partial R(t))},$$

it is a simple matter to verify[1] that a solution to the problem must satisfy

$$\frac{\dot{M}(t)}{M(t)} = r \quad \text{or} \quad M(t) = M(0)e^{rt} \tag{4}$$

so that the present discounted value of the marginal revenue is the same in all periods. If $\eta(R(t)) \leqslant 0$ is the elasticity of demand at supply $R(t)$, then (4) implies that

$$\frac{\dot{p}(t)}{p(t)} = r - \frac{\dot{\gamma}(t)}{\gamma(t)} \tag{5}$$

where $\gamma(R(t)) = 1 + 1/\eta(R)$. A comparison with the equivalent competitive case in (2) is now simple: the difference between the price paths depends solely on $\dot{\gamma}(t)/\gamma(t)$. A very simple case is that of a constant-elasticity demand function: in such a case, $\dot{\gamma}(t) = 0$ and the monopolistic and competitive price paths are identical in all respects. Such a case is clearly rather striking.

More generally, of course, there are differences, and these depend on the nature of the demand function. Clearly

$$\dot{\gamma}(t) = -\frac{d\eta}{dR} \cdot \frac{R}{\eta^2}$$

and hence

$$\text{Sign } \dot{\gamma} = \text{Sign } \frac{d\gamma}{dR}$$

---

[1] Details are in Chapter 11 of Dasgupta and Heal (1977).

Consequently:

$$
\left.
\begin{array}{ll}
\text{if } \dfrac{d\eta}{dR} > 0, & \dfrac{\dot{p}}{p} < r \\[3mm]
\text{if } \dfrac{d\eta}{dR} < 0, & \dfrac{\dot{p}}{p} > r
\end{array}
\right\}
\tag{6}
$$

and it appears that the behaviour of the price will depend upon whether the elasticity of demand increases or decreases with output. Either situation seems possible – for example, one could argue that as the price of a resource such as oil is lowered, it cuts into markets which by virtue of some particular technological or geographical characteristic had traditionally been the preserve of other fuels. In such cases, oil's advantage would be marginal and easily lost by small price changes – implying that lower prices and higher outputs lead to larger absolute demand elasticities and lower values of η.

Unfortunately, the contrary is equally plausible: it might be true that as the price is raised, this increases the incentive to invent substitutes that did not previously exist, or to speed up work on alternatives whose development had been held in abeyance while the resource price was low. In such a case, increasing price and lowering output would reduce η.

Let us consider the implications of these two cases *seriatim*: initially we suppose demand to become more elastic as the market expands, so that $d\eta/dR < 0$ and $\dot{p}/p > r$. In such a case, the relationship between the monopolistic and competitive price path is as in Figure 3:1.

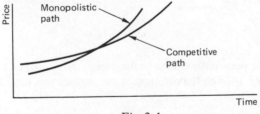

Fig. 3:1

The former has a greater slope at every price: total sales on both paths must of course be the same, so that they intersect once, as shown. The monopolist charges a lower price in the short-run, but a higher one in the long-run. In the converse case, where demand becomes more elastic as the market contracts, $\dot{p}/p < r$ and matters are as shown in Figure 3:2. The monopolist initially charges a higher price, and conserves the resource relative to the efficient, competitive outcome, but maintains lower prices in the long-run. This is obviously because he wishes to avoid price levels at which demand becomes highly elastic – the influence of the availability of substitutes is again apparent, as it is this availability which might lead the monopolist to expect demand to become elastic at high prices.

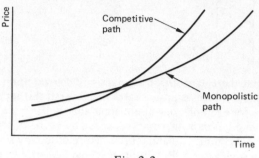

Fig. 3:2

3:2 Oligopoly

Oligopoly is usually difficult to analyse, and one would expect the imposition of dynamics, so essential for the study of resource depletion, to compound this difficulty. Interestingly, this is not so: if there are N identical and competing sellers of a resource, then one can show[1] that in an intertemporal Nash equilibrium (where each takes as given the entire price profile of each of his rivals) the price once again moves according to

$$\frac{\dot{p}(t)}{p(t)} = r - \frac{\dot{\gamma}(t)}{\gamma(t)} \tag{7}$$

where $\gamma(t)$ is now

$$\gamma = N + 1/\eta(R)$$

Qualitatively, the price path relates to the competitive case exactly as in the case of monopoly, though the differences are smaller and tend to zero as N increases without limit.

3:3 Asymmetrically placed oligopolists

For many resources, the assumption that oligopolists are identical is unacceptable. What one observes in many markets (such as oil or bauxite) is the presence of a dominant supplier or group of suppliers (typified by OPEC in the case of oil, and referred to hereafter as the cartel) and a group of smaller and relatively independent producers, whom we shall refer to as the competitive fringe. In such a situation, Nash's equilibrium concept is probably not appropriate: one would expect the cartel to announce its policies having taken into account the response of the competitive fringe, with this latter then

[1] Idem.

responding passively. An equilibrium concept which describes such a situation well is that of von Stackelberg, and we shall analyse such an equilibrium in some simple cases.

Suppose that a resource can be extracted at negligible cost, and that there is a cartel consisting of all resource owners. Suppose further that there is a perfect substitute for the resource that can be produced at a price $\bar{p}$ — we shall refer to this as the backstop technology. Many producers have access to this backstop technology, and they collectively form the competitive fringe.

The market equilibrium that results in such a situation is easily discovered. Clearly the resource price will never exceed $\bar{p}$: equally clearly, if there is an interval of time over which the price is less than $\bar{p}$, the cartel will wish to ensure that equation (4) holds and the present value of marginal revenue rises at the rate of interest. It would thus be reasonable to expect a period during which prices rise in such a way as to keep present value marginal revenue constant, followed by a period during which the price is infinitesimally less than $\bar{p}$, and it can indeed be shown formally that a market equilibrium has this character.[1] Of course, in the case of an isolelastic demand function, matters are somewhat simpler: if the elasticity exceeds one in absolute value, then during the initial interval prices will rise at the rate of interest (see the discussion following (5)). If the elasticity is less than unity in absolute value, the cartel will of course price just below $\bar{p}$ as long as it supplies the resource.

It is obvious that equilibria of the type we have just described involve a form of limit pricing: the cartel prices to keep the competitive fringe and the backstop technology out of the market. This has a very important implication for the conduct of technical change designed to lower the cost $\bar{p}$ of the backstop. The point is that a reduction in $\bar{p}$ will just result in an equal reduction in the cartel's price, with the substitute still being priced out of the market. The private return to such cost-reducing technical change will therefore be zero. The social return, however, may be very great — for the market price of the resource will have been forced down by the amount of the cost reduction, with a corresponding increase in consumer surplus generated.

We have been led once again to the conclusion that the price of a substitute is a crucial determinant of the long-run movement of a resource price. However, we now have the valuable additional insight that limit pricing by a cartel of resource-suppliers may well annihilate any private incentive to develop new substitutes or reduce the costs of those already in existence. In such cases, price-guarantee programmes have an obvious role to play.

Although our discussion so far has been premised on the assumption that the cartel controls the stock, and the fringe the substitute, a relaxation of this assumption makes no difference to the conclusions enunciated. If, for example, the competitive fringe also controls a 'small' resource stock, then price movements prior to the attainment of $\bar{p}$ may be somewhat more complex, with the possibility of the cartel and the fringe alternating in supplying the market:

---

[1] Idem.

there is some gain in descriptive realism, but the limit-pricing phenomenon remains.[1]

IV EMPIRICAL STUDIES

4:1 The work of Barnett and Morse

No survey of our knowledge of long-run resource price movements would be complete without reference to the pioneering work of Barnett and Morse in this field. They compiled and analysed data on the prices and costs of a number of resources produced in the USA over the period 1870–1957. The salient features of their data are

(1) that for almost all extractive products, the average cost of extraction, in constant prices, fell over this period;

(2) that for almost all extractive products, price fell slightly relative to an index of output prices during the period studied. The data supporting this second conclusion are reproduced in Figure 3:3.

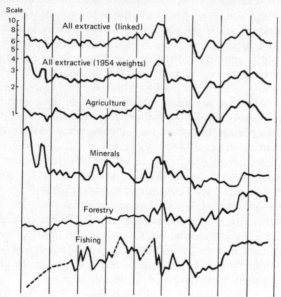

Fig. 3:3   Trends in unit prices of extractive products relative to non-extractive products in the USA, 1870–1957

Note: Solid lines connect points in annual series; dashed lines connect points over a year apart.
Source: Barnett and Morse, p. 210.

[1] Details are again in idem.

Barnett and Morse use this data to test the hypothesis that resources were becoming increasingly scarce in the USA during this period: and they concluded that as neither prices nor costs rose, this could not have been the case — the assumption here being that increasing scarcity would manifest itself in cost or price increases. In fact, it is not at all clear that this is the only interpretation, or indeed, the most persuasive interpretation, that can be drawn from this data. To see this, we consider it in the context of the models analysed earlier. The fact that average extraction costs declined over the period suggests that the most appropriate model will be one with extraction costs independent of the level of cumulative extraction, but perhaps declining at an exogenously given rate because of technical progress in the extractive industries. In such a case, equation (1) would hold in a competitive situation. This implies that

$$P(t) = C(t) + (P(0) - C(0))e^{rt}$$

where $P(0)$ depends on the size of the initial stock of the resource. A change in the perceived resource stock at some date after the initial one would lead to a change in this constant and hence to a discrete jump in price, downwards in the case of unanticipated discoveries of new stocks. For the moment we take it that known resource availabilities are constant, and consider the movement of prices in this situation. If extraction costs decline over time at a rate α to a constant C

$$P(t) = C(0)e^{-\alpha t} + (P(0) - C(0))e^{rt} + C \tag{8}$$

so that the price path may show an initial period of decline, but in the long-run will rise approximately exponentially.

Now we have a theory and some data: what conclusions can be drawn? Barnett and Morse chose to phrase their conclusions in terms of 'increasing scarcity' of resources. It is not clear that this is a felicitous choice of terminology, as in some absolute sense exhaustible resources are by definition scarce, and must in the long-run become more so. But this is essentially a terminological point, and it is certainly open to anyone to propose as a measure of scarcity the marginal or average extraction cost. If we accept the latter as a measure scarcity, then the Barnett—Morse data make the conclusion of decreasing scarcity unavoidable. But it is not really clear that this definition of scarcity, and the question to which it naturally leads, is the most penetrating and helpful approach to the issue. In many ways it seems more natural to take as a benchmark the rate of depletion that would be attained in competitive markets with full information, and then inquire whether depletion thus far has exceeded or fallen short of this rate. In the former event, there would seem to be grounds for worrying about excessive scarcity. Of course, a sufficient condition for depletion to date to exceed the competitive depletion level is that prices to date should have fallen below their competitive levels: in approaching this matter it is thus natural to proceed by comparing the actual and competitive price paths.

Unfortunately, there is no single (or even complex) way of computing the competitive path for the whole period 1870–1957: however, it does seem reasonable to claim that it would have taken exceedingly high and sustained rates of cost-reducing technical progress in extractive industries to generate a competitive price path that was declining over so long a period — especially in view of the undoubted incidence of diminishing returns in several sectors of the extractive industry. We can, therefore, suggest rather tentatively that while the actual prices of extractive products fell over the period studied, competitive equilibrium prices would have shown a rising trend for at least the later part of this period. Now, of course, this observation on its own is not sufficient to establish that there is any part of the period during which the competitive path lay above the actual, as Figure 3:4 demonstrates. To establish convincingly what one is tempted to infer from this observation — namely, that for at least part of the period resources were under-priced and over-consumed — requires considerably more research. But the inference is nevertheless tempting, because for a period as long as that studied the positive exponential term in (8) seems bound to dominate. Thus setting $r = 0.10$ at $t = 87$, e^{rt} exceeds 15,000 and is growing rapidly, whereas for $t = 87$ the first term will be approximately constant at zero. One would thus expect that the price would be high by historical standards, and rising rapidly. Such an inference is obviously contrary in spirit to the rather comforting conclusions that Barnett and Morse drew from their own study.

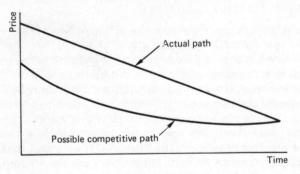

Fig. 3:4

It must however be emphasised that any conclusions on this subject must be very tentative, as it is still the subject of active research. A recent un-published study by Barrow indicates that the long-run time series on prices may conform more nearly to the theoretical model than the Barnett–Morse study suggested. He uses data produced by Potter and Christy and updated by Manthy to analyse the movements of the prices of pig iron, copper, lead, zinc and fuels over the period 1870–1973. These data series are significantly longer than those used by Barnett and Morse, and are also disaggregated and so correspond more closely to the variables with which the theory is concerned. Barrow fitted both linear and quadratic time trends to the data, and found that for pig iron, copper and fuels the quadratic had significantly more explanatory power than the linear trend, and that these series had minima in respectively 1920, 1938 and 1924. Further analysis using spline functions suggested that all series but lead (i.e. pig iron, copper, zinc and fuels) underwent at some point a structural change, prior to which they had a small but significant negative slope, and subsequent to which they had a small but significant positive slope. Barrow's findings thus indicate that when one looks at disaggregated data over the longest possible period, there is some evidence of the kind of pattern the earlier theory would predict.

The above arguments are all based on the premise that at the beginning of the period under discussion the total available resource stock was known with certainty. Such a premise is evidently unreasonable, as over the interval studied there have been large increases in the known reserves of most resources, with the great majority of these increases being unanticipated. A simple and appealing intuitive argument might suggest this as the source of the disparity between the theoretical model just constructed, and Barnett and Morse's results. After all, it seems reasonable that an increase in supply might drive price down.

Such an argument is in fact very misleading. The situation under analysis can presumably be formalised in the following terms. At some initial date $t = 0$ is known with certainty that a stock of S_0 units of the resources exists: in addition it is believed that in the future further discoveries may be made, though the magnitude and timing of these discoveries is uncertain. It is easy to see the nature of an equilibrium price path in such a situation. Whenever a new deposit is discovered, the price of the resource will undergo a quantum drop on to a path which is lower than the previous one, but which rises in a similar manner. This adjustment is necessary because equality of supply and demand over the entire consumption period now requires a higher cumulative consumption: a downward shift in the price path achieves this end.

Now, it is clear from this that those who hold resource stocks at the time of a discovery will experience capital losses on their stocks. As discovery dates and sizes are random and cannot be predicted accurately, an element of risk is introduced into the activity of holding a resource. Resource-owners must be compensated for bearing this risk, and the only form that such compensation can take is a higher rate of price increase between discovery dates. We thus have the conclusion that random discoveries of new resource deposits will lead to occasional discontinuous drops in price, and to paths which rise more rapidly than otherwise between such drops. Figure 3:5 illustrates the two types of path. The effect of stock discoveries is thus more complex than simply to depress the trend of prices. It produces a downward drift of the price path, while at the same time reinforcing its upward movements.

Because of the complexity of this effect, it is difficult without further

detailed quantitative study to know how far it should be allowed to qualify
the earlier very tentative inference that resource price paths have been below
their competitive levels. Indeed, the answer would almost certainly vary from
case to case, because additions to known reserves have varied greatly from
mineral to mineral.

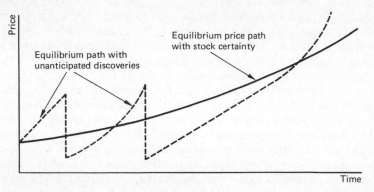

Fig. 3:5

4:2 The strength of arbitrage

We referred earlier to the fact that an equation such as (1) can be regarded as
an asset market equilibrium condition, to be achieved (if at all) by arbitrage
between other assets and resources. Indeed, this interpretation is particularly
clear for equation (2). In this last section we report briefly on an attempt[1] by
the present author to test directly the strength of this arbitrage effect. The
data used were drawn from several metals (copper, lead and zinc) and the
market for UK government short-term debt.

It is assumed that there is a basic demand for the metal which is a function
of its price and the level of industrial output: this is written as

$$D = P^{\eta_P} Y^{\eta_Y} \tag{9}$$

where P is the price, Y is industrial output, and η_P and η_Y the elasticities of
demand with respect to price and output, assumed constant. The equation (9)
is not a complete specification of demand conditions: it is assumed that, as
well as depending on price and output, demand depends on anticipated price
movements. If users expect the future price to exceed the current price, they
are encouraged to buy now and add to stocks, and similarly expectations of
price falls encourage them to delay purchases and run down stocks. To be
more precise, expectations of price increases lead to anticipatory buying if the
proportional increase in prices is expected to exceed the return available on
other assets that might be held instead of resource stocks.

[1] Full details are in Heal (1975).

In order to allow for these effects, (9) is modified to

$$D = P^{\eta P} Y^{\eta Y} \left[\frac{\tilde{P} | P}{\tilde{0} | 0} \right]^{\alpha_1} \tag{10}$$

where $\tilde{P}$ is the expected future price of the resource, 0 is the price of some other asset, $\tilde{0}$ its expected future price, and $\alpha_1 \geqslant 0$ is a constant. The expression within the square brackets is thus equal to unity if the expected return to holding the commodity equals the return expected elsewhere: if the former exceeds the latter, it exceeds unity, and vice versa. And provided $a_1 > 0$, this means that demand is scaled up or down in a way that depends on expected rates of return in commodity and other asset markets. The sensitivity of current demand to these expectations depends on the value of a_1, which is of course something we would like to measure empirically.

In order to complete the model, it is still necessary to specify several other components – a supply equation, and equations describing how the expectations $\tilde{P}$ and $\tilde{0}$ are formed. The supply function is very simple. Supply is just a function of price, though to allow for lags in the response of supply to price changes supply is a function of a weighted average of past prices, rather than of current prices only. We thus write:

$$S = S(\tilde{P})$$

where $\tilde{P}$ is a weighted average of past prices. The equality of supply and demand thus implies that

$$S(P) = P^{\eta P} Y^{\eta Y} \left[\frac{\tilde{P} | P}{\tilde{0} | 0} \right]^{\alpha_1} \tag{11}$$

It is perhaps worth remarking that there is in principle no reason why speculative behaviour of the type modelled by the term in the ratio of the rates of return should be confined to the demand side. It would be natural to have the supply function multiplied by a similar term, raised perhaps to the power β. It is however quite clear that if such a term were to be included α_1 and β could not both be identified. The most that could be identified would be $(\alpha_1 - \beta)$, the net exponent when both terms were grouped on the right. We shall henceforth suppose α_1 to be this net exponent. Taking logarithms of both sides of (11) and differentiating with respect to time,

$$\frac{\dot{S}}{S} = a_1 \left(\frac{\dot{\tilde{P}}}{\tilde{P}} - \frac{\dot{\tilde{0}}}{\tilde{0}} \right) - a_1 \left(\frac{\dot{P}}{P} - \frac{\dot{0}}{0} \right) + \frac{\dot{P}}{\eta_P P} + \frac{\dot{Y}}{\eta_Y Y} \tag{12}$$

For simplicity of notation, set $\dot{P}/P = r_c$ (the return to the commodity, $\dot{0}/0 = r$ (the return on other assets), $\dot{\tilde{P}}/\tilde{P} = \tilde{r}_c$, $\dot{\tilde{0}}/\tilde{0} = \tilde{r}$, and $\dot{Y}/Y = g$, the growth rate.

It is assumed that $\tilde{r}_c$ and $\tilde{r}$ are exponentially weighted averages of past values of r_c and r respectively, so that

$$\dot{\tilde{r}}_c = a_2(r_c - \tilde{r}_c) \tag{13}$$

$$\dot{r} = a_3(r - \tilde{r}) \tag{14}$$

which means that $\tilde{r}_c$ and $\tilde{r}$ are formed by a process of adaptive expectations — expectations are always revised in such a way as to narrow the gap between actual and expected values of the variable, so that $\tilde{r}_c$ is raised if $r_c > \tilde{r}_c$, and vice versa. This is a very natural way to form and revise expectations, and one which has survived fairly extensive use in empirical analysis.

The weighting which determines $\tilde{P}$ as a function of past values of is more complex: instead of declining exponentially, the weights rise to a peak in the recent past, and then tail off exponentially. This weighting scheme has been chosen because delays in the production of resources are often such that current supply is influenced more strongly by path than by current prices. $S(P)$ is assumed to take the form

$$S(\tilde{P}) = P^{a_4}, \ a_4 > 0, \tag{15}$$

commendable largely for its simplicity.

Substitution and manipulation produces

$$\ddot{r}_c(a_1 + a_4 - \eta_p) + \dot{r}_c(a_1 a_3 + a_2 a_4 + a_3 a_4 - \eta_p a_2 - \eta_p a_3) + r_c(a_2 a_3 a_4 - \eta_p a_2)$$
$$= a_1 \ddot{r} + a_1 a_2 \dot{r} + \ddot{g}\eta_Y + \dot{g}(a_2 + a_3)\eta_Y + g a_2 a_3 \eta_Y \tag{16}$$

which is a second-order differential equation relating the rate of change of a commodity price (r_c) to the rate of return on other assets (r) and to the rate of growth of output (g). In order to test this, it was reformulated as a difference equation: the appropriate reformulation is

$$r_c(t) = A_1 r_c(t-1) + A_2 r_c(t-2) + A_3 r(t) + A_4 r(t-1) + A_5 r(t-2)$$
$$+ A_6 g(t) + A_7 g(t-1) + A_8 g(t-2) \tag{17}$$

where (t) denotes the value of a variable this period $(t-1)$ a value last period, etc., and

$$A_1 = 2 - a_3 - \frac{a_2 a_4}{a_1 + a_4 - \eta_p} \frac{\eta_p a_2}{a_1 + a_4 - \eta_p} \frac{a_2 a_3 a_4}{2(a_1 + a_4 - \eta_p)} + \frac{\eta_p a_2 a_3}{2(a_1 + a_4 - \eta_p)}$$

$$A_2 = -1 + a_3 + \frac{a_2 a_4}{a_1 + a_4 - \eta_p} - \frac{\eta_p a_2}{a_1 + a_4 - \eta_p} - \frac{a_2 a_3 a_4}{a_1 + a_4 - \eta_p} + \frac{\eta_p a_2 a_3}{a_1 a_4 - \eta_p}$$

$$A_3 = \frac{a_1}{a_1 + a_4 - \eta_p}$$

$$A_4 = \frac{a_1 a_2 - 2a_1}{a_1 + a_4 - \eta_p}$$

$$A_5 = \frac{a_1 - a_1 a_2}{a_1 + a_4 - \eta_p}$$

$$A_6 = \frac{\eta_Y}{a_1 + a_4 - \eta_P}$$

$$A_7 = -\frac{2\eta_Y}{a_1 + a_4 - \eta_P} + \frac{\eta_Y a_2}{a_1 + a_4 - \eta_P} + \frac{\eta_Y a_3}{a_1 + a_4 - \eta_P} + \frac{1}{2}\frac{\eta_Y a_2 a_3}{a_1 + a_4 - \eta_P}$$

$$A_8 = \frac{\eta_Y}{a_1 + a_4 - \eta_P} - \frac{a_2 \eta_Y}{a_1 + a_4 - \eta_P} - \frac{a_3 \eta_Y}{a_1 + a_4 - \eta_P} + \frac{1}{2}\frac{a_2 a_3 \eta_Y}{a_1 + a_4 - \eta_P}$$

The estimation of the coefficients A_1 to A_8 in (16), and of the parameters η_Y, η_P and a_1 to a_4, poses severe econometric problems. For present purposes it is sufficient to note that (17) and similar equations based on slightly different assumptions about the lags involved in the response of supply to price and in the formation of expectations, give quite good explanations of observed price movements for some resources (lead and zinc in particular), and that those of the parameters η_P, η_Y and a_1 to a_4 that can be estimated from the data generally have values that accord with reasonable prior expectations. For example, when (17) was tested against monthly data from three-month forward transactions in zinc on the London Metal Exchange over the period December 1963 to December 1976, the values of the coefficients were:

$$A_1 = 0\cdot768* \qquad A_2 = 0\cdot0007 \qquad A_3 = 0\cdot540* \qquad A_4 = -0\cdot680*$$
$$A_5 = 0\cdot147 \qquad A_6 = -0\cdot131 \qquad A_7 = 0\cdot153 \qquad A_8 = -0\cdot071$$

Those marked by asterisks were significantly different from zero. In this estimation, r, the return on the other asset, was taken to be the return to 91-day treasury bills, and g was taken to be the rate of growth of an index of industrial production for all OECD countries. All variables were expressed in real terms. It is clear, then, that the basic hypothesis being tested has reasonable explanatory power, and that there are significant relationships between the return to holding a commodity and that on other capital assets. But in fact it is interesting to note that the empirical work just quoted suggests that this relationship is rather different from that which theory would predict in a set of efficient intertemporal markets.

This point is best seen by noting that the three interest rate coefficients in equation (17) sum to zero – i.e.:

$$A_3 + A_4 + A_5 = 0$$

Clearly the numerical estimates reported above confirm that the estimated coefficients do indeed satisfy this restriction – and, as reported in detail elsewhere, this confirmation is strikingly repeated in studies of other markets. Now, an equation with this adding-up property can be written

$$r_c(t) = b_1 r(t) + b_2 r(t-1) - (b_1 + b_2) r(t-2)$$

or

$$r_c(t) = b_1(r(t) - r(t - 1)) + (b_1 + b_2)(r(t - 1) - r(t - 2))$$

or

$$r_c(t) = b_1 \Delta r(t) + b_2' \Delta r(t - 1)$$

where $\Delta r(t) = r(t) - r(t - 1)$, etc. The rate of change of the resource price is therefore seen to depend not on the level but on the rate of change of the interest rate — a subtle but important difference from the relationship that would characerise an efficient allocation. As the model analysed above predicts this outcome, it should be possible to use it to provide an explanation of the phenomenon: to derive this, it is necessary to consider the full relationship between r_c and r:

$$r_c(t) = A_1 r_c(t - 1) + A_2 r_c(t - 2) + A_3 r(t) + A_4 r(t - 1) + A_5 r(t - 2)$$

Collecting terms, this can be rewritten as

$$B_1 r_c(t) + B_2 \Delta r_c(t) + B_3 \Delta r_c(t - 1) = b_1 \Delta r(t) + b_2 \Delta r(t - 1) + A_6 g(t) \\ + A_7 g(t - 1) + A_8 g(t) + \epsilon(t) \quad (17)$$

where b_1 and b_2 are as before, and

$$B_1 = 1 - A_1 - A_2, B_2 = A_1 + A_2, B_3 = A_2$$

The relationship between r_c and r in this equation is asymmetric, in that one has on the left hand side both the current value of r_c and its current and lagged rates of change: r, however, appears *only* in rate of change form. This reflects an asymmetry to be found in equation (16), where $\ddot{r}_c$, $\dot{r}_c$ and r_c all appear on the left, while only $\ddot{r}$ and $\dot{r}$ — the rates of change but not the level — appear on the right. In fact the basic asymmetry can be traced back further, to the demand function (10). Here demand is shown as depending on both the level of the resource price (via $P^\eta P$) and on its rate of change (via $\tilde{P}/P$), while it depends only on the rate of change of the price of the other asset. It is easy to confirm that if one were to set $\eta_p = 0$ and $a_4 = 0$, establishing a symmetric treatment of the two prices in the demand and supply functions, then $A_1 + A_2 = 1$ and $B_1 = 0$, so that in (17) both r_c and r appear only as current and lagged differences. An alternative condition that would yield symmetric treatment is that $a_2 = 0$ or $a_3 = 0$ — that is, that in one of the two markets concerned, traders should have static expectations about rates of return. This would also imply that $A_1 + A_2 = 1$. But it is easy to confirm from the empirical estimates that $A_1 + A_2 \neq 1$, so that it is neither the case that η_p, $= a_4 = 0$, nor that $a_2 = 0$ or $a_3 = 0$, and the asymmetry postulated by the model seems justified.

Of course, the causes of this asymmetry give us some indication of the reasons why the present model behaves rather differently from the efficient, competitive model. Let us consider carefully the two possible sources of this discrepancy, which are

(1) the asymmetric treatment of the two prices in the demand and supply equations and
(2) the processes by which expectations are formed.

What, in economic terms, is the justification for the differences in the treatments of the two prices and thus of r_c and r? The point is that the model reflects two types of demand for the resource – speculative demand depending on price changes, and a user demand which is essentially a derived demand depending on the demand for final products and the prices of substitutes. This latter is naturally a function of the price level – hence the inclusion of this term in the demand function – whereas the speculative demand is a function of resource price movements relative to movements elsewhere. This is clearly as it should be, and cannot of itself be the source of the discrepancy between the present model and an efficient outcome. For in a competitive market the price would, under suitable and familiar assumptions, rise at the rate of return elsewhere, leaving resource owners completely indifferent about the date at which they supply their resource. The time-pattern of use would then be determined by users (i.e. by derived demand), who would equate the marginal productivity of the resource to its price at each date.

It thus seems completely natural that both the level and the rate of change of price should enter into the demand function for the resource, so we must seek the source of the discrepancy under discussion in the facts that $a_2 \neq 0$ and $a_3 \neq 0$. Heal (1975) presents direct evidence that these coefficients are non-zero. Consider for a moment the implications of $a_2 = a_3 = 0$. These are that $\dot{\tilde{r}}_c = \dot{\tilde{r}} = 0$, so that $\tilde{r}_c$ and r_c are constant. The return on the other asset is expected to be constant, as is the return on the resource. The resource price is thus expected to grow exponentially over time at a constant rate. Hence, if $a_2 = a_3 = 0$, expectations may be compatible with efficient functioning of the market, in that efficiency requires that if r is constant then the resource price rises at rate r, and when $a_2 = a_3 = 0$, traders may expect such a situation. We emphasise that one can say only that they may expect such a situation: they are not precluded from doing so, though whether or not they actually do so depends on initial conditions, which are historically given and exogenous to the model. It is also worth noting that in the context of growth models with several capital goods, such as those discussed by Hahn (1966) and Shell and Stiglitz (1967), static expectations, which are implied by $\dot{\tilde{r}}_c = \dot{\tilde{r}} = 0$, have been found to be more conducive to efficiency than many other more sophisticated forms of expectation formation.

The general, albeit tentative, conclusion from this empirical work seems to be that there is a relationship between the movements of resource prices and the returns to other assets, and indeed this relationship is quite strong, though it is not of the form that would be generated by efficient markets. The principal cause of this difference would seem to be the manner in which expectations are formed.

V SUMMARY

We have reviewed parts of the theoretical and empirical literature bearing on resource price movements. The theoretical literature is now quite well-developed, and leads to clear conclusions. In market equilibrium under conditions of either perfect or imperfect competition, resource prices will rise in the long-run at a rate which is dependent upon (and in some simple cases equal to) the rate of return on other assets: they will continue to move in this fashion until they approach limits set by the costs of substitutes. In so far as these costs are influenced by research and development, then the upper limits that they pose are not exogenous, but will depend on expectations about price movements and upon the ability of cost-reducing innovators to secure the full social return to their activities.

The empirical studies cited are far from conclusive about any of the interesting issues, and suggest that the theory still remains to be tested seriously. However, work by the present author does indicate a clear connection between resource price movements and interest rates, though the nature of the connection is at first a little puzzling, and the role of the process by which expectations are formed appears to be very important. This is not of course surprising, though it is not a point that was emphasised at all in the theory. The difference arises because the theory presented is about *equilibrium* situations, where by definition people have full information about future developments. There have also been a limited number of theoretical studies of market behaviour under conditions where traders hold expectations about the future rather than having definite information, but these have also been equilibrium models in the sense of being concerned with situations where expectations are always realised. One would naturally hope that equilibrium models are a reasonable guide to actual behaviour, but the point remains to be substantiated.

The work of Barnett and Morse is again suggestive but far from conclusive: at first sight, their findings appear to contradict our *a priori* expectations about long-run price movements. However, there are many factors which could reconcile the two – increases in known stocks, cost reductions in the production of substitutes, and disequilibrium behaviour of markets, to name only a few. What we have is more an agenda for further research than a set of conclusions.

REFERENCES

M. Barrow (1977), 'An Econometric Study of Long-Term Price Movements of Certain Natural Resources' (Unpublished thesis, University of Sussex).

P. S. Dasgupta and G. M. Heal (1977), *Economics and the Allocation of Exhaustible Resources*, Cambridge Economic Handbooks (Cambridge University Press).

F. R. Hahn (1966), 'Equilibrium Dynamics with Heterogenous Capital Goods', *Quarterly Journal of Economics* (November).

G. M. Heal (1975), 'The Influence of Interest Rates on Resource Prices', Cowles Foundation Discussion Paper (Yale University Press).

G. M. Heal (1976), 'The Relationship between Price and Extraction Cost for a Resource with a Backstop Technology', *Bell Journal of Economics and Management Science* (Autumn 1976).

H. Hotelling (1931), 'The Economics of Exhaustible Resources', *Journal of Political Economy*.

R. Manthy, Unpublished update of *Trends in Natural Resource Commodities*.

M. Potter and F. T. Christy (1962), *Trends in Natural Resource Commodities,* Resources for the Future (Johns Hopkins Press).

K. Shell and J. E. Stiglitz (1967), 'The Allocation of Investment in a Dynamic Economy', *Quarterly Journal of Economics* (November 1967).

R. M. Solow (1974), 'The Economics of Resources or the Resources of Economics', *American Economic Review,* Papers and Proceedings (May 1974).

Discussion of Professor Heal's Paper*

Professor Csikós-Nagy,[1] who opened the discussion, said that it would be
desirable to examine the problem of the price of natural resources in a more
complex way than had been done in Professor Heal's paper. The Programme
Committee of the Congress had, however, limited the discussion, giving room
only for treating the questions in the form of short comments:

(i) The past and prospective price trends of natural resources were closely
linked with the so-called 'North—South problem', since the production
structure of advanced countries was poli-cultural, whereas most of the
developing world had an oligo-cultural character. Exports of the developing
world comprised mostly agricultural goods and minerals. Under such conditions, any increase in the relative price of natural resources was considered
by the developing countries as the firmest basis to finance fast economic
growth.

This process, however, was rather contradictory, since the increase in the
relative prices of natural resources could not be interpreted as unequivocally
advantageous for the developing countries. From time to time, the different
price movements, while favourable to some groups of countries, caused serious
economic problems to others. In fact, the revaluation of natural resources was
one of the main items of the developing world put on the agenda of the New
International Economic Order.

(ii) It had been assumed, said Professor Csikós-Nagy, that the disparity
between the price level of products in extractive and non-extractive sectors
was unfavourable to the former and that this affected mainly the developing
countries. If this assumption was correct, then how could the continued
exploitation of natural resources in the developed areas be explained? The
USSR and the USA were the main producers of natural resources in the developed areas. Concerning the USSR, one could argue that price structure did
not play a decisive role in its structural policy of planned development. But in
the case of the USA, we had to deal with a free market economy in which the
profit motive had always been decisive in investment activities.

Marx explained the specific features of the pricing of natural resources by
the transformation of surplus-profit into ground rent. According to him, when
the utilisation of a parcel of land ensured only the average rate of profit, then
only the landlord was in a position to cultivate it. Any contract of lease pre-
supposed, in addition to the average rate of profit, an absolute ground rent.
Therefore, under capitalist conditions, the market prices of agricultural goods
had to be determined by the production conditions of the least productive
land in cultivation. The rent of mining was similar to that of agricultural land,
but the price of some extractive products that could be exploited under
particularly favourable natural conditions also contained a monopoly rent.[2]

These circumstances had changed in one respect only since the Second

*The numbered footnotes within the discussion section that follows are the speakers'
own.
[1] A volume by Dr Gikós Nagy entitled *In For a New Price Revolution?* is in preparation
and will be published in 1978. The comments here are a summary of some theses which
will be discussed in more detail in that work.
[2] K. Marx, *Capital,* vol. III (Moscow: Progress Publishers, 1966) pp. 614–802.

World War. Due to European agrarian protectionism, the world price level of agricultural goods was lower than it would have been without the intervention of the European governments.

What was actually detrimental for the developing countries lay in their historic background, in their having been partly colonies and partly otherwise dependent on industrially advanced countries. This dependence had brought about and maintained their economic structure. Second, enterprises of industrially advanced countries had exploited the better part of natural resources. Thus these enterprises had accumulated – partly or entirely – the ground rent and the monopoly rent. And, lastly, the price policy of the multinational enterprises – as it will be referred to later – had been controlled in the interests of industrially advanced countries.

(iii) According to the conventional view, in the long-run the relative price of agricultural goods and of minerals could only increase. The Ricardian law of the diminishing return of land was in the background of this hypothesis. Economists usually considered diminishing returns as a fundamental law of economics and technology. However, if we considered the rules of socio-economic development as fundamental, the above hypothesis was open to debate.

It was worth while, he continued, to evoke Lenin's dispute with Bulgakhov in which Lenin pointed out that additional input in itself presupposes changes in the method of production and reforms in technique. Clearly, if an additional input of labour and capital into the same parcel of land produced not a diminishing but an equal quantity of products, then there would be no sense in extending the area of land under cultivation.[1] Ricardo had formulated the law of diminishing returns in close connection with the extension of arable land. It was his hypothesis that parallel with its increasing needs mankind would be obliged to utilise usable land with ever-decreasing efficiency.

Forecasts for the last quarter of the twentieth century seemed to justify this idea. In the so-called Leontief model, representing the future of world economy, the generalisation of specific inputs of the USA assumed that the average relative prices of minerals would increase some 2·7 times between 1970 and the year 2000; the average price of agricultural goods would do so by 14 per cent, while the average price for manufactured goods would decline by 6·8 per cent. Prices of minerals would, in 2000, be 2·9 times as costly in relation to manufactured goods as they were in 1970 and agricultural commodities would be 1·2 times as expensive.[2]

The remarkable study by Harold J. Barnett and Chandler Morse[3] made it impossible to accept the law of diminishing returns as interpreted by Ricardo. Investigating the costs of extractive output in the USA for the period 1870–1957, the evidence mainly showed increasing, not diminishing, returns. The Barnett and Morse study drew our attention to the circumstances under

[1] V. I. Lenin, *The Agrarian Questions and the 'Critics of Marx': The Iskra Period 1900–1902*, Book 1 (New York: International, 1929) pp. 184–5.
[2] UN Department of Economic and Social Affairs, *The Future of the World Economy* (United Nations, 1976). This Report was prepared under the direction of Wassily Leontief and included Anna P. Carter and Peter Petri, p. 41.
[3] H. J. Barnett and Ch. Morse, *Scarcity and Growth: The Economics of Natural Resource Availability* (Baltimore, 1962) pp. 7–9.

which Ricardo formulated his hypothesis. These circumstances had been created by the specific features of British agricultural policy, which had hindered the importing of corn, and also by the Continental blockade during the Napoleonic Wars. All this had compelled Britain to extend the areas of arable land and bring the poorer soils into cultivation. This was really a specific situation, hardly one on which to base a 'universal law'.

The likelihood of diminishing land returns in the last decades of this century could not be excluded, said Professor Csikós-Nagy. Nevertheless, it seemed that the price of natural resources between 1970 and the year 2000 would be determined less by input than by scarcity, and efforts to get the highest ground (monopoly) rent; that is to say, by related conflicting interests.

(iv) The relative prices of natural resources were usually measured on the world market by the terms of trade. The course of the terms of trade showed that demand and supply could bring about price movements of different intensities and, sometimes, in different directions, in the case of extractive and non-extractive goods. One could say, without ambiguity, that the price dispersion intensity around the average price was greater for extractive goods than for non-extractive ones.

Short-run price fluctuations brought about elements of instability. This instability meant grave disadvantages. In the case of an excessive decline of prices, difficulties arose concerning exporting countries, because of short-falls in foreign exchange earnings compelled them to cut down imports if they were to avoid international balance of payments deficits. An excessive increase of prices caused difficulties for the importing countries, because imports could be maintained only by increasing exports; otherwise, again, international balance of payments deficits could not be avoided.

The 1973 oil price explosion seemed to have created a profoundly new situation. Since that time dramatic price rises could be experienced in the sphere of natural resources. But whereas in the case of most natural resources the business cyclical sensitivity of prices had remained more or less unchanged, the relative price of oil had stabilised for nearly four years at the top point reached at the time of the price explosion. Nevertheless, the price of oil deserved special attention; amongst other reasons, because two-thirds of the value of minerals produced in the world fell to energy carriers, and 40 per cent fell to oil alone.[1]

(v) His intention, said Professor Csikós-Nagy, was to approach the expectations for the price tendency of natural resources through the oil price, although there were several specifics in the background of the universal laws which were valid only for some of them. However, one could make the general assumption that the dramatic price movements of natural resources in the world market could not be explained entirely by market price theories.

According to market price theories, demand was determined by prices, and it changed as a function of prices. The 1973 oil price explosion had increased the world price of crude oil five times overnight. According to the course prescribed by the demand curve, demand should have decreased. But the price explosion had had hardly any influence on oil demand. What had actually happened was that development projects rejected in the past for their in-

[1] F. Friedensburg, 'Die Entwicklung der Bergwirtschaft der Welt in den letzen Hundert Jahren', *Glückauf*, 6 (January 1965) pp. 63–77.

efficiency had been revived and energy savings had been given greater importance. All this was significant, yet in its character differed from the suppositions
of conventional price theories.

For the most part, it was the theories of imperfect competition and of
monopolistic competition that provided a basis for a scientific analysis of price
movements in modern market economics.[1] According to the theory of monopolistic competition, the substitution of products transformed the competition
between enterprises into a competition between products. Owing to its suit-
ability for heating purposes, oil could be brought to a common denominator
with other energy carriers: e.g. coal. Comparison, in this case was based on
heating values. It could be supposed that the relative world market prices of
energy carriers would adjust themselves to their relative heating values. In fact,
divergencies from parity prices were substantial in both directions; the coin-
cidence of the two was only incidental.

It was possible, of course, to define price determinant factors in mathematical formulae, as Professor Heal's paper had done in a sophisticated way.
But we would be confronted with an insoluble task if we attempted to explain
ex post the 1973 oil price explosion, or to forecast ex ante the future price
of oil by applying the mathematical model presented in his paper. To take just
one factor, he said, the cost of oil substitution, considered today as the most
important price determinant, Table 3:1 showed the different evaluations of
these costs.

TABLE 3:1 PROGNOSTICATED RELATIVE
WORLD MARKET OIL PRICE IN ABOUT
THE YEAR 2000 (at 1975 $ US value)

	$ *per barrel*
Lowest price limit	7
Basic price /1976 price/	11·5
Top price limit	
Estimation I	18
Estimation II	20–30

The price of $7 per barrel was the lowest limit – confirmed in the declara
tions of several industrially developed countries – encouraging entrepreneurs
to invest in sectors capable of producing substitutes. The price of $20–30 per
barrel was explained in the H. Ager-Hanssen paper, on the basis of which the
'Offshore North-Sea' oil conference held in Stavanger in the autumn of 1976
had investigated the costs of substitutes.[2] At the November 1976 meeting of
the Oxford Energy Policy Club, several experts had considered a price of $18
per barrel as reasonable for the future.

(vi) The question we had to put could be formulated in the following way:
was it at all possible to work with criteria developed in a price theory representing on an abstract basis a marker situation? This was the really debatable
point. The prices of natural resources operated as equilibrium prices. But

[1] J. Robinson, *Economics of Imperfect Competition* (London, 1954); E. H. Chamberlin,
The Theory of Monopolistic Competition (Cambridge, Massachusetts, 1947).
[2] H. Ager-Hanssen, *'Norwegian Oil and Alternative Energy Resources'*, manuscript.

behind them a definite price policy was to be found, which in its character was power policy. That is why, in the analysis — both present and future — of the prices of natural resources the limits set for the market mechanism to operate were rather narrow. What differentiated the future from the past in this respect could be summarised in the point that the price policy of natural resources was slipping under the control of multinational enterprises, and that the role of the exporting developing countries was increasing in significance all the time.

The oil resources of the developing world used to be exploited mostly by international monopolies of the western world, he said. Through foreign investments these enterprises could establish favourable market relations for their own — i.e. industrially developed — countries. It was their real business interest, too, that part of the ground and monopoly rent should not be realised in the price of crude oil; and that as big a part as possible of the rent should be realised in the higher vertical stages of production — i.e. in the domestic stages of production. This was the way in which the oil price policy could mostly contribute to the general industrialisation of the home countries.

Multinational enterprises used to keep the price of oil generally below its relative use value. This price structure had brought about a definite production structure very favourable for the industrially developed countries and had contributed to the financing of industrialisation. The price policy was supported by a specific budgetary policy, in which two elements are of major importance: (a) The import duty system in which the imports of natural resources were free of duty and customs tariffs increase — as a general rule — as a function of the degree of processing. (b) The turnover tax system, according to which a part of the ground rent of natural resources was charged at the stage of consumption goods (petrol, sugar, etc.); i.e. not at the place of exploitation of natural resources, but at the place of consumption of the end products.

Thus, the historical price structure could be explained only if we knew the power structure that characterised the oligocentric world economy, together with its organic parts — the countries of colonial or semi-colonial status. Consequently as the former colonies had become independent countries, the criteria of economic decisions, among them pricing, had changed. The developing world pursued a price policy to revaluate natural resources. The OPEC price policy was the most spectacular manifestation of the challenge. In essence, it transformed an end product-centred price policy dictated by multinational enterprises into a raw product-centred price policy pursued by the oil exporting countries. This was the very point which — with a certain generalisation — could be considered as relevant in the assessment of future prices of all natural resources.

OPEC had raised the oil price above its relative use value. A new production structure policy was concomitant with that price policy. That was why the hypothesis according to which secular change in the world economy could be characterised as having brought about a structural crisis could be considered justified.

(vii) The 1973 oil embargo decided upon by OPEC and the price explosion following it (or rather the success of those actions) pointed to the relative vulnerability of developed capitalist countries, to their conflicting interests and to the limits of possible retaliations. Beyond this, the OPEC countries had evidently taken into account the rigidity of demand, determined by basic interests in steady economic growth and full employment.

When all was said and done, said Professor Csikós-Nagy, it was hardly possible to see a rational conventional solution: i.e. within the framework of a market mechanism. One was led to believe that the free market system was workable only in a period when power-imposed political discipline – and as a last resort, war – could be used.

For the time being, the forces aiming at price stability at levels that were adequate for producers and equitable to consumers were rather weak. Conflicting interests made agreement difficult: whereas exporting countries wanted to stabilise a high price level, importing countries wanted a low one.

The problem of the relative prices of natural resources grew even more intricate because it arose in inflation, and was thus connected with the problem of indexation. But indexation itself raised the rate of inflation, by giving the raw materials block a privileged position: for them, the average rate of all price increases became the lowest limit of a price rise.

Such a challenge by the developing world had obviously played a part in changing the export price policy of industrially advanced capitalist countries. Up to the 1970s there had been relative price stability on the world market in spite of ever-growing inflation in some countries. This inflation, however, extended in the 1970s to the whole world market.

From the Second World War up the 1970s the industrially advanced capitalist countries had attempted to avoid the effects of home inflation by invading the international market. The business policy of enterprises considered this important if they were to preserve their international competitiveness, an endeavour supported by the state in the interest of preserving the value of its currency. Thus, in a way, domestic inflation had helped to finance the policy of relatively stable export prices. But in the 1970s a change had taken place. In that period – at least in some industrially advanced capitalist countries – an attempt to exploit world market inflation for the purposes of an anti-inflationary policy at home could be observed. This was one of the new features to be taken into consideration when examining the future prices of natural resources.

The influence of government policies on the formation of world market prices was steadily increasing. Consequently, economic stability could be achieved only by an internationally harmonised price policy at governmental level. Agreement on the interpretation and practical application of the basic principles of a new international economic order should be reached as soon as possible, to be followed by a co-ordinated operative price policy of all governments.

*

The second speaker was *Professor Winckler*,[1] who said that, attracted by the public recognition of studies such as the *Limits to Growth*, startled by its

[1] Professor Winckler was grateful to H. Abele and H. Selinger for helpful comments on earlier drafts of his remarks.

gloomy aspects, shocked by the apparent success of the oil cartel of OPEC, many economists had shifted their interest towards questions of inter-temporal price and extraction paths of exhaustible resources. In fact, the interest in this topic had grown so fast that a surprised Solow pursuing his own research in this area had once said:

> it seemed that every time the mail came in it contained another paper by another economic theorist on the economics of exhaustible resources. It was a little like trotting down to the sea, minding your own business like any nice independent rat, and then looking around and suddenly discovering that you're a lemming.[1]

However, taking Heal's paper and most of the recent studies concerning this 'contemporary but somehow perennial topic' (Solow), one had an uncomfortable feeling about the adequacy of the underlying Walrasian thought experiments.[2] The difficulty of an application of Walrasian modes of thought to the economic questions of resources like oil, copper a.s.o. might be that the area chosen was especially inapt for this type of reasoning. Walrasian theory hardly explained the dynamics of disequilibrium (e.g. due to speculation) or that of oligopolies.

The fundamental principle of the economics of exhaustible resources, didactically well presented in Professor Heal's paper, was quickly stated: in the competitive case, if costs are negligible relative to price, the price of the resource rose exponentially at the rate of interest. In monopolistic markets, it was the marginal revenue which, in equilibrium, had to grow at a rate equal to the rate of interest.

The introduction of extraction cost might complicate but does not invalidate the main theorem: that equilibrium in the competitive case now required that net price, i.e. price minus marginal cost (scarcity rent or royalty), grew at the rate of interest. There could be some refinements: one might consider high-cost and low-cost producers of upper price limits due to a 'Nordhaus backstop technology'. Or one could ask which mix of capital (its production requires the input of resources) and resource assets should be saved for the future if future welfare was to be maximised and the cost of substitutes was uncertain?[3] In all these models the efficiency result concerning the exponential growth of price or net price still somehow held.

Of course, the fictitious nature of the variable called rate of interest could be criticised. Was it the rate of return on investment? Did this presuppose a

---

[1] R. Solow, 'The Economics of Resources and the Resources of Economics', *AER PP*, 64 (May 1974) p. 2.

[2] The economics of exhaustible resources mostly deals with partial equilibrium problems. Hence the term 'Walrasian' may be regarded as a mislabel. However, the salient feature of Walrasian economics is not its general equilibrium approach (recent researches indicate a wide variety of general equilibrium theories), but rather that it lacks a time-intrinsic structure, because all decisions are made prior to any transaction. For further clarifications on this point see e.g. E. R. Weintraub, 'The Microfoundations of Macroeconomics: A Critical Survey', *JEL*, 15 (March 1977) pp. 1–23.

[3] See D. A. Hanson, 'The Allocation of a Natural Resource When the Cost of a Substitute is Uncertain', *Annals of Economic and Social Management*, 6 (Spring 1977) pp. 189–201.

state of equilibrium in the capital markets and what happened to this equilibrium if the resource market was out of equilibrium? Was this rate identical with the suppliers' or society's rate of time preference? What happened if the market rate of interest systematically exceeded society's rate of time preference? How much did this divergence impinge on issues of intergenerational equity? These intriguing questions had been seen from the very beginning in the development of the economics of exhaustible resources.[1] Questions about governmental interventions had usually focused on such considerations.

A fundamental critique of the modes of thought implicit in the economics of exhaustible resources was the predominance of the partial equilibrium analysis along Walrasian lines. Another critique demonstrating the limited usefulness of this equilibrium approach referred to the stability of various equilibria in these models. What kinds of equilibria were involved in Professor Heal's analysis?

The exponential growth of the resource price or net price could be interpreted as a *stock equilibrium condition* for the asset market. Equilibrium there required that the rate of return of all assets should be equal. Hence in stock equilibrium, resource owners were left completely indifferent between selling the resource or holding it in the ground as an investment. This indifference of suppliers in turn allowed the time-pattern of use to be fixed by demand in each period. Thus the existence of *flow equilibria* in all successive periods was guaranteed: the flow demand determined the rate of extraction of the resource and thus the market was cleared.[2]

Intertemporal efficiency further required that the initial resource price or net price should be just so large that precisely at the time when demand reached zero the resource would be exhausted. Assuming the stock and flow equilibrium case, and hence an exponential growth of price or net price, only the initial price determined the sum of flow demands of the resource. As the total supply of the resource was given it was analytically simple to find out the equilibrium value of the initial price.[3] This solution then satisfied the intertemporal equilibrium or intertemporal efficiency condition.

Taking for the moment the market guess of an efficient initial price as granted, problems of disequilibrium dynamics still remained. As Professor Heal had tried to analyse in his section on the strength of arbitrage, there might be speculators acting on the resource markets and adding a stock demand to the (resource-consuming) flow demand. Furthermore, one had to conceive of unanticipated supplies of newly discovered amounts of the exhaustible resource. These unanticipated supplies posed a delicate problem of market entry because one had to take into account the refusal of the owners of old deposits 'to jeopardize the value of their present assets by looking for additional ones'.[4]

[1] 'The Economics of Exhaustible Resources', *JPE*, 39 (April 1931) pp. 137–75; H. Solow, op. cit., p. 8 and elsewhere.

[2] See Solow, op. cit., p. 3.

[3] For this reduction of the problem see e.g. M. C. Weinstein and R. J. Zeckhauser, 'The Optimal Consumption of Depletable Natural Resources', *QJE*, 89 (August 1975) p. 374.

[4] H. S. Houthakker, 'The Economics of Nonrenewable Resources', in *Die Versorgung der Weltwirtschaft mit Rohstoffen: Beihefté der Konjunktur-politik*, vol. 23 (Berlin, 1976) p. 123.

Some possible adjustment paths could be analysed.

Supposing that the speculators' stock demand depended on the expectation of the future price movement; and assuming further that the elasticity of expectation (in the Hicksian sense) was rather high. If, then, the temporary price rose, speculators would expect a further price rise in the future and would keep buying. The same instable result could be obtained for the stock supply. Solow had described this process.[1] In both cases disequilibrium was self-reinforcing.

These disequilibrating tendencies were due to anomalously sloped curves for the stock demand and for the stock supply, said Professor Winckler. Instabilities in those cases were classical results in stability analysis. Of course, there were a number of arguments against a long-run prevalence of such disequilibria. Solow, for example, argued that producers' expectations about future price changes were not so responsive to current events, because 'producers do have some notion that the resource they own has a value anchored in the future, a value determined by technological and demand considerations, not by pure and simple speculation'.[2] However, this optimism about a perceivable, in the long-run relatively stable, value of the resource might not be shared. Professor Heal showed (p. 99) that unanticipated discoveries of new deposits and of new technologies produced a downward drift of the equilibrium price path while at the same time reinforcing its upward movement between discovery dates as a compensation for the capital risk of new discoveries. Fearing new deposits, new substitutes, new resource-saving technologies, and so on, the sensitivity of a resource owner to speculative price changes might be quite high.

The occurrence of unstable market processes was however not only linked to an anomalously sloped stock demand or stock supply curve, as could be seen if we assumed normal conditions for the supply and demand side, but regarded the intertemporal equilibrium (intertemporal efficiency condition).

To satisfy this condition a curious dichotomisation of admissible price effects caused by demand changes was needed. Let us suppose, first, that the (resource-consuming) flow demand curve shifted to the right, e.g. due to an unexpectedly increased volume of the industrial production. Then, given an exponential growth of the resource price (the required stock equilibrium condition) and hence given the determination of the time-pattern of extraction by flow demand (the required flow equilibrium condition), it was necessary that the (current-initial) resource price should increase. Otherwise the condition of intertemporal efficiency was not fulfilled (demand reached zero precisely when the resource was exhausted).

If we supposed, second, the occurrence of a (normally sloped) stock demand, e.g. due to speculation, intertemporal efficiency required that the current resource price should *not* be changed since the speculators' demand, however large, would not alter the remaining amount of the resource. In other words, a shift of the flow demand curve should have price effects, a shift of the stock demand curve, however, not. Hence if changes of the speculators' stock demand (exogenous changes or changes due to disequilibrium processes) had price effects, the flow demand would be accelerated or decelerated and a

[1] Solow, op. cit., p. 6.
[2] Idem.

new source of instability for the intertemporally efficient price path would occur.

In a more technically oriented paper contributed to the Congress, Professor Winckler continued, he and a colleague had summarised some results of their study of the stability problem in the models of exhaustible resources.[1] Of course, the solutions depended in a crucial way on how price expectations and market reactions were specified. However, one result seemed to be recurrent: due to exogenous shocks, resource prices shifted away from the efficient price path and might finally settle down around another exponentially growing path, where the stock and flow equilibrium conditions might be met. However, this path was intertemporarily efficient only in very special cases. That meant that the exhaustion date of the resource would generally *not* coincide with the moment when the resource price would choke off demand.

There still remained the problem of oligopolies, said Professor Winckler. Professor Heal correctly rejected the notion of identical and competing oligopolists and the intertemporal Nash equilibrium solution.[2] Instead, he stressed the case of asymmetrically placed oligopolists. Although his political conclusion about price-guarantee programmes was interesting, his analysis remained inconclusive. One was reminded of Shubik's verdict that 'oligopoly theory provides one of the clearest examples for the malaise in microeconomics. It is here that the contrast between institution free and detail-rich approaches is the most striking.'[3]

For instance, the oil market was a classic example that there was no *a priori* way to reduce the study of oligopoly to Nash or Stackelberg solutions. The power of an oligopolist in the oil market might depend in a knotty way not only on its ability to control the price, but also on its ability to carry through embargoes or on its disposal of a retailing and distribution set-up in the oil consuming countries. In addition, latent competitors might enter the market and might further complicate the analysis of oligopolies.

Despite all these problems, Professor Heal accepted the fundamental message of the economics of exhaustible resources, namely that their prices grew exponentially at the rate of interest. So he tried to test this hypothesis empirically.

The task did not seem to be very promising, said Professor Winckler. Barnett and Morse had found out that for almost all extractive products real price fell slightly during 1870 and 1957. One has also to remember recent studies by the World Bank and by UNCTAD that the terms of trade of the countries exporting raw materials had deteriorated at least until 1972. These studies apparently contradicted the interest rate hypothesis of the microeconomic models based on Walrasian thought experiments.

Reformulating his fundamental equation (p. 90) Professor Heal had demonstrated (p. 00) that given constant marginal costs decreasing in time at

[1] G. Pflug and G. Winckler, 'Speculative Stocks and the Stability in the Market of Exhaustible Resources', paper contributed to the 5th World Congress of the IEA, Tokyo, 1977.

[2] This solution is present in the literature of exhaustible resources and states that the oligopolistic price path relates to the competitive case exactly as in the case of monopoly.

[3] M. Shubik, 'A Curmudgeon's Guide to Microeconomics', *JEL,* 8 (June 1970) p. 415

an exogenously given rate due to technical progress the price path might show an initial period of decline and would rise approximately exponentially only in the long-run. But how long could the 'initial period' last? Perhaps eighty-seven years, in order to explain the price decline in the time period studied by Barnett and Morse? This explanation seemed unlikely. As Professor Heal had mentioned, for eighty-seven years an interest rate of 10 per cent yielded a growth of the resource price which exceeded 15,000 times the initial value ($p_t = p_0 e^{0.1t}$, $t = 87$). This price increase probably exceeded any cost decreases which could have occurred in the meantime.

There must be other factors which were responsible for the reported decline of resource prices. It might be that the actual price started from an initial value which lay well above the initial value calculated by the standard microeconomic efficiency model. The actual decline of prices could then be interpreted as a convergence towards the (Walrasian) efficiency price path. Explanations along these lines posed a delicate problem for an empirical test: who knows the location of the Walrasian efficiency price path?

Considering all the possibilities of unanticipated discoveries, unanticipated technological advances, shifts in the oligopolistic power, and so on, any empirical study about the interest rate hypothesis of the long-run movement of the prices of exhaustible resources needed first to separate these disturbing side-effects. If this was not done, as in Professor Heal's study, it was difficult to determine the time period in which the interest rate hypothesis was most likely to be true. As Professor Heal had demonstrated, cost considerations spoke for the long-run; however, unanticipated discoveries of new deposits and of new technologies spoke for the short-run. Thus the question remained open whether the interest rate hypothesis was valuable for the explanation of the short-run or long-run movement of the prices of exhaustible resources.

If Professor Heal concluded that the interest rate hypothesis was substantiated by the data ('clear connection between resource price movements and interest rates', p. 29), did this mean that in the eight years studied by Professor Heal there were no unanticipated discoveries or no increased extraction costs? Or perhaps both with a zero net effect? Furthermore, the observable price increase might perhaps be caused by a 'secular' shift in the market power in favour of the suppliers due to the oil shock of 1973 or by the commodity speculation in 1973/74 as a consequence of notorious monetary instabilities (inflation and currency instabilities).[1] The equilibrium hypothesis that the price of assets grew at the rate of interest, then yielded only a spurious correlation.

He would not discuss Professor Heal's estimation procedure, said Professor Winckler, although specialists could probably find a lot of econometric problems caused by collinear variables, autocorrelated errors and under- or over-identified parameters. Turning to economic issues again, he said, it was not clear which kind of equilibrium Professor Heal was going to estimate in equation (11) on p. 101. Did the condition 'supply equals demand' refer to an overall (stock and flow) equilibrium? If not, then what part in the adjustment processes did this temporary equilibrium condition play? As already noted there were several pitfalls in the disequilibrium analysis of the economics of

[1] See e.g. W. C. Labys and H. C. Thomas, 'Speculation, Hedging and Commodity Price Behaviour: An International Comparison', *Applied Economics* (December 1975).

exhaustible resources.

He wished to make two points, said Professor Winckler, summing up. First, although the interest rate hypothesis might partially explain the price movement of exhaustible resources, the explanatory power of this hypothesis was exaggerated in Walrasian microeconomic thought experiments. Due to unanticipated discoveries of new deposits, of new technologies, due to shifts in the oligopolistic power, due to speculative activities, it was not even clear whether the interest-rate hypothesis was more valuable in testing the short-run, medium-run or long-run price movements.

Second, disequilibria, instabilities, oligopolistic market situations all cast serious doubts on the usefulness of the Walrasian framework in the economics of exhaustible resources. These phenomena and our ignorance about their adequate methodological treatment seemed to point more in the direction of structural, institutional studies, simply in order to increase our understanding of the subject under scrutiny.

*

Opening the discussion from the floor, *Professor Houthakker* expressed doubts about Professor Heal's reliance on Hotelling's rule, according to which the royalty (or 'net price') increased at the rate of interest. This rule needed modification when extraction costs depended on the rate of extraction and on cumulative production, as was likely to be true in reality. In that case the royalty equation had a second term and it was possible that the royalty did not rise steadily. When there were several deposits, moreover, the difference between price and extraction costs could no longer be identified with royalty since there would be rents and quasi-rents. Professor Houthakker also expressed reservations about Professor Heal's suggestion that in oil extraction costs were a small fraction of the price; that might be true for OPEC, but there must always be marginal producers for whom the extraction cost was close to or equalled the market price.

Professor Kravis said that there was some doubt that the price data cited from Barnett and Morse provided the basis for rejecting the hypothesis that resources had become increasingly scarce in the USA between 1870 and 1957. The Barnett and Morse series did indeed fail to show a rise in the relative prices of all extractive goods to non-extractive products. It was not, however, implausible to believe that the extractive-non-extractive price ratios were biased downward. At least this would be the case if, as was likely, our price indexes failed to capture adequately the improvement in quality and if quality improvements had been more important in non-extractive goods than in extractive products. The deficiencies of our price indexes, particularly with respect to non-extractive products, increased as one went backwards in time. Even the price indexes for recent decades tended systematically to exclude products for which technological progress was most rapid, and this tendency was even more notable for the price indexes for the early decades of the period which were based on the most simple kinds of manufactures.

*

Replying to the discussion, *Professor Heal* said that he would like to begin by answering the questions raised by Professors Kravis and Houthakker. Professor Kravis's point about the likely downward bias in Barnett and Morse's price index was an interesting and persuasive one, which he would certainly accept: unfortunately it was extremely difficult to produce even a rough estimate of the order of magnitude involved.

Professor Houthakker has queried the appropriateness of equation ($1'$) of his paper in situations where extraction costs were endogenous. This was clearly an important point, and it was certainly true that Hotelling's original analysis, and most subsequent works, had been concerned with situations where costs were exogenous. In fact the equation in question was equation (10) of Heal (1976), and in that model he had been explicitly considering the effect of cumulative extraction on extraction costs. There were three separate effects that one could be concerned with here:

(1) the effect of cumulative extraction on extraction costs;
(2) the effect of the rate of extraction on extraction costs; and
(3) the effect of the rate of extraction on the total recoverable stock.

Equation ($1'$) of his paper is derived from a model which took due account of the first of these effects, and which could be readily modified to include both the second and the third. In general, modification to allow for effects (2) and (3) led to some slight change in equation ($1'$), though in certain special but by no means uninteresting cases it led to no change at all. In particular, the incorporation of effect (2) {costs depending on the rate of extraction} led to an equation identical to ($1'$) in the long-run, and incorporation of effect (3) led to no change in ($1'$) if the dependence of the recoverable stock on the extraction rate was linear. In summary, then, equation ($1'$) was quite generally valid — substantially more so than much previous analysis.

Professor Houthakker had gone on to remark that, when there were several deposits, the difference between price and extraction costs could no longer be identical with royalty. He would not dispute this, said Professor Heal, but he was not clear what implications it was supposed to have for the present discussion. Finally, he was a little surprised to find it alleged that he had suggested that oil-extraction costs were a small fraction of price. He had merely suggested that this might be 'an acceptable approximation for Middle Eastern oil' — precisely Professor Houthakker's point.

As regards the formal discussion by Professors Csikós-Nagy and Winckler, said Professor Heal, he found the former's remarks interesting in a general sense, but sufficiently unrelated to the contents of his paper for a detailed reply to be unnecessary. Professor Winckler's comments were certainly related to the paper: indeed, one could say that they went to the other extreme, and focused so exclusively on points of detail as to omit the more general issues. Most of his points were probably not worth a detailed reply, though he did feel sufficiently irritated by Professor Winckler's comments on the empirical work to respond. Professor Winckler had alleged that the empirical study of interest rates and resource prices 'only yields a spurious correlation', and had gone on to say of the econometric methodology that 'specialists could probably find a lot of econometric problems'. Neither comment was substantiated by the slightest vestige of evidence, an absence which he took as a sure sign of an absence of such evidence. Of course, the empirical evidence was not unambiguous, said Professor Heal. No one with experience of empirical work would expect it to be, and he had said this quite explicitly in the paper. Equally clearly, he would welcome carefully considered comments on how it might be improved or reinterpreted, and could only regret that no such comments had been offered by the discussant. Professor Winckler had also commented, very much *en passant*, that the work of Barnett and Morse 'apparently contradicts the interest rate hypothesis'. He thought his paper made it reasonably clear, said Professor Heal, that (a) the data used by Barnett and Morse, being aggregated over broad groups, were not ideally suited to testing this hypothesis, and (b) that the use of disaggregated data extending over a longer period suggested, albeit tentatively, that the essential qualitative predictions of the theory might be correct.

Professor Winckler was, he believed, on much sounder ground when he argued that the paper was possibly deficient in considering mainly equilibrium situations. The basic issue here was that all the theoretical models referred to in the paper were models of situations where people's expectations about future prices and outputs were fulfilled: it was in this sense that they were equilibrium models. Of course there were, in practice, many situations where expectations turned out to be false and had to be revised: ideally our models should specify how traders formed their expectations about the future, and how they revised these in the light of differences between actual and expected outcomes. This was an issue that was addressed in the empirical work discussed in Section 4:2, with equations (13) and (14) representing particular hypotheses about the ways in which people formed expectations about future rates of return. Any empirical work had to face this issue, but much theoretical work had not done so. It was, however, an active research field at present, and the emerging consensus was that the behaviour of resource markets in which expectations were not always fulfilled was very sensitive to the assumptions made about how these expectations were formed. Two cases had been considered: those where future price expectations were influenced primarily by past price data, and those where future price expectations depended primarily on quantity rather than price data — for example, on the relationship between the current consumption rate and the remaining stock. Models where expectations depended primarily on price data seemed to predict rather unstable behaviour, whereas those where quantity signals were more influential seemed both more stable and more likely to resemble in their behaviour the equilibrium markets discussed in the paper. The influence and importance of disequilibrium considerations were therefore still unclear, he said, and it seemed to him appropriate to end by emphasising the need for more research on this issue.

4 Planned Growth and Rational Utilisation of Resources

T. S. Khachaturov
ASSOCIATION FOR SOVIET ECONOMIC SCIENTIFIC
INSTITUTIONS, MOSCOW USSR
and N. P. Fedorenko
ACADEMY OF SCIENCES, USSR

The postwar period, and especially the last decade, is characterised by significant changes in the economic development of the world, an increasing rate of scientific and technological progress, strengthening of the socialist system and development of the underdeveloped nations.

At the same time, the further growth in the production of many countries becomes more and more linked with the problem of sources for economic growth, scarcity of natural resources and pollution of the environment. That is the reason, especially in the western countries, for conducting research work aimed at investigation of resources for future growth.

We should mention the work of J. Forrester, D. Meadows *et al.* and M. Mesarovitch, E. Pestel *et al.* These authors make an attempt to build models of world development.

The Forrester and Meadows model consists of five blocks: population, industry, agriculture, natural resources and environment. Those blocks are analysed simultaneously. The world is analysed as one system, with features of a capitalist society. That system does not provide any possibility to influence the process of development by man. As a result, the authors arrive at a pessimistic conclusion and attention is mainly focused on the period after which world catastrophe takes place due to lack of resources, hunger and pollution.

The Mesarovitch and Pestel model is a more differentiated one because all the states are grouped into ten regions, each of which is described by a system of sub-models. The control is conducted in accordance with the scenario chosen. The main difference of these models as compared with the Forrester and Meadows global model is that the maintenance of the existing development trends will lead to regional catastrophes in different periods of time and for different reasons. The conclusions are also pessimistic. There are a number of other papers by B. Commoner, B. Ward, R. Dubos and J. Tinbergen which discuss the problem of resources from the point of the time period during which there may be sufficient resources, and the population of the world is seen only as an ever-increasing consumer of the produced commodities.

Nevertheless, rational activity on the part of man is assumed in some papers. For instance, there are proposals for co-ordinated international action in management of systems and for their differentiated development in various time periods, although these models seem to be very much over-simplified.

The main stress in these papers is on the necessity to stop population growth, to limit production growth and to control pollution as the chief conditions for the survival of mankind in the next century.

The main weakness of those papers is that, while attracting attention to the hazards to the existence of mankind arising from limitation of resources, uncontrolled growth and pollution, they do not focus on the possible ways of achieving social and economic objectives. It is doubtful whether these objectives can be achieved in a society based on private ownership of the means of production.

Artificial limitation of the growth of production is hardly possible, especially in the present situation where the growth rate is very unequal in different countries and at different times. Every country tries to accelerate its growth in every way because this is a condition of survival. Long-term perspective forecasts which are now being elaborated in the socialist states are aimed at formulating scientifically possible general trends in the economic development of the whole socialist commonwealth of nations based on rational utilisation of labour and other resources. The aim is to raise the material and cultural living standards of the people. It should be pointed out that the term 'living standard' includes not only the increase in consumption of consumer goods and services. In a socialist society, the full development of personality and of all the capabilities of the individual is put first. This includes the creation of equal opportunities for development of all members of society, equal rights for every citizen to work, to education, to participation in important decision-making affecting the community. These objectives are being achieved in balance with the development of productive resources and relationships in production.

All these considerations are included in the long-term forecast. Such questions as demand, its priorities and the extent to which the demand can be met are being investigated in the forecasts and plans. Such work helps to determine the levels of production, of scientific research, of education and of cultural development. A very important part of this work is concerned with scientific and technological progress, more intensive use of production capacity, and growth of labour productivity.

In accordance with these principles, in the USSR and other socialist states short and middle-term plans and programmes are being elaborated. As a very important part of the work in this field, we must mention 'The comprehensive programme for scientific and technological progress, with its significant social and economic consequences, for the period down to 1990. The importance of this work was stressed at the Twenty-Fifth Communist Party Congress in the USSR.

When one begins to study the possibilities of economic growth, it is necessary to answer the questions: what are its bases, what are the main factors
determining it?

We cannot agree with those who regard natural resources as the only
principal factor in growth, and who see the human factor as thereby that of
consumer of the commodities produced.

In fact, the first and the most important contributor to economic growth
is the human factor — population — for it is the main source of productive
resources. Of course, we mean by this not mankind in general, but people as
members of a given society, living under a given social system which provides
to a given extent opportunity for development of human capacities, of knowledge, of professional qualifications, and of culture — all the factors which
contribute to the expansion of production.

The second principal contributor to economic growth takes the form of the
means of production, industry, transportation, agriculture, cities — all the
wealth created by man, created by the labour of man. This second source of
progress of mankind depends, as did the first, on the social system of the
country concerned and its features.

The third contributor is that of natural resources — the soils, the forests,
the rivers, the seas and oceans, the mineral resources and the rest. These
resources are extremely important sources of economic growth although they
themselves do not produce anything but are used by the nation for production
purposes.

The main planning objective in the USSR and other socialist nations is the
utilisation of the three factors mentioned — those of labour available for
economic growth, means of production and natural resources.

Changes in the labour force are determined by population growth. Man is
a producer and at the same time a consumer.

A very important role is played by the ratio between the indices of production and consumption for the population as a whole. Thanks to the progress
in production, the difference between the net production of any individual
working in the sphere of production during his life span, and his net consumption during the same period becomes larger and larger.

Some calculations made in the USSR confirm this. The rate of growth of
national income in the USSR is much higher than the population growth.
During the twenty-five-year period 1950—75, national income increased seven-
fold as compared with a population growth of 1·4 times.

The increase in numbers of those occupied in the production sphere has a
positive result because it leads to economic growth and as a consequence to
growth of consumption.

During the twenty-five-year period 1950—75, real income *per caput*
employed in industry, agriculture and services increased 3·4 times. Real
income includes, besides the earnings of workers and peasants (more than
200 billion roubles), other forms of payments received from social consumption funds amounting to 90 billion roubles in 1975. (Free education, free

medical services, social insurance, pensions, paid vacations, and the like.) These figures do not include apartments received free of charge (during the ten-year period of 1965–75, 84 million people were provided with new apartments), and large subsidies of the state thanks to which the payment for apartments is not more than 4–5 per cent of a family budget.

During the postwar period, the birth rate in the USSR decreased and this decrease is linked with the rise in the material and cultural level of population, with urbanisation, with the rise in the social and economic role of the woman in Soviet society. It is unlikely that in the near future there will be an increase in the population growth rate. Decrease in the population growth rate raises the question whether it is better to make some changes in the population policy designed to increase the growth of labour resources and adopt an extensive growth of production by increasing the number of working jobs or to accept the existing demographic situation and develop production by intensifying utilisation of all resources both of labour and materials.

The Soviet state has chosen the path of more intensive technical progress, based on the advantages of the socialist system, and as a consequence regards the growth of labour productivity as the main factor in the expansion of production. This does not mean that we neglect measures concerning demographic policy aimed at increasing the birth rate and decreasing the death rate.

The planned development of the USSR national economy secures full employment of the labour force. Unemployment in the USSR was eliminated in the prewar years. The ever-increasing demand for labour has brought the country to a situation where the remaining reserves of labour are being brought into the national economy. These reserves include: women occupied in the household, students, pensioners, all of whom would not be engaged the full working day.

The main method of planning the labour force is the balance method. This balance implies a comparison of the demand for manpower in all professions with the calculated population of working age in a situation of full employment.

The state planning system determines measures which affect the growth of birth rate and decrease the death rate. The training of the labour force includes: compulsory secondary school education; industrial and technical schools and higher education at institutes and universities.

During recent years, the number of those employed in the sphere of physical production has decreased. The number of those employed in industry increased during the last decade by approximately 1·5 to 1·7% per year and the number employed in agriculture decreased. In this situation, professional qualifications become extremely important. Quite apart from any social significance, this has a very important economic significance and leads to growth of the production potential of the labour force. In 1939, 16 million persons in the country had received secondary and higher education. In 1976, this number rose to 122 million. In 1939, 108 in every 1000 persons over the age of ten had received secondary and higher education. In

1976, this figure reached 570. In 1975, there were 714,000 graduates of institutes and universities. Educational expenditure in the country amounted to 30 billion roubles per year. The number of research staff reached 1,223,000 persons in 1975, or 25 per cent of the research staff in the whole world. Expenditure on research work reached 17·5 billion roubles in 1975, or 5 per cent of the national income.

During the last twenty-five years, labour productivity in the USSR grew 6·7 per cent per year and this was due to growth in professional qualifications, in culture, in education and to technological progress. This means that the labour productivity during this period increased fivefold.

For the future, the USSR looks forward to a significant increase in the number of employed with high professional qualifications. This will lead to an increase in labour productivity during 1976—80, of 31 per cent in industry, 28 per cent in agriculture, over 30 per cent in the building industry. About 90 per cent of the growth of national income will result from growth in labour productivity.

Another important source of economic growth is the increase of production capacity in manufacturing industry, agriculture, transportation, the construction industry, and the trading and distribution system. In this production capacity, composed of the production funds, buildings, machinery and other equipment, as well as in infrastructure, the labour of the nation is being accumulated.

During the past decade, about 30 per cent of the national income has been accumulated in the Soviet Union. The national wealth of the USSR (apart from land, forests, mineral resources and water) reached almost 2000 billion roubles. Production funds are the main part of national wealth.

Since the Soviet state came into existence, all fixed funds have increased 25-fold and production funds 30-fold. During the last decade, they increased 2·1 and 2·25 times respectively. In 1975, all fixed funds were estimated at 1260 billion roubles and fixed production funds at 807 billion roubles.

This enormous increase in production funds opens the way for further development of the Soviet economy. The swift growth of production funds derived from the advantages of the centralised planning system, which makes it possible to manoeuvre and redistribute resources so as to concentrate them on the most important areas. These advantages are used to facilitate accumulation at a comparatively high level.

At the same time, the advantages of the socialist economic system made it possible to use the production funds very intensively. We may illustrate this with the following figures: the average capacity in the power stations in the USSR is used for 5555 hours per year as compared with 4261 hours in the US. The capacity of the blast furnaces in the USSR is 70 per cent of the capacity in the US. Nevertheless, the quantity of pig-iron produced in the USSR is 15 per cent higher than in the US.

One of the most important parts of the national economic development plan is the plan to expand production capacity, utilising the latest scientific and technological research designed to improve productivity. These plans cover the development of science and technology, improvements in production efficiency, the development of industry, agriculture, the transportation system, the building industry, education, culture, medical treatment, amongst other things. The implementation of these plans involves full utilisation of production capacity, the maximum possible meeting of demands, and the balanced development of the national economy.

Long-term forecasts of the main constituents of the national economy for the period 1990–2000 have recently been completed at the Central Economic and Mathematical Institute of the Academy of Science of the USSR. The aim of this forecast has been to establish the possible variants in the rate of development of the Soviet economy and the factors determining it, together with the efficiency of production, and the dynamics of production in sectors of the national economy. On the basis of this work, it became possible to calculate the future demand for energy resources, for the construction of primary energy transportation and the whole structure of energy consumption.

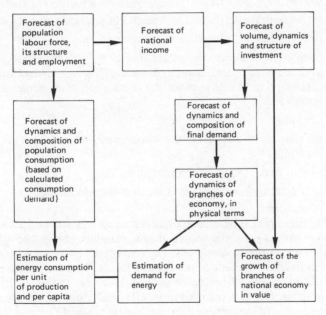

Fig. 4:1 Estimation of demand for energy

General economic calculations were carried out on the basis of simple econometric models and models of the input—output type, as well as on the basis of separate estimates by experts, who estimated general trends in the development of different sectors of the national economy.

The input—output model in physical or monetary form takes into account a special form of information used for planning purposes, i.e. that the cost of production is fixed for main items although all other expenses are not differentiated for every item and are fixed in a summarised form for the whole branch of industry. We used the following I—O model in physical and natural forms:

$$X_i = \sum_j \sum_l A_{ij}^l X_j^l + \sum_l A_{il}\tilde{X}_l + Y_i,$$

$$X_j^l = U_j^l X_j;$$

$$\sum_j X_j^l P_j^l + \tilde{X}_l r_l = \tilde{X}_l$$

X_i = level of production of item 'i' in physical form (for the national economy)

X_i^l = the same for the branch l

A_{ij}^l = technological coefficients in branch l in physical form for item j

$\tilde{X}_l$ = net production of branch l in monetary form

Ail = coefficient of direct consumption of item i (in physical form) per 1 rouble of net production in branch l. This coefficient shows the consumption of this item for the production of all other items in branch l

Y_i = final product of i-th type

U_j^l = the portion of branch l in the whole production of item j in national economy

P_j^l = price of item j produced by branch l

r_l = production of all other non-specified items by branch l

The third important type of economic resources — it was said above — are the natural resources — i.e. the source of raw materials, energy and all other things that make up the environment. The role played by those resources changes with the development of production forces. Technical progress opens new possibilities for the utilisation of natural resources. As the result of technical progress, fuel is being used more efficiently, the physical weight of equipment per unit of capacity is decreasing, new types of raw materials are being utilised, new man-made materials have begun to be widely used, etc. Oil started to be used as fuel only in the last decades of the nineteenth century and in the middle of this century it became the source of synthetic materials. Such elements as aluminium, uranium, titanium and others, not long ago known only by scientists, have begun to be widely used in industry.

Nevertheless, we must admit that utilisation of natural materials by man is in an unsatisfactory state. For instance, thermal efficiency at the largest power stations is about 40—42 per cent (on an average 35 per cent), but actually it is much lower if we take into account the losses which occur in supply lines and in the use of electricity (efficiency in an electric railroad system as a whole is about 20—25 per cent). Usually, the main part of the energy contained in the primary fuel is lost and this leads to some heat contamination of the environment.

Metals are also utilised in an imperfect way. Besides enormous losses at all stages of metal production large quantities of metal are lost during the fabrication of metal goods. Very often as much as 25 per cent of the metal is lost in processing.

As a whole, the world economy consumes every year (some 18—20 billion tons of raw materials, including fuel, ores, gravel and sand, stone, wood, agricultural products, fresh water, but the tonnage of final products is less than 1 billion tons. These figures illustrate the large potential economies in the utilisation of raw materials and at the same time the important problems to be solved by science and technology in this field.

In the future, it is necessary to decrease the use of materials per unit produced and this is a task that can be achieved by planning.

In the USSR, the rate of growth of the output of manufacturing industries during the last decade is 33 per cent higher than the rate of growth of the output of the extractive industries, the value of which in industry production as a whole decreased from 7·1 per cent in 1965 to 5·4 per cent in 1974.

Decreases in the rate of additional extraction of mineral resources in the USSR can be clearly illustrated by the following figures, which compare two periods — 1950—5 and 1970—5. The increases in production of coal were for the two periods 49 per cent and 12 per cent; of oil 87 per cent and 37 per cent; iron ore 81 per cent and 19 per cent, lumber 32 per cent and 4 per cent. Net industrial production increased, in the two periods, 86 per cent and 43 per cent and according to the plan for 1976—80, 38 per cent. Nevertheless, the increase in absolute quantities became much greater. For instance, during 1950—5 industrial production rose 45 billion roubles, and during 1970—5, 137 billion roubles; according to the plan for 1976—80, the rise will be 194 billion roubles.

The development of the economy in the USSR in the postwar period would be impossible without the utilisation of new mineral resources. During the existence of the Soviet state, new mineral resources have been discovered in many regions.

It may be realised that the amount of proved and probable reserves had decreased as a result of the increase in extraction. On the other hand, they have increased due to additional discoveries.

At the present time, the level of production in none of the main branches of Soviet industry is limited by the resources of raw materials, and in the foreseeable future none of these resources will become a constraint.

The main task in the area of mineral resources can be formulated as follows: geological field-work must secure such an increase of industrial reserves of raw materials as to balance the level of extraction with increased economically proven reserves.

The USSR has enough resources of coal for many hundreds of years even with an increase in its extraction. But it is very important to have a rational combination in the consumption of different mineral fuels: coal, oil and gas, especially taking into account more the limited resources of oil and gas which are used more and more as raw materials for chemical industry.

A number of scientific, technological and economic problems need to be specially tackled as a result of the possibility and necessity of utilising such sources of energy as atomic (and especially breeder) reactors, thermonuclear, geothermal and solar energy. Reserves of those sources of energy are unlimited, although efficient methods of utilisation must be thoroughly worked out.

At the present time, the planning administrations of the USSR prepare forecasts covering the whole energy and fuel complex. The demands for different types of fuel and energy are estimated, and at the same time technological progress in producing secondary energy and in supply systems is taken into account, as well as the effects on the environment.

The quantity of oil used as a raw material for the chemical industry is relatively low and oil is mainly used as fuel. The well-known price increase in oil led to investigation of new fuel and energy sources and more rational utilisation of existing sources of fuel and energy. There will be enough oil if its consumption as fuel is decreased, and its consumption as raw material for the chemical industry will also be increased as further steps are taken to increase the percentage of extracted oil.

As far as metals are concerned, a very important task is to increase the percentage of metals efficiently used. First of all, the percentage of manufacturing waste such as shavings should be lowered, the tensile strength of metals should be increased, the quantity of metals lost due to corrosion should be decreased, and there should be an increase in the secondary use of metals.

At the present time, metal stocks in use in the USSR have reached almost 1 billion tons. Out of that quantity, every year about 40 million tons of metals go out of the sphere of utilisation. Most of it can be recycled and used as secondary metal. Similar processes of recycling should be widely used in the field of paper, glass and other materials. Important progress can also be made in the more efficient use of lumber.

Special attention should be drawn to the problems of nutrition. On one hand, there are still large opportunities to add new land for agriculture purposes; on the other, there are great possibilities of increasing yields which are significantly different in different countries and regions. Important resources for nutrition are available in the form of producing synthetic food and the utilisation of the resources of the seas and oceans.

Serious attention in the USSR is being devoted to the problems of industrial pollution and protection of the environment. As a result of the measures taken, the atmosphere in Moscow has become much cleaner. These measures included the closing of various enterprises located in the city which were responsible for pollution. Power stations located in Moscow and Leningrad use gas and fuel with a very low sulphur content. A significant role is being played in establishing heat and gas distribution systems which has resulted in the closing down of a large number of small boiler-houses.

The Soviet government has taken serious steps to prevent pollution of the Volga river and the Black, Baltic and Azov Seas. Important measures have been taken to introduce technology based on the utilisation of recycled water. For instance, consumption of fresh water by refineries built twenty years ago was 8 cubic metres per 1 ton of refined oil. About ten years ago, the best oil refineries consumed 0·8—1·3 cubic metres of water per 1 ton of refined oil. Now the consumption of water has decreased to 0·1—0·2 cubic metres per 1 ton of refined oil.

Another important measure is that dealing with the development of new technology based on recycled waste. For instance, in the metallurgical plants and power stations, waste is used for the production of building materials.

Important steps are being taken in the USSR to prevent pollution. For instance, it is prohibited to flush water into the sea after washing out oil-tankers. Comprehensive measures are being taken to prevent the pollution and contamination of Lake Baikal.

A safe way to guarantee the supply of resources for future generations is their rational utilisation on the basis of comprehensive planning of the existing natural and labour resources. This, of course, will require significant social and economic changes in society. There are reasons to hope that the further development of science and technology will help in the discovery of new resources and secure better utilisation of existing ones.

It should be stressed once again that the welfare of mankind is linked not only to increase in consumption of the physical goods produced, but to an even greater extent depends on the cultural, educational and social improvement within society.

A very important aspect of more economic utilisation of natural and labour resources may be the limitation of military expenditure. Humanity daily spent 0·5 billion dollars during the Second World War and lost 30,000 lives per day. Military expenditure in the world has increased progressively and now amounts to 1 billion dollars per day. Apart from that, the resources used for military purposes are of the highest quality as well as labour with the highest skills. These gigantic expenditures of material and labour resources should be brought to an end as soon as possible. This can become a very important source of increased resources for mankind.

In conclusion, we should like to stress that the ever-increasing scale of industrial production, in combination with increasing rates of growth, makes the problem of available resources more and more acute. Natural resources are finite, although their quantity is much greater than mankind believes them to be.

Under those conditions, the need for an economical, planned and comprehensive utilisation of resources in combination with decrease in the waste of resources becomes more and more important. Production must become waste-free. Resources must be fully utilised in the interests of the economic and cultural development of mankind.

What are the real chances of society being able to solve this most important problem? Science and experience should give us the answer to the question.

Discussion of Academician T. S. Khachaturov and Academician N. P. Fedorenko's Paper*

Mr Michael Kaser, making the first comments, said that Academicians Khachaturov and Fedorenko had performed a service to the Congress by placing before it unequivocally and unhesitatingly the Soviet view of resource economics. That approach had two important connotations for the discussions that were in progress.

One was implicit and could be characterised in two words: technological optimism; the other was explicit: preference for central planning over decentralised pricing as a mechanism for allocating resources. There was, one must immediately say, a relationship between the two in selecting a procedure to evoke the dissemination and innovation which underlay their critique of the 'limits-to-growth' postulate. The link was the investment initially in research and subsequently into productive capacity which was required to relax the constraints shown by a setting of projected consumption trends against known resource availabilities and contemporary techniques. The funding of that investment must either depend on a forecast of effective relative prices, so that it was made by profit-seeking entrepreneurs (including, of course, nationalised as well as private corporations) or be furnished by conscious public decision from taxation (in its widest sense and including again, of course, profits of nationalised corporations). Other papers were directing attention to the broad issues that arose in resource allocation, and he wanted to focus his comment on the forecasting and planning of energy provision and use to which Academicians Khachaturov and Fedorenko had devoted a large part of their paper. The forecasting model developed in the latter's Institute (in the flow-chart, though not explicitly in the formulae) separated energy constraints from all other resources, while the second part of their paper immediately following the model drew most of its examples from energy policy.

It was, he hoped, fair for him to begin by characterising the authors as 'optimistic', if only because they rightly termed the limits-to-growth school as 'pessimistic'. They recorded the Soviet state as 'having chosen the path of intensifying technical progress based on the advantages of a socialist system'. They fortified their belief in man's ingenuity to make ever better use of the natural endowment by the stark contrast of 20 billion tons of world raw materials input with less than 1 billion tons of finished outputs. That comparison was new to him, said Mr Kaser, and would have been still more telling had it also specified the ratio as exhibited in the USSR, for there had been ever since the USSR was created sixty years ago controversy over whether socialist planning was more or less efficient than capitalism in resource allocation. The conventional assessment for capitalist systems concentrated on the labour and capital, and a project which he was directing with Ford Foundation funds at St Antony's College, Oxford, was applying it to planned economies. It was too early not only to provide results, but also to state whether the methodological obstacles to a systemic comparison of two factor productivities could be solved.

*The numbered footnotes within the discussion section that follows are the speakers' own.

Looking beyond that, perhaps formal, comparison, one could assert that the contribution of other production factors to total output had been seriously neglected even for capitalist economies, such that the assessment of the relative efficiency of capital and labour was distorted in international comparison. Attention was increasingly being paid to the contribution of technology and the evaluation of the natural resource factor was one of the reasons for the convocation of the Congress. Zdenek Drabek, a lecturer at University College, Buckingham (formerly research assistant, said Mr Kaser, on a project he had been directing at St Antony's College, Oxford, funded by the UK Social Science Research Council), had been testing a resource allocation hypothesis on the basis of inter-country comparison. Czechoslovakia was taken as a typical socialist planned economy and Austria was used as a comparable capitalist market economy. Both countries were highly comparable in the sense that they had similar factor endowments, had achieved a comparable rate of growth and had reached a comparable level of development. In addition, the social and historical background could also be considered as broadly common to each. The method for empirical testing was input—output, and natural resource products were used as surrogates for the natural resource factor. This assumed that any inter-country difference in the efficiency of the natural resource factor would be reflected in differences in the efficiency of the natural resource industries and in the use of natural resource products. Hence the differences in the use of natural resource products between the two countries could be due to, first, differences in final demand (one subject to private, the other to planners' preferences); second, differences in technology; and third, differences in each set of industries' consumption of natural resource products (i.e. in the absolute level of natural product consumption of individual industries). The efficiency comparison in which they were interested must refer to the last, i.e. to the comparison of the level of intermediate consumption of natural-resource products. The comparison was made on the basis of input—output coefficients and, as a first phase at least, only to direct coefficients. This appeared to be the model underlying the input—output procedures described by Academicians Khachaturov and Fedorenko.

The study he was recounting, said Mr Kaser, made no comparison of total coefficients (i.e. direct and indirect requirements per unit of output). The direct input coefficients of Czechoslovakia shown in Table 4:1 were considered as similar to those of Austria if their values were in the range of an arbitrary ± 10 per cent of the corresponding coefficients of Austrian industries. In the comparison of input coefficients four natural resource product sectors (the first four rows), the input coefficients were significantly higher in Czechoslovakia in three — even after allowing for + 10 per cent in the level of import coefficients characteristic for Austrian natural resource sectors. In the remaining sector (food processing), the natural resource product content was lower. However, almost 30 per cent of total costs in that sector were accounted for by the value of supplies of agricultural products in the case of Czechoslovakia and 40 per cent in Austria, and the natural resource product of processed food was dependent on a natural resource product content of agricultural products which was almost twice as high in Czechoslovakia.

The Czechoslovakia bias towards higher natural consumption of natural resource products was characteristic also among non-natural resource product industries. There were five non-natural resource product industries in Czechoslovakia with higher material consumption of natural resource products while there were only three in Austria. In total, the material consumption of natural resource products was higher in 8 out of 18 sectors in Czechoslovakia but only in 4 sectors in Austria.

TABLE 4:1 DIRECT NATURAL RESOURCE REQUIREMENTS PER UNIT OF GROSS OUTPUT IN SELECTED SECTORS IN CZECHOSLOVAKIA (1962) AND AUSTRIA (1964)

| | Input coefficients from input–output tables | | |
Sectors	Czechoslovakia	Austria	Sign
Agriculture	0·158,306	0·079,133	>
Fuels	0·028,442	0·011,983	>
Mining	0·069,751	0·045,890	>
Food processing	0·322,604	0·435,349	<
Textiles	0·105,416	0·113,732	=
Footwear, clothing, leather	0·038,729	0·025,297	>
Wood processing	0·166,596	0·375,586	<
Rubber	0·089,380	0·069,217	>
Chemicals	0·111,126	0·045,547	>
Oil, coal processing	0·380,471	0·492,567	<
Non-ferrous metals	0·063,572	0·066,945	=
Base metals	0·191,961	0·181,395	=
Transport vehicles	0·004,434	0·006,109	=
Engineering	0·008,047	0·009,110	=
Electricity	0·214,569	0·107,327	>
Construction	0·005,713	0·122,379	<
Trade	0·008,692	0·100,227	<
Transport	0·046,082	0·015,038	>

The interpretation of this comparison must obviously be cautious, said Mr Kaser, particularly since the degree of disaggregation of the input–output table was relatively small. Nevertheless, there were strong indications that the above findings reflected higher material consumption of natural resource products per unit of output in Czechoslovakia rather than technological differences between the two countries. First, the degree of homogeneity of the natural resource industry was fairly high and the coefficients were, therefore, directly comparable. Second, the higher intermediate consumption of natural resource products in Austrian industry as a whole was artificially inflated by different forms of food marketing and by different technology employed in the construction sector in Austria. Finally, it was unlikely that the different natural resource intensity of production was due to a disparate structure of final demand. Thus, despite the pro-investment bias in the chosen socialist planned economy, the structure of private and public consumption was biased towards natural resource products.

On the other hand, there are some countervailing factors which tended to increase material consumption in general and intermediate consumption of natural resource products in particular in a typical advanced market economy. An excessive use of raw materials for purposes other than those directly necessary in production (e.g. packaging) was perhaps the best-known example. It was likely, however, that such macroeconomic comparison showed equipollent resource inputs only between economies at significantly different levels of development, of access to markets, or of natural resource endowment, rather than countries for which these parameters were similar. Where the relativities were microeconomic, the extensive, critical comparison in Soviet technical and professional journals of domestic and western machinery in embodied raw materials suggested that the transformation of resources was more efficient when monitored by active price and market mechanisms.

He would not like to rely, as did Academicians Khachaturov and Fedorenko, on simple appositions of global outputs over time. They had noted that the rate of growth during the past ten years of manufacturing industry had been one-third greater than that of the extractive industries. But global output was the sum of enterprise outputs and might not necessarily reflect changes in values added.

While whatever might be proved by empirical investigation was of relevance to the debate 'between price and quota', it was a common tenet of Soviet, and one could probably say all Marxist, economists that man could dominate his environment and that planned, socialist organisation could assure increments in labour productivity that maintained positive growth in welfare. 'In the foreseeable future', Academicians Khachaturov and Fedorenko had written, resources of raw materials would not limit Soviet industrial growth. They had drawn attention to the measures of conservation that would prove necessary — more recycling, greater efficiency in metal use, better nutritional structures and ways of meeting food demand. But they had rightly laid emphasis on energy, and although this Congress was not making a fetish of any 'Energy Crisis' that there might be, the arena of energy was certainly germane to choice between pricing and administrative allocation.

It was unnecessary to emphasise that nowhere was the choice a blunt one between extremes. Academicians Khachaturov and Fedorenko had observed that the world oil price rise had stimulated the search (in the USSR also, they had implied) for alternative sources. Well before the western price explosions, Soviet pricing policy had been used as an instrument in inducing changes in energy consumption. In the major wholesale price reform of 1967 prices of oil products had been brought up closer to that for coal to help shift demand back to coal. The rise desired by the planners could not be implemented because the price of too many fuel-using outputs would have been affected. Within oil products, the price of aviation gasolene had been increased 2·3 times while that for high-octane petrol for vehicles had been cut by 28 per cent. The predominant use of oil for fuel remained and it was not until the Twenty-Fifth Party Congress in Moscow in 1976 that the *mot d'ordre* had been given to shift it more towards petrochemical feedstocks. President Brezhnev, in calling for this policy change, had not used the same terms as the Shahinshah of Iran, who had stressed the need for 'nobler' uses of petroleum, but both had been motivated by the opportunity costs of its use as fuel. Academicians Khachaturov and Fedorenko had noted that feedstock use in the USSR was 'relatively low' and that 'oil is mainly used as fuel'.

But was there a higher constraint on Soviet energy supplies than the authors of the paper before us would have us credit? Because it was an office of the

US government, the CIA should be listened to and it was right to record that its paper of April 1977, 'Prospects for Soviet Oil Production', contended that Soviet oil production would peak in the early 1980s and thereafter would be insufficient to supply both domestic and Comecon demand; the USSR would hence have to compete for OPEC oil as a net importer. Exports of gas would rise but not enough to offset the disappearance of oil earnings, while neither hydroelectric nor nuclear capacity could afford relief for more than a decade.

The CIA believed that because the oilfields of the USSR in and west of the Urals area were relatively shallow, further extraction from these areas would have to be much more deeply drilled; moreover the present Soviet preponderance on turbo-drilling would have to be reduced. A recent book by Robert Campbell[1] found (p. 20) that the changeover had been frustrated ('oil industry officials have either changed their minds or have been unable to carry out their intention') and emphasised 'how little [of] this deep drilling the Soviet industry is actually doing – far less, in fact, than the planners had expected' (p. 18). But the technology for the deep rotary drilling required was available in the west and could be imported.

The CIA also believed that the incursion of water into the west Siberian fields threatened expanion east of the Urals. Here again, imports from the west of a suitable technology were being sought. Campbell did not mention that Soviet experience with gas-lift oil extraction had begun as early as 1967 (when the US company Camco equipped the Pravinsk field in west Siberia, which had since run at 8 million tons a year quite successfully), and the Soviet decision to call for western tenders was only very recent. Two contracts were expected to be signed by the end of 1977 to convert the entire basin to gas-lift over a period of ten to fifteen years. This would affect some 3200 wells in Samotlor and 1200 in the Fyodorovsk field. The vast size of the undertaking suggested a high level of Soviet purchases in the west during the 1980s and hence the virtual certainty that the USSR would continue to sell oil and gas to earn the currency required.

The Soviet official prognoses did of course rely substantially on opening up new fossil fuel deposits east of the Urals and, as Academicians Khachaturov and Fedorenko had stressed, on the development of nuclear power. It was in the choice of degree of reliance on the latter that non-market forces would play their largest role within the forward energy decision in the west. But in the east, paradoxically, the nuclear decision had been made more on market relations. The difference in the factors influencing the respective governments was the strength of what for want of a more precise term was called the environmental lobby, which was far greater in the capitalist than in the socialist world. So little expression did such a lobby have in the USSR that only occasional rumours emerged that the issues were discussed – as the few remarks that Zhores Medvedev put together in the London *New Scientist* in November 1977 showed. Hence the Soviet Gosplan was free to select that share of nuclear power (including fast breeder reactors) which it preferred on cost grounds. It was evident that the transportation costs were heavy for fossil fuels from remote Siberian deposits to the areas which would remain at least to the end of the century the main consumers of energy. He did not need to rehearse the foreign exchange cost of developing the oil and gas of

[1] *Trends in the Soviet Oil and Gas Industry* (Baltimore, 1976).

Siberia to which he had just referred. In the case of South Yakutian coal, the large Japanese investment must, at some time be paid off. For users west of the Urals, therefore, nuclear power represented the choice that the market would have made.

He had not found a recent Soviet figure for that country's projected reliance on nuclear power in the longer-run, added Mr Kaser, and Academicians Khachaturov and Fedorenko did not quantify their affirmation that the USSR found it necessary to develop 'atomic (especially breeder) reactors', but N. V. Melnikov[1] had projected 16 per cent of the energy required in the year 2000 as nuclear. Every Comecon member either had, or would have by 1983, a nuclear power plant in operation.

It was hence another paradox that the socialist countries would rapidly expand nuclear power when they were relatively better off in terms of fossil fuels. One estimate he had seen put Comecon's aggregate reliance on nuclear power at 6 per cent in 1990 (M. Szöcs, in the organ of the IEA's Hungarian member association, *Gazdaság*, January 1974), whereas, as Table 4:2 showed, that group had 25 per cent of world reserves (excluding China) of oil, 32 per cent of natural gas and 62–3 per cent of coal. By the year 2025, on a forecast

TABLE 4:2 FORECASTS AT THE INTERNATIONAL INSTITUTE FOR APPLIED SYSTEMS ANALYSIS OF ENERGY DEMAND IN THE YEAR 2025

	Demand			Reserves (bn tce)		
	Low	High	Oil	Gas	Coal	
	prognosis				10%	50%
	terawatt-years				use of geological reserves	
Comecon	152·0	152·0	78·4	73·0	527·0	2709·0
China	204·8	262·4	–	–	–	–
Socialist group	356·8	414·4				
West Europe and Japan	229·4	229·4	15·3	12·4	41·2	205·8
North America	177·5	177·5	38·5	37·0	260·0	1228·0
Latin America	63·8	80·6	71·0	58·0	27·9	139·4
Africa & other Asia						
OPEC	24·0	30·1	106·0	46·5	–	–
Capitalist world	602·6	655·6	230·8	153·9	329·1	1573·2
Total world						
(excl. China)	754·6	807·6	309·2	226·9	856·1	4282·2
(incl. China)	959·4	1070·0	–			

Source: W. Häfele, talk at Oxford Energy Policy Club, 14 May 1977.

of the International Institute for Applied Systems Analysis (Vienna) which he had heard at the Oxford Energy Policy Club and which doubtless had been published, Comecon would be using only 20 per cent of the planet's energy on a low estimate of world use (again excluding China) and 18 per cent on a high estimate. Least among most countries did the USSR, on physical

[1] *Toplivno-energeticheskie resursy SSSR* (Moscow, 1971)

quantities, need nuclear or other alternative sources of energy (see Table 4:2).

Since the Institute formulating this projection was principally and jointly run by the USSR and the USA, we might attach some credence to the figures and reflect on possible explanations, said Mr Kaser. One was that central planning would continue to keep energy demand below that which it would be in a free market. Quota would thus dominate price and the socialist world might well be deciding to keep its energy to itself and to exploit its rich reserves only slowly, putting off the use of fossil fuels by an early introduction of nuclear power. Indeed Comecon was already self-sufficient in energy, for in 1980 only 2 per cent of its large energy use would be imported (Szöcs, already quoted, aggregated consumption at 2·94 billion tce in 1980 against 1·8 billion in 1970 and 4·4 billion expected in 1990).

Alternatively, did this projection mean that the Comecon group would sell energy from its richer reserves, since in scarcity-price terms energy should be cheaper than where demand was higher in relation to reserves? This would be the 'price' option and could be given weight for probability in the light of relatively recent Soviet concern for aligning domestic price ratios to those prevailing in the world market. This was not incorporated even in the 1967 revisions to which he had referred earlier and which an American authority, Professor Gregory Grossman of Berkeley, had called 'a major landmark in the history of price formation'.[1] But in 1971 a Soviet book[2] observed that

> a necessary stage in the justification of (the new) price levels is comparison with prices of similar products abroad and on the world market. It should be noted that not enough attention is given to this in actual price setting. Comparison with world prices is a necessary element of the economic analysis of the levels of cost and price. If (specific) internal prices are above world prices, then it is necessary to inquire into the reasons . . . . The problem of bringing the prices of products of extractive industries closer to world prices can be solved primarily by lowering costs via increased labour productivity.

Two steps had been taken to bring Soviet domestic decision-makers into closer contact with external price relativities. The first was the revision of Comecon prices in January 1975 to reflect western prices, with a lag (an average of five years on world markets). The second was the Soviet foreign trade reform of August 1976 which gave Soviet exporters a share in the foreign-exchange profits of the transaction. That share, 10 per cent in fabricating, rather less in the extractive industries, might be spent on foreign goods and services at the discretion of the earning management.

The possibility of adopting the price option was heartening to those who looked to a continuing expansion of east—west trade, just as OPEC's projected 3 per cent use of world energy might be set against its 34 per cent of world oil and 20 per cent of world gas reserves. The scenario implicit for Comecon and declared by OPEC was of energy interdependence. At a World Congress, said Mr Kaser in conclusion, we must reflect on world issues and it was perhaps fortunate that we could expect that the gains of trade would be realised also in the arena of energy.

[1] In Alan Aboucher (ed)., *The Socialist Price Mechanism* (Durham, N.C., 1977) p. 142.
[2] A. N. Komin, *Problemy planogo tsenoobrazovaniya* (Moscow 1971) pp. T27—8.

Professor Takayama,[1] the next speaker, noting that the paper by Academicians Khachaturov and Fedorenko dealt with the problem raised by Forrester's *World Dynamics*, Meadows *et al.*'s *The Limits to Growth*, and other works of 'doomsday' prediction, said that the main stress of the paper could be summarised by the following two propositions:

(1) The analyses and the conclusions of those works contained serious defects in that their systems 'do not provide any possibility to influence the process of development by Man'. In particular, the authors duly emphasised the roles of the three factors determining growth: i.e., the 'human' factor, man-made productive capacities, and natural resources.

(2) Although the 'doomsday' predictions and the recommendations to limit growth by Forrester, Meadows and others could thus be avoided, the authors were 'rather doubtful whether these goals can be achieved in a society based on private ownership of a means of production'. In order to support this contention, the authors repeatedly cited certain figures, by which they hoped to illustrate the excellent performance of the Soviet Union under a socialist system.

Professor Takayama said that, although he basically agreed with the authors on the points raised in (1), he did not agree with the argument put forth in (2). For example, a rapid growth in *per capita* income during 1950–70,[2] a rapid increase in production and fixed funds, and an improvement of the educational standard (all of which apparently took place in the USSR) were cited by the authors to show the strength of the socialist system. However, as was well-known, these phenomena could also be seen in many non-socialist countries – Japan would be one such example. That is, the figures did not necessarily imply inferiority of the private ownership economy. Also, important technological innovations (including those which concern natural resources) were certainly not the monopoly of the socialist system. In fact, many (if not most) such innovations had been occurring in western countries such as the USA. He was also sceptical about the claim made by the authors that, in the USSR, unemployment had been eliminated and full employment of the labour force secured. Even in the economy of Robinson Crusoe, Robinson might not be able to engage in any productive labour during the days of heavy rains and storms. Furthermore, if full employment was to be achieved through the planning of demand for final goods and the planning of the population of working age, this might imply certain rather serious sacrifices of individual freedom.

He might add that there was another very important aspect of the problem.

---

[1] Gratitude is expressed to Ngo Van Long and Neil Vousden of the Australian National University for valuable discussions.

[2] Academicians Khachaturov and Fedorenko seem to identify the growth of *per capita* income with the growth of *per capita* consumption. Obviously, this cannot be correct unless a part of the national output which is used for capital formation, military expenditures, and wages and salaries for the bureaucrats is counted as a part of 'consumption'. Although these expenditures may directly and indirectly affect the welfare level of the public, the extent to which they affect welfare is obviously very debatable. Khachaturov and Fedorenko duly note that 'a very important role for more economic utilisation of natural and labour resources may play limitation of military expenses . . .. Military expenses of the world increases progressively and reached 1 billion dollars per day'.

Namely, if the present third world countries did not or should not remain in the underdeveloped stage, then world demand for natural resources would increase drastically when those countries reached the take-off stage of growth. This surge would take place even if western countries were able to agree on putting a restraint on their own growth so as to conserve resources (in spite of opposition from labour unions, etc.). Forrester's conclusion that the 'present efforts of underdeveloped countries to industrialize may be unwise' was unlikely to pursuade the people in the third world countries not to continue such efforts.

Although it was unfortunate that the third world aspect had been somewhat ignored in the present debate on resources, Professor Takayama said, he would like to concentrate his efforts on the question of whether or not such attempts to limit growth were necessary in the first place – the first issue raised by Khachuturov and Fedorenko – and to highlight some key economic issues involved in the resource problem. He hoped that his contributions would put the discussion of Khachuturov and Fedorenko in proper perspective.

'Doomsday' predictions, as was well known, were not particularly new in the literature. Economists could easily recall Thomas Malthus's *Essays on Population* (1798), for example. It is well known that Malthus's theory, and its subsequent predictions, had basically failed. By the same token, the current works of Forrester, Meadows, and others had been severely criticised. For example, Nordhaus branded *World Dynamics* as 'measurement without data',[1] and two control engineers, Graham and Henrick, asserted that it is 'essentially trivial'.[2] Kay and Mirrlees had also asserted that *The Limits to Growth* was 'essentially trivial', and that its 'most important models are naive in conception, amateurish in construction, and make negligible – and warped – use of empirical data'.[3]

What went wrong in those studies was quite apparent to western economists. One serious flaw in *World Dynamics* was that it lacked the concept of production functions. *The Limits to Growth* hypothesises a naive linear relation between the output and the stock of capital: i.e. a constant capital–output ratio, ignoring the possibility of substitution among capital, labour, and natural resources.[4] In fact, the failures of these studies could perhaps best be demonstrated by using the usual concept of production functions.

Letting Y be the vector of outputs, and letting K, R, and L, respectively, denote the vectors of man-made means of production (capital), the flow of natural resources, and human labour,[5] we would write the technical

---

[1] W. D. Nordhaus, 'World Dynamics: Measurement Without Data', *Economic Journal* (December 1973).

[2] D. Graham and D. C. Hendrick, 'World Dynamics', in IEEE, *Transactions of Automatric Control* (August 1973).

[3] J. A. Kay and J. A. Mirrlees, 'The Desirability of Natural Resource Depletion', in D. W. Pearce (ed.), *Economics of Natural Resource Depletion* (New York: Wiley, 1975) p. 147.

[4] See Nordhaus, op. cit.; Kay and Mirrlees, op. cit.

[5] The natural resource that was the centre of the discussion in the day of Malthus was land. In the 1970s, such natural resources are energy and certain metallic resources. The problem of pollution can be considered as that of depletion of environmental resources such as fresh air and water. The list of man-made resources (K) can include transportation services, cities, etc., as well as plant and equipments, as pointed out by Khachaturov and Fedorenko.

relations among these variables (production functions) as

$$Y = F(K, R, L), \tag{1}$$

where technological progress shifts the function F. Quite clearly, K, R, and L correspond to 'the three major factors determining growth' pointed out by Khachaturov and Fedorenko. Combining (1) with the accumulation or de-cumulation equations of K, R, and L, and with various economic equilibrium (and disequilibrium) relations, we could describe an economic system.[1]

Given (1), which allows for substitution among K, R, and L, and techno-logical progress, it would be rather difficult to see why *per capita* consumption should always have to cease to grow or have to decline when certain resources essential for production and their reserves were fixed. The use of such natural resources could be decreased by substitution of man-made resources K and human resources L, and by technological progress — which would enable us to increase the size of outputs with fixed inputs, as well as to expand the reserves or to save natural resources. Thus, the elasticities of substitution among various factors should play an important role in the properties of an optimal plan;[2] and technological progress plays an essential role in sustaining a constant level of consumption *per capita*.[3] For example, assuming the Cobb–Douglas technology with unit elasticities and aggregate inputs (K, R, L) and output, we might write the (aggregate) production function as

$$Y = e^{\lambda t} K^{\alpha_1} R^{\alpha_2} L^{\alpha_3}, \quad \alpha_i > 0, \quad \Sigma\alpha_i = 1, \quad \lambda > 0, \tag{1'}$$

where λ denotes the rate of technological progress. For such a production function, it had been shown that the magnitude of λ plays a crucial role in sustaining a constant level of *per capita* consumption.[4]

Quite clearly, there was another consideration in the resource problem: i.e., the reserves of natural resources were not known fixed quantities, as they could be increased by human efforts. The classic example would be the Ricardian theory of differential rent: a given resource (say 'land') was *not* homogenous and use of the resource would proceed according to grade (i.e., better grades being used first, poor grades later).[5] Obviously, the same theory could be applied to other natural resources such as energy resources.[6] Khachuturov and Fedorenko, apparently aware of limited oil and natural gas reserves, had pointed out the existence of large reserves of coal in the USSR,

---

[1] Nordhaus, op. cit., p. 1182, points out that 'the basic notion of system dynamics — usually called simultaneous difference and differential equations — have been used extensively in economics and elsewhere for decades'.

[2] See, e.g., P. Dasgupta and G. Heal, 'The Optimal Repletion of Exhaustible Resources', *Review of Economic Studies*, Symposium Issue (1974).

[3] See, e.g., J. E. Stiglitz, 'Growth with Exhaustible Natural Resources: Efficient and Optimal Growth Paths', *Review of Economic Issues*, Symposium Issue (1974); R. M. Solow, 'Intergenerational Equity and Exhaustible Resources', ibid.

[4] Stiglitz, op. cit., Prop. 4, p. 128.

[5] Strictly speaking, this statement is not accurate. See M. C. Kemp and N. V. Long, 'On a Folk Theorem Concerning the Extraction of Exhaustible Resources' (September 1977, unpublished).

[6] See R. M. Solow and F. Y. Wan, 'Extraction Costs in the Theory of Exhaustible Resources', *Bell Journal of Economics*, vol. 7 (autumn 1976).

and the 'possibility and necessity to utilise such sources of energy as atomic (especially breeder) reactors, thermo-nuclear, geothermal and solar sources'.[1] Also, just as oil and natural gas could be replaced by coal, etc., some resources could be replaced by other materials. The use of plastic in place of metal and the use of aluminium instead of copper might be some notable examples. Furthermore, the stock of any particular resource was not a known fixed quantity. For example, Colin Robinson[2] reports a quadrupling of the world reserves of oil in the last twenty years, which has kept the reserves/production ratio of oil approximately constant in spite of a rapid increase in the consumption of oil.

The 'doomsday' conclusions were in essence arrived at through the assumptions of fixed reserves of natural resources, no technological progress in the resource and other industries, and no productive substitution of man-made resources (capital) and labour for natural resources. Professor Takamaya believed that this was rather absurd, and welcomed the paper by Khachaturov and Fedorenko, for it, too, clarified some of these points. Doomsday might still come, for the parameters of the economic system might not be correct or might be too slow to adjust, and the transition to a new phase of technology might not be smooth. However, the models used for the current 'doomsday' conclusions were too naive to provide serious conclusions.

One important question could still be asked, he added. Could an efficient and optimal plan of growth be achieved solely by the market forces of the private ownership economy? Although he might agree that some planning and government intervention might be necessary in view of certain market imperfections and the absence of future and risk markets,[3] he also believed that the importance of market forces under the decentralised private ownership economy should not be underemphasised. Even setting aside the theoretical issues involved, history was full of examples of past 'energy crises' (see Robinson, pp. 25—6) which had been avoided by market forces through a relative increase in prices of those resources whose stock became scarce.[4]

[1] Khachaturov and Fedorenko also correctly realise that 'there will be enough oil if the consumption of oil as fuel is decreased'.

[2] See C. Robinson, 'The Depletion of Energy Sources', in D. W. Pearce (ed.), op. cit., p. 29.

[3] See J. E. Stiglitz, 'Growth with Exhaustible Natural Resources: The Competitive Economy', *Review of Economic Studies,* Symposium Issue (1974).

[4] C. Robinson concludes that 'the probability is that what we are now observing is no more than a transition from oil and natural gas to new energy sources, during which energy prices will increase substantially' ([5], p. 55). Needless to say, the fact that the past transition to new energy sources have been rather successful does not necessarily imply that the present (probable) transition will also be successful. Note also that in spite of a sharp rise in the early 1970s, the present *relative* price of oil is lower than that of 1950s. On the role of price changes reflecting scarcities, one might also be reminded of the classical treatment of natural resources by W. Stanley Jevons (*The Coal Question,* 1865), in which he was concerned about the exponential growth of the demand for coal and the limit of coal reserves, but anticipated a rise in the price of (British) coal. His concern was, however, that this would destroy Britain's comparative advantage in manufactured goods, rather than that this would induce substitution of other resources for coal and coal-saving technological progress. On the other hand, some countries may well take warning from Jevons that the present 'transition phase' from oil to some other resources may be particularly harsh to them.

Indeed, economists in the western countries had long been aware of the importance of prices as an adaptive mechanism by which the economy could adjust to changes in relative scarcities: i.e., prices and the market mechanism were the keys to the efficient and optimal allocation of resources over time and between sectors. A satisfactory discussion on such a mechanism was completely missing not only in the works by Forrester, Meadows, and others, but also in Khachaturov and Fedorenko.

Setting this important question aside, Professor Takamaya said, we might return to the problem of investigating the properties of an efficient and optimal plan of growth and the conditions for sustaining a constant (or even increasing) level of *per capita* consumption. As mentioned earlier, it was known from the literature that technological progress played a crucial role in such a problem. On the other hand, there were serious shortcomings in such studies: i.e. technological progress was assumed to be costless.[1] Clearly much of technological progress was not free, and 'doomsday' was not likely to be avoided only by 'merciful rain from heaven'. Constant human efforts in improving technology would be necessary. His remaining comments, he said, would investigate that problem. To save space, he would consider only two cases, corresponding to whether a part of human resources was allocated to research for increasing the reserves of natural resources, *or* for increasing the size of output for given inputs. Among other results, we would discover that the efficiency of human resources in the research sector must be sufficiently large to ensure sustainable growth in *per capita* consumption as well as to ensure the optimal programme. The principal analytical technique was optimal control theory as developed by Pontryagin and others.

For *Model 1,* that of technological progress which expands the resource stock, we should assume the Cobb–Douglas technology, and write the (aggregate) production function as

$$Y = K^{\alpha_1} R^{\alpha_2} L_P^{\alpha_3}, \quad \alpha_i > 0 (i = 1, 2, 3), \quad \Sigma \alpha_i = 1, \tag{2}$$

where Y = aggregate output, K = (aggregate) stock of capital, R = input of natural resources, L_P = labour price in the productive (or material) sector. Output could be used either for consumption (C) or capital accumulation (K), and the total labour force would grow at a constant rate n: i.e.,

$$Y = C + \dot{K}, \quad \text{and} \quad \dot{L}/L = n. \tag{3}$$

The stock of natural resources (S) would deplete as it was used for production (i.e., R) but it would increase at the rate of $\psi(L_R/L)$, where L_R is the labour force allocated to the research (or the knowledge) sector: i.e.

$$\dot{S} = -R + S\psi(L_R/L), \quad L_P + L_R = L \tag{4}$$

Loosely speaking, ψ signifies the rate of expansion of the resource stock (net of extraction costs associated with R) due to new discoveries of reserves and

[1] See, e.g., Solow, op. cit.; J. E. Stiglitz, 'Growth with Exhaustible Natural Resources: Efficient and Optimal Growth Paths', *Renew of Economic Issues,* Symposium Issue (1974).

invention of substitute materials, where we assume $\psi > 0$ and $\psi(0) = 0$.[1] We would then consider the problem of maximising

$$\int_0^\infty u(C/L)e^{-\delta t}\, dt, \quad u' > 0, \quad u'' < 0, \quad u'(0) = \infty \tag{5}$$

subject to (2)–(4), $0 \leqslant L_P$, $L_R \leqslant L$, $S \geqslant 0$, $Y \geqslant 0$, $C \geqslant 0$, $K \geqslant 0$, and $R \geqslant 0$, where δ signifies the rate of discount. This problem could equivalently be converted to the problem of choosing c, r, and θ so as to maximise (5) subject to

$$\dot{k} = y - nk - c, \quad \dot{s} = -r - ns + s\psi(1 - \theta), \tag{6}$$

$$y = k^{\alpha_1} r^{\alpha_2} \theta^{\alpha_3} \tag{7}$$

and $0 \leqslant \theta \leqslant 1$, $s \geqslant 0$, $y \geqslant 0$, $c \geqslant 0$, $k \geqslant 0$, $r \geqslant 0$, where $c \equiv C/L$, $s \equiv S/L$, $y \equiv Y/L$, $k \equiv K/L$, $r \equiv R/L$, $\theta \equiv L_P/L$.

Following much of the literature on this topic, we could assume that $u(c)$ was specified by $u'(c) = c^{\beta-1}$, $0 \leqslant \beta < 1$. Among the necessary conditions for an interior solution, we would have

$$p = c^\beta - 1, \quad \alpha_2 py = qr, \quad \alpha_3 py = q\psi' s\theta \tag{8}$$

$$\hat{p} = (n + \delta) - \alpha_1 y/k, \quad \hat{q} = (n + \delta) - \psi \tag{9}$$

where the circumflex (ˆ) would denote the rate of change ($\hat{p} = \dot{p}/p$, etc.) and where p and q would be the multipliers associated with (6); p and q, respectively, would signify the (shadow) prices of output and natural resources.

To illustrate the solution of the above maximisation problem, we could assume $\beta = 0$,[2] and that ψ is linear: i.e. $\psi = (1 - \theta)a$, where a is a positive constant. Then, after the usual procedure, we would obtain

$$\hat{x} = -(1 - \alpha_1)x + (\alpha_2 a + \alpha_3 n)/\alpha_1, \tag{10}$$

$$\hat{z} = z - v + (\alpha_2 a + \alpha_3 n)/\alpha_1, \tag{11}$$

$$\hat{v} = -(1 - \alpha_1)x + v - \delta, \tag{12}$$

where $x \equiv y/k$, $v \equiv c/k$, and $z \equiv r/s$.[3] In obtaining (10) and (11), we might note that the following relation holds, due to the linearity of ψ

$$\theta = \alpha_3 z/(\alpha_2 a). \tag{13}$$

The steady state values of x, v, and z are readily obtained from (10)–(12) as

$$x^* = (\alpha_2 a + \alpha_3 n)/\alpha_1(1 - \alpha_1), \quad v^* = (\alpha_2 a + \alpha_3 n)/\alpha_1 + \delta, \quad z^* = \delta. \tag{14}$$

---

[1] For simplicity, the factors other than labour in the function ψ are assumed away. Also, more efforts will be needed as S depletes, i.e., it may be more desirable to write $\psi = \psi(L_R/L, S)$ where $\partial\psi/\partial S < 0$. We also assume away this complication.

[2] See Stiglitz, op. cit.

[3] Note that $x = Y/K$, $v = C/K$, and $z = R/S$. I.e., x, v, and z, respectively, signify the output-capital ratio, *per capita* capital consumption, and the flow-stock ratio of the natural resources.

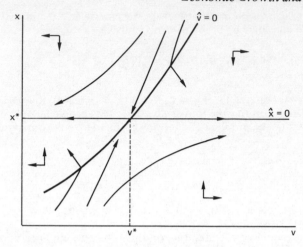

Fig. 4:2

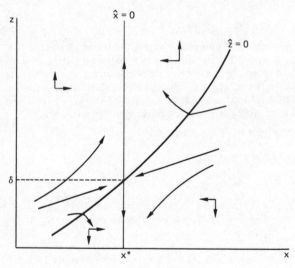

Fig. 4:3

The dynamic path of (x, v) would be completely specified by (10) and (12), and this is illustrated in Figure 4:2. From that phase diagram, it is clear that (x^*, v^*) is a saddle point, which means that if $x \to x^*$, then we could solve for the path $v = v(x)$, $v' > 0$. Along this path we could illustrate the dynamic path of (z, x) in Figure 4:3. Since z decreases along the path in which x decreases, we might also conclude from (13) that the ratio of labour allocated to the research sector $(1 - \theta)$ over total labour increases along the path in which capital increases over time with respect to output (i.e., x decreases). Since our solution is such that $0 < \theta \leqslant 1$, we must have $a \geqslant \alpha_3 z/\alpha_2$ (in the steady state $a \geqslant \alpha_3 \delta/\alpha_2$) to ensure the optimal programme.

We should also note that the following relation holds in general.

$$\hat{c} = \alpha_1 x - (n + \delta). \tag{15}$$

Substituting the expression for x^* in (14), into this, we obtain

$$\hat{c} = [\alpha_2 a - (1 - \alpha_1)\delta - \alpha_2 n]/(1 - \alpha_1). \tag{16}$$

Hence, a necessary and sufficient condition for $\hat{c} > 0$ in the steady state is

$$a > (n + \delta) + \alpha_3 \delta/\alpha_2. \tag{16'}$$

I.e., the efficiency coefficient (a) must be sufficiently high to ensure $\hat{c} > 0$. Since $x > x^*$ along the path in which x decreases over time, we might conclude that $(16')$ is sufficient for $\hat{c} > 0$ along such a path. Also, along the path in which x increases over time, $(16')$ is necessary for $\hat{c} > 0$. Along such a path, $\hat{c} < 0$ if the inequality in $(16')$ is reversed. Thus we could establish

Proposition 1: Under the specification of the present model, there exists a unique optimal path of (x, v, z) which converges to (x^*, v^*, z^*), provided that the efficiency coefficient in the research sector (a) is greater than certain critical values. Positive values of x^* and v^* are ensured as long as $a > 0$. In the steady state, the rate of utilisation of the natural resource must be equal to the rate of discount (i.e., $z^* = \delta$). In the steady state, *per capita* consumption increases over time if and only if $(16')$ holds. Namely, the efficiency coefficient (a) must be sufficiently large to ensure $\hat{c} > 0$. Along the optimal path in which x decreases over time, *per capita* consumption increases over time if $(16')$ holds. Along such a path, more of labour should be allocated to the research sector. Along the path in which x increases over time, $(16')$ is necessary to ensure $\hat{c} > 0$.

The last conclusion of the above proposition may be contrasted to that of Proposition 2 below, and to Stiglitz's conclusion.[1]

In the model just discussed, human efforts for research are solely dedicated to the expansion of the stock of natural resources. In the case of *Model II*, that of technological progress which expands the size of the output, we investigate instead the case in which natural resources are used solely to expand the size of output. That is, we write the production function as

$$Y = A(t)K^{\alpha_1} R^{\alpha_2} L_p^{\alpha_3} \quad \alpha_i > 0 (i = 1, 2, 3), \ \Sigma \alpha_i = 1, \tag{17}$$

where the rate of technological progress is specified by:[2]

$$\dot{A}/A = \lambda(L_R/L), \quad \lambda' > 0, \quad \lambda'' \leqslant 0, \quad \lambda(0) = 0. \tag{18}$$

On the other hand, the stock of natural resources simply decumulates as $\dot{S} = -R$.

With these changes, we can now specify the maximisation problem. In *per capita* terms, our problem would be to choose c, r, and $\theta \, (\equiv L_P/L)$ so as to maximise (5) subject to

$$\dot{k} = y - c - nk, \quad \dot{s} = -r - ns \tag{19}$$

$$\dot{A}/A = \lambda(1 - \theta), \quad 0 \leqslant \theta \leqslant 1, \quad y = A(t)k^{\alpha_1}r^{\alpha_2}\theta^{\alpha_3}, \tag{20}$$

$$\int_0^\infty re^{nt} \leqslant S_0 \ (= \text{constant}), \tag{21}$$

and $s \geqslant 0$, $y \geqslant 0$, $c \geqslant 0$, $k \geqslant 0$, $r \geqslant 0$. Again we would have to specify the utility function by $u'(c) = c^{\beta-1}$, $0 \leqslant \beta < 1$. Then, among the necessary conditions for an interior solution, we would have

$$p = c^{\beta-1}, \quad \alpha_2 py = qr, \quad \alpha_3 py = \mu\lambda'A\theta, \tag{22}$$

$$\hat{p} = (n + \delta) - \alpha_1 y/k \quad \hat{q} = (n + \delta), \quad \hat{\mu} = (\delta - \lambda) - py/A\mu, \tag{23}$$

where p, q, and μ are multipliers.

To illustrate the solutions of the above maximisation problem, we would again assume $\beta = 0$, and that λ was linear (i.e., $\lambda = (1 - \theta)b$, where b is a positive constant). Then, after the usual procedure, we would obtain,

$$\hat{x} = -(1 - \alpha_1)x + [\alpha_3 n + \lambda + b\theta/\alpha_3]/\alpha_1, \tag{24}$$

$$\hat{v} = -(1 - \alpha_1)x + v - \delta, \tag{25}$$

$$\hat{\theta} = -v + [\alpha_3 n + \lambda + (1 + \alpha_1)b\theta/\alpha_3]\alpha_1, \tag{26}$$

$$\hat{z} = z - v + [\alpha_3 n + \lambda + b\theta/\alpha_3]/\alpha_1, \tag{27}$$

where $x \equiv y/k$, $v \equiv c/k$, and $z \equiv r/s$. The steady state values of x, v, θ, and z would be obtained as

$$x^* = \frac{1}{\alpha_1(1 - \alpha_1)} [\alpha_3 n + (1 - \alpha_3)\delta + b], \quad v^* = \frac{1}{\alpha_1} [\alpha_3 n + (1 + \alpha_1 - \alpha_3)\delta + b],$$

$$\theta^* = \alpha_3\delta/b, \quad z^* = \delta. \tag{28}$$

With $b > 0$, x^*, v^*, and θ^* would all be positive. We should note that $\theta^* \leqslant 1$ requires $b \geqslant \alpha_3\delta$. Also, that the matrix

$$-\begin{pmatrix} \dfrac{\partial \dot{x}}{\partial x} & \dfrac{\partial \dot{x}}{\partial v} & \dfrac{\partial \dot{x}}{\partial \theta} \\[2mm] \dfrac{\partial \dot{v}}{\partial x} & \dfrac{\partial \dot{v}}{\partial v} & \dfrac{\partial \dot{v}}{\partial \theta} \\[2mm] \dfrac{\partial \dot{\theta}}{\partial x} & \dfrac{\partial \dot{\theta}}{\partial v:} & \dfrac{\partial \dot{\theta}}{\partial \theta} \end{pmatrix} = \begin{pmatrix} (1 - \alpha_1)x^* & 0 & -a_1 x^*/\alpha_1 \\[2mm] (1 - \alpha_1)v^* & -v^* & 0 \\[2mm] 0 & \theta^* & -a_2\theta^*/\alpha_1 \end{pmatrix}$$

has a negative trace and a positive Jacobian, where $a_1 \equiv (1 - \alpha_3)b/\alpha_3$ and $a_2 \equiv (1 + \alpha_1 - \alpha_3)b/\alpha_3$. From this, we could deduce that (x^*, v^*, θ^*) was a saddle point, where two of the eigenvalues are negative, and one eigenvalue is positive. Noting that (15) holds for the present model, we could obtain for the steady state

$$\hat{c} = [\,b - \alpha_2 n + (\alpha_1 - \alpha_3)\delta\,]/(1 - \alpha_1). \tag{29}$$

Hence a necessary and sufficient condition for sustainable growth in *per capita* consumption in the steady state would be

$$b > \alpha_2 n + (\alpha_3 - \alpha_1)\delta \tag{29'}$$

Since we must have $b \geqslant \alpha_3\delta$ in the steady state, we might also conclude that *per capita* consumption always increases in the steady state if population stays constant. This would give us

> *Proposition 2:* Under the present specification of the model, the steady state (x^*, v^*, θ^*) is a saddle point, where x^*, v^*, and θ^* are all positive. In the steady state, the rate of depletion of the stock of the natural resource is equal to the rate of discount. The magnitude of b must be sufficiently large to ensure the optimal programme. *Per capita* consumption increases in the steady state if and only if (29') hold.

*

In the discussion from the floor, *Professor Józef Pajestka* said that three observations had come to mind as afterthoughts when he had studied the paper presented by Professor Khachaturov and Fedorenko. They all concerned the state of economics and certain desirable lines of change in its profile:

(1) The paper was right in indicating and opposing the pessimistic conclusions of the first two reports to the Club of Rome, and Mr Pajestka said that he believed that the vivid discussion which followed the publication of the two reports had demonstrated a very wide conviction that it was not the natural environment, nor techno-scientific factors, which created obstacles and barriers to economic development, but essentially the social, managerial, institutional and political factors. Hence his first conclusion: *When dealing with world development issues we have to turn more and more from economics, narrowly conceived, to political economy.*

It was worth noting, he said, that the above-mentioned identification of the main obstacles to progress was shared by the last two reports to the Club of Rome: the RIO report by Jan Tinbergen and the report 'Beyond Waste' by Dennis Gabor and Umberto Colombo.

(2) Professors Khachaturov and Fedorenko had put a very strong emphasis on the proper understanding of development goals. They had stressed improving the human qualitative traits, developing creativity, assuring social justice, and peoples' participation in decision taking. This they had linked with the human factor as the most decisive factor for progress. Hence his second conclusion: *Socio-economic linkages and feedbacks had to become a core of development analysis.* Unless the social aspects and dimensions were considered, no proper analysis of long-run development, could be made, whether retrospective or prospective. This implied the need for a multidisciplinary approach to all important development issues on the national and international scale.

(3) From the above it also followed that economic science should deal

with the most important, though also most difficult subject — that of societal goals. By and large economists were shying away from considering the goals of economic development. In certain theories they were assumed as exogeneously given; in others their primitive quantitative treatment was being proposed; in most, however, they were simply ignored. The conclusion therefrom: *Economic sciences, particularly when dealing with development issues, should necessarily include into their sphere of interest the societal development goals.* As it happened, he said, attempts at finding new approaches in dealing with societal goals were appearing already and seemed to be bringing about some results. They needed appropriate theoretical analysis. If someone was to remark that, as a consequence, economics (one part of it) would turn into some kind of social philosophy, he would agree. This was just what was needed in the critical periods of development of humanity.

Professor Evgeni Mateev said that, in regard to the factors of economic development he would like to outline certain considerations which related to matters of principle.

The planet on which we lived was the one it actually was. That was why, if for purposes of predictions in this field we took any single independent variable in its capacity of growth factor and extrapolated its increase at whatever rate we chose, we would reach a limit of economic development and of the development of society as a whole. This was such a trivial result that it should hardly evoke any emotions at all. What was worthy of our attention was, rather, the question whether such an approach was admissible or not.

If on the eve of what was called the Neolithic revolution predictions had been made in terms of the existing extensive approach to the factors of growth, then the economic development of the world should have stopped some 10,000 years ago, because the number of hunters and the members of their families would have reached the limit set by the number of game animals. The planet would have been too small as early as at that time for the several million people inhabiting it.

The dynamic and intensive approach to the factors of growth was manifested in several directions, said Professor Mateev:

(1) The number of deposits of each one of the minerals of interest to us have been steadily increasing with the success of the geological surveys carried out. On the basis of the deposits known fifty years ago the crude oil should have been exhausted by now. Instead, the deposits known today are much larger than the ones known then.

(2) There really exists a theoretical limit to the discovery of new deposits and in many instances this limit is already in sight. However, parallel with the increase in known deposits and long before this limit has been reached, there develops a process of improved extraction of the mineral from the rock or material incorporating it, or a process of improved extraction of the useful component of the mineral.

(3) The number and types of minerals from which a certain useful component is obtained has been steadily expanding, e.g. the initial materials for obtaining aluminium, the oil shales, etc.

(4) The complex utilisation of the useful components and the existing

tendency towards manufacturing processes without residual material leads to a relative decrease, per unit of the useful components, of the overall mass of the initial minerals obtained.

(5) It is possible to obtain higher effects per unit of useful component used. By way of example we might refer to the efficiency coefficient in power engineering, to the strength and other characteristics of metals, etc.

(6) Recycling, i.e. secondary utilisation of materials.

(7) As a result of the extension and complication of its further treatment or processing, a given material with given properties can be used to obtain finished products of a higher degree of economic performance.

(8) These seven factors lead to the growth of the economy as a whole, this growth being calculated relatively, i.e. per unit of each one of the initial natural factors. Nevertheless, they do not abolish the problem of its theoretical limitation but can only postpone the moment of its exhaustion. However, long before the growth of the economy has reached or even approached this limit, the respective natural factor ceases to be a resource or loses its previous significance, being substituted by another factor which starts its growth from zero, reaches a certain significance, and is in its turn substituted by a third factor, etc. Metals came long before the deposits of suitable resources for Neolithic tools had been exhausted, the coal came before the forests had been felled for charcoal, and so on, with the atomic power plants and the plastic materials, following in the same way.

(9) The growth of final consumption in an intensive sense, i.e. per head of the population, as a general growth factor of the economy, does not signify in itself and under all conditions a similar growth of the substances and of the energy taken by the economy from nature. It would be quite incorrect to extrapolate the present-day dissipation of materials and energy, which is quite irrelevant from the point of view of the standards of the human individual.

(10) A dynamic approach along the above lines practically removes the mirage of the economic apocalypse. However, the earth as a whole is a *locus standi*. That is why, if we extrapolate the population growth with some exponential function, no matter how small the exponent may be, we reach a limit, theoretically at least. Nevertheless, the exponential approach in such a prediction is not admissible even in this general aspect. In the case of Bulgaria, for example, the birth rate was 42·2 per cent in 1900, as against 17·2 per cent in 1974, without any measures being applied to reduce it but, on the contrary, under a policy of containing this process of decrease.

The tendencies referred to did not lead to any underestimation of the ecological problems, said Mr Mateev. On the contrary, they were the basis for an active attitude by society towards their solution.

On that background, one basic factor of economic growth, and hence of solving the ecological problems, proved to be the capacity of society to control entirely its economy and, in particular, to co-ordinate its scientific and technical progress, the investment necessary for introduction of this progress into the economy, the qualifications of the labour force as a contributor to growing productivity, the numerical strength of the labour force, and the pattern of consumption as well as its improvement.

This complex incorporated and provided the solution of the basic problems of economic development, of the further improvement of society and of the individual, and of the protection – or more correctly the ennoblement – of the natural environment.

He wanted, he said, to reiterate that optimism in this respect was not only justified, provided there was a sufficiently careful analysis of the laws of economic development, but at the same time served as the general basis for solving the problems raised by that development.

The factors he had listed, which showed the harmony that existed between economic growth and the resources it depended on, emphasised the crucial importance of the problem which the socialist countries were systematically and persistently trying to resolve: that basic problem of our epoch – disarmament.

Mr John Hardt observed that Mr Kaser and Professor Takayama had both commented with approval on Academician Khachaturov and Academician Fedorenko's critique of the Forrester–Meadows projection as being 'technologically pessimistic' because 'that system does not provide any possibility to influence the process of development by man' (p. 122). Michael Kaser appeared to interpret this critique as being related to the lack of decision – making in the Forrester–Meadows model, thus making it 'technologically pessimistic' since it ruled out changes that would improve performance by the more effective use of technological change. Mr Kaser also appeared to find this interpretation of the Khachaturov–Fedorenko critique applicable to a critique of CIA projections of Soviet energy production. Following the Kaser line of reasoning in commenting on the Khachaturov–Fedorenko critique, he would ask two questions said Mr Hardt: one on the microeconomic CIA Soviet energy projections, and the other on the macroeconomic CIA projection of Soviet GNP performance:

(1) Was the 'technological pessimism' that Kaser found in the CIA energy production relative to potential importation of western exploration and extraction technology? Was Kaser arguing, along with Jeremy Russell and others of his UK colleagues, that importation of improved technological means for exploration and extraction plus more investment in building up the energy infrastructure would raise the output projections. This would presumably be introducing the 'process of development by man' into the Soviet projections.

(2) Recent CIA macroeconomic projections[1] indicated a sharp slowdown in Soviet performance to a 'worst case' annual performance with oil shortages and bad crop years of zero or negative growth. The question of 'technological pessimism' in Question (1) might also be applied to this macroeconomic projection, i.e. decisions especially involving importation and effective use of western technology and shift in domestic investment, would markedly change the outcomes.

---

[1] The testimony of Director Turner, 'Soviet Economic Problems and Prospects', released by the US Congress Joint Economic Committee, 8 August 1977.

This was not to suggest that a reasonable range of technological options could shift performance from its downward trend, but the degree of retardation might be markedly influenced and ameliorated.

Applying this correlation of the Khachaturov—Fedorenko critique to the CIA energy projections of Kaser, one might thus ask the general question: was the critique by Academicians Khachaturov and Fedorenko of the Forrester—Meadows/Club of Rome projections as technologically pessimistic also applicable to the CIA macroeconomic projections of the Soviet economy?

*

Replying to the discussion, *Professor Khachaturov* said that he wanted, first, to answer Michael Kaser's comments on his and Academician Fedorenko's paper. Beginning with the title Mr Kaser had given to his critique — 'Natural Resources in the Conflict between Price and Quota' — he could not agree that this reflected in the slightest degree the contents of the paper he and Academician Fedorenko had written. In the USSR, there was no such conflict. To think that there was, was to misunderstand the essence of the economic mechanisms of the Soviet system. The USSR had never underestimated pricing. Prices there were a very effective and necessary means of planning. Someone might ask why Russian prices were so stable, why they did not change following shortages or surpluses of production. He would like to say that it was an advantage that the Russians did not increase their prices in the years of bad harvests. But with great pleasure they reduced prices when they had the slightest possibility of doing so. He and Academician Fedorenko had had no intention of discussing pricing in their paper. If such a discussion was wanted, it could take place elsewhere at some other time. For the present, he was against diverting the discussion into a quite different channel.

One could receive the impression from Mr Kaser's comments, said Academician Khachaturov, that he had had in mind the rational use of only natural resources, in his country only and only by means of centralised planning. But the purpose of the paper was different. They had wanted to prove that there was not just one category of resources — i.e. natural resources — but three, and that the well-being of the whole of mankind depended not only on nature, but also, and perhaps to an even greater extent, on human resources — human brains, knowledge, experience; and on technology — means of production, their progress and perfection.

Michael Kaser had tried to show in his comments that in a socialist economy the consumption of natural resources per unit of output was higher than in a market economy, and as proof had used a comparison of data from Austria and Czechoslovakia. He had said that in only three sectors out of eighteen material consumption in Czechoslovakia was lower than in Austria. This was a curious mistake. If one referred to Mr Kaser's own Table on p. 135 one could see clearly that nine positions out of eighteen were in Czechoslovakia's favour. But the comparison as a whole was not convincing, because both countries were rather limited in their resources and the structure of their economies was different.

He had been rather surprised, said Academician Khachaturov, by the reference in the paper to the US Central Intelligence Agency data on oil output in the USSR, for Mr Kaser had written that this agency was a government office. It was known, of course, that governments had various unpleasant agencies, like the secret police, the Intelligence service, and so on. He did not know who was the author of the CIA report and what his sources were, but was sure that these were dubious data obtained from dark and evidently espionage sources.

Mr Kaser's references on p. 139 of his comment to Soviet purchases in the West, and his conclusion that the USSR would continue to sell oil and gas abroad to earn the currency it needed were quite irrelevant to the subject under discussion, he added. As for the so-called paradox that the socialist countries would rapidly expand nuclear power when they were relatively better off in terms of fossil fuels, why was this called a paradox? Mr Kaser had himself written a few lines earlier about the heavy transportation costs of fossil fuels from remote Siberian deposits to the areas of consumption. That was why in many regions of his vast country it was more effective to produce energy from nuclear power.

As regards Professor Takayama's comments, he would like to say again that the main purpose of his and Academician Fedorenko's paper was to underline that natural resources are not the only source of production. There were *three* important sources of growth – human resources, technology and nature. This was a very important point in their paper, for their aim had been to show that the population of this planet was not entirely dependent on the continued existence of visible and potential resources, because human resources and the means of production created by man were much more considerable.

Professor Takayama recognised the importance of human resources and technology for the further progress of production. It was broadly recognised that economies of human resources, their development, the rise of productivity, improvement of social conditions, etc., were highly important, and, as everyone knew, human resources and their development is to be the subject of the next Congress of the IEA.

The paper he and Academician Fedorenko had written could not be regarded merely as an answer to doomsday predictions of an impending catastrophe. In this connection they wanted to say that it was impossible to stop artificially the growth of population and production, especially in an atmosphere of insoluble contradictions between states, between monopolies.

Professor Takayama had not objected to our statements on rapid growth of income, production, fixed assets, educational standards, and so on, in the USSR, but in his view that had also occurred in non-socialist countries, for example, Japan. Of course, nobody would deny that in Japan the rate of growth in the third quarter of this century was very high, and it was possible to explain why this had occurred if one took into account the high abilities of the people and their hard work, successful development of science and technology and liquidation of the remains of feudalism.

At the same time, he agreed with Professor Takayama's two models and his analysis of them, said Academician Khachaturov. His excellent and elegant application of the production function was very convincing. Certainly, economies of materials through rationalisation of production, including utilisation of by-products, was more effective than the use of new resources of raw materials. Analysis showed that extraction of raw materials was more and more costly and at the same time technological progress required less use of materials per unit of production.

As far as the discussion from the floor was concerned, he wanted to make the following comments:

He agreed in general with Professor Pajestka's observations on the usefulness and desirability of turning our attention more and more to the socio-economic conditions of world development and therefore to the tasks which confront economic science – both theoretical and applied. That fully corresponded with the contents of the paper they had written.

He supported also Professor Mateev's considerations, which as a matter of fact, were in line with some of the main points of the paper. In particular, that there were large latent resources within our planet, which could be used as we acquired increased knowledge and greater scientific and technological ability. They looked forward to the progressive exploration of the hidden possibilities of the productive forces. At this point in time we did not know what was hidden in the entrails of our planet deeper than seven or eight kilometres under the surface. Probably the unknown resources were very large.

As regards the questions raised by Mr Hardt, he would first of all like to repeat that CIA assumptions concerning future economic growth of the USSR and its energy situation, based on unknown shady sources, were groundless and could hardly be seriously discussed in the Congress, said Academician Khachaturov. His country was successfully fulfilling its tenth five-year plan; the planned rate of growth for next year was not zero or even negative as somebody had suggested, but + 4 per cent for the whole national economy (national income) and 4·5 per cent for industrial output.

As to the importation of western technology and its effective use, he agreed that they could play an important role in the further rise of the Soviet economy; but even without such importation into the country, its people could certainly maintain the USSR's projected rates of growth.

In conclusion he would like to say that although he and Academician Fedorenko had not finally solved the problems dealt with in their paper, they had given the correct direction for further research and hoped that this would be useful.

5 Barriers to Development

K. N. Raj

CENTRE FOR DEVELOPMENT STUDIES, ULLOOR,
KERALA, INDIA

Barriers to development are of two kinds: those that can be attributed to
factors within the countries concerned, and those that might be traced to
their external environment. Low levels of productivity to begin with, poverty
of natural resources (such as limited availability of land for agriculture), and
high rates of growth of population can all be serious impediments to development, and explain no doubt to a large extent the predicament of many parts
of the world that remain economically backward. But there have been
instances enough of such impediments being successfully overcome, partly by
institutional adaptation or innovation within and partly by resort to solutions
which depend on the external environment. The interaction between the
internal and the external has a profound effect on the processes of development as well as on their outcome. It is therefore with reference to this interaction that we shall consider the barriers to development experienced earlier
and those now in evidence.

I

It has been generally recognised in the literature on the subject that the
obstacles to development are on the whole more formidable now than was the
case for the presently developed countries in their pre-industrial phase. The
reasons listed in this context (under what have been broadly categorised as
'initial conditions') suggest, however, that it is to be traced almost wholly to
factors internal to the underdeveloped countries today – such as lower *per
capita* product, lower *per capita* supply of agricultural land, lower per worker
productivity in agriculture, greater inequality in the size-distribution of income,
higher rate of growth of population, lower levels of literacy, weaker political
and administrative structures, and various socio-cultural characteristics.[1] Even
failures to exploit adequately the factors favourable to them now, such as the
accumulated knowledge and experience available to be drawn upon and the
opportunities offered by the existence of several developed countries, is not
infrequently attributed to these internal characteristics.

[1] S. Kuznets, 'Present Underdeveloped Countries and Past Growth Patterns', in Easton
Nelson (ed.), *Economic Growth: Rationale, Problems, Cases* (University of Texas Press,
1960).

While there are good reasons for focusing attention on internal impediments, it is important not to overlook the extent to which the external environment can help to overcome the constraints so imposed. This is evident nowhere more clearly than from the experience of the countries of western Europe in the nineteenth century.

Though the availability of land per worker in agriculture in western Europe at the time was at least three times as high as it is in the countries of south Asia today, and the rate of growth of population only about half as high, the main barrier to development as seen then was, as now, the pressure of population on land. This was reflected in considerable concern not only with the problem of meeting the minimum food requirements of the population, but with the possibility of the rising cost of food and/or inadequate purchasing power acting as deterrents to the expansion of manufacturing industry. It is obvious in retrospect that improvements in agricultural technology and organisation within these countries helped only in part to overcome these obstacles – the output of corn in Britain, for instance, seems to have at best kept pace with population growth[1] – and that there was perceptible relief only after the phenomenal expansion of cropped area in America, Australia and Canada made available substantial imports to supplement domestic production. As internal pressures grew, large-scale emigration also provided an important outlet, with well over 9 million people leaving Europe between 1846 and 1875 (the greater part of them for the USA).[2] Economic expansion in new territories, and penetration of older markets through free trade, offered at the same time the growth in demand needed for the development of manufacturing industry.

That manufacturing had not itself progressed much beyond the handicraft stage in the rest of the world, and required as yet relatively small amounts of fixed capital, was also an important feature of the external environment at the time. Though the range and variety of the machinery needed for manufacturing was growing, and the production of such machinery was itself becoming a specialised activity, the fixed capital requirements were still relatively modest, generally no more than could be accumulated in each case by a small enterprise within a relatively short period.[3] One result of this was that development through industrialisation could be sustained until the 1840s with much less than 10 per cent of the national income being devoted to net capital formation. It also minimised the displacement of labour through technological change. There was evident, in fact, an organic continuity in the industrialisation process, such that even as late as the 1830s and 1840s it was difficult in Britain to distinguish between the craftsman–tradesman and the manufacturer; and, though more than two-fifths of the labour force of the

[1] Phyllis Deane and W. A. Cole, *British Economic Growth, 1688–1959: Trends and Structure* (Cambridge University Press, 1969) p. 65.

[2] E. J. Hobsbawm, *The Age of Capital, 1848–1875* (Weidenfeld & Nicolson, 1976) p. 193.

[3] David S. Landes, *The Unbound Prometheus* (Cambridge University Press, 1970), p. 78.

country was reported to be engaged in manufacturing, mining and building in the middle of the nineteenth century, 'most people were working either in their own homes as self-employed craftsmen or outworkers, or in small workshops, than in large-scale factory industry'.[1]

Japan was also in a position to take advantage of some of these features of early industrialisation, and of expanding demand for its exports, in the initial phases of its development. It was, however, much less well-endowed in respect of agricultural land, comparing unfavourably in this respect with even the countries of south Asia today. Consequently the development process needed a much greater degree of institutional adaptation within, and also imposed more severe pressures on levels of consumption (including food intake).

The adaptations within took various forms. Important among them was the technology of agriculture. Since almost the entire area under paddy had been irrigated even by the beginning of the Meiji era, the steps taken in the subsequent period to raise productivity included not only the breeding of higher-yielding varieties of rice and the use of chemical fertilisers but, more crucially, measures to introduce underground drainage and increase the efficiency of control over water supply.[2] (It is evident that it is the lack of such basic investment in irrigation, drainage and flood control that keeps agricultural productivity much lower in countries of south Asia today than in Japan.) Another adaptation, more slow to evolve, was through the development of nutritional science for making efficient use of the available food. Since the average daily availability of food provided less than 2200 calories *per capita* until the second decade of the twentieth century, and did not exceed 2400 calories until the 1960s, proposals for improving dietary habits through education were promoted more than half a century ago. The experience Japan has acquired in this field since then shows that a high level of nutrition and national health is attainable with a largely vegetarian diet, high in carbohydrate, low in fat, and using fish and animal food as complementary sources of protein, a finding of great importance for the less developed countries of today.[3]

The pressure on food supplies in the face of population growth, and the need for markets for its manufactured products, drove Japan also outward in the direction of colonial expansion. In the process, the same measures as were adopted for raising agricultural productivity within Japan were extended to Taiwan and Korea as well. This would not have been possible, of course, but for the external political circumstances being favourable to such expansion.

[1] Phyllis Deane, *The First Industrial Revolution* (Cambridge University Press, 1965) pp. 255–7.
[2] S. Ishikawa, *Economic Development in Asian Perspective* (Kinokuniya Bookstore Co., 1967), pp. 96–8.
[3] William Insull and Kenzaburo Tsuchiya, 'Diet and Nutritional Status of Japanese', *The American Journal of Clinical Sciences*, vol. 21, no. 7 (July 1968).

That nevertheless, after eight decades of industrialisation, Japan's *per capita* income was still below $200 in 1952–4 – lower than in any European country and even in most of the Latin American countries – has been attributed to paucity of natural resources.[1] It is important to note, however, that this did not prevent its growing at a phenomenal rate in the two decades thereafter when Japan was in a position to compete effectively in the rapidly expanding trade in sophisticated manufactures between the developed countries. Acquisition of scientific and technological capability, particularly during the Second World War, had apparently more than compensated for the deficiency in other resources and helped it to take advantage of the changed external environment.

II

The countries now grouped together in the category of the 'developing' differ among themselves even more than the countries of western Europe, Japan and the USA in the nineteenth century. One must therefore be careful when making generalisations about the obstacles they face and what they imply.

If one were to go by the rate of growth of output achieved over the last two decades by this group of countries as a whole, and compare it with the rate achieved earlier by countries that could have been so categorised by the same criteria in the nineteenth and early twentieth centuries but have since become developed, one might easily be tempted to conclude that the constraints on development are much less severe now for the former than they were for the latter. The rate of growth of output in Great Britain did not exceed 3·5 per cent per annum over any length of time in the nineteenth century; few other countries did much better. On the other hand, in the 1950s, the growth rate of the developing countries taken together was about 4 per cent per annum; by the late 1960s it was very nearly 5 per cent per annum; in the first half of the 1970s it has been around 6 per cent per annum for the group as a whole, and over 5·25 per cent per annum even if the petroleum exporters among them are excluded.

The performance of the developing countries today would appear to be better than of those that developed earlier even if allowance is made for the higher rates at which their population has been growing. Thus, while the rate of growth of product *per capita* was less than 1·5 per cent per annum in Great Britain between 1801 and 1871, and did not exceed 1·75 per cent per annum even in the following three decades, it has touched over 2·5 per cent per annum among the developing countries (excluding the petroleum exporters) in the period 1971–5.[2]

The intensity and scale of the problems facing the underdeveloped countries today come into focus only when attention is specifically directed to countries

[1] Kuznets, op. cit.
[2] Committee for Development Planning, *Report on the Thirteenth Session* (11–21 April 1977) United Nations Economic and Social Council, Official Records, Sixty-Third Session, Supplement no. 4.

with *per capita* income of less than $200 per annum. The average annual rate of growth of *per capita* income of countries belonging to this poorest group has been hardly 1·5 per cent over the last decade and a half, as compared to the rate of around 3·5 per cent recorded in other developing countries. All but a few of them are located in two regions, one extending across the middle of Africa ('stretching from the Sahara in the north to Lake Nyasa in the south', including all countries within this area except some on the West African coast) and the other beginning with Afghanistan and Pakistan in the west and stretching eastward across south Asia and some South-East Asian countries.[1] In more recent years, the *per capita* output (valued at 1970 prices) of countries belonging to this poorest category (excluding the petroleum exporters) rose by hardly $1 a year, from $103 in 1970 to $108 in 1975.[2] Together they account for about one-third of the world population.

The obstacles to development today are however more wide-ranging and serious than indicated by these figures. For, even where the level of *per capita* income and its rate of growth have been relatively high, the ability to absorb labour in productive activity has generally lagged far behind its availability, resulting in growing mass unemployment (both open and disguised), depressed wage rates, and accentuation of inequalities in income. In some regions, particularly in certain countries of Latin America and in several of the petroleum-exporting countries, high rates of growth have resulted mainly in creating and expanding enclaves of affluence with no significant impact on the living standards of people outside these enclaves.

The reasons for these and other barriers to development now in evidence can be traced in part to the external environment, in part to factors within these countries, and not least to the interaction between them.

III

The most important change in the external environment since the Second World War has been that the already developed countries have become their own best customers and suppliers and, with the exception of some important items, have acquired a high degree of self-containedness as a group. Consequently, even when world trade was expanding at a relatively high rate, the most dynamic element of it was the trade amongst the developed countries themselves, while exports from the developing countries grew at but a much lower rate. Moreover, since the developed countries have been in a position to meet the greater part of even their requirements of agricultural products, exports of food and raw materials to them from the developing countries have been growing more slowly than their exports of manufactures and semi-manufactures. But the scope for expanding their exports of manufactured

[1] United Nations, *International Finance, Depressed Regions and Needed Progress: Views and Recommendations of the Committee for Development Planning* (1976), p. 21.
[2] Committee for Development Planning, op. cit.

products has been also affected by import restrictions of various kinds imposed by the developed countries.

This change in external environment means not only that expansion of world trade cannot be depended on to promote growth to anything like the same degree as was possible earlier for most of the new developed countries, but also that the lack of adequate purchasing power in the form of foreign exchange restricts the access of developing countries to the supplies of food that could otherwise be drawn upon from the world market to supplement internal production. While land is still available in many parts of the world for growing more food, there is now greater incentive to use it for producing the animal proteins that are in growing demand in the relatively affluent countries than to meet the grain requirements of the poor in the less developed countries. Their access to grain supplies from these sources is therefore confined largely to times of crisis when special aid programmes make them available. Migration on any large scale to countries with more abundant land (and other natural resources) is also not any longer a feasible alternative.

Aid from developed countries does of course supplement the foreign exchange earnings of the less developed. But the scale of such aid (expressed as a percentage of the national income of either category), as also the grant element in it, have been declining. The high rates of interest charged on commercial credit, as well as the constraints on exports which affect the ability to repay, restrict the scale on which external borrowing can be resorted to by most developing countries. Moreover, on account of the terms and conditions on which external aid is forthcoming (whether stated explicitly or not), a high degree of dependence on it has usually the indirect effect of forcing adherence to policies that have the approval of the donors and closing thereby some of the options that might otherwise be available. Countries in this position would, for instance, certainly find it difficult to follow the highly restrictive policy that Japan adopted towards foreign equity participation in its corresponding phase of development.

Above all, the fact that over a century of development has raised living standards elsewhere to levels hitherto unknown, and introduced new products and services which have begun to be regarded as essential components of development, is itself part of the external environment which the less developed countries face today. This new range of products and services is not only in general highly capital-intensive but its production results in most cases, through technological change, in considerable displacement of labour engaged in traditional economic activity. The discontinuities in the development process are therefore much greater, and their economic and social consequences far more serious.

All these factors add up to changes in external environment that are not merely differences in degree; they involve certain qualitative differences that imply almost a total transformation. While circumstances vary no doubt from country to country, and some may be more fortunately placed than others, the external environment confronting the underdeveloped countries as a whole poses so many more problems than the now-developed countries had to face a century ago that one could well regard it as the most formidable of all the barriers to development today.

One must however take into account also the features of this environment that are favourable to development. They include not only the scientific and technological knowledge accumulated over several decades but the experience gained from different patterns of development under different circumstances, which makes it possible to perceive how the mistakes committed earlier can be avoided and what are the choices to be made to achieve more quickly at least some of the objectives of development. If such perceptions have not in fact had much impact on development policy and practice, the explanation is to be found partly in the factors within the different countries concerned and partly in the interaction between these factors and the particular features of the external environment which happen to be conditioning them most powerfully.

IV

The most important of the factors internal to these countries which determine their success in facing and overcoming the barriers to development are the economic and political power structure, the interests and values it upholds, and the choices that can (and cannot) be effectively made within such a framework.

As indicated earlier, the pressure of population on land was much more severe in Japan in the closing decades of the nineteenth century than it is in countries of south Asia today. Consequently, though agricultural technology was adapted to make possible intensive use of land and productivity per hectare was high even in the early Meiji era, productivity per worker engaged in agriculture does not appear to have been very much higher in Japan at that time than in these countries now.[1] In fact, despite productivity of land under rice being 1·5 to 2 times as high in Japan in 1878–82 as in India and Pakistan in 1953–62, productivity of the labour engaged in rice cultivation in Japan was possibly only one-half to one-third as high on account of the area of arable land available per farm worker being much lower.[2] That Japan was nevertheless able to extract an adequate surplus out of agriculture to sustain the process of industrialisation – apparently more effectively than in India or Pakistan today – must be explained in large part by the power that the propertied interests in land and business together wielded at that time and the social and political milieu in which it all took place.

---

[1] K. Ohkawa, 'Initial Conditions: Measures of Economic Levels and Structure and their Implications – Rough Notes', paper prepared for private circulation at a Research Planning Conference on 'Japan's Historical Development Experience and Contemporary Developing Countries: Issues for Comparative Analysis' organised by the Japan Economic Research Centre in April 1976.

[2] See Allen C. Kelley and Jeffrey G. Williamson, *Lessons from Japanese Development: An Analytical Economic History* (University of Chicago Press, 1974) pp. 164–7.

With the rather different balance of forces in the countries of south Asia today, higher levels of agricultural output *per capita* and a much higher rate of growth of output are essential to secure the necessary surpluses. The relatively low initial level of the productivity of land is of course an advantage from this point of view, since the scope for raising it is correspondingly greater. However, at the same time, the basic investment needed in irrigation, drainage and flood control to raise the productivity of land requires not only consolidation of the fragmented holdings, but also mobilisation of both manpower and financial resources on a scale that poses major problems given the present alignment of social and political forces in these countries.

Much the same kind of conflict of interests and values is involved also in the choice of the product-mix and in the choice of technology in the non-agricultural sector. For maximising productive employment, as well as for avoiding the use of scarce resources, the case for selectively adapting traditional techniques using locally available labour and materials as far as possible, instead of replacing them with machinery and materials that are more capital-intensive, is obviously a strong one. Yet the appeal of a wide range of new products that have been popularised in the developed countries is very strong for the upper-income groups in the less developed countries today; the more open their economies, the more vulnerable in this respect are even the income groups below. Given strong preference for these products, the range of choice open in respect of technology is often limited, and a much higher degree of capital intensity thus gets built into the development process than is strictly required for the meeting of the needs involved.[1]

The high degree of capital intensity introduced into the development process through transplantation of new tastes, and the further inequalities of income which this in turn generates, can become mutually reinforcing. This is perhaps the main explanation for the enclaves of affluence that have grown rapidly in many countries (such as Brazil). Just as trade among the developed countries has been a source of high growth rates in the period since the Second World War, so economic activity within such enclaves can also be a source of rapid growth. At the same time, though land is available in relative abundance, concentration in ownership keeps the majority of the people outside the enclaves fairly close to the subsistence level.

Whether such growth can be characterised as development in a meaningful sense does however become then a very pertinent question. Moreover, since the product-mix on which it is based − consisting to a considerable extent of items such as aluminium, stainless steel, synthetic fabrics, structural steel, plastic, glass and cement − tends to highly energy-intensive,[2] one may doubt

[1] Cf. K. N. Raj, 'Linkages in Industrialization and Development Strategy: Some Basic Issues', *Journal of Development Planning,* no. 8 (United Nations, 1975).
[2] The energy requirements, expressed in KWH, per tonne of output have been estimated at nearly 77,000 for aluminium, well over 65,000 for stainless steel, about 28,000 for nylon fabrics and 21,000 for structural steel, about 13,000 for mill-made cotton fabrics, nearly 8000 for glass, about 3200 for plastics, and over 2500 for cement.

how far this kind of growth is compatible with the limits set by the energy potential from known sources and the need for its being distributed fairly equitably. Indeed it has been suggested on this ground that

> it is essential to halt and reverse the changing pattern of demand which over the past few decades has been shifting from wood to aluminium (e.g. for furniture and building), from handloom cloth to mill cotton, from cotton fabrics to nylon fabrics, from one- or two-storey buildings to high-rise buildings, from lime mortar to cement, from earthenware to stainless stell, etc. [1]

Much progress in this direction is, however, unlikely to be achieved without major institutional changes and shifts in the distribution of income within the societies concerned.

Not the least of the internal factors which determine the ability of the less developed countries to overcome the barriers with which they are faced is the extent of investment in human capital in the initial phases, particularly through the spread of basic educational and health facilities that could help to increase the responsiveness of people to the options available to them. Though there has been considerable literature on the potential benefits of such investment, the priority given to it has in practice varied a great deal.

In the past, the value of spreading education was recognised in some cases as the result of religious or social movements within (as in western Europe from as early as the seventeenth century), and in some others in response to challenges from outside (as appears to have been the case in Japan in the last quarter of the nineteenth century). More recently there has been increasing awareness of the beneficial effect education can have on labour productivity, and also in reducing social and economic inequalities. The progress made in this respect continues to be very uneven, however — even as between different regions within the same country (as in India now on account of the differences in policy followed in different states) — partly because the value of education is not understood widely enough, partly for the reason that there is resistance to bearing the fiscal burden involved in extending educational services on the necessary scale, and in some cases for fear of mass education promoting social unrest and radical political movements.

The importance of extending health services in the initial phases of development has been much less clearly grasped, as it is generally associated with precipitous declines in mortality rates and consequently with explosive increases in population which are considered detrimental to development. It is beginning to be appreciated that considerable decline in overall mortality rates can take

[1] Amulya Kumar N. Reddy and K. Krishna Prasad, 'Technological Alternatives and the Indian Energy Crisis', theme paper presented at the National Seminar on Energy organised by the Institute of Asian Studies and the Administrative Staff College of India in December 1975.

See C. and J. Steinhart, *Energy: Sources, Use and Role in Human Affairs* (Duxbury Press, 1974).

place merely in response to the control of epidemics through general measures of public health; but that, in order to create conditions favourable to significant decline in fertility rates, it is essential to extend medical facilities that can help to bring down infant and child mortality rates still more sharply, raise the life expectation at birth, and thereby give assurance of higher survival rates to parents who seek in surviving children the assistance they need in their household enterprises as well as the main insurance they can rely on in times of sickness and old age.

Economic historians have recently drawn pointed attention to the finding that even in Europe birth rates began to fall sharply (except in a few countries such as France and Ireland) only after a sharp decline in infant mortality rates had been achieved (as in England after 1900); and that such decline offers the most plausible explanation for the time sequence and the geographical pattern of the decline in fertility rates recorded in most European countries.[1] This kind of relationship is also becoming evident now in some of the underdeveloped countries that have made significant progress in the extension of educational and health services.[2] Though the factors determining the time-lag between decline in infant mortality rates and fertility have yet to be studied the important policy implications of this relationship are clear enough.

Nevertheless, conflicts of interest will still have to be resolved within these countries between those who find public investment in other kinds of infra-

---

[1] See the following statements in H. J. Habbakuk, *Population Growth and Economic Development since 1750* (Leicester University Press, 1971) pp. 59–65:

> The links which have been suggested between economic changes and the fall in the birth rate are all quite reasonable, but there is nothing in the economic data to explain why the fall should have started when it did . . .. It started towards the end of the nineteenth century when real incomes were rising, and it accelerated after 1900 in a decade during which the rise in real incomes appears to have been checked.

> From 1841–5 to 1896–1900, the rate fluctuated [in England] within the limits of 145 and 157 infant deaths per 1000 live births. . . . the sharp decline in infant mortality did not start till after 1900.

> The fall in infant mortality threatened to increase the size of surviving family and to offset this threat the traditional remedies – postponement or avoidance of marriage – were clearly not adequate. The age of marriage might accomodate itself to the pressure of economic circumstances over a long period . . .. But it could not respond adequately to relatively rapid change in mortality . . .. It was the people who married in the 1880's and 1890's who reaped the advantage of the marked fall in infant mortality after 1900; the high rate of survival of their children compelled them at some stage to consider the question whether they should have another child . . .. At the lower levels of mortality prevailing after 1900 parents could reasonably expect that most of their children would grow up; that is, the size of surviving family came to approximate fairly closely to the number of children born.

[2] Cf. Centre for Development Studies, *Poverty, Unemployment and Development Policy: A Case Study of Selected Issues with reference to Kerala* (United Nations, 1975) ST/ESA/29; also T. N. Krishnan, 'Demographic Transition in Kerala', *Economic and Political Weekly*, vol. XI, nos. 31–3 (August 1976).

structure such as transport, power and irrigation more profitable and those who, taking a more long-run view, attach higher priority to the extension of educational and health services. The more limited the resources available for such investment the more severe these conflicts within are likely to be.

V

Where the internal power structure has been so radically changed as to widen considerably the range of options available within, and the external environment found to be on balance unhelpful to the mobilisation and redeployment of the domestic resources, the tendency has been to rely on mechanisms and processes of development which need external stimulus and support to only a limited degree. China has apparently adopted this course with success. On the other hand, where the internal power structure has itself a strong external orientation for geo-political or economic reasons, there have been in evidence tendencies to depend primarily on forces from outside to stimulate and sustain the development process. South Korea, Taiwan and Hong Kong are examples of countries that have opted for the latter course.

It is generally agreed that, on account of differences in political conditions, the example of China is not capable of being repeated in most of the countries remaining underdeveloped, at any rate in the foreseeable future. South Korea, Taiwan and Hong Kong are, however, often held up for emulation, on the ground that exports of labour-intensive manufactures from them to the developed countries have been growing at a phenomenally rapid rate over the last decade, and that the adoption of similar policies should make it possible for other developing countries to raise their rate of growth of exports, output and employment all in one go.

The most dynamic segment of these exports, it would appear, however, has been of products for which the necessary material inputs are almost wholly imported from the developed countries, and manufacture is thereby confined to certain labour-intensive processes and component specialisation within vertically integrated international industries.[1] Precisely for this reason, such manufacture tends to have relatively limited linkage effects within the exporting countries, import requirements are high, the value added by manufacture is much lower as a percentage of the gross value of the products, and a high proportion of even this is apt to be repatriated as profits. Further, since attracting international sub-contracting work of this kind requires very often the offer of various incentives such as tax holidays and subsidised credit and it may still be shifted at little notice to other countries offering more generous terms, the direct and indirect social costs involved could be considerable.[2]

[1] G. K. Helleiner, 'Manufactured Exports from Less Developed Countries and Multi-national Firms', *Economic Journal*, vol. 83, no. 329 (March 1973).

[2] Paul Streeten, 'Policies towards Multinationals', *World Development*, vol. 3, no. 6 (June 1975); Michael Sharpston, 'International Subcontracting', *World Development*, vol. 4, no. 4 (April 1976).

Apart from these considerations which countries opting for such manufacture need to take into account, one must bear in mind that imports of these and other manufactures using low-wage labour in the poorer countries can be acceptable to the developed countries only so long as the scale of such imports does not pose a serious threat to the wage demands and levels of employment among their own workers. With stagflation in the developed countries already imposing severe constraints on the feasible rates of growth of output and employment within them, it seems unrealistic to assume that a strategy of development based on rapid expansion of exports of manufactured products to them can be viable for the developing countries as a whole; it can at best be regarded as a supplementary measure for exploiting such opportunities as might still be available.

VI

Given the internal and external constraints that the majority of the developing countries are faced with, most of the measures advocated for tackling problems such as rural under-employment and poverty are difficult to implement. Even when technological advances make it possible to accelerate the rate of growth of agricultural output, gross inequalities in the distribution of land, credit, etc., make its impact on employment and levels of living among the poor almost negligible. The bulk of the population in the countryside continue therefore to have incomes too low to generate any significant demand for non-agricultural products. The impact of such development is then confined mainly to the top one or two deciles of the population in the countryside, and the use of the surpluses generated reflects the preferences of these upper strata. The demand for some non-agricultural inputs increases in the process but, in the absence of a more widely diffused growth of incomes, the stimulus that agricultural development gives to manufacturing industry is confined to a limited range of products, a good many of which (for reasons mentioned earlier) are of a capital-intensive nature. Consequently, the pattern of industrialisation that tends to emerge fails to reflect the basic needs of development of poor countries and reflects instead the tastes and requirements of the relatively affluent in these countries; and it assumes particularly grotesque forms when multinational companies assume positions of dominance and acquire the power to influence significantly both the distribution of incomes and the product-mix in the growth process.

Various fiscal measures, as well as extension of the public sector, are often proposed in this context to correct such distortions. While such measures can in principle make some difference, and perhaps do so to a degree, there is little evidence as yet to suggest that they can have a significant effect on the distribution of wealth and income under conditions in which more direct measures for dealing with the problem, such as land reforms, are found to be not feasible for political and administrative reasons.

Much the same is true of proposals for appropriate technology. While correct in principle, and potentially of great value, such technology can get adopted only when the institutional framework and the values it promotes are also appropriate.

The recorded rates of growth of agricultural output, as also of output as a whole, in the poor countries since the Second World War compare favourably with the secular rates of growth observed in the now advanced countries of the world at their corresponding stage of development. If, nevertheless, the impact of such growth on the levels of living of the vast majority of the people in these countries has not been very significant, it is only in part explained by the higher rates of growth of population in evidence in these countries; the rest of the explanation lies in factors such as those mentioned above.

In the ultimate analysis, the barriers to development are basically political in nature. Poor countries tend to emphasise the barriers imposed by the prevailing system of international economic relations, while the rich draw attention to the vested interests within the poor countries. Unless, however, the interrelationship between the two is recognised, and solutions which take adequately into account the power equations within each sphere are explored, the progress made in dealing with these barriers is not likely to be greater in the future than it has been hitherto.

Discussion of Dr Raj's Paper *

Professor Bela Balassa was the first to comment. He said that he wanted to put forward an alternative view of the internal and external barriers to economic development today. In drawing comparisons with the experience of European countries — in particular Great Britain — at the early stage of their economic development, Dr Raj had asserted that 'the main barrier to development as seen then was, as now, the pressure of population on land' (p. 157). He had further claimed that 'the external environment confronting the underdeveloped countries as a whole posed so many more problems than the now-developed countries had to face a century ago that one could well regard this as the most formidable of all the barriers to development today' (pp. 161–2). Finally, according to Dr Raj,

> the most imporant of the factors internal to these countries which determine their success in facing and overcoming the barriers to development are the economic and political power structure, the interests and values it upholds, and the choice that can (and cannot) be effectively made within such a framework [p. 162].

His intention, said Professor Balassa, was to subject all these statements to scrutiny and offer an alternative view which put the emphasis on the importance of policy choices.

To begin with, questions arose concerning Dr Raj's interpretation of the British, and more generally European, experience of economic development. First, rather than the pressure of population on land being the main barrier to development, as Raj alleged (p. 157), 'recent research has done much to emphasise the part played by population increases in easing the labour scarcity which seems to have been an outstanding feature of the British economy in the late seventeenth and early eighteenth centuries, and in providing the labour force on which the industrial system rested'.[1]

Second, in citing the lack of growth of British corn production per head to support his claim that improvements in agricultural technology were inadequate (p. 157), Dr Raj failed to note that, in line with her comparative advantage, which became fully operative following the enactment of the Corn Laws, Britain changed from being a net exporter to becoming a net importer of corn and a large importer of beef and dairy produce.[2] It was also incorrect to say that 'there was perceptible relief only after the phenomenal expansion of cropped area in America, Australia and Canada made available substantial imports to supplement domestic production' (p. 157), since even during the period of the Second Industrial Revolution (1830–50) imports came from other parts of western Europe.

Third, large-scale migration did not provide an important outlet for the

---

*In the discussion section which follows, all the numbered footnotes are the speakers' own.

[1] Phyllis Deane and W. A. Cole, *British Economic Growth* 1688–1959: *Trends and Structure* (Cambridge University Press, 1969) p. 89.

[2] Ibid, pp. 63–74. The authors further note that the contemporary estimate of Gregory King shows a much smaller agricultural output in 1700, corresponding to a higher growth of output during the eighteenth century.

growth of population of the industrialising countries of Europe, as Dr Raj claimed. In the period he considered (1846–75), Great Britain accounted for only one-fifth of emigration from Europe[3] and experienced a net population growth of 1·2 per cent a year.[2] Also, net emigration had hardly amounted to more than 3 per cent of Europe's population in the mid-nineteenth century and to 15 per cent of the increment in population, and it came largely from the pre-industrial countries, such as Ireland.[3]

As regards the developing countries of today, in insisting on the importance of land scarcity, Dr Raj generalised from the Indian experience to the developing world as a whole. Yet, this experience was largely irrelevant for Latin America and tropical Africa, where land limitations were rarely binding. And, in the case of India, too, there was considerable scope for increasing agricultural output, that had not been utilised in large part because of the price and incentive policies applied, which favoured import substitution in manufacturing at the expense of agriculture.

Agriculture had also suffered discrimination in Sri Lanka and, until the policy changes undertaken in the last two years, in Argentina and in Uruguay. All of these countries had experienced unfavourable trends in agriculture, with stagnation or decline in the *per capita* output of food. The relevant index numbers for 1971–5 on a 1961–5 basis were 98 for Argentina, 99 for India, 92 for Sri Lanka, and 88 for Uruguay.[4]

Furthermore, in China, which Raj considered to be a success (p. 166), food production per head was below the level attained during the 1930s[5] And, while increasing reliance had been placed on imports, according to Colin Clark, 'food consumption levels are still far below those of 1929–33'. Nor could Tanzania be considered a successful case as food production per head declined by 6 per cent between 1965 and 1970 and in 1971–5, and substantial foreign aid was necessary to compensate for the adverse effects of the policies followed.

By contrast, in developing countries where agriculture suffered little or no discrimination, food production per head had continued to increase. The relevant index numbers for 1971–5 on a 1961–5 basis were 132 for Israel, 111 for Japan, and 108 for Korea. Also, with the introduction of policies more favourable to agriculture in the second half of the 1960s, the index of *per capita* food production had reached a level of 107 in Brazil.

According to a recent study carried out at the Free University of Amsterdam, said Professor Balassa, it would be technically possible to sustain a world population thirty times its present size[6] And, while the economic aspects of

[1] Brinley Thomas, *Migration and Economic Growth* (Cambridge University Press, 1973) Tables 92–6. Data refer to migration into the United States which accounted for about 80 per cent of the total.

[2] Deane and Cole, op. cit., p. 288.

[3] A. M. Carr-Saunders, *World Population* (Oxford, Clarendon Press, 1936) p. 42.

[4] Data on food production originate in the FAO, *Production Yearbook*.

[5] Colin Clark 'Economic Development in Communist China' *Journal of Political Economy* (April 1976) p. 244. Official published estimates are higher but, following recent political changes, the 'Group of Four' have been accused of having falsified crop statistics. Note further that, over the last year, China placed orders for 11·8 million tons of wheat imports (*Barron's*, July 25 1977).

[6] F. Rabar, 'Food and Agriculture: Global Aspects of Supply and Demand', in *Proceedings of the IIASA Conference* (10–13 May 1975) vol. 1, pp. 102–3. The paper

the corresponding increase in food production had not yet been investigated, the results of the study pointed to the need for taking appropriate policy measures to increase agricultural output. This would require, first of all, re-forming price and incentive policies. Price and incentive policies would further need to be supplemented by irrigation, investment in infrastructure, extension services and other measures designed to increase agricultural productivity.

The next point he wished to challenge, said Professor Balassa, was the claim advanced by Dr Raj that the developing countries of today faced a more unfavourable external environment than was the case in the nineteenth century. In Dr Raj's view, 'the most important change in the external environment since the Second World War has been that the already developed countries have become their own best customers and suppliers and, with the exception of some important items, acquired a high degree of self-containedness as a group' (p. 160). He further claimed that 'the developed countries have been in a position to meet the greater part of even their requirements of agricultural products' and that 'the scope for expanding exports of manufactured products has also been affected by import restrictions of various kinds imposed by the developed countries' (idem).

As far as primary commodities other than tropical beverages were concerned, the problem had been chiefly one of supply rather than demand. Thus, in the 1953—66 period, the exports of primary products other than fuels from the developing countries had increased at a rate of 1·8 per cent a year as com-pared to a rate of 5·7 per cent a year for the developed countries.[1] And, in 1936—8 and 1959—61, the share of the industrial countries of North America and western Europe in world exports had risen from 3 per cent to 17 per cent in rice, from 4 per cent to 28 per cent in beef and veal, from 9 per cent to 56 per cent in maize, from 41 per cent to 67 per cent in wheat, from 20 per cent to 72 per cent in barley, from 33 per cent to 86 per cent in pork, from 13 per cent to 68 per cent in cottonseed oil, and from 11 per cent to 82 per cent in soya bean and oil.[2]

The observed results had been greatly influenced by the policies applied. With domestic demand for food rising, the adverse effects of import substitu-tion policies on agricultural production had had unfavourable repercussions *a fortiori* on the exports of agricultural products. Policies of import substitu-tion behind high protective barriers had adversely affected manufactured exports too. In turn, countries pursuing export-oriented policies had achieved high rates of export growth.

The differential effects of the policies followed by particular countries were apparent from the data on manufactured exports. At one extreme, with con-

---

[1] I. B. Kravis, 'Trade as a Handmaiden of Growth: Similarities between the Nineteenth and the Twentieth Centuries', *Economic Journal,* vol. 70, no. 320 (December 1970) p. 862.
[2] R. C. Porter, 'Some Implications of Postwar Primary-Product Trends', *Journal of Political Economy,* vol. 78, no. 3 (May/June 1970) pp. 590—1. The comparison would be even more unfavourable to the developing countries if agricultural exports from Australia and New Zealand were also considered.

---

provides alternative estimates of the world population that can be sustained if food resources are fully utilised, ranging up to 150 billion.

tinued discrimination against manufactured exports that were presumed to be subject to market limitations abroad, the share of India in the exports of manufactured goods by developing countries had declined from 33 per cent in 1960 to 7 per cent in 1975. At the other extreme, while Taiwan and Korea started out with negligible exports in 1960, as a result of the adoption of export-oriented policies the manufactured exports of each of the two countries had surpassed India's exports by 1970 and were more than double the Indian figure by 1975.[1]

At the same time, one could not agree with Dr Raj's assumption that the kind of goods exported by Taiwan and Korea 'tend to have relatively limited linkage effects within the exporting countries, import requirements are high, the value added by manufacture is much lower as a percentage of the gross value of the products, and a high proportion of even this is apt to be repatriated as profits' (p. 166). To begin with, it had been shown that in Korea 'import substitution for intermediate inputs has been carried back to the stage where only the unprocessed natural resource product is imported',[2] where this was economical.

Also, the approximately 50 per cent share of value added in world market prices (net foreign exchange earnings) in the manufactured exports of Korea and Taiwan might well be higher, rather than lower, than the value-added share of import replacement in countries pursuing inward-oriented policies. In the latter group of countries, the use of direct and indirect inputs, and the relatively high cost of domestic operations, reduced value added in world market prices that had even been negative in some cases.[3] This conclusion was strengthened if we considered the repatriation of the profits of foreign companies obtained in replacing imports at a high cost, which entailed a transfer from the domestic consumer to the foreign firm. There was no such transfer in exporting where the firm got the world market price rather than the domestic price that had been raised by protection.

At any rate, foreign direct investment was of much less importance in the export-oriented economies of Korea and Taiwan than under import substitution in Latin America. Thus, as Westphal and Kim had shown, in 1970 foreign direct investment had accounted for less than 5 per cent of the capital stock in the manufacturing sector and for only 11 per cent of manufactured exports in Korea.

Nor could one explain rapid export expansion in Korea and Taiwan by reference to a special relationship with the USA and Japan. For one thing, the combined share of Korean exports to those countries had declined from 70 per cent in 1960 to 56 per cent in 1975. For another, sales in Vietnam had never exceeded 5 per cent of exports and, while such sales had come to an end

[1] Unless otherwise noted, data on international trade originate in UN, *Monthly Bulletin of Statistics* and *Yearbook of International Trade Statistics,* and IMF, *International Financial Statistics.* For Taiwan, the source is *Statistical Abstract of the Republic of China.*

[2] Larry Westphal and Kwang Suk Kim, *Industrial Policy and Development in Korea,* IBRD, World Bank Staff Working Paper no. 263 (August 1977) pp. 4–41.

[3] Bela Balassa, *The Structure of Protection in Developing Countries* (Baltimore: Johns Hopkins University Press, 1971) p. 74, and Jagdish Bhagwati and Padma Desai, *India: Planning for Industrialization* (New York: National Bureau of Economic Research, 1970) Appendix 1.

in 1973, the total value of Korea's manufactured exports had risen by 150 per cent in the next three years.

It should be noted further, said Professor Balassa, that, by leading to specialisation according to comparative advantage, contributing to increased capacity use, and permitting the use of large-scale production methods, export orientation in Taiwan and Korea had reduced the capital requirements of the growth of output. This explained why in the two countries the incremental capital-output ratio hardly exceeded 2. The high cost of import substitution was indicated by the fact that countries following such a policy, such as India and Chile, had had incremental capital-output ratios exceeding 5.[1]

In turn, with the rapid growth of labour-intensive exports and the consequent expansion of manufactured output, industrial employment in Taiwan had increased at an average annual rate of 10 per cent between 1961 and 1971 whereas the corresponding figure was 3 per cent for India.[2] Finally, real wages in manufacturing had risen 10 per cent a year between 1966 and 1973 in Korea and 6 per cent in Taiwan but had remained unchanged in India.[3]

At the same time, it would be incorrect to assume that Taiwan and Korea were the only successful exporters. In fact, in the mid-1960s several important developing countries, which had hitherto followed inward-looking policies, adopted export promotion measures. Particular interest attached to the experience of Brazil, which had a domestic market for manufactured goods similar in size to India. Following changes in incentive policies in the mid-1960s, the value of Brazilian exports of manufactured goods rose from $124 million in 1965 to $2182 million in 1975, now surpassing the level of Indian exports, whereas Brazilian exports of manufactures had been less than one-sixth of Indian exports a decade earlier. The rapid expansion of manufactured exports in Brazil had, in turn, contributed to a decline in the incremental capital-output ratio from 3·8 in 1960—6 to 2·1 in 1966—73 and to an acceleration of the annual average rate of growth of *per capita* incomes from 1·1 to 6·4 per cent.[4]

All in all, the volume of exports of manufactured goods (SITC classes 5 to 8 less non-ferrous metals) of the developing countries (excluding exports to the socialist countries) had risen nearly fivefold between 1965 and 1975, reaching $30 billion in terms of 1975 prices. As a result, the share of the developing countries in the imports of manufactured goods by developed nations had increased from 3 per cent in 1965 to 7 per cent in 1975.

As regards the future, according to Dr Raj,

> it seems unrealistic to assume that a strategy of development based on a rapid expansion of exports of manufactured products [to the developed nations] can be viable for the developing countries as a whole; it can at best be regarded as a supplementary measure for exploiting such opportunities as might still be available [p. 17].

[1] IBRD, *World Tables* (1976). Data refer to the period 1960—73 and pertain to the national economy taken as a whole.
[2] R. Banerji and J. Riedel, 'Industrial Employment Expansion under Alternative Development Strategies: Some Empirical Evidence' (1976, mimeo).
[3] Ibid, ILO, *Yearbook of Labor Statistics*, and IMF, *International Financial Statistics*.
[4] Data on *per capita* incomes originate from IBRD *World Tables* (1976) and *World Bank Atlas* (1977).

This statement failed to consider the possibilities open to developing countries for exporting manufactured products.

As he had already pointed out, said Professor Balassa, despite the rapid expansion of manufactured exports from the developing countries, those countries accounted for only 7 per cent of manufactured imports in the developed nations; their share hardly reached 1 per cent of the domestic sales of manufactured products in the latter. If we were to assume that the domestic sales of manufactured products in the developed nations would increase at a rate of 5 per cent a year over the next decade and that the developing countries would supply 5 per cent of this increment, those countries could increase their exports of manufactured goods to the developed nations from $21 billion in 1975 to $80 billion in 1985 (in 1975 prices).

Needless to say, such an expansion of exports could not take place in textiles and clothing and a few other labour-intensive manufactures which Dr Raj had considered.[1] In fact, the leading developing country exporters of manufactured goods had increasingly diversified their exports. This conformed to the continuing shift in comparative advantage, with countries such as Korea and Taiwan taking the place of Japan in exporting some skill-intensive products, and countries such as Brazil and Mexico showing signs of doing so in the future in regard to more capital-intensive products, e.g. automobiles and steel. In turn, newly emerging exports could take the place of those countries in exporting products that utilised largely unskilled labour.

The shifting pattern of comparative advantage, determined largely by the accumulation of human and physical capital, had important implications for the alleged market constraint for the manufactured exports of the developing countries. As he had noted elsewhere, Professor Balassa said,

> to the extent that one developing country replaces another in the imports of particular commodities by the developed countries, the problem of adjustment in the latter group of countries does not arise. Rather, the brunt of adjustment will be borne in industries where the products of newly graduating developing countries compete with the products of the developed countries.[2]

Also, there were possibilities for replacing imports from developed nations in the markets of other developing countries.

Shifts in comparative advantage had taken place throughout the postwar period, entailing the transformation of the export structure of Japan and the countries of southern Europe, which had passed from the ranks of developing to those of developed countries in applying a strategy largely oriented towards exports. Between 1953 and 1975, the value of the exports of manufactured goods of Japan grew from $1 billion to $52·6 billion while the corresponding figures for the countries of southern Europe were $0·2 billion and $11·5

[1] At the same time, it should be recognised that in 1973 the developing countries provided only 4 per cent of sales of textiles and clothing in the developed countries. In turn, despite the restrictions applied, these exports approximately tripled between 1973 and 1976 (the data originate in an unpublished study by D. B. Keesing of the World Bank).

[2] Bela Balassa, 'A "Stages" Approach to Comparative Advantage', paper presented at the Fifth World Congress of the International Economic Association, held in Tokyo on 29 August–3 September 1977.

billion.[1] As a result, in terms of *per capita* incomes, those countries had 'leap-frogged' Chile and Uruguay, and some of them even Argentina, all of which had continued with inward-oriented policies.[2]

In the present-day developing countries, too, *per capita* incomes had been rising more rapidly than in nineteenth-century Britain. Dr Raj had noted, however, that income growth rates had been much lower in countries with *per capita* incomes of $200 or less, adding that 'the *per capita* output (valued at 1970 prices) of countries belonging to this poorest category (excluding the petroleum exporters) rose by hardly $1 a year, from $103 in 1970 to $108 in 1975' (p. 160).

At the same time, the experience of the first half of the 1970s could hardly be regarded as representative. During this period, the quadrupling of oil prices entailed an income loss of over $3 per head for the poorest countries,[3] and increases in oil prices aggravated the world-wide recession that adversely affected their exports. Taking instead the 1960–70 period, a *per capita* income growth of 1·8 per cent a year was shown for the poorest countries; the corresponding figure was 1·7 per cent a year for 1960–75 if we adjusted for the terms of trade loss due to the rise in oil prices.

These results compared favourably with *per capita* income growth of less than 1·5 per cent in Great Britain between 1801 and 1871 (p. 159). And while, expressed in 1970 prices, *per capita* incomes in Great Britain had reached $200 in 1800, increases had averaged only 0·5 per cent a year during the eighteenth century.[4]

Furthermore, the presentation of data for countries that had had *per capita* incomes of less than $200 in 1970 gave rise to a 'statistical illusion' since, by definition, the group excluded countries that had 'graduated' into the above-$200 group as a result of their rapid economic growth. Expressed in terms of 1970 prices, Taiwan and Korea had *per capita* incomes only slightly above $100 in 1950, reached incomes per head of $380 and $250, respectively, in 1970, and $510 and $370 in 1975. These countries experienced increases in *per capita* incomes averaging 6–7 per cent a year between 1960 and 1975, in contrast with increases of 1·1 per cent a year in India, the largest of the poor countries.

Among exporters of primary products, note might be taken of the experience of the Ivory Coast and Ghana, two countries with similar resource

[1] During the same period, India's manufactured exports grew from $0·5 billion to $2·1 billion.

[2] *Per capita* incomes expressed in 1970 dollars were, in 1950 and 1975, respectively: Japan, $360 and $2370; Greece, $330 and $1360; Portugal, $220 and $870; Spain, $410 and $1270; Argentina, $800 and $1280; Chile, $520 and $620; Uruguay, $940 and $780. It may be added that in the early 1950s Japan did not have eight decades of industrialisation behind it, as Raj alleges (p. 158). Thus, at the time, primary products and semi-finished materials still accounted for three-fourths of Japanese exports and their share fell below one half only in the mid-1960s (K. Ohkawa and H. Rosowsky, *Japanese Economic Growth,* Stanford: Stanford University Press, 1973, p. 304).

[3] UN, *Yearbook of International Trade Statistics* (1975) and *Demographic Yearbook* (1975).

[4] Deane and Cole, op. cit., pp. 78, 282, 329–31. The data have been translated into 1970 US dollars by the use of price indices provided in the IMF *International Financial Statistics.* Needless to say, these figures should be treated with considerable caution.

endowments but widely different growth performance. Thus, between 1960 and 1975 *per capita* incomes rose at an average annual rate of 3·7 per cent in the Ivory Coast as against a decline of 0·1 per cent in Ghana. As a result, while *per capita* incomes in Ghana were nearly twice as high as in the Ivory Coast in 1960, by 1975 the Ivory Coast had surpassed Ghana.

In the cases indicated, differential growth performance had been determined to a large extent by the policies followed, with outward orientation characterising Taiwan and Korea, as well as the Ivory Coast, and inward-oriented policies being pursued in India as well as Ghana. Empirical evidence on this point was provided in his paper 'Export Incentives and Export Performance in Developing Countries: A Comparative Analysis',[1] said Professor Balassa, which had already established an industrial base. The evidence indicated that export incentives and export performance, as well as export performance and economic growth, were highly correlated.

He had shown in the same paper that the application of export incentives had favourably affected the distribution of incomes also. Countries such as Taiwan and Korea, where export orientation had begun the earliest and had been the most far-reaching, had experienced the most rapid increases in the incomes of the poor and had the most equitable income distribution among developing countries.[2] This had to do with the increased demand for labour in labour-intensive manufactured goods, the exports of which were growing rapidly, as well as with the improved performance of agriculture.

He had demonstrated, said Professor Balassa, that economic performance in developing countries was greatly affected by the incentive policies applied. In particular, policies oriented towards export promotion had favourable effects for economic growth and the sharing of the benefits of growth. Prices and incentive measures also had an important role to play in the future in accelerating economic growth and improving income distribution.

Dr Raj, however, in rejecting reformist solutions out of hand, had given no attention to these measures. At the same time, the effects of land reform on agricultural production were far from clear in his paper. Furthermore, in arguing that a redistribution of assets in agriculture could become the mainstay of industrial development, Dr Raj disregarded the possible adverse effects on savings.

While agreeing with Dr Raj that the internal power structure exerted an important influence on the course of economic development, and that in agriculture and in industry vested interests in the form of large landowners or protectionist industrialists and monopolistic labour unions had often stood in the way of the adoption of more rational policies,[3] at the same time, as far as industry is concerned, it was the adoption of the inward-looking policies Dr Raj appeared to be advocating that had led to the emergence of powerful vested interests.

*

[1] World Bank Staff Working Paper no. 248 (January 1977).

[2] Shail Jain, *Size Distribution of Income: A Compilation of Data* (Washington DC: World Bank, 1975).

[3] For a discussion of reforming economic policies, see Bela Balassa. *Policy Reform in Developing Countries* (London: Pergamon, 1977).

Professor Victor Urquidi spoke next. He observed that, if he was not mistaken, when Dr Raj, in his paper, placed emphasis on the interaction of external and internal barriers to development, had in mind the conditions prevailing in the least developed countries – namely, those with an average *per capita* product of less than 200 dollars – which comprised one-third of world population (over 1300 million people) located mostly in two regions: one 'extending across the middle of Africa' and the other stretching from Afghanistan 'across south Asia and some South-East Asian countries'. *Per capita* output, in effect, had barely risen by $1 a year to $108 in 1975. (It might be remarked in passing, he said, that there were two and possibly three countries in this category in Latin America and certainly vast regions within countries.) Dr Raj had also drawn some historical comparisons with early development in Western Europe and Japan.

In focusing on this category of poorest (non oil-producing) countries, Dr Raj had undoubtedly directed attention to the greatest problem in the world economy: one which touched directly upon the problem of international inequality and its prospects – a topic which the RIO report, co-ordinated by Professor Tinbergen, had recently dealt with. The question was essentially the following: given existing and foreseeable resources and institutions, and given external conditioning factors, as we now knew them, could economic growth and structural change take place in the poorest countries in such a way that better living conditions could be assured over a reasonable period for those 1300 million inhabitants who would be 2600 million in thirty to thirty-five years' time?

Concerning the internal barriers singled out by Dr Raj, Mr Urquidi said that he was not too sure that the pressure of population on land was as absolute a negative factor as might be inferred. Population density was certainly strong in some areas; nevertheless, technological change through high-yielding varieties of grain had shown the way to raising productivity per hectare and farmers' income (with due allowance for the side-effects of the Green Revolution). Whether population pressure had itself induced technical change *à la* E. Boserup (recently reinforced by Salehi) was open to question. Whether the technological optimists were right in asserting that agricultural productivity could be raised immensely in less developed countries – enough to support many times the present population – was also arguable. But we could accept at least that it was possible to organise farming in backward areas, with the aid of technical inputs, irrigation and drainage, better marketing, crop conservation and the like, in a manner which would induce rural development, meaning by rural development not only an increase in cash income from crops and animals, but an improvement in health and sanitation, education and training, housing, and community services. This would depend, of course, on many conditioning factors, both internal and external, and it was not a matter for economic policy alone. It might be that the cultural barriers were very strong. Institutional factors, particularly land tenure conditions, might be difficult to overcome. In many cases, self-reliant development methods might be the answer, as was increasingly being proposed and experienced in many places. Appropriate rural technologies were being studied and applied in numerous instances. The case of China should not be dismissed too easily as a way out of backwardness, in spite of the difficulty of transplanting the experiences of one country and system to another.

It was also useful to consider population policy in relation to rural development. When population pressure was already high and/or fertility and consequently growth rates were high, a major factor in facilitating future development might be fertility control through family planning programmes. This was easier said than done, of course. In recent discussions, the problems of extending family planning methods to rural areas had been shown to be difficult. They were, however, not intractable, as was evident at the Tokyo International Symposium on Population held in April 1977. Such programmes could not succeed fully in isolation but only as part of integrated rural development projects. There were many good examples in the regions defined by Dr Raj, although the difficulties of those regions should not be minimised.

A corollary of fertility control was rural-urban migration. Dr Raj had cited international emigration in the nineteenth century. Today we had a new type of migration, directly to the industrialised countries from the poor countries. There was also intense migration to cities in the search for education and employment. This brought some relief to poor rural areas, although it created new problems in the cities when the expansion of manufacturing and services was not sufficient to absorb working-age people into useful employment.

Was more rapid industrialisation partially the answer? Here again, said Professor Urquidi, there were internal barriers, which had to be overcome, frequently with the help of external factors — trade and aid. The simple import-substitution theory of industrial development had, he hoped, been laid to rest. Export opportunities in manufactures should also be fully exploited, but the developed countries did not yet seem ready, in view of their restrictive trade policies, to allow such opportunities to become generalised (in spite of the well-known success stories of certain semi-industrialised developing nations). Even if protectionism by the developed countries were to decline, there was still the question of how to get industrial development started in the poorest countries or regions Dr Raj was referring to. Skills and entrepreneurship scarcely existed. Institutional conditions were not favourable — financing, marketing, technical assistance, export promotion. The domestic market itself was weak. There were obvious vicious circles. Knowledge of technologies appropriate to a smaller scale of production or to labour-intensity was either very scanty or in the experimental stage. Even knowledge of existing resources — raw materials and foodstuffs that might be processed — was poor. Energy scarcities and cost were an additional negative influence.

Here again, there was an interaction of internal and external barriers, but if he had interpreted Dr Raj correctly, said Professor Urquidi, the situation was not hopeless. Domestic policies and programmes could be formulated and implemented, with appropriate technical support from international organisations and concessional financial backing from multilateral and bilateral aid programmes (including the oil producers). Private foreign investment might be helpful where it was welcome and conformed to national policies, (though caution should be exercised in the case of the transnational corporations). Trade integration policies and schemes among the developing countries themselves, which had not been mentioned by Dr Raj, could also be helpful. Unilateral generalised trade preferences on the part of the advanced industrialised countries were also necessary, in much wider and unrestricted form than up to the present. Deliberate deployment of labour-intensive industries from high-wage developed countries to lower-wage developing countries was part of the future picture. The redirection of technological research and development in industry towards the design of efficient capital-saving equipment and processes was increasingly important for the poorer countries, together with support for such research and experimentation as already took place; Tanzania, Swaziland, India and other countries well known to UNIDO were case in point. Training programmes under UN auspices should be multiplied, encompassing basic skills, small-scale entrepreneurship, packaging and marketing, public administration, and so forth.

On the purely economic side, the low rate of savings in the poorest countries was undoubtedly a hindrance. In addition, income inequality, as Dr Raj had pointed out, restricted the domestic market. Inequality was, however, bound up closely with low productivity in agriculture. External financial resources for food and raw material production and small-scale industry should supplement domestic savings sufficiently to raise the rate of productive investment and allow some social investment in health, sanitation, education, local transportation and community development, which in turn would help raise productivity. Cultural barriers might be strong – for instance, in parts of Africa – but they were not totally rigid.

According to Dr Raj, in the last analysis 'the barriers to development are basically political in nature'. Professor Urquidi said that, while agreeing entirely with Dr Raj's statement, this was nothing new. However, as economists, it was necessary to identify the barriers; and as economists concerned with development, it was necessary to strive to overcome them. As for the 'political' nature of the obstacles, internally, in most cases, this was a question of the survival of entrenched agrarian or commercial interests – often reinforced by neo-colonial pressures and by corruption – which had short-term aims of economic power and failed to see the long-term basic needs of the people, including the need for change. These were the interests that did not read history correctly until reality hit them in the face. These were the interests that did not understand human misery, that ignored the need for human solidarity. On this score, one should not be too pessimistic about the long-term future. One might hope, too, that the solutions would be consistent with basic human rights and freedom.

Externally, the situation was much more complex. The superpowers, whose influence predominated, were not only behaving mainly in accordance with their military security interests but were also promoting or, as the case might be, protecting their particular social systems – neither of which might be suitable for the poorest third of the world, or for the rest of the less-developed countries. Expenditure on defence and the sale of arms, economic protectionism, insufficient and often highly conditional external aid, the abuses of transnational corporations, the use of force or threats of force, the charades that took place at international conferences, the role of misrepresentation played by most sectors of the communications media, mental lethargy, unconcern for the global problems of humanity, waste and pollution – these were but a few of the negative external factors that had to be dealt with. In that area, one could not help but feel less hopeful. The western industrial nations were still negative towards the idea of a new international economic order; and the second world countries as a whole were not co-operating fully in that direction.

The RIO Tinbergen report had directed its attention mainly to the question of international co-operation and redesign of the international order to enable the present 13 : 1 gross international inequality to be reduced to a more tolerable 3 : 1 over a span of some forty years. All main areas of concern to economists − not to mention politicians − were covered in the report. He urged economists to read it and throw more light on the issues and possible solutions, said Mr Urquidi, and to talk to the political leaders. The stakes were too high for improvisation, *laissez-faire*, indifference or one-sided, doctrinaire attitudes.

*

Opening the discussion from the floor, *Professor Martin Bronfenbrenner* said that he wanted to mediate between Dr Raj's distrust of export-led growth strategies, emphasising low wages in light industries, and Professor Balassa's critique in favour of just such strategies. But he was afraid that he could not satisfy either principal in this debate.

In a regime of 'Smithian' or 'Manchester' freedom or near-freedom of LDC access to MDC markets, he could hardly side more strongly with Professor Balassa and against Dr Raj. But in regimes of MDC protection to high-wage organised labour and its agricultural counterparts, one could hardly fault, say, India for what currently seemed undue pessimism in its assumptions about the degrees of effective US and EEC protection, or to praise Korea and Taiwan too strongly for guessing right, up to now at least; Indeed, India might still turn out to have been more nearly right than Taiwan−Korea in the long run.

What mattered to the LDCs was less the *present* level and variety of US, EEC, or Japanese protective devices than the *potential* ones which might be erected against expanded LDC exports. Uncertainty, especially of the pessimistic variety, was a real barrier to investment of the types required for exported growth.

In terms of Dr Raj's analyses, said Professor Bronfenbrenner, he would class developed-country protectionism, both *ex ante* and *ex post*, as perhaps the most important single 'external' barrier to LDC development. Even accepting, as he did, essentially free trade and export-led strategy as an optimal 'engine of growth', one could hardly fault the LDCs for accepting UNCTAD's New International Economic Order (NIEO) as a second-best solution over accepting the present and prospective MDC protections of its labour and agriculture aristocracies at their (the LDCs') expense.

In *Dr Iyengar's* opinion, Dr Raj was right in concluding that despite the fact that the developing countries were facing more formidable problems than those faced by HDCs at similar periods, they had done better. Dr Raj's other comment, that the new range of products whose development raised living standards to high levels in HDCs, were capital-intensive and labour-displacing, needed modification, however.

The industrial revolution had produced technologies which were a mere extension of the old craft technology. The economics of the new technologies favoured complexity, gigantism and labour elimination. Adoption of these technologies by the LDCs would be costly and disruptive of the present

labour-based production in LDCs as visualised by Dr Raj. But LDCs need not
follow this path. What had to be realised was that a great qualitative transformation had taken place in technology since the Second World War, brought
about by the infusion of science. Examples of second- and third-generation
technologies were electronics and microbiology. If the first generation favoured
capital and size, with the new technologies it was the other way round. For
instance the first-generation computer in 1950 based on the thermionic valve
had occupied 100 cubic inches per logic function and was valued at $100 per
logic function. The fourth-generation computer evolved in 1970 used large-
scale integration, had a speed 10,000 times that of the first and occupied only
0·05 cubic inches per logic function, and was valued at only $0·01 per logic
function. A communication satellite weighed only 250 kgs and performed
much more than the 150,000 tonnes transatlantic cable.

The FAO had estimated that to produce 4·26 million tonnes of protein by
the conventional animal husbandry process to meet the requirements of the
LDCs would involve capital of $10,290 million. If the same were to be pro-
duced by fermentation using methane, ethanol or petroleum as substrate it
would cost only $930 million, which was only 9 per cent of the conventional
process.

The LDCs should therefore refrain from retracing the traditional patterns
of development followed by the HDCs and opt not for labour-intensive or
'intermediate' technologies, but for the sophisticated new technologies which
would enable them to have much higher rates of growth with the same
investments.

The history of economic developments had shown that it was always
advantageous to be a latecomer, for a new, accelerating path of growth could
be taken from the 'critique' of the old, said Professor Iyengar. The LDCs had
an opportunity to 'take off' higher in the technological scale with a much
faster rate of growth through hindsight and a different background of values.
The LDCs had the opportunity to explore innovative structures for socio-
economic and technological development and new models for institutional
and individual relations to society. It was possible for them to 'leapfrog' into
higher levels of growth and convert all the disadvantages that Dr Raj
enumerated to advantages.

Professor Costin Murgescu said that the report by Dr Raj had helped to give
everyone at the Congress a better understanding of the obstacles to economic
development in the countries of the third world.

He was in agreement with many of Dr Raj's conclusions, but there was
little to be gained in the debate from dwelling on details of historical accident
or on specific situations. The important thing was to fix one's attention upon
the difficult problems which at present faced the developing countries as a
whole.

It was from this point of view, he said, that he wanted to make two
observations connected with two of the basic ideas which they in Romania,
and the Romanian President, Nicolae Ceausescu, thought should be the
principles of the new international order.

The first concerned the question of internal obstacles. He had in mind, said
Professor Norgescu, the problem of capital accumulation. Any country making
a determined effort to break out of its state of economic underdevelopment

needed to work out an appropriate scale of priorities for the use of its own resources. All human, natural and financial resources must be brought to bear upon the creation of a modern economy and its balanced growth, and a major portion of the national income must be allocated to these ends for a long time. No foreign aid could be a substitute for a nation's own effort. Making due allowance for each country's specific conditions, it was therefore the primary responsibility of developing countries themselves to speed up domestic, national capital accumulation, with all the difficulties such an endeavour involved and with all its implications.

His second comment, said Professor Murgescu, had to do with external barriers to development. There was no need to explain at length that the world economic environment today made the task of the developing countries more difficult and sometimes indeed frustrated their efforts. The conclusion must be that international relations needed to be reshaped in a democratic spirit. They should be governed by effective respect for the principles of national independence and national sovereignty, equality of rights and non-interference in domestic affairs; all states should renounce the use of force and the threat of the use of force; and suitable measures should be adopted, at world level, to ease the task of the developing countries and to put an end to under-development, in the common interest of all mankind.

Dr Uka Ezenwe said that, drawing on the experiences of European countries, especially Britain and Japan at the early stages of their development, Dr Raj had stressed the 'growth-promoting' or 'growth-thwarting' effects of internal and external factors in the process of economic development.

Dr Raj contended that both for the former less-developed countries (LDCs) of Europe and the present LDCs of the third world 'the pressure of population on land' consituted 'the main barrier to development' (p. 157). But, while in the case of the former a favourable external environment permitted emigration, which in turn enhanced domestic output *per capita*, this escape hatch was not available to the latter today. Furthermore, Dr Raj held that

> the most important of the factors internal to these countries which deter-
> mine their success in facing and overcoming the barriers to development
> are the economic and political power structure, the interest and values it
> upholds, and the choices that can (and cannot) be effectively made within
> such a framework [p. 162].

The immediate inference from Dr Raj's thesis was that, in so far as the economic development of the present LDCs was concerned, the cards were stacked against them both internally and externally.

Unquestionably, Dr Raj had handled the subject of his paper very thought-fully, said Dr Ezenwe. The paper was interesting and essentially well-written. Indeed, with some qualifications here and there, he was generally in agreement with the main stream of Dr Raj's line of thinking. But he found himself unable to accept the generalisations and seemingly gloomy conclusions which emerged from the analysis.

He was not quite sure that 'the pressure of population on land' was 'the main barrier to development' for the generality of LDCs today (p. 157). If one still accepted this aspect of the Malthusian theory, which in his view should now be largely laid to rest since available technological innovations could multiply productivity *per capita*/hectare several times more, this might be true to some extent of south Asia, especially India, where Dr Raj came from and with which he was very familiar. But the same could not be said of other LDCs.

In West Africa, for example, the average population density for the 14 states of the sub-region was 21 persons per square kilometre (55 per square mile) in 1973. At the national level the figure varied very widely from 1 in Mauritania to 77 persons per square kilometre in Nigeria. Only three countries (Togo, Ghana and Nigeria) had up to 30 persons or more. However, defined, these figures could not be regarded as alarming. On the contrary, the West African countries exhibited varying degrees of underutilisation of land resources. Nigeria, which was the most densely populated in the area, had a total land area of 91·2 million hectares. Of this the total cultivable land was estimated at 71·2 million hectares, while the total land currently under cultivation was no more than 34 million hectares: i.e., the total land under cultivation was only 47·8 per cent of the potential arable land and slightly more than one-third of the total land area (see *The Third National Development Plan*, 1975–80). The Nigerian experience, with minor variations, was quite representative of the general situation in the LDCs.

It was against this background, said Dr Ezenwe, that one must reject Dr Raj's generalisation that the pressure of population on land is the main barrier to the economic development of LDCs today. Instead, he was of the view that the apparent inability of the vast majority of LDCs to maximise the utilisation of their land resources constituted a major brake on their development. The areas of policy manoeuvre should focus on the importation, adaptation and application of improved agricultural technology rather than on emigration or control of the agrarian population. Emigration in the form of brain drain had proved to be a curse rather than a blessing for many LDCs; and, needless to say, while population planning was important, in most LDCs the question of control at this stage was hardly imperative.

Another point central to Dr Raj's argument was the conviction that 'the external environment confronting the underdeveloped countries as a whole poses so many problems than the now-developed countries had to face a century ago that one could well regard it as the most formidable of all the barriers to development to-day' (p. 00). He agreed with Dr Raj there, he said. Admittedly, LDCs had formidable internal barriers to rapid economic development; but it was the reinforcement of these internal constraints by external barriers to development to-day. (p. 157). He agreed with Dr Raj there, he said. development efforts rather than their own domestic problems. The activities of transnational companies, which often enjoyed the clandestine support of their home governments and their local agents and stooges, could be cited as a case in point here.

The proclamation of the New International Economic Order in 1974 could be interpreted in part as an open admission of the failure of the external environment to meaningfully assist the development of the LDCs. Some influential economists (Johnson, 1967; Kravis, 1970; Little, Scitovsky and Scott, 1970) had blamed the plight of LDCs mostly on their so-called export pessimism and the import-substitution strategy; but he would like to add that any attempt to ignore the impact of external factors in the economic development of LDCs merely raised more questions than answers.

However, he did not see the situation as being as hopeless as one could infer from Dr Raj's exposition, said Dr Ezenwe. He was persuaded that the vast majority of LDCs had considerable areas for policy manoeuvre. As he had already said, they could increase their agricultural productivity, and needed to. The Green Revolution was a *sine qua non* if rapid industrialisation was to be sustained in the next few decades. China had set the pace here. Also, emphasis on labour-intensive techniques of production could lead to increased exports of cheaper manufactures from LDCs to developed countries. Furthermore, opportunities existed for the expansion of intra-LDC trade through the formation of regional economic groupings and/or other trade arrangements. Needless to say, many LDCs had reached or were about to reach the limit of import-substitution in simple, consumer goods manufactures. It was about time that those countries moved into intermediate and capital goods industries.

The existence of local vested interests likely to obstruct modernisation, to which Dr Raj had referred, was a common phenomenon. Internal resistance of some sort was to be expected in any society that wanted to make a clean break with the past. The present industrialised countries had had to deal with the rich aristocracy and landowners who considered modernisation measures a threat to their dominant status. Economic development as a historical phase necessarily called for a good deal of sacrifice and dedicated involvement of the masses, though the road to this might differ from society to society. In the final analysis, the LDCs had to realise that they had to pull themselves up by their own bootstraps.

Professor Tibor Scitovsky's brief comment was that he had found Dr Raj's approach very helpful, but would like to point out an implication of it that Dr Raj might have missed. It was a handicap of a latecomer, which affected the demand for his output rather than its production or supply.

The industrial countries, at the time of their development, had faced an outside world that was less advanced than they were themselves — and that fact had assured a ready, even eager export market for their manufactures. Today's LDCs, and especially the least advanced among them, had to seek an export market for their manufactures in a world which economically was ahead of them. Their products were typically inferior substitutes for the local article and had to rely on the attractiveness of a lower price. Unfortunately, however, price competition was much more resented and was considered more unfair than quality competition; and it was this irrational resentment and hostility to price competition that confronted the manufactured exports of many of the LDCs today.

Professor Zdzlslaw Sadowski's view was that the question of what the developing countries of the world could and should do in their development strategies about exports of manufactured goods to advanced countries emerged from the Raj—Balassa controversy in the shape of an either-or question: either they had to promote such exports or they had to concentrate an internal market solutions. It followed that the actual choice depended on the estimates of the existing potential for such exports. But in his view, said Professor Sadowski, it was not an either-or question. The real choice was not between export promotion and import substitution: for any developing country the promotion of structural change through the exports of manufactured goods was not an option, it was a must; and the real choices related to how to achieve it, taking into account all the constraints. It would not, therefore, seem to serve any useful purpose to say that constraints on the world market were non-existent. He did not think anybody could seriously maintain that the South Korean or Taiwanese development pattern could be followed by all the developing countries acting in concert. It was doubtful whether the potential for manufactured goods exports from the developing to the developed countries could be estimated — or even illustrated — by assuming a steady growth of demand of 5 per cent per annum. But it was not only the arithmetics of it that was in question. A joint export drive on the part of all developing countries would be bound to evoke a protectionist response on the receiving end. The choice of strategy for individual developing countries would therefore be a complex question even if no other constraints were in existence. And such constraints could be seen in the limiting role of the internal power structure which Dr Raj had so rightly underlined.

*

Replying to the discussion, *Dr Raj* said that, evidently, the reference in his paper to the pressure of population on land had been misunderstood. His intention had not been to endorse the view that it was the main barrier to development, but to place it in a broader perspective by pointing out that it was so regarded even in western Europe (though the availability of land per worker in agriculture was at the time at least three times as high there as it was in the countries of south Asia at present) and that the problems posed by scarcity of land had been sorted out under much more unfavourable conditions later (as in Japan, where the pressure of population was more acute than even in south Asia). Dr Ezenwe appeared to underrate the extent of the institutional changes that might be needed in certain countries if all available labour was to be put to productive use and agricultural technology improved, but otherwise he was in agreement with Dr Ezenwe's observations on the underutilisation of land and the potentialities of technological adaptation.

The main difference of opinion that had emerged from the discussion related to the external environment confronting the underdeveloped countries. While most of the participants had expressed agreement with the view that this was now the most formidable of all the barriers to development, and some had specifically identified developed-country protectionism, Professor Balassa believed that there were still enough opportunities left for rates of development to be significantly accelerated through export promotion. Indeed the main barrier, as Professor Balassa saw it, lay in the inward-looking policies followed by many countries, which disregarded such opportunities.

Professor Balassa's alternative view raised two sets of questions. One related to the circumstances which made it possible for individual countries such as South Korea and Taiwan to increase their exports so phenomenally; the other to whether it was valid to generalise from their experience and argue that export-led strategy could be viable for the underdeveloped countries as a whole.

Professor Balassa saw this simply as a shift in the comparative advantage of Japan helping South Korea and Taiwan to take its place, and such success-

ive replacement as the mechanism which unfailingly promoted the development of countries that followed the right pricing policies and were appropriately oriented to foreign trade. He did not mention the exceptional factors
that had brought about the rapid economic growth of Japan during this period,
a subject on which Professor Abramovitz had had some very pertinent observations to make in the first plenary session of the Congress; nor the special
political and other ties which served to keep up high rates of inflow of foreign
savings to these two countries (touching levels as high as 10 per cent of the
GNP of South Korea over several years); nor all the factors that made possible
in South Korea 'labour's acceptance, until recent years, of wages that lagged
behind productivity'.[1]

Nor did the literature on the export performance of South Korea, Taiwan,
etc., and similar countries usually reveal the crucial role played by Japanese
trading companies (*shōshas* and *sōgōshōshas*) there. The financial power of
these companies and their control over marketing channels had been immense,
and this had helped to develop not only Japanese foreign trade with the USA
and elsewhere but third country trade wherever the Japanese trading
companies operated.[2] The fact that the share of the USA and Japan in Korean
exports had been declining did not therefore necessarily mean that the links
with those countries had been weakening.

It was necessary to add, too, that the policies followed for export promotion had not been free from the kind of dangers which Professor Balassa
associated exclusively with import substitution, such as encouragement of
inefficient resource use and the creation of vested interests. The South Korean
experience itself in this regard appeared to be open to question. Not only was
there extensive subsidisation of exports, but the forms of subsidy given had
evoked the comment that 'indiscriminate subsidisation of all export-
manufacturers will not only induce them to rely on the government's import
subsidies but may also encourage them to develop industries which yield low
− or even negative − value added measured in international prices'. It had
also been observed that most of the capital export from Japan to Korea had
been 'a kind of movement of superannuated industry in the form of sub-
contract into Korea' and that, while small and medium-scale industries had
played a major role in Korea's industrialisation, their investment performance
revealed 'a virtual absence of efforts to increase labour productivity' and that
'Korea's export promotion drive tended to interest industrial firms in quick-
return and short-sighted development patterns'.[3]

Even if one were to ignore all this, said Dr Raj, it was obvious that, should
the same kind of strategy be adopted on a more extensive scale, it could show
comparable results only if the demand for imports from developed countries
grew at a vastly accelerated rate. There was no such prospect in the foreseeable

[1] Parvez Hasan, *Korea: Problems and Issues in a Rapidly Growing Economy* (Johns
Hopkins University Press, 1976) p. 29.
[2] N. Shioda, 'The Sōgōshōsha and its Functions in Direct Foreign Investment', *The
Developing Economies* (Tokyo: Institute of Developing Economies, December 1976),
vol. XIV, no. 4.
[3] See Nak Kwan Kim, 'Is Korea's Export Promotion Scheme consistent with her
Industrialisation?', and Park Tong-sup, 'Japanese Capital and Korea's Economy', in
Asian Economies (Seoul, Korea, June 1972 and September 1973).

future, apart from the consideration mentioned by Professor Bronfenbrenner that the uncertainty in this regard was itself a strong enough deterrent. But he agreed with Professor Sadowski that the choice between export-promotion and import-substitution was not really an either-or question but one that had to be decided in the light of the circumstances facing each country. His intention had been, in fact, not to deny that there were important lessons to be drawn from the experience of either South Korea and Taiwan, on the one hand, or mainland China, on the other, but only to suggest that they were unique cases moulded by conditions significantly different from those faced by most other countries.

The main difficulty in dealing with these and other issues raised in the course of the discussion was that the countries grouped together as 'underdeveloped' or 'developing' were so highly heterogeneous. The focus of his analysis, said Dr Raj, was on the poorest among them, as Professor Urquidi had noted, and, though a few had graduated/out of the group over a period, its composition had not only by and large remained unchanged, but they also presented the really hard core of the problems of development in every sense of the term. Potentially, latecomers have several advantages, but it was their handicaps that had been most in evidence, and it was the dilemmas they faced that he had tried to highlight in his paper. Despite the differences in viewpoint expressed in the course of the discussion, there appeared to be considerable agreement that the cards were stacked against them both internally and externally.

6 Costs of Economic Growth[1]

Edmond Malinvaud

PRESIDENT IEA, PARIS, FRANCE

In the contemporary world, the costs of economic growth have become a matter of great concern, and economists are expected to devote the most serious attention to them. We owe it to ourselves to respond to this challenge as best we can.

We could, of course, argue that the now fashionable disparagement of economic growth is exaggerated in view of the enormous needs which have to be met. We could point out that this is simply a reaction against the naive convictions cherished by the general public in contradiction to the views of economists. After the last war it was indeed hard to gain a hearing for any of us who contested the notion that if the gross national product per head doubled, people should be twice as happy. Yet there were warning voices.[2]

Nevertheless we cannot, in good conscience, sidestep the issue at this Congress. It is a matter of concern to many, and it is up to us to look for the truth in it. It is our duty to help the lay public to advance beyond the stage of summary judgements and to submit the problems concerned to rigorous analysis. Only then can choices regarding the pace and the nature of future growth be well-advised and have a better chance of furthering the progress of mankind.

The task is not an easy one. Like other men of science, economists dislike topics involving an answer to ill-defined ethical questions. The mere word 'cost' implies reference to a norm by which certain facts may be classified as unfavourable, which means, in the particular case, 'socially unfavourable'. In discussing the costs of economic growth, therefore, it will be necessary to call attention to certain normative questions, however embarrassing they may be.

The term 'growth' itself is not unambiguous, for an economy may develop along very different lines. Mere demographic growth involves costs and benefits. These will not be discussed here. Instead, attention will be focused upon the difficulties connected with the fact that progress in technology and in social

---

[1] The translation is by Elizabeth Henderson. I am also indebted to A. Desrosières, G. Henry, C. Sautter and Y. Ullmo for their helpful advice during the preparation of the paper.

[2] The whole body of neo-classical theory deliberately avoided reference to any cardinal scale of levels of satisfaction. Moreover, it was stressed that there was no simple connection between the size of GNP and the ordinal comparison of satisfactions. See, e.g., Paul A. Samuelson, 'Evaluation of Real National Income', *Oxford Economic Papers* (January 1950).

organisation entails continuously increasing division of labour and rising output per head.

The problems meant by the term costs of economic growth have, in fact, not been neglected by economists as much as some people claim. This will become apparent presently, in a brief survey of various aspects of the problem. Yet, admittedly, we have left some gaps, and I shall put forward a few proposals for filling them, at least partially.

In surveying past work, a distinction must be made between two types of research, concerned, respectively, with describing the facts as such, and with working out an analytical framework for the choice of measures to reduce costs. Such work has on the one hand shown up deficiencies in the world's economic growth, and on the other hand led to recommendations on how to make our economies work better. It is not only the results of these studies which concern us here, but also the methodological problems which beset them.

Each particular case actually requires two types of research, forming two successive stages of a complete treatment in a logical sequence of purposes:

(1) identify certain effects of growth, such as modification of the natural environment or quickening mobility of labour;

(2) look for choice alternatives between these effects and the pace or nature of economic growth, and so provide a basis for decisions by which harmful effects can be obviated.

It is at the junction of these two stages that the question of costs arises, when we have to ask which of these growth effects are harmful. How far we can go in trying to answer this question is debatable.

Attempts have been made to quantify the costs of growth, and some economists have even proposed systematic schemes for doing so: all the costs of growth were to be evaluated in the national currency and deducted from the gross national product, leaving the 'corrected GNP'. But on further consideration and in the light of a few trial applications, it appeared that it was neither possible to go that far without an element of arbitrariness, nor necessary to do so for the sake of more enlightened collective choices.[1] Even the most precise evaluation of the corrected GNP would still fail to describe certain aspects of reality which are relevant for our purposes; some of the critical observations in Section III below are directed at the very process of aggregation which serves as a basis for defining the GNP.

Hence, special attention will not be given systematically here to the evaluation of costs. The main purpose will rather be to study the unfavourable effects of growth and to inquire whether they could not and should not be avoided, even when some slowing down of the tempo of growth would result.

[1] The two outstanding examples are *Measuring Net National Welfare of Japan* (Tokyo: Economic Council of Japan, March 1973) and W. Nordhaus and J. Tobin, 'Is Growth Obsolete?', in National Bureau of Economic Research, *Economic Growth* (New York: Columbia University Press, 1972). See also O. Arkhipoff, 'Peut-on mesurer le bien-être national?', *Collections de l'INSEE*, no. 41, C (Paris, March 1976).

Considering successively each one of the major unfavourable effects, I shall try to comment on its significance, on the theoretical and empirical works that were devoted to it and on decisions that could reduce it in the future.

In the brief survey which follows, the first part deals with the physical costs of production and the second with the social costs of growth, while the third is concerned with attempts at a synthesis; that is, with the relations between growth and the satisfaction of people's needs or aspirations.

Needless to say, the discussion will keep its distance from some of today's most topical questions. Nothing will be said about the costs occasioned by the crisis of 1974 and after, nor about those due to present unemployment. They are heavy costs, but both are well identified and both are, in any case, the concern of other analyses than those which should underlie the debate on growth.

Furthermore, attention will be focused exclusively on the most highly developed industrial countries, for it is only to them that this debate is relevant. The main problems facing developing countries are obviously quite different. Finally, some costs of economic growth have international implications. They, too, will not be considered here; international problems are assigned a prominent place in the programme of this Congress, and brief mention of them here would not do them justice.

I PHYSICAL COSTS

Economic growth is often held responsible for a deterioration in the quality of products, for increased pollution and other external effects, and for wasteful use of the earth's resources. Let us examine these three types of cost separately, and see how they can, or should, be first identified and then reduced.

A Product quality

It is in the nature of technological progress that products change and that new goods and services are produced, both for the direct satisfaction of human needs and for the efficient use of human labour and natural resources. This transformation of products is an extremely complex process. It should be no surprise to anyone that it is not beneficial in all respects. So many dimensions are necessary to describe the qualities of all goods that it would be presumptuous to want to make progress in all directions at once; to try to do so would in practice mean ruling out all progress.

This, then, is not the question. Rather, it is to find out what truth there is in two arguments underlying certain critical statements, namely:

(1) that the measurement of total output fails to take correct account of deterioration in the quality of some products;
(2) that in modern economies growth is misdirected in so far as it gives priority to quantity to the detriment of quality.

To deal with the first of these arguments in depth would lead us into questions of measurement, which we do not need to stress here, as I said. We should require a full investigation of the logic underlying the evaluation of global quantities and of the methods used to this end. The upshot would be that no principle can be perfectly satisfactory so long as different social categories attach different values to the replacement of some goods by others.

But most of the current criticism is rather less sophisticated. All it amounts to is the charge that the statisticians responsible for measuring the increase in the volume of total output, and at the same time the rate of price increase, introduce a systematic bias into their calculations by neglecting deterioration in the quality of some goods and overestimating quality improvements in others. This seems to me to be an entirely gratuitous accusation, and its authors do not even seem to have taken the trouble to read the handful of investigations devoted to the precise study of the question.[1] I have had a lot to do with statisticians, and I have found them to be persons of sufficient intelligence, independence of mind and concern for accuracy to be aware of the risk of bias and to avoid it.

The second argument is much more difficult to scrutinise. One would have to compare actual growth with some other hypothetical growth, which would likewise have been possible and would have done more to improve the quality of products to the detriment of their quantity. The question then has to be put in these terms: would the quantity of products have had to be reduced much or only a little in order to obtain a marked improvement in their quality? Who would have benefited by the quality improvement, and who suffered from the quantity reduction?

Given the difficulties of any direct and full exploration of these questions, one might try a different approach to the same subject. Is there anything in the working mechanism of market economies or planned economies which suggests that in either case quality must necessarily be sacrificed to quantity? Is there some failure of the price system or of planning practices in this respect? We know that in centrally controlled economies the setting of quantitative targets may indeed work to the detriment of quality: there are numerous examples to prove it. If we think in terms of a market economy and of well-defined goods and services in demand for their own sake, such a failure of the price system could result from imperfect knowledge on the part of buyers. Where they understand little about quality differences, bad merchandise perforce drives out the good.[2] Certainly, the public are well informed about the main features of products, but in some cases perhaps do not know quite enough. In a system with a high degree of division of labour there is a danger that qualities not commonly described may be systematically neglected.

[1] For a discussion of these investigations see, e.g. G. Malignac, 'Indices de prix et changements de qualité', *Annales de l'INSEE* (September—December 1970).

[2] See G. Akerlof, 'The Market for Lemons: Qualitative Uncertainty and the Market Mechanism', *Quarterly Journal of Economics* (August, 1970).

In addition to information gaps, the consequences of 'non-convexities' affect production in various ways in our era of mass production. Both explain the part played by the strategies of big firms in the determination of the choices open to consumers.

If, among the costs of economic growth, those occasioned by qualitative deterioration have their origin in imperfections of knowledge, the remedy surely lies mainly in providing more and fuller information. In addition there have long been regulations to enforce certain quality standards especially with respect to such characteristics of a product as the buyer cannot personally ascertain. Such regulations can and should be multiplied. In concentrated sectors of production, finally, there is a case for intervention by government and consumer organisations.

In recent years much interest has been attracted by the development of certain important services and by their role in economic growth.[1] A number of fairly distinct problems arise in this connection, which it will be convenient to mention at this point.

The expansion of health services is often regarded as exaggerated, at least in some respects. It is argued that this may to some extent be due to lack of information on the part of patients, who accept and often even ask for expensive and useless treatment. In some part it is no doubt due to the care lavished on elderly patients or on those who have little chance of survival; but this is a matter of moral choice on which the economist has no right to pronounce judgement.

The general spread of secondary and higher education answers a desire for access to culture and knowledge, and to that extent is certainly welcome. But there is another explanation too; students want to rise in the social scale, but it is obviously not possible for all of them to do so.[2] This is one of the most notorious cases of a difficulty discussed later in Section III.

Finally, the growth of transport services is largely a cost of urbanisation. To that extent it should not enter into the calculation of final production. But the fact that these services develop does not mean a misallocation of resources. If such a misallocation existed, it would rather come from an exaggerated preference given to private as against collective transportation. Analysing the phenomenon would raise issues similar to those concerning pollution.

B Pollution

The production of goods and services has external physical effects, some favourable, some decidedly unfavourable. The latter are subsumed under the term pollution, in the broadest sense. Pollution's existence has long been

[1] For a deliberately and exaggeratedly critical discussion, see 'L'économie du contre-sens', in J. P. Dupuy and J. Robert, *La trahison de l'opulence*, Part I.

[2] This point is developed and discussed in F. Hirsch, *Social Limits of Growth* (Harvard University Press, 1976).

recognised, but its scale has greatly increased in recent decades with the vast expansion of industrial zones. The problem has taken on new dimensions and is causing alarm among experts no less than among the public at large.

There is a wide variety of pollutants. To establish their presence and their consequences requires techniques unfamiliar to economists, who nevertheless cannot afford to neglect the problem. In their response to the anxieties of modern societies about pollution, economists then have to get used to collaborating with other technical experts.

Pollution definitely constitutes a cost of economic growth; if our national accounts could claim perfection it ought to be deducted from the national product as measured. It is more important to note that, in any specific case, economic decisions may have a major influence on the extent of the harmful external effects of production.

Some of the currently most widely debated forms of pollution create collective risks. Opposition to the construction of nuclear power stations or to the development of fast breeder reactors comes from those who, rightly or wrongly, attribute more than negligible probability to the risk of serious accidents or of fissile material falling into the hands of criminals. Another reaction of the same kind is the fear of possible biological or climatic imbalances due to the emission of heat or carbon dioxide.

In the treatment of pollution, as in many other fields, careful observation and measurement of the facts goes a long way towards solving the problems they occasion. In recent years efforts to this end have followed two lines of approach, one intensive, the other extensive.[1]

A system of regular statistical observation of the environment in which men live requires in the first place the regular measurement of the quality of the main natural elements, air and water. The presence of certain pollutants and their concentration in relation to certain thresholds of damage are matters of primary interest[2] Industrial countries are now setting up statistical monitoring systems, but much remains to be done to develop them and make them fully adequate. Some of the hardest questions are these: how do we aggregate observations made in specific places? How do we distinguish in observed developments what is due to variations in natural conditions (wind, hydrology) and what to variations in human activity (industry, motor traffic)?

Second, attempts are being made to collect and bring together all the information relating to the environment of certain urban zones. The idea is to devise a set of indicators of the urban environment, a task in which the Organisation for Economic Co-operation and Development has been playing a

---

[1] I am indebted to C. Henry for the information which follows.

[2] The definition of thresholds of damage is not easy. To take a case in point: experts are tracing the path and measuring the accumulation of the effects of certain toxic substances like DDT, mercury, asbestos, where accumulation comes about by progressive diffusion and is in practice irreversible. In such cases, the thresholds of damage are very low.

leading part.[1]

Data now at hand show that pollution has greatly increased in most cases, but not in all. Where deliberate action has been taken to restore the quality of air or water, it has most often met with distinct success.[2] This demonstrates the practical importance of measures of pollution control. If present evaluations are correct, such measures are not unduly expensive and their cost by no means rules out a satisfactory growth rate.[3]

Economic theory itself has not neglected the question of pollution control.[4] Two questions in particular have been examined: who should meet the cost of control measures, and in what cases it is more effective to rely on penalties rather than on regulations and prohibition.

One of the most awkward aspects of the problems of pollution control is that certain decisions are irreversible. The collective risk created by some present investments will durably affect the future, but nobody quite knows how. We must henceforth make it a habit to give a correct definition of the choices concerning irreversible decisions having distant and hazardous effects. We should be helped in this by modern theoretical research on irreversibilities in economic calculations.[5]

C Exhaustible reserves

While the earth's natural resources have allowed an increase in production far beyond the expectation of economists of the beginning of the nineteenth century, attention has been focused in recent years on the fact that some resources do not renew themselves naturally, as does the productivity of fertile soil. Once mineral or fuel reserves have been extracted (or certain soils been destroyed by use), they are gone for ever. What our generation consumes will not be available to future generations. The likely size of some of these

---

[1] See OECD, 'Urban Environmental Indicators: A Tool to Assess the Quality of Man's Urban Environment', preparatory report to the meeting of a group of experts (Paris, September 1976).

[2] The most difficult forms of pollution, if indeed they were shown to be such, would seem to be the most diffuse; e.g. the heating up of certain seas, the deterioration of the upper atmosphere. But for the time being anxieties on this score appear to have no very solid foundation. In any event, it is not physically impossible to combat such pollution, as W. Nordhaus, for example, explains in a recent work ('Economic Growth and Climate', *American Economic Review,* February 1977). But this would require concerted action on the world scale — an obvious difficulty.

[3] See e.g., J. Fisher and R. Ridker, 'Population Growth, Resource Availability and Environment Quality', *American Economic Review* (May 1973), or M. Evans, 'A Forecasting Model Applied to Pollution Control Costs', *American Economic Review* (May 1973).

[4] As an example of such theoretical work, see W. D. Montgomery, 'Markets in Licences and Efficient Pollution Control Programs', *Journal of Economic Theory* (December 1972).

[5] See especially K. Arrow and A. C. Fisher, 'Preservation, Uncertainty and Irreversibility', *Quarterly Journal of Economics* (May 1974).

reserves is small enough to raise the serious question of the rate at which they should be exploited. The consumption of these reserves must then be counted at a cost well in excess of the actual cost of extraction.

But how should this cost be calculated? At which rate should reserves be exhausted? In theory[1] there is an answer: 'it is enough' to set out fully a model describing all possible cases of future growth, on the world scale and with reference to the distant future; one then has to choose the growth path that looks best among all feasible alternative ones and hence is most likely to be followed; the cost imputable to each use of reserves is then given by the dual variable associated with the constraint expressing the fact that this reserve is limited. In effect, the choice of the programme of resource utilisation and the cost calculation have to be carried out simultaneously, like two facets of one operation.

This is a formidable task for scientists, given the vastness of the problem and the considerable uncertainties regarding both our knowledge of all possible alternatives and the collective choices of future generations. Yet there is no short-cut, no viable method for arriving more easily at a first approximation to the costs to be measured.

It is obvious enough that the net discounted cost (excluding extraction costs) of one unit withdrawn from an exhaustible reserve is independent of the date of this withdrawal. It follows that this cost depends directly upon the conditions of production prevailing in the distant future. To estimate it, therefore, is exceedingly difficult.

This difficulty throws doubt upon most of the evaluations worked out so far, for they all rest upon hazardous assumptions. This is no reason, of course, for setting the question aside. On the contrary, it is so important that we must do our best to define the options open to mankind with regard to the use of the earth's exhaustible resources, so that an at least provisional choice can be made.

At present it would be premature to formulate any conclusions about the amount of costs involved, which look like being worth considering at the macro-level only in the possible case of energy. But limitations on the expansion of agricultural output may well turn out to be a much more restrictive barrier to economic growth than are those of fossil energy resources. So far it has not been proved that recent growth has been too fast in terms of the rate at which natural resources have been used up.

II SOCIAL COSTS

Physical costs alone do not account for the whole of the present, and in many cases long-standing, disenchantment with economic growth. Often human costs rate much higher in these attitudes, even though they are passed over in silence in most of the technical literature of economics.

[1] On this point, see G. Heal, 'The Long-Run Movement of the Price of Exhaustible Resources', Chapter 3 in this volume.

Economic growth transforms the social structure. It would obviously be wrong to say that everything about this transformation is bad. But some of its aspects clearly are harmful or at any rate less beneficial than had originally been believed.

Full treatment of this topic would require close collaboration between sociologists and economists. No such collaboration exists at present. As economists, we are ill-equipped for the study of social transformations, and, if only for this reason, I do not propose in the brief survey which follows to deal with all the adverse aspects of social transformation deriving from economic growth. I shall mention only those which seem to me most important.

Some social costs are associated with the transition from one social structure to another; they would diminish if structural transformation were slower, and would disappear if it came to a halt. Other social costs appear in a direct comparison between the present and the past structures of the most highly developed countries, independently of the transition between the two systems; these would continue even if economic growth were now to stop. Costs of the first type arise largely in connection with occupational and geographical change; those of the second type claim our attention in connection with persistent inequalities or with the growth of concentration.

A Occupational and geographical change

Economic growth entails many occupational changes. These show up in statistics in two main ways. First, changes in the structure of final consumption and the transformation of production techniques alter the relative importance of different branches and, hence, the distribution of the labour force among them. The number of farmers diminishes, that of people working in the services rises. Second, within each branch the adoption of new techniques transforms the structure of employment. More skilled and fewer unskilled workers are needed, but sometimes, on the contrary, fewer people expert in some skilled craft and more workers for assembly lines.

Such changes in turn require a change in the structure of the labour force. In large part, this happens by the mere succession of generations: the sons of farmers go to work in industry or construction, their daughters in trade or in services.

These are matters which have been thoroughly investigated and about which we know a good deal. Taken as a whole, they cannot be counted as genuine costs of economic growth. The progressive changes they entail have caused little hardship to the people of developed countries, who on the contrary have often regarded them as beneficial.[1] On the other hand, we are on much less certain ground in explaining another type of structural change.

---

[1] Resistance was strongest in the case of changes in the international division of labour, and it came from workers in those branches which as a result were facing decline in developed countries.

In some countries economic growth is, at certain periods, accompanied by structural changes on an uncommonly large scale. More enterprises are set up than usual and more close down; workers frequently change their jobs, their residence and even their trade, all without proper preparation. In France, it seems, the years 1963–73 were such a period.[1] At such times quickened mobility and a large number of occupational and geographical changes, added to those mentioned earlier, would seem to be the counterpart of efforts either to promote more rapid growth or to overcome specific obstacles. The implication is that there exists a choice between dynamic growth accompanied by a great deal of structural change as well as by large-scale frictional unemployment, on the one hand, and on the other hand moderate growth, less successful but also less demanding in terms of mobility and of adaptation efforts on the part of people.

If this view is correct, as it probably is,[2] it should be possible to illuminate this choice by improving our knowledge of the human costs occasioned by additional changes and unemployment. These costs have to be considered at two levels. At the level of the individual, they are no doubt acceptable provided the change is a success in the sense that it enables the worker to take up a new trade without destroying the balance of his family life. But what is the proportion of failures? We need sociological studies to provide an answer to this question. At the collective level, these costs affect the whole of society, for they introduce an additional uncertainty into family life. Many of those who keep their jobs are afraid that they may lose them. To the extent that this could have been avoided by less dynamic growth and that individuals naturally have an aversion to risk, this is truly one of the costs of economic growth.

B Social inequalities

Often in the past, and especially immediately after the last war, people entertained two ideas which both seem to have been disappointed. They thought, first, that economic growth would automatically reduce inequalities as regards income, wealth, access to education or any other factor of social differentiation. No doubt this notion owed more to intuition than to precise analysis of future developments, but it found fairly wide acceptance. Second, people thought that, even if inequalities persisted, they would be more readily tolerated as and when everybody's standard of living rose.

By and large, inequalities have remained as great as before. This statement of course, needs to be interpreted correctly. It applies in overall terms, whereas inequalities are of many different kinds and magnitudes and cannot be fully expressed by any common aggregate numerical index; hence it necessarily rests

[1] See, e.g. C. Thélot, "Mobilité professionelle plus forte entre 1965 et 1970 qu'entre 1959 et 1964', *Economie et Statistique* (December 1973).
[2] One way to test it would be to construct a theory giving precise formulation to this view and facilitating its verification by facts. Such a model would have to trace how economic growth comes about through more or less marked imbalances, and this is not easy to do.

upon summary judgement.[1] So far as income inequalities are concerned, it is the *relative* dispersion of incomes which has remained more or less unchanged; the growth of real incomes has done little to alter the distribution of the ratio between individual incomes and the average income of the entire community at any given moment.[2] Finally, it would be wrong to take no account at all of the relatively slow changes which in some countries have come about as a result either of economic growth as such or of policies specifically designed to reduce inequalities. These changes have often been significant, but much slower than had been hoped. Changes in income inequalities in particular do not seem to contradict Simon Kuznets's view that the relative dispersion of incomes tends to increase in the early stages of economic development, but to decrease progressively in developed countries.[3]

There is yet another aspect to the question. Some aggravation of inequalities may be one of the costs of accelerated growth. The quickening of occupational change must surely have such an effect to the extent that it involves severe hardship for those who cannot adapt themselves to the new pace. More generally speaking, an active growth-promoting policy accepts, or even calls forth, the appearance of many imbalances having very unequal effects on individual incomes and living conditions, and this often happens in a rather haphazard, and hence inequitable, manner. Such a policy is bound to lead to windfall gains and losses.[4] Finally, rapid economic growth presupposes rapid

---

[1] A complete description would have to take account of each of the social characteristics affected by inequalities, and not income alone. For France, for example, wealth would need to be considered (P. L'Hardy and A. Turc, 'Patrimoine des ménages: permanence et transformations', *Economie et statistique,* March 1976) as well as access to higher education and health (*Données sociales,* INSEE, 1973, pp. 98–114 and 127–39). Serious attention should also be given to international inequalities and to the fact that the intercountry relative dispersion of average income per head seems to have increased rather than decreased during the recent decades.

[2] Relative dispersion certainly seems to be the most natural measure of income inequalities. But it has been argued that income inequalities have increased since the absolute dispersion of differences between real individual incomes and real average income has increased.

For a thorough treatment of this question it would be necessary to work out a formula for the collective value judgement of what is the best measurement of the satisfaction of needs in a society where individuals receive unequal incomes. If it should turn out that this best measurement is the sum of the logarithms of individual consumption volumes (a formula which has often been suggested), then it is the relative dispersion of real incomes that must indeed be considered, simultaneously with the rise in the average real income.

Incidentally, this question of the measurement of inequality has recently been treated in a whole spate of theoretical works. See, e.g., S. C. Kolm, *Justice et équité,* (Paris: CNRS, 1972); A. B. Atkinson, *The Economics of Inequality* (Oxford: Clarendon Press, 1976); A. Sen, 'Ethical Measurement of Inequality: Some Difficulties', paper read at a conference of the International Economic Association, at Noordwijk-aan-Zee (1977).

[3] See especially E. L. Bacha, 'The Kuznets Curve and Beyond: Growth and Changes in Inequalities', Chapter 2 in this volume.

[4] This is the proper place to mention the views according to which inflation would be one of the costs of economic growth. Indeed, on the one hand inflation may be expected

accumulation of capital and this cannot happen without some rise in the rate of profit; this, too, increases income inequalities. Thus the choice ventilated at the end of the preceding section must take account of yet one more cost of dynamic as against moderate growth: dynamic growth is less egalitarian.[1]

In any event, it seems that, contrary to general expectations, inequalities are less readily tolerated now than they used to be. Or at least this is the view of F. Hirsch (op. cit.), who regards the constraint of a more egalitarian distribution (the 'distributional compulsion') as a social limit to economic growth.

If indeed inequalities are less readily tolerated nowadays this must certainly be due to the fact that hopes of quick improvement were, on the whole, disappointed. But to understand the full extent of this disillusionment, we must remember that it is not merely, or perhaps not even mainly, a question of a nation being disappointed with the slowness of desired social change. It is a question also of any particular individual's being disappointed when he finds that higher income and consumption, and better education, have failed to help him rise in the social scale, as he had expected. With reference to the demand for education, F. Hirsch has explained the nature of this disillusionment very well.

In sum, the reason why people are so impatient nowadays with the persistence of inequalities is that some of the expected satisfactions have proved in part to be illusory. I shall have more to say about this aspect of things in Section III.

C Concentration

Economic growth in most cases leads to intensified division of labour and to the introduction of new techniques, some of which are applicable only in large production units. Growth is always accompanied by increased urbanisation.

In market economies and in centrally planned economies alike, people have to work and live in more and more complex and more and more concentrated systems of organisation, where individual action is hemmed in by constraints necessary for the efficiency of the whole and where individuals

[1] The notion that it is possible to strike a balance between the rate of growth and inequalities is widespread today. But to lend it precision one would have to define clearly the range of alternative feasible situations as well as the instruments of economic or social policy which make it possible to pass from one situation to another. It would then become apparent that often some measure intended to reduce inequalities has secondary effects which make its long-term impact uncertain. This is the message of a paper entitled 'Equality, Taxation and Inheritance' which J. Stiglitz read at a conference of the International Economic Association at Noordwijk-aan-Zee in 1977.

to result from growth only when particular efforts have been made to promote an acceleration of production or to overcome specific obstacles; only then may inflation be expected to be cured by a moderation of growth. On the other hand, the costs of inflation are directly related to its impact on inequalities, on the occurrence of windfall gains or losses and on the disruption of fair economic relationships.

have little chance of assessing their own responsibility in relation to overall results.

The precise manner in which this transition to a world of highly concentrated activities comes about merits a serious factual investigation, which I cannot undertake here. Some speak of 'bi-polarisation of skills': taks of conception, it is said, will require more and more competence and intelligence, while other tasks, including those of production, will become more elementary and fragmented. This prediction does not seem to me very convincing. Perhaps belief in such bi-polarisation is no more than a reflection of current discontents. But even if this belief is wholly erroneous, the fact remains that increased concentration means for most people that they will be further removed from the point of strategic decisions.

Common sense suggests that this hinders the full flowering of the human personality both in individual and in social activities, that it must be a source of discontent and bafflement, and generates resistances on a disproportionately large scale.

Psychologists and sociologists no doubt have a whole battery of scientific theories to underpin this commonsense view. Some economists, too, have developed it with conviction. E. F. Schumacher[1] devotes to it the fourth part of his plea for small units. J. P. Dupuy and J. Robert (op. cit.) speak of the 'structural counterproductivity' of organisations in which individuals have no chance of independent action and production. In all developed societies today individuals insistently demand more direct control over their own affairs and claim the right to participate in the major decisions of the great organisations in which they live and work.

Since concentration of human activities definitely seems to have a social cost, growth planning should take account of it. Just as economic expansion can take place with less physical pollution than it would do without pollution control, it can equally take place with at least partial avoidance of concentration and its harmful effects. But, in one case as in the other, efficient planning presupposes precise knowledge of all the relevant facts. The time for ideological confrontation is past; let us look closely now at the facts we know to be important.

Clearly, much stands to be gained from more intensive research into the human consequences of decisions affecting the structure of economic activities. Town planners have recognised this and have adopted a new approach which relies heavily upon sociological research. A similar attitude is advisable in the organisation of production activities. This may be the reason why economists nowadays devote serious study to the societies in which these activities are worker-managed.[2]

It is probably right to assume that such major measures as are often taken

[1] *Small is Beautiful* (New York: Harper & Row, 1975).

[2] See especially J. Vanek, *The General Theory of Labour: Managed Market Economies*, Ithaca, Cornell University Press, 1970, and J. E. Meade, 'The Theory of Labour-Managed Firms and Profit-Sharing', *Economic Journal*, 1972, p. 402–28.

by government in developed countries to contain the growth of capital cities and to encourage industry to locate factories in the poorer regions, rest upon the view that this should make it possible to avoid not only certain external physical diseconomies, but certain social costs as well. But in the absence of methods of analysis by which each case can be examined on its merits, these measures remain rough and rather ineffective — much less effective no doubt than they could be if planners knew more about how people react to concentration of their activities.

III ECONOMIC GROWTH AND HUMAN SATISFACTIONS

To speak of the costs of economic growth implies the assumption that there are alternative patterns of growth, possibly proceeding at different rates and occasioning different costs (and our discussion so far suggests that there are in fact many alternatives). Those who draw attention to the costs of growth indeed often take the simple view that these are directly dependent on the rate of growth, and conclude that it would be best to opt for moderate growth.

But to warrant such a conclusion one would have to take account not only of the costs of growth, but also of the satisfactions it affords, and it would have to be established that beyond a certain growth rate these satisfactions cease to offer genuine rewards. Hence the champions of moderation take pains to prove that these satisfactions are in part illusory.

In what follows, I shall first examine their argument. Having done so, I shall discuss how, taking account both of costs and satisfactions, we can clearly define the options open to a community as regards its economic growth. Finally, I shall briefly survey the means at our disposal for redirecting economic growth.

A Illusory and real satisfactions

Critics of the consumer society restate the old proposition that a general rise in consumption would not be conducive to better satisfaction of needs.[1] When an individual takes steps to increase his material resources, he does so with reference to the society in which he lives. More or less unconsciously, he supposes that living conditions in that society are stable, and on this basis imagines the additional satisfactions he might gain from increased consumption. But if all individuals manage to raise their purchasing power simultaneously, part of these satisfactions will not materialise.

[1] The classical work on the subject, of course, is T. Veblen, *Theory of the Leisure Class* (1899). A less well known but particularly relevant reference is G. H. Bousquet, *instituts de science économique,* tome I, (Paris: Marcel Giard, 1930); see in particular Chapter V, § 4 to 6). Among numerous modern works I would recommend P. d'Iribarne, *La Politique du bonheur* (Paris: Editions du Seuil, 1973). A precise model will be found in J. S. Duesenberry, *Income, Saving and the Theory of Consumer Behavior* (Cambridge, Massachusetts: Harvard University Press, 1949). Hirsch, op. cit., speaks of the 'paradox of opulence'.

The chief reason for this perverse effect is that it is impossible for everyone to rise in the social scale at the same time. To the extent that anyone's consumption rises faster than that of his fellow citizens, this would signify to himself, and to others, that he was going up in social status. Obviously, no such 'sign effect' can occur in the case of a general increase in individual consumption levels. Similarly, when an individual gives his children the means of pursuing their studies, he imagines that this will give them access to responsibilities and rank which he assesses with reference to his present situation. But the spread of higher education means that an equal number of years spent studying leads on the average to progressively less elevated rank. Or else, any person who, thanks to his work or his savings, has bought a house in a good residential quarter, will feel thwarted if other, identical houses spring up in his neighbourhood, crowding it and lowering its quality.

This argument rests upon correct observations amply confirmed by sociological research. Not only is individual satisfaction not proportional to the volume of consumption, but, at any given volume of individual consumption, satisfaction tends to decrease with an increase in the volume of global consumption. Any general increase in the level of individual consumption has the result that each individual's additional utility is less than it would be if only his personal consumption were rising. This is a point that must not be overlooked in comparing any increase in individual consumption with the costs of growth which make it possible.

However, it has never been proved that the resulting decrease in the progression of individual utilities goes so far as to bring it to a halt; it has not been proved that, as some maintain, utility depends solely upon the ratio between the volumes of individual and of global consumption, in which case only the sign effect, or some analogous effect, would be operative to the exclusion of any direct cause of satisfaction. Common sense and observed facts alike contradict this notion. In all countries there are always many unsatisfied individual needs which owe nothing whatever to such effects, and while to neglect these needs would perhaps be in order so far as the upper classes of society are concerned, it would certainly not be so in the case of the average citizen.[1]

---

[1] Some readers might be tempted at this point to refer to the results of some opinion surveys (see in particular R. A. Easterlin, 'Does Money Buy Happiness?' *The Public Interest*, New York, winter 1973). Indeed, if such surveys show, within any country and at any time, a clear correlation between one's income and the fact of declaring oneself happy, no correlation appears between national income per head and the proportion of people finding themselves happy, when comparison is made between different countries or even between different times for the same country. But on reflection such results do not bear on the point under discussion here. On the one hand, the satisfaction of human needs and the feeling of happiness must not be confused; economic progress aims at enriching human life and not at generating a happy feeling. On the other hand no absolute scale exists for measuring happiness; hence, the meaning of answers given to opinion surveys on such a question is obviously relative to the times at which they take place and the countries where they are conducted.

The argument according to which growth does not increase the satisfaction of human needs is often put forward with exaggerated insistence in relation to global consumption, but it is more compelling when applied to some particular types of consumption or to some particular manner of consumption in modern societies. It follows that nuisance control should extend not only to physical pollution but also to 'external consumption effects'. There is no reason why regulations, prohibitions and tax disincentives should not be used to this end.

Thinking over these questions leads us to two rather important conclusions. First of all, we must accept as highly plausible F. Hirsch's intuitive notion that, as economic growth proceeds, the effects associated with relative consumption become increasingly more important in the determination of satisfactions than those associated with absolute consumption. Second, these thoughts give us new reasons for understanding why mankind will never attain the ideal of a society so affluent that all spontaneous wants can be satisfied. Given a limited supply of physical resources, individuals today cannot hope to improve their satisfactions merely by increased consumption; no doubt we need also a new social ethic which checks the growth of individual wants and enhances human solidarity.

B A conceptual framework for finding a better economic growth

The term 'costs of economic growth', then, expresses misgivings of many kinds. But in reviewing them, we also perceive that corrective action of many kinds is possible, at the microeconomic and at the macroeconomic level. We are then led to consider the choice of policies designed to reduce the costs of growth, or even the prior collective choice concerning the type of growth mankind is to enjoy once the present crisis is overcome.

To organise our thoughts on this matter we can proceed in two stages, as is customary in economics. Let us leave aside, initially, the problems connected with the implementation of growth policy; these will be discussed in the next section. Here I propose to state as clearly as possible the terms of the macroeconomic choices which have to be made at the very outset of growth planning.

During the last fifteen years theoretical tools have been devised for the study of the choices involved in growth planning. The theory of optimum growth, which takes simultaneous account of costs and satisfactions, has increasingly proved its analytical power in multiple applications, even though mathematical economists often incline to be unduly hermetic in their work on the subject.[1]

The foremost merit of this theory is that it requires a perfectly explicit statement of many notions which remain vague in common language or in less rigorous reasoning. Collective aims must be precisely defined, and so must the

[1] The theory is well set out in Chapters 10–14 of G. M. Heal, *The Theory of Economic Planning* (Amsterdam: North-Holland, 1973).

constraints. The models enable optimum growth to be calculated, together with the appropriate prices and rates of discount. Two types of lesson can be learnt from these models. Directly, they show up the major options of a development plan adapted to future growth conditions, and also show how to carry out economic calculations in a system of more or less decentralised planning. Indirectly, they introduce a dialectic method of research, which, going back from the results to the formulation of the aim and the constraints, makes it clear which are the most crucial elements for the choice of the rate and the nature of future growth. In this way we are helped to an increasingly better understanding of the social ethic regarding future development and to more precise knowledge of the objective constraints to which it is subject.

Along these lines of thought, we would do well, no doubt, to incorporate our misgivings about the costs of economic growth into the theory of optimum growth. I cannot do this here, of course, for it would take me too far and require a whole paper to itself. But I can suggest the premises of the model that would have to be constructed, as well as the main questions to which it should provide an answer.

The model must contain a correct explicit statement of alternative choices between quality and quantity in the broad sense, which means introducing them into both the objective function and the constraints. As we have seen, insistence on quality may entail two types of sacrifice; it may mean that producers have to incur costs implying a smaller volume of output (reduction of pollution, or avoidance of more concentrated forms of production), and it may mean slowing down certain humanly costly developments (occupational mobility, urbanisation).

The objective function, therefore, must be stated in terms not merely of the volume of consumption per head in each period (C_t in period t), but also in terms of two quality indicators. The first, Q_{1t}, would be an independent variable in the production function, alongside the traditional variables K_t for capital input and L_t for labour input (output Y_t would be a decreasing function of Q_{1t}). The second indicator Q_{2t} would have to do with the speed of structural transformation in production; it could be, say, a decreasing function of capital accumulation, e.g. $Q_{2t} = K_t - K_{t+1}$.

To state the problem in such aggregate terms involves great intellectual courage. We must not be deterred by certain major difficulties. Not only must we work with aggregates representing the volume of production, of capital and of labour. Not only must we disregard the well-known objections to the definition of a global production function. We must also take into account two aggregates representing qualities of growth. Yet reflections on the measurement of an enlarged GNP and the search for social indicators suggest that in this matter aggregation involves even more serious arbitrariness than it does in the case of purely economic magnitudes.

The only really different alternative approach, however, is even more inadequate.[1] This would be to take full account of all the inherent complexity from the outset. We would have to construct an extremely complicated model, which would not only be difficult to use but probably even more arbitrary, for many of its relations would rest upon very sketchy knowledge and they would be so numerous as to preclude thorough examination.

This is why research would be better employed in trying to provide an answer to the questions involved in quantifying an aggregate model of the type here proposed. But the first step is to find out what characteristics of the model exercise a crucial influence upon optimum growth and its rate.

For example, one might concentrate on the case where the objective function is the sum of utilities at any one period, $U_t(C_t, Q_{1t}, Q_{2t})$, possibly discounted and weighted by the size of the population. The precise significance of the function U_t would have to be examined in detail so as to make sure that the factors which determine satisfactions are correctly expressed. Everything, obviously, would depend upon the definitions of quality indicators. The marginal rates of substitution between the qualities Q_{1t} or Q_{2t} and the consumption volume C_t would be important for the choice of optimum growth, but so would the variation of these rates as a function of the volume of consumption (they would probably be increasing, but according to what law?). Similarly, the elasticity of final output with respect to Q_{1t} is relevant, and so is the variation of this elasticity as a function of the volume of capital K_t (is it an admissible approximation to assume the elasticity to be independent of K_t?).

We begin to perceive how many questions need to be answered. We also realise that these questions are pertinent: they throw light on what must precede any lucid choice of growth policy, and they show the directions in which our factual knowledge needs improvement.

C Redirecting economic growth

If it is difficult enough to identify the costs of economic growth, it is a much more formidable task still to find the means of effectively altering the nature of economic growth.

Supposing that, in the light of more or less thoroughgoing study of the points discussed here, it were decided to go for moderate growth, involving careful husbandry of natural and human resources, or priority for the qualitative aspects of life, for the individual and for society alike. How is growth to be redirected to correspond to such a choice? There is no simple answer to this question.

---

[1] It is, of course, perfectly possible not to push aggregation as far as the model here proposed requires, but intellectual courage is still needed in any exercise having to do with the quest for optimum growth. For example, we might try to take account of the aim of reducing inequalities by introducing negative inequality indicators into the definitions of Q_1 and Q_2. Or we might disaggregate consumption into two magnitudes, of which one concerns the poor classes of society and is given greater weight in the definition of the objective function. This is really what H. Chenery and his collaborators do in *Redistribution with Growth* (Oxford University Press, 1974).

To some extent it can be done by modifying the principles accepted at the moment of decisions affecting a large number of microeconomic projects or regulations. The calculations carried out when projects are examined may be based on formulae in which some weight is accorded to previously neglected elements, such as the pollution resulting from certain production processes, scarcity of certain resources, the human costs of certain changes, the socially illusory character of certain projects which may appear attractive from an unduly individualistic point of view, effects on inequalities, etc. Such elements as cannot be quantified may be systematically enumerated and presented alongside the results of the calculations which omit them. Similarly, new ideas that take account of all the costs of economic growth may come to prevail with the adoption of regulations concerning the treatment of industrial wastes and effluents, or urbanisation, industrial location, etc. The same may apply to taxes or subsidies designed to have a disincentive or an incentive effect on certain kinds of production and consumption.

But all this may not be enough, since any radical redirection of economic growth involves also a change in the individual attitudes of producers and consumers. Their whole outlook must become very different from what it was in the years 1950—74. Failing widespread adherence to a long-term view defined at least in its qualitative aspects, individual decisions are only too likely to be governed by old habits and, moreover, often to be mutually inconsistent.

On top of all these difficulties there are the inherent conflicts of modern societies. Any redefinition of the pattern of economic growth is bound to re-awaken old antagonisms which had somehow come to terms in the past in a common *modus vivendi*. It is naive to think, as many have done or pretended to do, that an overthrow of the now prevailing powers is the necessary and sufficient condition for a new course in economic growth. Yet the changes that are needed assuredly include some that are likely to benefit certain countries to the detriment of others, or certain social groups more than others. The resulting conflicts will be hard to settle.

We need a long-term view to serve as reference for individual decisions and to make them mutually consistent. We need a new economic order in relations among countries and among social groups. Here, surely, are two fundamental and compelling reasons for organising all the consultations and all the applied studies which are the essence of planning. The fact that we must do our planning on the international scale makes it exceptionally difficult. We have no time to waste.

In public debates about the costs of economic growth economists are often put into the dock as though they were responsible for the way economic growth has gone in recent decades. I have too little faith in the direct influence of our work to accept this accusation. Having neither a guilt-complex nor ambitions of facile success, I refuse to join the ranks of the prophets of zero growth.

But I do think that the subject here discussed is one of those to which we, as economists, should devote our best efforts. I have tried to outline the main tasks awaiting us.

Discussion of Professor Malinvaud's Paper*

Professor Bagchi, the first speaker, said that Professor Malinvaud had given a fairly comprehensive picture of the problems raised by economic growth in developed capitalist countries. By implication, he had also demonstrated how simple-minded the analysis and prescriptions of advocates of zero growth were. In all this, he had deliberately confined himself to a single economy without going into the international dimensions of economic change.

In considering the issues facing the less developed capitalist countries, however, it was hardly possible to confine the analysis to the framework of an isolated economy. One basic reason for this was that a less developed capitalist economy acted less often on its own account than it was set into motion by impulses propelled from abroad. Furthermore, the costs incurred in the past by a typical less developed economy would have been incurred not on account of its own growth, but on account of the growth of others. In spite of these two contentions, he did not mean to assert that there were no costs of economic growth in less developed countries which were incurred on their own account. On the contrary, he thought that many of the costs incurred by the less developed capitalist countries were unnecessarily high for the existing pattern of growth, and that the existing pattern of growth was quite out of line with the basic needs of the majority of the people in those countries. But in order to grasp the roots of such waste, and worse, it was necessary to delve into the international factors that directed the less developed countries into the familiar course of underdevelopment and dependent capitalism.

Essentially, he said, uncompensated costs of economic growth had been incurred by the countries of the third world because of serious antinomies in development along capitalist lines. These antinomies could be classified into three different categories: (a) the contradiction between the capitalist class and rentiers and the rest of the population within a country; (b) the contradiction between capitalist strata or ruling classes of different countries or different groups of countries; and (c) the contradictory nature of the economic processes set into motion by capitalism, which had led inevitably to phenomena of cyclical growth, inflationary recession, and stagnation. That third component, at least in its purely cyclical aspect, was often regarded as a process of 'necessary correction' (as, for example, in the early work of D. H. Robertson), such a view personified the whole society as a single entity and failed to take into account the immense costs incurred by workers at the receiving end of the processes of correction.

In setting out his argument, said Professor Bagchi, he would largely ignore, however, the purely cyclical or short-term aspects of the working of a capitalist economy, although it would be difficult to deny that long-run tendencies were in actual fact worked out in a series of spasmodic pulsations. He would do this partly because of lack of time, and partly because, in his view, in the case of countries of the third world long-run trends emanating from their interaction with the advanced capitalist countries dominated any changes brought about through purely cyclical variations.

The central antinomy in the international sphere for the third world countries sprang from their exploitation by the mercantile and industrial

*In the discussion section that follows, all numbered footnotes are the speakers' own.

capitalist classes of the countries of western Europe and, later, of the countries of western Europe and North America, extending over several centuries. Ultimately the exploitation took the form of appropriation of the produce of third world peoples without anything like an adequate payment (the adequacy could be defined in terms of needs of subsistence including the needs of re-production, or in terms of some notion of equivalence of exchange). This process was starkly clear in the case of the Spanish and Portuguese empires in the Americas up to the beginning of the nineteenth century, in the case of India up to around 1850, and in the case of the Dutch empire until the very beginning of the Second World War. When Amer-indian labour had proved intractable, as in the Caribbean islands and in most of Brazil, or when it had declined in numbers through over-exploitation and the diseases brought in by the Conquistadores, slaves had been transported in their millions from the continent of Africa. The 'surplus product' had been extracted from the slaves, the Amer-indian peasants and Indian and Indonesian peasants. That most of the fruits of exploitation in Portuguese and Spanish America ended up in London, Antwerp and Amsterdam rather than in Madrid or Lisbon should not blind us to the fact that it was the western European capitalists as a group who had gained at the expense of the peoples of the Americas, Africa and Asia.[1]

With the growth of industrial capitalism in Europe, and with the increasing sophistication of methods of exploitation exercised by the European (and subsequently, North American) capitalists, the tracks of the surplus extracted became more difficult to uncover. This was because Europeans and North Americans then sold manufactured goods and various kinds of services to third world countries, and apparently invested vast amounts of capital there.[2] Some of the mystification about the real nature of the payments extracted from the colonies and near-colonies had been deliberate, of course: political tribute paid to Britain by India, for example, had been designated as 'home charges' during the period of British rule. Again, the amount of goods bought up by the East India Company for sale in Britain and Europe out of excess revenues had been styled as its 'investment' in India.

However, apart from deliberate mystification, said Professor Bagchi, the usual, supposedly neutral, balance of payments accounting procedure was seriously defective from the point of view of assessing the true magnitudes of transfer of capital from third world dependencies to the advanced capitalist countries ruling them. Most of the problems centred on payments for services, the valuation of goods imported and exported, and the proper accounting of capital raised as 'loans'. First of all, most of the colonies had been saddled with the cost of conquering them in the first place: this might be called the cost of

[1] The literature on the exploitation of these continents is too vast to be given in even a capsule form in this comment. Much of it has been cited in the speaker's forthcoming book on the processes of economic retardation. The argument and evidence regarding de-industrialisation in third world countries are given in a fuller form in A. K. Bagchi, 'De-industrialization in India in the Nineteenth Century: Some Theoretical Implications', *Journal of Development Studies,* 12(2) (January 1976).

[2] As had been shown by the work of Herbert Feis, C. K. Hobson, and Matthew Simon, among others, the total amount of investment in third world countries, as computed even by conventional accounting methods, turns out to be only a fraction of total foreign capital invested in the developed capitalist countries.

self-ransoming. Thus the colony had had to service the 'public debt' incurred in connection with this initial calamity imposed on it. Second, the colony had had to pay the cost of policing itself (something akin to the 'protection money' levied by gangsters) and sometimes, as in the case of India, the cost of conquering and policing other territories. Third, the colony had been required to pay for the administrators imposed on it by the ruling power. These administrators had generally earned salaries which were way above what they could have earned at home. The colonial authorities had taken good care to ensure that for as long as possible natives were denied the opportunity either to learn the skills of the colonial administrators or to exercise their authority. As a result, in most colonial territories a large part of the superior administration and technical services had remained a heavily protected preserve of the Europeans ruling the country. Thus, payment for these services — such as they were — had also been jacked up by straight monopoly control (the technical services such as the Geological Survey of India, or the Survey of India, had themselves been run largely in the interest of foreign businessmen or had served the strategic interest of the rulers).

If we turned to other goods and services which were more tangibly put to the use of the people of the third world countries, Professor Bagchi said, we met the element of monopoly and other forms of restriction of entry against the 'natives' at every turn. The services of shipping, organised banking, insurances, etc., were generally monopolised by firms from metropolitan countries. Shipping and shipbuilding had played key roles in the protection of the national interests of European capitalists throughout the seventeenth, eighteenth and nineteenth centuries. Naturally, they had tried to prevent the growth of colonial shipping and shipbuilding industries wherever they could. In India and the British empire in general, first the 'Old Shipping Interest', and then the P & O and BISN companies, had enjoyed various kinds of state patronage and had been able to keep out competitors by using a variety of weapons. In Indonesia, the Dutch shipping company KPM had enjoyed similar privileges. In India, the government had chartered the so-called Presidency Banks, which were dominated by European interests throughout their career. Later on, European-controlled exchange banks had monopolised the foreign exchange business in India, China and many other third world countries. Thus a large part of the payment for these services had also been extracted from the colonies or semi-colonies by denying them the opportunity to develop any alternative facilities.

Second, foreign enterprises had dominated the public utilities, extractive industries, wholesale trade and, in later phases, the processing industries in many third world countries. Generally, these enterprises had had a monopolistic structure, with interlocking interests in many different fields,[1] and most of the enterprises in trade, plantations, mining, and crude processing had been established by foreign nationals who had amassed their capital in the third world countries, and who owed much of their success to explicit or implicit barriers against the entry of natives into European preserves. Racial discrimination had been a much-used and potent weapon for excluding the natives from

---

[1] For a vivid picture of such monopolising in the French colony of Madagascar, see Rene Dumont, *False Start in Africa* (London: André Deutsch, 1966) Chapter 2.

those vantage points which yielded very high rates of profit.[1] However, the capital acquired by foreign nationals by such means had shown up as 'foreign investment' in the balance of payments, neatly concealing the fact that in most cases there had been no real transfer of capital from metropolitan countries to the colonies. Third, when loans had been floated in the metropolitan country by the colonies, their expenditure had generally been tied to the products of the lending country. A large percentage of the loans never had reached the colonies anyway.[2]

Fourth, even when goods had not been bought with loans – that is, in normal transactions, most of the time – their import had been tied to the ruling country either through explicit government instructions or preferences or through accepted codes of conduct on the part of the importers and the users. Thus British India before 1914 had continued to import from Britain many categories of iron and steel products which had ceased to be competitive with Belgian and German products on the basis of the accepted maxim, 'British is best'. Even where there were no explicit colonial ties, tying of imports had been achieved through the activities of the foreign capitalists in third world countries. Thus, in nineteenth-century Argentina, British capitalists had played the dominant role, raising loans in London, floating railway companies and getting much of their cost underwritten by the Argentine government and importing all their requirements of capital goods and manufactured intermediate goods from the UK. This had been happening when the USA, France and Germany had established their own manufacturing complexes to serve the need of their own railway development and then to cater to the railways they had floated abroad.[3] This sort of excess cost arising from the tying of imports to particular metropolitan countries had yet to be computed for the period before the Second World War, he said. A similar kind of tying had taken place also in the case of export: Indian raw jute and tea exports had continued to be tied to London (and Dundee, in the case of jute) long after the USA, Germany and other countries had emerged as major buyers of jute and tea. Finally, many colonial and semi-colonial countries had been more or less forced to buy commodities which were often positively harmful to the health and welfare of the people. The most notorious case was that of the forcing of opium on China: between 1867 and 1910, for example, the annual imports of opium into China averaged roughly between £7 million and £12 million[4]

[1] For examples of such discrimination, see W. F. Wertheim, *Indonesian Society in Transition* (The Hague: W. Van Hoeve, 1959), Chapter 6, and A. K. Bagchi, *Private Investment in India 1900–1939)* Cambridge University Press, 1972), Chapter 6.

[2] For accounts of the misappropriation of the loans at the source, see L. H. Jenks, *The Migration of British Capital to 1875* (London: Nelson, 1963) Chapters 2 and 3; and R. E. Cameron, *France and the Economic Development of Europe, 1800–1914* (Princeton, New Jersey: Princeton University Press, 1961) Chapter 15.

[3] This comment does not explicitly discuss how the colonies or semi-colonies chiefly populated by non-Europeans (or as in the exceptional case of Argentina, by the people of southern Europe) differed from the countries settled mainly by Europeans in respect of transfer of capital, pattern of economic development, and so on. For a brief discussion of these questions, see A. K. Bagchi, 'Some International Foundations of Capitalist Growth and Underdevelopment', *Economic and Political Weekly*, Special Number (Bombay, August 1972).

[4] This had been computed on the basis of figures given in Hsiao Liang-Lin, *China's*

Professor Bagchi went on to say that, while the costs in question were difficult to compute, they were *in principle* computable, using standards derived from the payments made by the advanced capitalist countries to one another.[1] There were other costs which were not computable except on the assumption of a different world economic order — an order in which the growth of a few capitalist countries would not have imposed enormous costs on the rest of the world. These sprang from the thwarting of industrialisation in the colonised countries, the forced de-industrialisation of traditional manufacturing nations, such as India or China, their forced commercialisation — with an orientation towards serving the needs of the advanced capitalist countries — and the forcing of their societies into the pattern of retarded development that was familiar today. These distortions, caused in the first place by capitalist colonialism, had had the most lasting consequences and it was with these that he would be concerned in the rest of his comment. But before doing so he first wanted to cite some illustrative computations of the external costs imposed on third world countries by growth in advanced capitalist countries.[2]

The proper method of computation would be to correct the figures of external transactions so as to enter all payments arising out of political subjugation, monopolisation of crucial areas of economic activity, and effective tying of loans and imports of goods to metropolitan countries as unrequited capital transfers to metropolitan countries. However, the usual accounting procedures had camouflaged such transfers so successfully that it would take a tremendous effort on the part of a team of researchers to accomplish the needed corrections. As a first approximation to the true state of balance of transactions between individual third world countries and the rest of the world

[1] It is to be noted that many of the usual accounting conventions are perfectly sensible when applied to trade between the advanced capitalist countries themselves, for there the typical phenomena of unequal exchange and monopolisation of key sectors of the economy by foreigners are less likely to occur. For the same kind of reason, the usual terms of trade calculations, taking into account only the border prices, make good sense in the case of trade between advanced capitalist countries, but not for the terms of trade of third world countries, particularly in their colonial phase. For the latter, the terms of trade calculations should be based on a comparison of the returns obtained by the peasants and workers and the prices paid by the ultimate consumers. Most of the present trend analyses of terms of trade of third world countries are vitiated by the failure to make this distinction between border prices and true internal prices.

[2] The maintenance of the world imperialist order involved not only a one-way flow of real capital from the third world to the metropolitan countries; it also involved the passing on to the third world of most of the costs of cyclical adjustment in primary commodity markets, and of the transition from a bimetallic to a gold standard in the advanced capitalist countries (India, China and Indonesia were made to absorb enormous quantities of depreciating silver at a time when European countries were moving over to the gold standard). On these monetary aspects of the costs imposed on third world countries, see R. Triffin, 'The myth and realities of the so-called Gold Standard', in R. N. Cooper (ed.), *International Finance* (Harmondsworth: Penguin Books, 1969); A. G. Ford, *The Gold Standard 1880–1914: Britain and Argentina* (Oxford: Clarendon Press, 1962); and M. De Cecco, *Money and Empire: The International Gold Standard, 1890–1914* (Oxford: Blackwell, 1974).

Foreign Trade Statistics, 1864–1949 (Cambridge, Massachusetts: East Asian Research Centre, Harvard University, 1974).

he would take the simple difference between merchandise exports and merchandise imports of those countries. This would avoid the problem of valuing the services – dubious and real – rendered to the third world countries by the advanced capitalist groups. If in so doing the value of the real services obtained by third world countries from abroad was understated, it had to be remembered that the commodities imported and exported were still valued at the going market price which, as he had pointed out, would lead to an over-valuation of commodity imports and undervaluation of commodity exports. Furthermore, the products imported would include those consumed by the resident Europeans (who had a far higher standard of living than the average 'native') and the military stores needed for the army of occupation. Hence the export-import gap was as likely to understate the true capital outflow from the third world as to overstate them.

This method would show that the total capital outflow from Indonesia over the period 1867–1930 was 12,400 million guilders.[1] This contrasted with an estimate of 4000 million guilders as the total foreign capital invested in that country around 1929[2] (in order properly to compare the sum of capital transferred out of Indonesia with this estimate, the series of annual capital transfers would have to be accumulated at some notional rate of interest between the year in which the capital transfer occurred and 1929). The latter figure showed that, even after remitting vast sums out of Indonesia, foreign capitalists had managed to tot up a claim of some 400 million guilders (assuming a rate of profit of 10 per cent) annually against the Indonesian economy.

Making similar calculations for India, we would find that the total capital outflow from India from 1871–2 to 1938–9 was about £1811 million.[2] This was in addition to an estimated foreign investment in India of about £664 million in 1938,[4] which would imply a claim to at least another £66 million annually on the part of foreign investors.

Regarding the distortions in the economic and social organisation produced by the impact of capitalist imperialism, he said, we had to note the destruction of traditional craft industries in such regions as India, China, the Ottoman empire, and Latin America – particularly in the nineteenth century – without anything like a compensating growth of modern manufacturing industries. Unlike, say, in England or Germany, the destruction of craft industries had not been the consequence of growth of modern machine-paced industry, nor

---

[1] The figures of exports and imports are taken from W. F. Wertheim: *Indonesian Society in Transition,* p. 101. For most of the time, twelve guilders may be taken to have equalled one pound sterling. In all these calculations, we have taken the simple sum of money values of export surplus over time. A more sophisticated calculation would involve the deflation of the money values by a suitable price index, and the use of an appropriate discount or compounding rate to arrive at a proper figure of the present value of the export surplus flows over time.

[2] John de La Valette, 'The Netherlands East Indies Today', *Journal of the Royal Society of Arts,* vol. 87 (16 December 1938).

[3] The conversion rate for the rupee was taken as Rs 12 to the £ from 1871–2 to 1885–6, Rs 15 to the £ from 1886–7 to 1915–16, Rs 10 to the £ from 1916–17 to 1920–1 and Rs 13·33 to the £ thereafter.

[4] The figure is taken from A. K. Banerji, *India's Balance of Payments* (Bombay: Asia, 1963) p. 183.

had it been in any sense preparation for such growth. When the new manufacturing industries had begun to grow, the capital goods, human skill and
many basic raw materials had had to be imported, generally on quite unfavourable terms. This process of growth of modern industry had thus continued
the general pattern of orientation of third world economies towards the reception of impulses from advanced capitalist countries, which had started at a
time when the colonies were forced — often at the point of a bayonet — to
grow exportable agricultural products or produce valuable minerals.

There was a misconception in some quarters, he went on, that the displacement of millions of artisans from craft industry had been compensated
by the growth of agricultural products — as demanded by the general direction
of comparative advantage at that time. This betrayed a naive idea that displaced artisans had been automatically and profitably fully employed in
agriculture. In fact, the redeployment of such vast numbers would have
involved vast amounts of capital investment in agriculture. Despite the
apparently enormous investment made in the irrigation network of Egypt and
India, the total amount of investment in agriculture had not been more than
a fraction of the surplus extracted from those countries. Furthermore, the
investment had been made on a centralised basis in the interest of capitalists
operating with an eye to the external market (producing cotton in the case of
Egypt, and cotton and wheat in the case of India—Pakistan). The irrigation
works had been conceived without adequate attention being paid to the costs
incurred in the process: they had led to the spread of bilharzia in Egypt, and,
in combination with the railways, to that of malaria in India. They had had
the side-effect of making vast tracts of land alkaline or saline and unfit for
cultivation. In many areas, furthermore, they had rendered the earlier sources
of privately controlled irrigation, such as seasonally or annually constructed
wells, inoperative.

There were vast areas where no public investment at all in agriculture had
taken place. Yet in those areas also, the production of exportable crops took
place at the behest of the world capitalist market. Part of this was supported
no doubt by small amounts of private investment. But most of the increase
took place through the more intensive utilisation of existing land, the cultivation of hitherto uncultivated land, and the substitution of exportable crops
for crops supplying local or exclusively national needs.

In the process not only had labour-intensity of cultivation enormously
increased,[1] but the careful husbandry of generations and the balance of crops
needed to conserve the nutrients of the soil had been destroyed, never to be
restored without conscious and costly effort; and in most underdeveloped
capitalist countries that effort had yet to be made. Furthermore, pasture lands
had been converted into cropland in the interest of government revenue from
land, and private profit. In Kenya, and South Africa, for example, the best
land had been reserved for European farmers. Minor irrigation works had often
been destroyed as in Spanish America or had fallen into disuse through lack
of public support or interest as in India. The result was a precipitate decline
in fertility of the soil in some areas, soil erosion on a vast scale, as in central
and eastern India, and depletion of the livestock at the disposal of tribal and

[1] Cf. C. Geertz, *Agricultural Involution* (Berkeley: University of California Press,
1963).

peasant populations.[1]

The commercialisation of agriculture in the colonial and semi-colonial countries had been achieved by leaving the peasants no other alternative for survival than to grow crops for export, said Professor Bagchi, with the result that they became heavily dependent on consumption loans for carrying on from one harvest to the next. The implicit and explicit rates of interest on such loans had been very high – partly as the result of practices under pre-capitalist regimes and partly as the result of the high rate of surplus value exacted by Europeans, either through trade or commerce or through the state apparatus. Under pre-capitalist conditions, the peasants or tribal peoples had had security against dispossession of their means of production, however indebted they might be. The economic liberalism of the nineteenth century had deprived the peasants of such protection, without opening out new avenues of investment and without leaving them the wherewithal for sufficient investment.

While, in the rural areas, this kind of perpetual indebtedness for small and middle peasants had been effected in the interest of generating an exportable surplus, the towns erected under colonial or semi-colonial rule had served as the collecting centres for this surplus. The surplus had been sucked into the ports from the rest of the country and had then been siphoned off into the metropolitan lands. In Spanish America, towns had been explicitly organised as centres for dominating the countryside. That role continued into the era of the Latin American republics, which had been integrated into the world system of industrial and mercantile capitalism. In India also the pre-British towns had been administrative and military centres dominating the countryside. But they had been inward-looking, rather than outward-looking, and there had been a wide dispersal of such towns, particularly in the days of breakdown of the Mughal empire. The British had achieved a far greater degree of centralisation than the Mughals, and had turned the towns and cities outwards. One paradoxical result was that, although on balance the urban population as a percentage of total population had probably declined in the period up to the last quarter of the nineteenth century, the importance of a few cities of metropolitan dimensions as the centres for collection of the surplus had increased enormously. The objective difference between town and country had vastly increased, because, while new towns and growing cities had been blessed with some of the new comforts and amenities imported from advanced capitalist countries, the villages and the decaying towns had lost the earlier facilities they had enjoyed without acquiring much that was new. With the extremely low (and quite often, negative) rate of capital accumulation, the use of non-market methods of coercion in fields, plantations and even factories, the exercise of monopolistic control at various levels of economic activity and

[1] For illustrative accounts of soil erosion in colonial countries, see R. Maclagan Gorrie, 'The Problem of Soil Erosion in the British Empire, with Special Reference to India', *Journal of the Royal Society of Arts*, vol. 86, (26 July 1938); A. D. Hall, *The Improvement of Native Agriculture in Relation to Population and Public Health* (London: Oxford University Press, 1936); On the policy of preserving the best areas for Europeans in Kenya, see C. Leys, *Underdevelopment in Kenya* (London: Heinemann, 1976). For an analysis of the impact of the British revenue system on peasant holdings of livestock, see A. K. Bagchi, 'Reflections on Patterns of Regional Growth in India', *Bengal Past and Present* (Calcutta, January–June 1976).

access to income-earning opportunities, many pre-capitalist forms had survived and had been put to conscious use by the alien rulers for the maintenance of their power. In the politically independent countries of the third world, these forms of symbiosis of pre-capitalist *force majeure* and capitalist exploitation continued to thrive and exact their costs not only in the field of economic activities, but also in social life, politics and culture.

When a conscious effort at industrialisation had been made in the third world, the basic structure of society fashioned in the nineteenth century had remained unchanged. The top crust, now consisting of indigenous capitalists, landlords and bureaucrats, continued to use the methods of exploitation that had been current in colonial or semi-colonial times. The capitalists investing in industry continued to look for a rate of return that was very high by the standards of advanced capitalist countries. The towns continued as the centres for collection of the surplus, and town-and-country differences continued unabated, and, in fact, increased in most cases.

With a small home market, a highly unequal distribution of income, assets and educational opportunities, the base for research and development on capitalist principles (even when supplemented by state help) in most third world countries remained small, he said. Furthermore, the tastes of the rich in those countries had become geared to product developments and fashion changes abroad. Hence industrialists in those countries found it the path of least resistance to imitate the product changes and methods of production in advanced capitalist countries. In such imitation, they faced a very great number of obstacles springing from their lack of knowledge of what they were imitating, their limited financial resources, the small scale on which they operated, and the lack of personnel with the requisite training. Foreign companies — particularly transnationals — enjoyed a number of advantages in these respects even when operating on alien ground. Naturally, the indigenous capitalists then tried to intensify the exploitation of workers and peasants as a defensive measure. If workers' unions were granted some advance in wages, work was allotted to the unorganised sector where no powerful unions existed.[1] Since the rate of investment in most third world countries was too low by most criteria, most governments were anxious to encourage private investment at almost any cost. Naturally, protests about environmental damage, particularly by propagandists from developed capitalist countries, fell on deaf ears in the third world. The wanton neglect of measures to prevent environmental damage and the intensive exploitation of workers were not the prerogative of private indigenous capitalists: they were resorted to by transnationals and state enterprises. If pollution at Zuari (in Goa, India) was caused by a local enterprise in collaboration with foreign giants, much of the pollution in the Damodar valley (in West Bengal) was caued by public enterprises working in the area.

Along with these internal costs exacted by the sluggish and retarded capitalism of most third world countries, the external costs continued to be paid on a very large scale, so that, for example, even with conventional methods of accounting, the outflow of capital from Latin America in the 1960s far exceeded the inflow — even after taking into account the much-touted official aid from the USA and other sources. But the ruling classes of the underdeveloped capitalist countries continued to pay this kind of price for their dependence

---

[1] Thus the so-called 'informal' sector acts as an essential adjunct of the formal sector.

on the advanced capitalist countries – because they benefited directly from the process, and because their survival as rulers was itself contingent on such dependence.

It would be noticed, said Professor Bagchi in conclusion that he had not distinguished between costs that could be properly accounted for by a perfectly functioning market system and costs that arose from various externalities.[1] This was because, as far as the vast majority of the peoples of the third world were concerned, such a distinction was almost entirely ir-relevant. A market system which was so heavily weighted against them would produce the results it had produced in the past – namely, poverty, unemploy-ment, illiteracy, and famines – however perfectly it might function in some dream-world of neo-classical economics.

*

Professor Franco Modigliani, who spoke next, said that President Malinvaud's invitation to him to discuss his paper was an honour but also something of a challenge, since the topic of Professor Malinvaud's paper was not one on which he could claim any particular expertise.

He had done his best to meet this challenge by pondering over Professor Malinvaud's paper and brushing up a bit on some of the literature, but none the less he remained no expert. All he could do was to record the reactions of a man who approached the problem afresh – except, of course, for that un-avoidable bias, instinctive to an economist, that more 'value' was better than less value.

Professor Malinvaud's main concern was with reviewing the array of recent criticisms of the supposed benefits of growth. The bulk of his analysis focused on the question of whether the growth of output, as conventionally measured by GNP or analogous indices, systematically overstated the improvement in welfare. His other main theme was that of how growth policies might be redirected so as to get more true benefits out of development.

In reviewing Professor Malinvaud's analysis and assessment, said Professor Modigliani, he found it convenient to classify the factors that could cause the growth in measured output to overstate systematically the improvement in welfare under two headings rather different from those chosen by Professor Malinvaud. They were:

(1) *measurement errors or bias,* causing the growth in conventional measures of output to overstate the true growth in *net* output;
(2) *externalities,* causing the growth in correctly measured net real output to overstate the increment in net benefits received by the consumer.

In so far as one's concern was with percentage growth over some base, what mattered here was not the presence of bias *per se,* from either source, but whether the bias tended to grow proportionately more than output.

---

[1] The misleading nature of the conventional theory of external effects has been brought out in two different contexts by Stephen Hymer and Frank Roosevelt: see their 'Comment' (on Assar Lindbeck's *The Political Economy of the New Left*) in *Quarterly Journal of Economics,* 86(4) (November 1972); and also by J. H. Dales in 'Beyond the Marketplace', *Canadian Journal of Economics,* 8(4) (November 1975).

He would review, he said, the various sources of possible bias, proceeding from those which appeared most evident and relatively easy to measure, to those which were most controversial, and whose measurement posed enormous, if not insurmountable, problems.

In so far as measurement errors were concerned, Professor Malinvaud had explicitly called attention to the possibility of growth being overstated because of a presumed failure to take quality deterioration properly into account. But he had promptly added that, from his personal experience, errors on this score were most unlikely to produce significant systematic upward bias. He had also alluded to a more vaguely defined purported conflict between quantity and quality, or, as he himself would put it, said Professor Modigliani, mass consumption and refinement. It was quite likely that economic development, by producing some affluence for lower social classes less educated and less 'cultivated', might give rise to the growth of consumptions that were offensive to the upper crust of society, the so-called *nouveau riche* syndrome. But he certainly shared Professor Malinvaud's view that this was hardly a good reason for discounting measured growth. Indeed, this criticism of the consequences of growth, which he had frequently heard, particularly in Europe, had led him to the view that there was something more obnoxious than the *nouveau riche*, namely the *vieux riche*.

There were, however, several other sources of measurement bias that had not been systematically covered in Professor Malinvaud's survey, he said. A potentially important one arose from failure of the conventional measure to net out certain intermediate outputs which did not produce direct satisfaction but were only instrumental in the production of the true final output. A prime example was the case of substantial portions of government expenditure. This had been explicitly recognised in some of the early attempts to measure national income: e.g. by Gini. Indeed, until fairly recently, Italian national income statistics had been constructed on this basis. The conventional procedure was dictated only by pragmatic considerations of convenience and of avoiding debatable 'judgemental' allocations. One could imagine that in the process of development such expenditures might rise proportionally faster than output. But empirical evidence, such as that provided by the estimates of Tobin and Nordhaus,[1] for the USA, provided little support for this view. To be sure, in the estimates of these two writers 'intermediate government output' had risen faster than GNP between 1927 and 1965, but only because of the great rise in defence expenditure in the USA — surely not a necessary concomitant of development. The remaining items seemed to have moved pretty much in proportion to GNP. Tobin and Nordhaus had also endeavoured to identify and measure other types of intermediate expenditure, notably the cost of commuting to work (which Professor Malinvaud had also mentioned); and again they had found that, in terms of their measures, such expenditures had moved roughly in proportion to GNP.

A third potential source of measurement error was the omission from the conventional measure of the value of many commodities and services that were not exchanged through the market: e.g. those produced and consumed

---

[1] J. Tobin, and W. Nordhaus, 'Is Growth Obsolete?', in, National Bureau of Economic Research, *Economic Growth,* (New York: Columbia University Press, 1972).

within the household or bartered, and leisure. Some of these items were actually included in the GNP measures through imputations. Tobin and Nordhaus had tried to carry out comprehensive estimates. One might think that since growth in productivity had been accompanied by appreciable reduction in working hours, the inclusion of leisure would raise estimated growth. It turned out, however, that the outcome might go either way, depending on how one measured the real value of leisure.

One last type of bias to be considered was that which arose from certain hidden costs incurred in order to make the expansion of output possible and which had to be subtracted. The same authors had pointed out, for instance, that increased productivity had been made possible, in part, by increased urbanisation, and had estimated the cost or dis-amenity of urbanisation from the cross-sectional relation between *per capita* income and population density. Their estimated aggregate cost was modest (some 6 per cent of GNP) and, rather surprisingly, moved again roughly in proportion to GNP. Professor Malinvaud had suggested that an analogous cost arose from the increasing concentration of employment and the dis-amenity of working in larger units, at more highly specialised tasks, etc. It was hard to know how serious this cost was; one might perhaps obtain some estimates by applying the Tobin–Nordhaus method, though this would almost certainly result in an upward bias because of the positive association between unionisation and size of the firm. But one should also note that the negative effect of concentration might be on the decrease rather than on the increase because of new ways of organising production and because concentration itself might not be increasing. In some countries, like Italy (and even France to some extent), the trend had been clearly reversed, though it was not clear how far this reversal was due to the endeavour to evade taxes and unions, rather than to an attenuation in the economies of scale.

One must conclude therefore that, except possibly for the debatable leisure effect, there was little ground for concern that the conventional measures of output tended systematically to overstate the expansion of *per capita* net output.

As regards the role of externalities, he went on to say, one must again distinguish between production and consumption externalities. The former arose when the production process affected other variables which in turn affected welfare. The classical case was that of pollution of air or water. This had been discussed by Professor Malinvaud, and he had little to add to the latter's analysis. Certainly pollution seemed to have grown faster than output, and failure to make allowance for its cost did mean a risk of upward bias to measured growth. The bias persisted when resources were expended to reduce or eliminate pollution, and this expenditure was included in output. A good example was the recent decision of the American Bureau of Labor Statistics to treat the addition of anti-pollution equipment to automobiles as an improvement in quality rather than an increase in cost.

But what deserved more concern than measurement bias, said Professor Modigliani, was the well-known effect of externalities in interfering with the ability of the competitive price mechanism to insure Pareto optimality. This failure could, in principle, be remedied through incentive schemes and regulation. On the whole, one could share Professor Malinvaud's view that these problems were beginning to be well understood, or at least well recognised, and that there was evidence of progress in handling them, including instances in which air and water had been successfully reclaimed — as in the conspicuous case of London.

There remained the case of externalities in consumption. Here again, one had to distinguish two types. One might be labelled physical externalities, where the physical circumstances which controlled the enjoyment derived by one person's consumption were affected by the consumption of others: e.g. congestion on highways or public facilities. He did not know of estimates of the size of this phenomenon and to what extent it might just reflect lags in adjustments rather than the systematic consequence of development; but he suspected that many of the problems in this area reflected the rise in population rather than *per capita* output growth. In part they also resulted from mistaken — but hopefully improvable — government choices with respect to public investment: e.g. the construction of roads rather than mass transit facilities.

The other, and by far the most controversial, source of consumption externalities was the one which Professor Malinvaud had discussed towards the end of his paper, namely social or positional externalities.[1] They would arise because satisfaction depended not on a person's income, but rather on his relative income or position in the social scale. Here again, said Professor Modigliani, he shared Professor Malinvaud's scepticism about the validity and relevance of the hypothesis for the purpose of evaluating the benefits of development or the design of policy. Admittedly, this scepticism might reflect a vested interest, for, if one were to accept the hypothesis in its extreme form, it would destroy the very foundation of economics. Indeed, since the level of output would then be irrelevant, the concept of social scarcity would disappear — even though, through the failure of the price mechanism, each individual might perceive a subjective scarcity. More than that, every possible allocation would be Pareto optimal for, starting from it, it would not be possible to make someone better off without making somebody else worse off! Fortunately, he did not regard the evidence for it as very convincing. For instance, he found the reference to Duesenberry's thesis, and evidence that the saving rate depended on relative income, of little relevance in view of the explanation of this phenomenon provided by later developments, such as the permanent income and life-cycle hypothesis.

As a good Bayesian, he said, it would need a lot more unequivocal evidence than so far offered to convince him that the absolute level of income did not play a major role in well-being, and he felt sure that Professor Malinvaud felt the same. Indeed, he suspected that anyone who really believed that a washing machine or a refrigerator, two prototypes of the fruits of economic develop-ment, were of no value if your neighbour had them too, had never had the opportunity to compare the life of housewives owning or not owning them.

Professor Malinvaud had also discussed the possibility that the benefits of development might be diminished by some hidden costs associated with the speed of development. The main instances he had given were the possible costs of occupational and locational changes which might be associated with faster

[1] Fred Hirsch, *Social Limits to Growth* (Cambridge, Massachusetts: Harvard University Press, 1976).

development, and the costs of the uncertainty that such rapid shifts might generate. It was an interesting and plausible hypothesis, said Professor Modigliani, but, here again, he felt that some attempt at measurement was essential before we could assess whether this phenomenon was or was not serious.

In a review of the growth-critical literature, he went on to say, Professor Malinvaud could not fail to devote some attention to the problem of exhaustible natural resources. Unfortunately, his analysis of those issues lacked the sharpness that had characterised the rest of his paper. In his own view, said Professor Modigliani, there were two main aspects that needed to be considered. The first was whether the market mechanism could be counted upon to produce an allocation of the resource over time which was efficient in the Pareto optimal sense. The second question was whether this mechanism also ensured distributional equity as between generations.

As regards the first issue, there seemed to be general agreement that with perfect foresight the price mechanism did generally ensure Pareto efficiency; the well-known condition that, with minor qualifications, the price of un-extracted reserves must rise in time at a rate equal to the rate of interest was simply one of the necessary conditions for Pareto optimality. In the presence of uncertainty, the market could, of course, price things 'wrongly' at least for a while, but analysis of the problem, e.g. by Stiglitz,[1] had not been able to establish any systematic bias in the direction or current over-utilisation. (Monopolisation or cartelisation of the resources could create a bias but of uncertain sign.) It was conceivable that producers were myopic, but the evidence on this point was at best unclear – nor was there evidence that governments could make better judgements than private markets! Thus, while there was room for continuous monitoring, there was no case for alarm in principle.

The second question was a much more complicated one and unavoidably involved value-judgements. As long as there were substitutes for the resource in production or in consumption (and abstracting for the moment from population growth), it would seem that it was always possible, in principle, for the current generation to compensate for the depletion of limited resources by an equivalent amount of capital formation – and this independently of the rate at which resources were being depleted. The question then was, does this happen, and should it happen? As to the first question, if the owners of the resources correctly computed income as the interest rate times the value of the reserves, then they should set aside the excess of depletion over this income as a reserve for depletion available for investment. This, however, was insufficient to offset the entire depletion. There remained the possibility that the existence of exhaustible resources might have other positive effects on saving. In an endeavour to investigate this issue, said Professor Modigliani, he had, understandably, tended to rely on the life-cycle model. His very preliminary results suggested that the introduction of exhaustible resources into the model, especially where the substitution was through consumption, did tend to result in additional accumulation of capital, aimed at offsetting the prospective reduction in return to labour and capital and/or the rising cost of

[1] Joseph Stiglitz, 'Growth with Exhaustible Natural Resources: the Competitive Economy', *Review of Economic Studies,* Symposium Issue (1974).

a given level of utility, measured in terms of the reproducible commodity. However, the increased accumulation would tend to be insufficient to totally offset the depletion, except in the limiting case, where the length of life was indefinitely long – or, equivalently, consumption decisions took heirs fully into account. Under more realistic assumptions, a deterioration in time of the production possibility set might well occur in the absence of *technological change*. But technological change could readily offset this tendency, depending on its magnitude and the importance of exhaustible resources – and past experience suggested that it had. Accordingly, even if the market system might fail to offset fully through capital accumulation the depletion of resources, there was, to say the least, no clear case to interfere with private decisions to protect future generations from encroachment by the present one – except possibly with respect to population growth. For, even though the neo-Malthusians had claimed to have generalised Malthus by showing that resources were threatened as much by *per capita* income growth as by the traditional growth of population, Robert Solow[1] had given an elegant demonstration of the fallacy of this proposition. As long as population was constant and there existed substitution possibilities, it was possible to offset the depletion through an increase in capital per man; but, as Solow pointed out, if population was growing at a constant rate this must eventually become impossible since we knew from the golden rule paradigm that, for any given population growth, beyond some point an increase in the capital: labour ratio decreased instead of increasing consumption per man. Thus, if there was need to be concerned with growth, it should be with population, not with productivity growth.

In the last Section of his paper, Professor Malinvaud had proposed a social utility function that explicitly recognised two arguments besides that of standard *per capita* consumption. The first summarised the quality of output (including externalities), the second dis-utilities associated with the speed of development. He had then suggested that this function, together with an appropriate representation of the constraints relating the three arguments and other controlled variables, such as the stock of capital, should be used to generalise the received theory of optimal growth. As Professor Malinvaud was aware, said Professor Modigliani, the difficulties in such an enterprise were formidable; they involved not only matters of measurement, but also the vexing question of a valid representation of social preferences. He hoped, nevertheless, that Malinvaud's challenge would be picked up, and looked forward to the results, including a new spate of suggestive golden rules.

In the meantime, he ended, he had to say that a reading of Professor Malinvaud's stimulating paper and a perusal of some of the other literature, had not shaken his economist prejudice that there was scant substance to the disparaging and alarmistic views of past and future economic development set forth by the critics of growth. The two valid concerns, population growth and physical externalities, had been recognised long before the anti-growth crusade, and were certainly receiving attention. The endeavour to correct externalities might well slow down the growth of conventional output measures, but no economist should regret this – except for the conceivable danger that it might, in the short-run, intensify social conflicts and contribute to the inflationary

[1] Robert Solow, 'Intergenerational Equity and Exhaustible Resources', *Review of Economic Stability*, Symposium Issue (1974).

pressures.

As for envy-based, positional externalities, these struck him at the moment as good conversation pieces; and, while conceding that the study of their empirical importance and operational implications deserved serious pursuit, his view was that, for the moment, they should not distract economists from their traditional concern with the most effective use of economic resources, including full utilisation of willing manpower in the short-run, and the rapid expansion of output *per capita* or, better, of productivity. The qualms, he said, should be not about whether the growth of productivity was worth while, but about the fact that there still were such wide gaps in our understanding of the forces controlling productivity growth. He hoped that the work of this Congress would make a major contribution to filling that gap.

*

Professor Tsuru was the next speaker. He opened by saying that the methodological approach suggested by Professor Malinvaud was admittedly an ambitious one if it was to be empirically tested. One was reminded of Walras's pioneering work on general equilibrium which sixty years later bore fruits in the form of Leontief's input—output table. But a quicker empirical result was desirable in the case of the problem now under discussion.

He would take as his starting point the suggestive remark in Professor Malinvaud's paper that 'the growth of transport services is largely a cost of urbanisation. To that extent it should not enter into the calculation of final production', and would propose a somewhat more modest approach which could be adopted immediately for empirical purposes.

He agreed with Professor Malinvaud that the process of economic growth in modern societies was almost inevitably accompanied by a process of urbanisation and very often by a phenomenon of urban sprawl and that this was likely to necessitate longer commuting hours via public transport and/or greater congestion on roads accompanied by a higher degree of air pollution. Both private and social costs, were involved here, and they might be classified as 'the cost of life'. There were other types of costs which were often associated with urbanisation, such as the cost of installing burglar alarms in private houses. This, we might also count as a part of 'the cost of life'.

We should remind ourselves, however, that it is often very difficult to draw a hard and fast line between cost-type consumption and end-object-type consumption and that thus it is not easy to say whether a certain item should or should not 'enter into the calculation of final production'. Heating costs in a cold country would be an item in 'the cost of life' when comparison was made with warmer countries. But it would be impossible to say at what temperature heating would go beyond the necessity of life. A more complicated example would be the case of the substitution of a private device for publicly supplied services — a circumstance which often created a new necessity for a certain category of people. Until around 1930, the provision of a private bathroom at home was considered to be a luxury in Japan; and public bathhouses prospered as a social institution for city-dwellers for whom taking a hot bath every day had long been considered a necessity. But in recent decades, as the economy had 'grown', more and more people had started installing bathrooms in their private homes, so that public bath-houses had become a 'declining industry'. When a public bath-house closed down in a typical district in Tokyo for example, about one-fourth of the residents in the neighbourhood would have to choose between two alternatives: either to go to a bath-house further away or to instal a private bath at home. For such people, what was once a semi-luxury suddenly became a necessity. A similar thing happened when a bus line discontinued service over a certain route due to the decline in the number of customers and the congestion of roads by private commuting cars.

In discussing 'the cost of life' type of consumers' expenditures he had deliberately used items closely related to residential housing to illustrate the point, said Professor Tsuru. There was a reason for this: in discussing 'costs of economic growth' — a topic which he saw as an exercise in welfare economics — it might be better, in the first instance, to limit the scope of the object of study to an area like housing and related amenities. There was an additional advantage in selecting this area because the usefulness of the stock-approach as against the flow-approach could be very well illustrated.

Taking two benchmark years like 1925 and 1975, *per capita* real GNP in Japan had risen by roughly eight times in the period, and the proportion of expenditure on housing out of total household expenditures had declined from 16·9 per cent to 9·7 per cent. 'Expenditures on housing' were divided, in both of these years, almost equally between those on 'houses' and those on 'furniture and utensils'. This meant that expenditure on 'houses' rose in real terms roughly by 4·5 times between those years. In other words, in terms of expenditure-flows on housing, it could be said that the Japanese had improved their living condition 4·5 times in fifty years.

Such a calculation, one might say, was a first approximation which could be successively amended by deducting 'costs of economic growth' such as external dis-economies of all kinds, distance for commuting, etc., provided that they were quantifiable.

But of course there was another approach: i.e., to adopt the Fisherian concept of 'capital' and 'income', and to make intertemporal welfare comparisons on the basis of 'stock' rather than of 'flow'. As was well known, Professor Usuru said, 'income' for Irving Fisher consisted solely of services as received by ultimate consumers, whether from their material or from their human environment, which together might be called 'social wealth' or 'capital'. Social wealth consisted not only of producers' real capital, such as plant and equipment, but also of what are nowadays called 'common property resources' as well as geological capital and consumers' real capital. In this conceptual scheme, 'production' was defined as an addition to this social wealth and 'consumption' as a subtraction from it. Since 'income' was essentially proportional to the stock of social wealth, 'consumption' would have a negative effect on 'income' while 'production' would have a positive one.

If we were to apply this Fisherian concept to the realm of housing, the first step would be to estimate the gross stock of residential buildings by (i) making tabulations of physical structures in terms of floor space, type of construction and age, and (ii) applying measures of valuation as if all the buildings were new. The net stock could be subsequently obtained by deducting an estimated value of depreciation for each type of structure. Measures of

valuation, however, did not usually reflect anything but the cost of construction and, therefore, were extremely limited as an index of welfare. Nevertheless, one might make a comparison of such physical stock figures between
1925 and 1975 as one's first approximation. For this, there were a number
of statistical studies; and they showed a range of percentage changes over
those fifty years of −15 per cent to +15 per cent on the average *per capita*
basis. Of course, one could be more precise and focus upon the housing
conditions of the urban middle class or of the working class. But it was likely
that even the most favourable figure showing improvement would not register
a rate of change greater than +50 per cent. If one compared such figures with
the 4·5 times improvement index obtained from the flow approach one would
see how big a discrepancy there was between the results of two approaches –
a discrepancy so large, he said, that he doubted whether it could be explained
by the deflator problem alone.

For the stock approach, we could and should go further by taking into
account the following items, he added:

(1) basic facilities for residential buildings such as provision of separate
washrooms and kitchens;
(2) environmental amenities such as access to the sun, freedom from noise
and air pollution, availability of playgrounds for children, etc.;
(3) cost of commuting, inclusive not only of transport cost but also of the
time cost involved;
(4) neighbourhood hazards of various kinds, such as road casualties by
automobiles;
(5) shopping conveniences.

Not all these items were quantifiable, of course, but they were usually reflected
in the rent paid or the property price itself or the price of residential land in
a relative manner at *a given point in time.* Comparison over time of rents or
property prices, even when deflated by a specific price index, did not, unfortunately, reveal the real changes over time as regards the various amenities
he had cited, said Professor Tsuru. Thus a basic difficulty of quantification
remained. But some of the relative rent (or property price) differentials at a
given point of time could be utilised to show historical changes in constant
value terms. This was definitely possible for items (1) and (3) in the list; and
possibilities are not excluded for some of the amenities and disamenities
under (2).

Of the five items listed, (1) was probably the only item that had shown
improvement over the last fifty years and (2), (3) and (4) would show a
negative sign reflecting what might be called 'costs of economic growth'. It
was most unlikely that one would be able to say anything definite as regards
(5) because urban dwellers' shopping habits had been greatly affected by the
use of motor-cars and also by the willingness of husbands to co-operate in
shopping nowadays. In this type of intertemporal comparison, one should
also take into account, as was mentioned earlier, the disappearance (or
appearance) of publicly provided services related to residential amenities,
such as public bath-houses, public libraries, school buses, garbage collection,
sewerage facilities, etc.

He did not propose to come out with any quantitative measure of comparison in terms of a single figure for housing conditions in urban Japan between 1925 and 1975, said Professor Tsuru, in conclusion. What he wanted to suggest, instead, was that the now fashionable discussion on 'costs of economic growth' had better adopt also a *sectoral stock* approach, as illustrated by the housing sector problem he had outlined, and use the results of such research as a check on the *aggregative flow* approach which might well proceed along the lines Professor Malinvaud had developed.

*

Professor Noguchi, who spoke first in the discussion from the floor, said that, while he had been moved by Professor Malinvaud's creative speech about the costs of economic growth, he had two questions concerning the categories used in the paper.

First, he thought that the costs of pollution and of using up exhaustible reserves were not physical ones; they were social ones since they went beyond private costs; physical costs should relate only to production and manufacturing processes. The category of social costs was a new creation; but it was questionable.

Second, multinational corporations had opened many types of subsidiaries, for example 'filliale relais' (intermediate subsidiaries) or 'filliale atelier' (factory subsidiaries). This was what was meant by internationalisation of production. Between such subsidiaries goods were directly exchanged within each country. In this case, the central offices of multinational corporations controlled only finance and personnel, and so were concerned with financial costs, while the foreign divisions controlled only the physical and private costs. What was Professor Malinvaud's opinion regarding this new phenomenon?

Professor Matthews, the next speaker, said that the possible social externalities of growth were an important matter, not just a subject for after dinner conversation, as suggested by Professor Modigliani. Concern about them was probably often at the root of the discontent with growth expressed, especially by the young, ostensibly on other grounds, such as environmental ones.

The mistake was to take too extreme a view. This mistake had been avoided by Professor Malinvaud. On the one hand it was absurd to say that satisfaction was a function exclusively of relative consumption — that refrigerators were just status symbols. But no less absurd on the other hand was a model of man according to which his aim was to stuff himself with consumables like a pig. Man was a social being and consumption was part of the fabric of social relationships. A starving man was interested in food and in satisfying his hunger, but he was a man reduced by starvation to the condition of an animal; he was not typical of the human state. An example of an alternative approach was that summarised by the saying of a British social anthropologist: 'Poverty is when you can't afford to ask someone else in for a cup of tea'. This represented just *one* possible approach. The social externalities involved in consumption were complex and not just a matter of relative income. It was natural that economists should have concentrated particularly on relative income, since this lent itself to the kind of formal expression to which they were accustomed. But the issue was really a more general one: how the social structure as a whole was affected by consumption and affected it in turn.

If it was agreed, he said, that both the physical and the social aspects of consumption were important, it was easily seen that there was no presumption that the physical aspect alone, as measured by conventional measures, was necessarily a good proxy for both.

What followed, from this? asked Professor Matthews. Certainly not necessarily zero growth. Personally, he said, he was not persuaded by the views of Hirsch and others that the social externalities were necessarily made worse by growth. In other words there was no necessary presumption that the ill-effects associated with these externalities were truly part of the cost of growth as such. Equally, however, there was no presumption that they were not. He doubted whether our understanding in that respect was yet sufficient to give us much guide at all to policy recommendations, but he would argue that clearer understanding of the social externalities of consumption, positive and negative, was high on the agenda for research. Without it economists had no entirely satisfactory answer to the charge of social and psychological naiveté sometimes levelled against them by their colleagues in the other social sciences.

Professor Dimitri Delivanis felt that Professor Malinvaud was right when he asserted that serious economists had not ignored the costs of growth. But they could be said to have neglected them somewhat, in the same way that everyone had the tendency to underestimate the dangers of increased velocity in transportation. He would refer very briefly, he said, to (i) the deterioration of quality, (ii) to pollution and to workers' exhaustion, (iii) to the advantages derived from the appropriate choice of investments in view of the quality required.

The deterioration of quality due to growth was a matter requiring serious consideration, but it should be noted that this deterioration does not particularly interest those who, thanks to growth, for the first time had the opportunity to use those goods. It might annoy more those who were rich before, as could be seen, for instance in the preference in the less-developed countries for made-to-measure clothes as against off-the-peg garments. If he had to choose between lower quality and increased quantity or equal quality with equal quantity, he said, he was for the first alternative, and even more so when the deterioration of quality was combined, especially in the case of durable goods, with better maintainance.

Deterioration of quality had, however, a great importance if it affected the whole environment or, if in consequence of increased claims, it affected unfavourably the health of the worker. In those cases the increase of quantity must be limited either by increasing prices substantially if demand was elastic, or which was preferable from the social point of view, by governmental measures. It had to be stressed that the struggle against pollution and against excessive exhaustion of workers had been until now rather satisfactory without undue limitation of production from the viewpoints of both quality and cost.

It was possible to foresee in both the public and the private sectors the quality with which consumers would be satisfied, and investments ought to be chosen accordingly. This would bring with it the great advantage that it should be possible to avoid investments which *ex post* would prove useless.

He believed that, when discussing the quality of output, this was the most important consideration, and one that warranted careful examination.

*

Replying to the discussion, *Professor Malinvaud* said that when we spoke of the costs of growth we had to turn our attention to the unfavourable effects of modern economic growth. But the study of these effects might aim at one or the other of two distinct objectives. The discussion had revealed that, in order to avoid confusing issues, we had to be very clear as to which objective we were pursuing. He now realised that his survey of the subject had not been clear enough in that respect.

A first objective might be to scrutinise and revise our measures of net output and of its growth rate. We should then look for all the factors that might be omitted in current GNP measures and we should estimate whatever bias this omission created in the level or growth rate of output.

Professor Tsuru had addressed his comments to that objective. He had pointed out a disturbing feature of the growth of measured output in Japan between 1925 and 1975; he had then suggested an approach that should be used in order to check the long-term trends that resulted from the year-to-year evaluation of real output. He fully associated himself with Professor Tsuru's suggestion. We indeed ought to make direct comparisons between distant periods more often and then to look both at the real costs of production and at the real consumption by ultimate users. He also fully accepted Professor Tsuru's conclusion and the notion that, in order to make scientific progress, we needed a detailed scrutiny of each one of the main changes that economic growth brought to our social life.

In the first part of his discussion, Professor Modigliani, too, had considered the conceptual deficiencies of the GNP. Broadly speaking, he agreed with Professor Modigliani and with his conclusion that 'there was little ground for concern that the conventional measures of output tended systematically to overstate the expansion of *per capita* net ouput'.[1]

But the study of the costs of growth might aim at a different objective, one which he considered much more relevant than the questioning of conventional GNP: namely, whether some of the unfavourable effects of growth could not be avoided and should not be avoided, even if, in some cases, this would imply slower growth. This had been the objective he had had in mind when he had written his survey.

To do so, he had tried to organise the subject using categories that he thought would be directly understood and that did not imply clear reference to any theoretical framework. Such a simple-minded approach had seemed to him to be appropriate since his purpose was to consider some of the concerns of non-economists. For this reason, he had not sharply distinguished external dis-economies from other costs of growth.

---

[1] On the minor point concerning whether, in some countries, and in France in particular, concentration is increasing or decreasing I should agree with Professor Modigliani that the picture is complex and cannot be fully given in a short survey. I should claim, however, that the 1960s were definitely years of accelerated concentration of enterprises in my country and that some human costs followed from this movement.

He might be criticised for this discussion, he said. In particular he could understand Professor Noguchi's misgivings as to his distinction between physical and social costs. He had used this distinction for convenience, classifying as physical those costs that were directly associated with changes in the physical produced and non-produced resources, and as social those costs that were not so associated. But economic theory had no reason to pay particular attention to such a distinction, since he had not meant to oppose two categories that would require completely distinct types of analysis. Professor Noguchi was referring to a different distinction, that between private and social (or collective) costs. He had to agree with Professor Noguchi, he said, that, from the Professor's point of view, most of the physical costs cited were 'social'.

When considering whether and how our economic growth ought to be redirected, he had two points of disagreement with Professor Modigliani. The first one concerned, of course, the significance of social externalities. He was very glad to have the support of Professor Matthews on this question. Like Professor Matthews, he thought that we should avoid both of the two opposite and extreme views about the significance of such externalities. He agreed that we knew too little about the reciprocal relationship between consumption and the social structure. We should discover some way of dealing more seriously with this relationship. His own guess was that aggregate consumption would then be found to be much less critical than some particular types or forms of consumption and that good reasons would be found for specific taxations or prohibitions, as well as for specific material incentives or obligations.

His second point of departure with Professor Modigliani, he said, arose from the difference in their respective beliefs as to how much the market mechanism could be counted upon to produce a good allocation of resources over time. Both of them knew the theories that had been built and were being continuously improved in order to clarify (i) what was meant by a good allocation of resources, (ii) how such an allocation could be reached in a planned but decentralised economy, and finally (iii) how well a market economy would perform in that respect under some idealised abstract conditions. But the question remained that of knowing what conclusion resulted from these theories when we wanted to understand the actual economic operations of our world. He was not one to declare the theories useless, said Professor Malinvaud; on the contrary, he was sure that our thinking about the real world would be very confused if we were not accustomed to scrutinising carefully a number of problems within abstract models. But the conclusions he drew from existing theories were less direct and less confident than the ones drawn by Professor Modigliani. In particular, he did not find in existing theories the proof that actual market economies correctly dealt with the allocation of resources over time; in other words, he did not rule out the possibility that some well-conceived public interference with the market mechanism might greatly improve this allocation.

The difference of opinion showed up more particularly in relation to the problems of exhaustible natural resources, problems which he had dealt with rather briefly in his report because they had been covered by Professor Heal in a different session of the Congress (see Chapter 3 of this volume).

In order to avoid misunderstandings, he said, he would like to say, first, that he considered as highly significant the theoretical papers by J. Stiglitz and R. Solow from which Professor Modigliani drew some of his comments. Similarly he would like to thank Professor Modigliani for his analysis of the phenomenon according to which increased use of exhaustible resources should result in increased capital accumulation. But these theoretical works having been considered, he remained less confident than Professor Modigliani was.

Was it 'always possible for the current generation to compensate for the depletion of limited resources by an equivalent amount of capital formation'? he asked. Yes, if and only if produced capital was, and would always be, substitutable for exhaustible resources: i.e. if a given level of output would always be possible, however small the input of exhaustible resources, as long as capital was made large enough. But the question of knowing whether such a favourable condition held or not could not be answered by theory alone. It depended on factual and technological data. If the minimum amount of exhaustible fuel resource that would be required in the future for each unit of output was bounded from below by a positive number, the condition did not hold and present marginal equivalence would only hide for a while an unpleasant fact.

One should not underestimate, either, the importance of uncertainties in the management of exhaustible resources. The fact that theory did not prove that uncertainty necessarily resulted in over-utilisation was of little comfort when we knew how large uncertainty was in that context. Moreover, since there was plenty of opportunity for speculation, rather myopic behaviour might be individually rational even when current prices did not agree with what would suggest the probability distribution of the best-informed long-term forecasts. Hence, his own reflection, he said, did not disprove the commonly held view according to which the management of exhaustible resources should be a subject of public concern.

He did not mean, he said, that public policy would be easy when it aimed at improving the allocation of resources over time. On the contrary, he had stated in his survey that the problems were more difficult than some writings suggested. They would be challenging in particular at the stage of implementation, as Professor Delivanis had reminded us for the special case of choosing the quality of products, though the difficulty occurred also, with at least equal force, in any other case that was under discussion at the Congress. He had left to the end Professor Bagchi's very interesting contribution. Professor Bagchi in his discussion paper had argued that exploitation of the third world had been a major cost of the economic growth experienced by developed countries. Lack of competence, said Professor Malinvaud, prevented him from being able to argue about the main substance of Professor Bagchi's thesis, which was supported by a large number of impressing and often convincing pieces of evidence.

Indeed, Professor Malinvaud continued, Professor Bagchi had taken a much broader historical perspective than he had, and most of his references concerned the three centuries of colonial domination in various parts of the world. While he found it difficult to believe that the same picture would emerge from the study of all countries and all times, said Professor Malinvaud, he accepted the view that, broadly speaking, western domination in colonies had imposed heavy costs on the people of those colonies and that whatever economic development occurred there had been of more benefit to a minority than to the bulk of the population.

As to the last few decades, Professor Bagchi's paper led one to inquire whether growth did not require exploitation of the developing countries and hence whether this should not be listed as one of its costs. He understood the question, he said, but he was sorry to say that he did not see how an objective answer could be given to it today.

In the first place, what was meant by exploitation? Economic theory did not seem to propose for this popular concept a definition that would make rigorous what the general public meant by it — and with the present pricing of oil he did not expect Marx's concept of exploitation to be widely accepted, he added. Even if we limited our attention to the terms of trade between industrial and developing countries, we could not claim to be able to measure exploitation, positive or negative, if we lacked an agreed definition on what was meant by 'fair trade'. In the present world the question was not only theoretical, but seemed to be a real stumbling-block on the road towards a new international economic order.

In the second place, he asked, would the growth of output in industrial countries have been slower if the changes in the terms of trade had been more favourable to the third world? When addressing this question we realised, of course, that the same output series in both industrial and developing countries, but with improved terms of trade to LDCs, would have implied either a smaller increase in the debt of developing countries or a less unequal evolution of the respective consumption levels; i.e. in a sense would have implied 'smaller costs' to LDCs. But if we considered the costs of the growth of *output*, as distinct from growth of consumption, we had to concentrate our attention on the induced changes of production.

We lacked a theoretical apparatus that would permit a convincing analysis of the question. Models for a world of two regions trading with each other certainly existed; but, so far as he knew, they were rather weak in explaining changes of capital accumulation or technical progress in either of the two regions.

Intuition suggested, he said in conclusion, that growth would, indeed, have been slower in the western world and faster in LDCs if terms of trade had experienced a course more favourable to the developing countries. Considering how our economies operated, one was inclined to think that the evolution of profits would have been less favourable in the west and more favourable in the south, which would have reacted on growth. Such a view was supported by what was observed during the first few years following the 1974 increase in the price of oil. It was necessary to remember, however, that these had been only the medium-term reactions and that, in the long-run, many possibilities existed for restoring a temporarily deteriorated profit rate.

In any case, we must recognise that Professor Bagchi had raised an issue to which we should pay a great attention today, when people's standards of living were so unacceptably unequal throughout the world.

7 Reports by the Chairmen of the Specialised Sessions

I Past Economic Growth and its Measurement

R. C. O. Matthews
CLARE COLLEGE, CAMBRIDGE, UK

The papers presented in this session were partly about measurement problems and partly about the picture shown by the measures we have. Naturally, the two aspects are related. Our picture of the past is affected by which measures we choose to look at. To some extent, too, the actual problem of events makes a difference to which are the most appropriate measures to look at, and also to their reliability.

I shall deal first with measurement problems, conceptual and statistical.

There was general agreement in our discussions that GNP, or GNP per head, is not likely in the foreseeable future to be displaced as the central measure in practice. Two papers were presented on the problems relating to the use of those measures in advanced industrial economies.

A case can be made for replacing GNP by a measure that includes allowance for increases in leisure, due to shorter hours or earlier retirement, the argument being, of course, that these are among the main points of economic growth.

There are a number of interesting empirical points that arise here. The proportional increase in leisure in the whole population is much smaller than indicated by reductions in hours of work. The reason is that reductions in hours of work affect only the working population. Another problem concerns the time spent in travel to work. Is Tokyo untypical, or has there been a significant general rise here, to set against reductions in hours at the place of work? This question was not actually discussed in our sessions. I think the answer is not obvious. In addition there are some difficult theoretical questions about how changes in leisure should be measured in an enlarged GNP measure.

It was shown in one paper that attentive ways of evaluating leisure can make a big difference to the measured rate of growth. On the other hand they make very little difference to the relative ranking of countries. So the question is perhaps of more interest theoretically than practically.

There was a fairly general consensus in our discussions that it is better not to try to refine the GNP measure to take account of leisure. This is not to underrate its importance. One thinks of the three traditional subjects of trade union bargaining: wages, hours, and conditions of work. All three are important to welfare; none of them can be described as non-economic. But most of those who spoke thought it was better not to try to boil them down into a single measure. A set of separate measures is more informative. An intermediate suggestion made in one paper was that two indices should be compiled: one of GNP, the other of the costs incurred in earning it – including costs of the type discussed by Professor Malinvaud in his address. Changes in those costs over time might be either positive or negative.

A rather profound point was raised about the concept of income *per head*. It was suggested that the meaning of this is affected if there are large changes in the length of life. The point is not merely that longer life is of value in itself. In addition, an increase in the life-span reduces the rate of depreciation of the investment in human capital that, from certain points of view, constitutes a significant proportion of income.

A further question of interpretation and measurement concerns the distribution of income. Should GNP measures be adjusted for changes in distribution, so as to give a better measure of welfare? Here, too, it was shown that, in advanced countries, changes in distribution have not been sufficiently large or variable to affect much the relative rankings of countries in regard to their rates of growth, or any reasonable allowance for them.

I should like to mention here in passing an interesting suggestion made in a contributed paper regarding the measurement of inequality itself. Conventional measures are static, showing in one form or another the income of one group as a percentage of the income of another group at a point in time. This can be supplemented by a dynamic measure: the number of years it will take one group to catch up another. This is a function partly of static inequality and partly of the general rate of growth. It can be applied not only to measuring inequality of income as a whole, but also to the inequality in the consumption of individual consumer goods. It was shown that it produces substantially different results in that connection from static measures of inequality.

Everyone is familiar with the statistical problems that arise in measuring growth when there are large changes in relative prices. These are likely to be greatest in times of very rapid growth, associated with rapid structural change. In this connection, a point arose that recurred often in our sessions. Recent rates of growth in the most successful countries, both developed and developing, have been far higher than in earlier periods. In particular, they have been far higher than in the classic eighteenth- and early nineteenth-century industrial revolutions. Hence it is not surprising that difficulties and ambiguities arise in the interpretation of some recent historical data. The index number difficulties are particularly great in measures of the rate of growth of groups of countries or of the whole world.

Rapid urbanisation may make measures of the growth of average income misleading as a description of what can be seen to be going on. Support was expressed for one measure devised by Kuznets: the average of the rates of growth of income of the rural population on the one hand and of the urban population on the other, weighted by constant weights. This measure in effect excludes the part of growth that is due to the shift of population from rural areas, where incomes are low, to urban areas, where they are higher. The urban–rural differential may be partly illusory; and even to the extent that it is not, it enters the life-experience of the individual in a different way from changes in average rural incomes or average urban incomes. This measure was shown in certain cases to yield very much lower growth rates than the conventional one.

So much for conceptual aspects of measurement. Now the statistical aspects. For advanced industrial countries in recent times, the problems here were not thought to be too bad, apart from the well-known difficulties of measuring quality change, particularly in relation to non-marketed goods. Far different is the situation regarding earlier periods of history or regarding many developing countries today. In both those, adequate price data are especially lacking. Statistics were presented showing disturbing differences between the estimates offered of the rate of growth of real GNP for the same country and period by different international agencies. It was suggested that for African countries the margin of error is about ±20 per cent for the level of real income, and about ±3 per cent for the rate of growth of real income. Such margins of error are very serious for policy purposes. But it wasn't clear from the discussion what can be done about it.

I now leave the question of measurement and proceed to those sessions in which we discussed the historical record of growth in advanced industrial countries. Since space is so limited, I shall confine my remarks to three particularly substantial papers. I hope that the authors of the several other interesting papers, invited and contributed, will forgive me. The three papers concerned were all very characteristic of their distinguished authors, and it would be artificial to proceed as I have done up to now without mentioning names.

Mr Maddison gave us new statistical series on real output and output per head in sixteen capitalist countries since 1870, based mostly on annual data for each country. His review covered some similar ground to Professor Abramovitz's paper to the plenary session, but with less particular emphasis on the post-war period. The size and persuasiveness of the differences of growth rates between historical phases revealed by Mr Maddison's figures should be enough to convert anyone, if there still is anyone, who believes that steady state growth is a good approximation to reality. The contrast in the growth rate of output per head between Mr Maddison's first phase, 1870–1913, and his third phase, 1950–70, is plain enough: 1·5 per cent compared with 3·8 per cent. The status, as a phase of his second phase, 1913–50, is more controversial. Not only did it include the two wars, but the 1920s were very different from the 1930s, and there were also large differences in the experience of the principal countries. The proper way to characterise the interwar period in the history of economic growth in capitalist countries remains, I think, rather obscure. Were there already present, but concealed by the disruptions of war and depression, some of the forces that permitted growth in the 1950s and 1960s to be so much faster than before 1914? Was the interwar period, on the other hand, as some contemporaries believed, a period of retrogression in economic performance compared with before 1914? Or were the disturbances themselves a major part of the forces that ultimately made for fast growth?

Mr Maddison himself saw the differences in phase as deriving from 'system-shocks' – changes in attitudes, institutions and, particularly, policies. For this reason he placed the beginning of a new phase in 1970, rather than in 1973 and 1974. His prognosis was optimistic in that he did not believe there had been much flattening in the rate of potential growth, except in Japan. It was pessimistic, in that he believed the system-shocks made it unlikely that the potential growth would be achieved. The likely shortfall of output below potential could have a more damaging effect on capital accumulation than slowdown in the rate of growth of potential output itself. 'Potential' here is a wider concept than full employment output. It is the output that could be achieved, given proper response of investment and factor mobility. I am sorry to report that there was no strong movement in the discussion to reject Mr Maddison's pessimism.

Professor Schultz's contribution was concerned less with the characterisation of phases than with the proper way to look at growth as a whole. Growth is usually seen in terms of quantities. It can alternatively be seen, and in his view better, in terms of prices: in particular in terms of the rise in the relative price of human time. Prices and quantities stand in a dual relationship to one another, so the opposition between the two approaches is not, perhaps, a stark one. The approach through prices is certainly less familiar, and no less certainly offers valuable insights.

Why has the price of human time risen? It has risen because of innovations and because of the accumulation of human and non-human capital. Why has the accumulation of human capital continued and accelerated? It has done so, said Professor Schultz, largely because of the complementarity of non-human and human capital. The absolute difference between the earnings of skilled and unskilled has increased, even though the proportional difference has diminished; so the inducement to acquire human capital has persisted and increased. Induced innovation has played an important part in this process. One interesting question traversed in the discussion was whether the process of innovation had served to reduce the cost of acquiring human capital itself. Professor Schultz's view was in the affirmative, particularly in relation to education outside the formal school system.

The third paper on advanced countries which I shall refer to had the widest historical sweep and linked the two topics of this Congress, growth and resources. It also linked the growth experience of the advanced capitalist countries with that of the rest of the world. Professor Landes posed the question how far the industrialisation of what he called the Centre, chiefly Europe and North America, was based on the drain of staples from the rest of the world. I cannot do justice in a short summary to his very substantial and learned paper. Between 1500 and 1800 what Europe drew from the periphery was not what would normally be considered the basic raw materials for industrialisation. Apart from precious metals, the most important imports from the periphery were addictive consumables: sugar, tea, coffee, tobacco. Maybe these products helped people endure the rigours of early industrialisation; maybe also, though I don't think Professor Landes actually said this, tea and coffee provided fuel to the human machine more promising for the generation of modern economic growth than the alcohol beverages which they partly replaced. But they were not staples of industrialisation in the usual sense. In the nineteenth century, too, though certain relatively minor raw materials had to be imported from the periphery, the main supplies of both food and minerals were drawn from within Europe and North America itself. It was natural that these supplies should be drawn on first. It was only in the twentieth century, when depletion of resources within the Centre had already become significant, that major reliance had to be placed on imports from the periphery, culminating in dependence on imported oil. The countries of the periphery were then faced with a depletion dilemma of a kind they had not faced before.

The relation between the Centre and the periphery in the era of industrialisation did involve the use of force and left some seriously damaging legacies to the countries of the periphery (along with some good legacies as well). But it was not the same as the zero-sum or negative-sum plunder practised by conquerors in earlier ages. It did, to an increasing extent as time went on, contribute to sustained economic growth — economic growth, admittedly, in the Centre itself.

In the discussion it was agreed, not least by Professor Landes, that there were other aspects to the relation between the Centre and the periphery during the period of industrialisation. The periphery was a market for exports as well as a source of imports; charges of exploitation and damage to the economies of the periphery have as often been based on that aspect as on drain of physical resources. No one, however, seriously challenged Professor Landes's rejection of the drain hypothesis in the particular form with which he was concerned.

I turn finally to the papers presented to this session about the less developed countries themselves. Postwar rates of growth of income per head have not been much higher in advanced countries than in the rest of the world, on the average. But it was difficult not to be struck by the difference between the tone of the discussion in our sessions about the developing countries and the tone of the discussion about developed countries. One speaks of postwar growth in developed countries with a mixture of admiration, puzzlement, and trepidation about the future. How did we manage to do so much better than in the past? This question was not at all in the forefront of our discussions of developing countries. Maybe the reason lay partly in some bias in the choice of papers; maybe partly in the lack of long-run historical data with which to compare postwar performance. But I think not wholly. The historically good average rate of growth in developing countries in the postwar period marks a wide dispersion between countries, and a wide dispersion, too, within many of them. So it is not surprising that we should have been concerned a good deal with the forces responsible for differences in the experience of different developing countries and also with the incidence of poverty within them.

Two papers presented on poverty had affinity in subject to Professor Bacha's paper to the plenary session. Lively debate was aroused by the suggestion in one paper that in many developing countries in recent years there has been not merely an increase in inequality, but an absolute increase in poverty. The explanation offered stressed structural conditions, notably the role assigned to itself by the government. Not all those present were fully persuaded by the statistical evidence. However the general picture was reasonably consistent with the historical evidence in the paper presented by Professor Adelman. This paper was concerned not with less-developed countries as such, but with all countries for which adequate information could be had relating to the nineteenth and early twentieth centuries. The range of evidence reviewed in this paper, and subjected to principal components analysis, was quite Rostowian in its sweep. A rich variety of experience was revealed. But certain general conclusions emerged, and here I can do no better than quote: 'The results . . . suggest that the major influences on poverty . . . were (1) the initial conditions with respect to resource constraints, colonialism, and land institutions; and (2) the nature and extent of labour displacement and labour absorption resulting from commercialisation and industrialisation'.

This is part of the pathology of economic growth. The comparative physiology of growth in developing countries was treated in several papers. One analysed the forces determining trends in shares in GDP of primary production, light and heavy industry, utilities, and services. The forces considered were changes in the structure of domestic demand, of imports, of exports, and of the matrix of input–output coefficients. Not surprisingly, some sizable differences between countries emerged. One of the contributed papers sought to test, by simultaneous equation methods, a specific hypothesis about the role of exports in growth, namely that they permit the purchase of imported capital goods. Hong Kong, Korea, and Singapore fitted this hypothesis well. Taiwan did not, apparently because investment was there a less important factor in growth. A theoretically oriented paper dealt in terms of a sequence of temporary equilibria with the forces determining the shift of factors out of agriculture. The resulting simulations fitted the Japanese case well.

One concluding observation. There does not exist for most of the developing countries a corpus of historical evidence about the course of past growth, such as we now have for the developed countries. The growth has not lasted long enough to create its own statistical documentation. Notwithstanding that – or perhaps because the phenomenon under study is so manifestly open-ended – the impression left by our sessions was that the sophistication and richness of the theoretical work addressed to its explanation has been at least as great as that of the theory that has actually been brought to bear on the explanation of growth in advanced economies.

II   Factors of Economic Growth

Herbert Giersch

INSTITUT FÜR WELTWIRTSCHAFT, KIEL, FR OF GERMANY

To summarise in so short a space a discussion which took place over two long days, and to do justice to every participant, is a task which goes far beyond my limited resources. I must, therefore, apologise in advance for all errors and omissions and for all imperfections and gaps in the subsequent account.

The subject was broadly called 'Factors of Economic Growth'. It attracted on the average around 50–60 attendants in the 9 meetings foreseen in the programme. We discussed 12 invited and 11 contributed papers. Omitted were 2 invited papers by Professors Bruno and Nelson, who had been unable to attend the Congress.

Of the 23 papers, 9 dealt with the development experience of individual countries. This list includes papers on

Brazil by Paulo Roberto Haddad,
Czechoslovakia by Josef Goldmann,
Italy by Vittorio Valli,
Hungary by Maria Augustinovics,
Sweden by Ragnar Bentzel,
USA by John Kendrick and Edwin Mansfield,
West Germany 2 papers, by Gerhard Fels and Frank Weiss and by Walter Frerichs and Knut Kübler,
In addition, 2 papers of a more general or philosophical character were placed at the beginning and at the end of our discussions, by Kenneth Boulding and by Koilpillai Charles from India.

There appeared to be widespread agreement on Boulding's proposition that economic development is a sub-set of societal evolution. He also argued that the theory of economic development had been greatly hampered by a false classification of production factors into land, labour, and capital, and by a 'cookbook' theory of a production function. Boulding suggested instead a distinction between know-how, energy, and materials, with know-how as the basic and energy and materials as limiting factors. Thus the spirit of the Club of Rome was alive and well amongst us, but Boulding was eager to point out that the limits to growth can be pushed back by increasing know-how.

The subsequent discussion failed to take full account of Boulding's suggestions. To nobody's surprise it dragged along the mere traditional lines of thought and centred on the following factors and aspects of economic growth:

(1) capital accumulation;
(2) technological progress;
(3) changes in the structure of production;
(4) inequalities in regional and personal income distribution; and
(5) economies of scale.

As Ranadev Banerji's paper on scale economies provoked no discussion, but only approval, I shall concentrate on the first four points.

Coming from a country which has experienced that rapid growth can take place from scratch and that sufficient capital will be generated or attracted in almost no time, if everything else, including know-how, is available, I take up technological progress first and capital accumulation afterwards. The field of technological progress was well covered by four papers from Mansfield, from Ruttan, Binswanger and Hayami, from Kapustin, and from Iyengar.

Mansfield supplied empirical evidence showing that the social rate of return from investment in R & D lies in the realm of 30 to 50 per cent per year both in industry and agriculture. He was careful not to draw any hasty conclusion from this. Whether or not there is under-investment in R & D in certain parts of the private sector in the US is something one could not say with any reasonable degree of certainty. But if it were decided that public support should be given to R & D, some rules on which there was broad agreement among experts in the field should be observed. They include five points:

(1) be selective and concentrate support on small-scale programmes so that you gain information for estimating the costs and benefits of larger R & D projects;

(2) do not support R & D in beleaguered industries that may already spend too much on R & D from the society's point of view;

(3) the government should not become involved in the later stages of development work, since it has no comparative advantage in development for commercial purposes;

(4) potential users should have a word to say in project selection;

(5) as the outcome of any R & D investment is highly uncertain, there is a good case for pluralism and for decentralised decision-making.

In their paper Ruttan and his associates gave an impressive survey of empirical tests which show how strongly inventions and innovations in the field of agriculture respond to relative prices at least in the longer run. Their theory of induced innovations implies that market and non-market forces are at work to allocate resources to research. That this is being done efficiently is critical for economic development. The theory gives rise to the hope that past and future changes in energy prices will have a major impact on the allocation of resources to research and subsequently on the direction which technical progress will take. To this I should like to add another hope. If the theory of induced innovations holds, there should also be a great chance for the transfer of technology from the rich to the poor countries and for adapting this technology to the factor environment and the relative factor prices in the third world. This draws attention to a contributed paper by Babatunde Thomas from Nigeria, who was much concerned with technology flows and to a contributed paper by Iyengar from India, who pointed out that the developing countries must look out for technologies which help to save energy and natural resources. Needless to add, how valuable it would be if more research could be devoted to inventions with a capital-saving bias.

Technical progress was also stressed by two participants from socialist countries. Miroslav Toms dealt in his contributed paper with the relation between growth and new technologies on a theoretical level, and Academician Kapustin presented the results of a survey of some 700 factories in the USSR. The Soviet study revealed that technical progress was more important for raising labour productivity than improved work organisation. Of course, he also pointed to socio-economic factors of productivity growth, such as improved planning methods, balanced growth, economic incentives, and moral stimulation.

The relationship between technological progress and investment was focused upon in the paper by Streissler. Although he did not contend that investment was the sole source of growth in labour productivity or that it had the same productivity effect at every stage of development, he nevertheless regarded investment as very important for growth and, moreover, as a factor which could more easily be influenced by public policy. In his view, the productivity advance via investment is brought about in a social learning process, a process of learning by doing. It largely takes place when the new investment goods are being incorporated and used in the production process.

The rise in labour productivity resulting from this learning process is strongest in enterprises which grow rapidly thanks to a high rate of investment. By stressing that growth could be accelerated through an increase in the investment ratio, Streissler came close to the classical position. He was told by a discussant that in The Netherlands increases in investment ratios were followed by increases in the capital output ratio with a lag of about ten years. This gave support to the neo-classical theory.

Like Streissler, Kendrick regarded capital formation as the most important factor of economic growth. Using a very comprehensive concept of capital, he reached the conclusion that the growth of output of the US business economy from 1929 to 1973 was to at least 70 per cent due to the growth of real capital and that the percentage for the total economy was even larger. The rest was due to learning by doing, to informal innovation activities, to the relative growth of public services, to economies of scale, to improved resource allocation, and to the effect of reduced average hours, which over-compensated such negative factors as declining labour efficiency, diminishing returns to natural resources and adverse changes in demand and supply conditions.

In the framework of a Kalecki model, Goldmann analysed the contribution of investment factors to economic growth in Czechoslovakia after the Second World War. He concluded that the contribution of the investment factor had increased over time. The non-investment factors had made a positive contribution from 1945 to 1950, a negative contribution from 1950 to 1965, and had been neutral since then.

While the papers so far mentioned had dealt with the supply side of the growth problem, Ostrowsky and Sadowsky focused attention on the fact that the public might express a demand for growth arising from high expectations with regard to future consumption − a pressure which they suppose to be relatively strong in semi-developed countries of both the capitalist and the socialist world. They envisage that this pressure is relatively low in LDCs before the take-off period and that it is likely to weaken in the most advanced countries. Work in this field has not yet gone beyond the stage of conceptualisation and no suggestions as to how to measure these growth pressures were put forward in the discussion.

Income distribution aspects came to the fore in the discussion of the paper by Nasilowski. He made a strong plea for political reforms in the least developed countries along the principle of redistribute first − grow later, so that all parts of the population could participate in economic development. At later stages of development the principle of equality of opportunities would lead to income inequalities. There would also be a need for having a growth-oriented incentive system.

The regional inequality problem played a central role in Haddad's paper on Brazil. He focused attention on the great income differentials between the various regions of his country. The inequality indicator which appeared most impressive was that the life expectancy in the most advanced regions was about twenty-five years higher than in the poor north-east. The author was sceptical *vis-à-vis* the growth policies pursued in Brazil and favoured a comprehensive plan with a national fund to be financed out of the income from the exhaustion of natural resources; this fund should be used for promoting investment particularly in footloose industries and human resources in the backward regions. In the discussion of regional inequalities it was pointed out that they were inevitably great in a large country and that it need not necessarily be optimal to remove them completely. Moreover, there was scope for migration.

The thesis that structural change is a necessary condition and consequence of economic growth played a crucial role in the paper by Fels and Weiss on West Germany. Apart from showing that the three-sector-hypothesis was consistent with data covering both less-developed and advanced countries, the authors pointed out that West Germany had grown in a particular fashion in the postwar period: the industrial sector had become too large and the service sector was too small for the *per capita* income attained at the end of the 1960s. The authors ascribed the anomaly to the undervaluation of the Deutschmark in the 1960s, which had favoured the export sector and the import substitution sector, mainly concentrated in industry, at the expense of services, which largely consist of non-tradables. A restructuring of the economy had become necessary after the Deutschmark had appreciated in real terms. West German industry had also become less competitive because of strong increases in real wages in recent years and because of the pressure of imports from low-wage countries. As the employment problem could not be solved by reducing real wages, the authors advocated a policy of stimulating investment in new lines of production with a high capacity to absorb human capital and to produce product innovations.

A similar diagnosis was given by a Dutch discussant for the situation in the Netherlands, but he was less pessimistic with regard to the possibility of lowering real wages.

Contrary to Fels and Weiss, who maintained that investment in new lines of production was very risky and uncertain and that, therefore, the search process would have to be left to decentralised business decisions, Frerichs and Kuebler said that they had produced a model which would give 'basically' all the information needed for a sectoral investment control.

Their model, which was based on input—output tables until 1967, contains twelve industrial sectors and consists of 1800 equations. The structure of world demand and of supply from competing countries would, however, enter the model as exogeneous variables.

Considering Italy, Vittorio Valli also observed deep structural changes in the economy. These included an accelerated rise of the modern sectors *vis-à-vis* the traditional ones, the emergence of a severe structural crisis in Italian agriculture and a process of radical change in techniques and labour organisation in those traditional sectors which had ceased to serve as a 'sponge' for labour released by other sectors.

Several country papers indicated that the period of rapid growth of the 1960s had ended in recent years: it would be followed by a period of slower actual growth in the immediate future. This view was expressed by Fels and Weiss for Germany, by Maria Augustinovics for Hungary and by Ragnar Bentzel for Sweden. Bentzel produced a vintage model with which he could explain the volume of production and total labour income during the period 1870—1975, with investment and interest rates as the only exogenous variables. (Incidentally, some of the refinements of vintage models in comparison with non-vintage models were also discussed in a contributed paper by Malcolmson.) The conclusions following from Bentzel's model were that growth rates in the future will be much lower than they had been in the 1950s or 1960s.

If similar conclusions have to be drawn for other advanced countries, the existing unemployment will probably not be absorbed as fast as we all might wish. Not much hope for the solution of the unemployment problem can be derived from the paper on employment and growth by Jørgen Gelting. He drew attention to the possibility that the capital stock might adjust to a lower level of employment. Gelting argued that when activity persists at a low level, firms, guided by the profit motive, would not keep investment at a level which would amount to maintaining excess capacity.

Two other factors are likely to aggravate the unemployment problem:

(1) the increase in the labour force due to higher participation rates and to demographic factors; and

(2) the labour augmenting bias in technological progress, which is likely to become more important with recent changes in relative factor prices.

Unemployment is not only unfortunate for the unemployed. It may also lead to more protectionist pressures in the advanced countries. This will make it more difficult for developing countries to pursue an export oriented policy, which was singled out as an important factor of growth in LDCs in a contributed paper by Roland Granier.

A final conclusion to be drawn would be that slower growth in the advanced countries will reduce the pressure on natural resources and may give rise to an accelerated flow of mobile resources to the third world. This may contribute to reducing the great income inequalities which exist on a world-wide scale and which have been so central to the discussions in many sessions of this Congress.

III   Resources for Future Economic Growth
Mogens Boserup[1]
UNIVERSITY OF COPENHAGEN, DENMARK

For the two days' discussion in Session III of the specialised programme we had twelve invited papers for presentation and discussion. In addition, we managed to accommodate a very brief presentation of three of the contributed papers, by O. de La Grandville, M. Mamalakis and A. Takayama. A further invited paper, by Academician A. Anchishkin, had to be left undiscussed, since the author was unable to attend the Congress.

Let me first try very briefly to characterise the general approach or 'mood' in the discussions, and in the papers. There was a remarkable degree of consensus in turning down, or rather ignoring, all 'doomsday' attitudes and opinions on natural resources. And even apart from that particular issue, there was an almost complete absence of sharp confrontation of opinions.

As we know, a gathering of economists which fails to produce disagreement on essential issues is a rare occurrence – and even a scandal, some would say. Indeed, it would be a poor meeting of monetary theorists, say, or experts in public finance, that could not find ground for disagreement. A question immediately comes to mind: Why do economists agree so largely on the issue of natural resources, not only at an IEA meeting in Tikyo, but in the profession as a whole?

Without trying to answer this question, I proceed to the report on our session.

---

[1] It is sad to report that Mogens Boserup suddenly died shortly after the Congress held in Tokyo. His very active participation in planning the programme, in chairing the session and preparing the publication of the proceedings was one of the last major tasks of a life devoted to economic and demographic analysis – (*E. Malinvaud*).

The twelve papers that were before us can be conveniently arranged under four heads:

(1) the transition from fossil to non-fossil sources of energy;
(2) food and agriculture;
(3) the sufficiency, or deficiency, of non-renewable natural resources, other than energy resources;
(4) the role and determinants of technological progress.

When I said above that there was little apprehension about the long-term problem of adequate natural resources, this must be understood with sharp underlining of the word *long-term*. For at the same time there was much awareness, throughout our deliberations, of the challenging tasks and difficulties of the transition, necessary over a range of decades, *from* depletable energy resources, that is to say fossil fuels, and *to* renewable or indepletable energy resources.

Three of the papers, complementing one another, were devoted to this problem of transition.

Tjalling C. Koopmans stressed that the transition from fossil to non-fossil energy sources was a problem of phasing *out*, over a considerable period, the technology associated with fossil energy, and of phasing *in* the new technologies of energy production. This problem could not be adequately solved, he said, without interdisciplinary work, involving not only economic theory, as exemplified by the much-noted work of Geoffrey Heal and Partha Dasgupta, but also disciplines equipped for energy modelling, such as operational research, mathematical programming, and engineering.

The goal of such interdisciplinary efforts would be to project an 'optimal' future path of energy use and of technology mix, and to test the sensitivity of that path to political choices, as well as to varying assumptions about such uncertain factors as future technologies and resource availabilities.

Koopmans also emphasised the need for communication and co-operation between economists and applied physicists, as exemplified by the joint study by H. E. Goeller and A. M. Weinberg, 'The Age of Substitutability'.

This need for the physicist's contribution was aptly exemplified by the paper presented by Wolfgang Sassin and Wolf Häfele, both of them from the International Institute for Applied Systems Analysis (IIASA) near Vienna.

Perhaps the gist of that paper can be best conveyed by mentioning just two of the theses the authors put forward.

The first thesis is as follows:

The problem is emphatically not whether economic growth can continue, but whether that *level* can be sustained (and further raised) which was reached by the kind of *quantum jump* in which energy consumption in the century since 1880 increased by a factor of 30. The implication of this is that zero economic growth and resource conservation are wholly inadequate means for solving the problems of transition we are faced with. The achievement, as from now, of zero growth of *per capita* energy consumption (if it were possible and desirable) would postpone the point of depletion for oil and gas by only *nine* years, according to some calculations quoted by Sassin and Häfele. And even if the world's extractable coal resources were to be fully mobilised, right up to the point of exhaustion, the immediate freezing of *per capita* energy consumption would push the depletion point only thirty to thirty-five years beyond what it would be under the assumption of continued growth of *per capita* energy consumption at historical rates.

The second thesis I wish to mention as particularly significant says that the distinction between so-called 'hard' and so-called 'soft' technologies in energy production is based upon a dangerous illusion. For instance, solar energy, if imagined at the appropriate size as a dominating form of energy, would appear to be a huge engineering task, and certainly a 'hard' technology if ever there was one. As one participant in the discussion put it, we must learn to see that 'big is beautiful'.

Lastly, among the papers dealing with strategies for the energy transition, was a report by Bruno Fritsch on the work done under his direction at the Research Centre of the Federal Institute of Technology (ETH) in Zürich. Essentially, this is an attempt to estimate for the transition period of the decades ahead the annual investment requirements for additional energy production. The exercise was done for several major regions of the world, and for four different scenarios. In this brief overview, I can mention only two of these scenarios.

The most expensive scenario is based upon the hypothesis that energy consumption will be allowed to continue to increase at the rates of recent years, and that all of the additional energy production will be derived from nuclear power plants. This would require an annual amount of energy investment corresponding to the following shares of total investment potential: 14 per cent in non-OPEC developing countries, some 20 per cent in Western Europe and Japan, and around 35 per cent in North America and Eastern Europe (including the USSR).

By contrast, another scenario assumes that the annual total (not *per capita*!) growth rate of primary energy consumption will henceforth be held down at 2 per cent, while all additional energy production will come from nuclear plants (as in the scenario first mentioned). This would require far lower shares of potential investment to be devoted to energy production: from as low a figure as 5 per cent in non-OPEC developing countries to a maximum of 20 per cent in North America.

This scenario, the author says, shows capital requirements which lie well within the adjustment capacity of the developed economies. But as regards developing countries (and perhaps Japan) Fritsch would probably agree that a target of 2 per cent annual increase in total use of energy is excessively restrictive, since it implies a zero or very slight increase in *per capita* energy consumption.

Of course, Fritsch was aware that the results of such model exercises are highly sensitive to future technical change, and he therefore stressed the need to give high priority to investment in energy research. Also, Fritsch stressed (as did Sassin and Häfele in their contribution mentioned above) that conservation of fossil fuels could be only a short-term measure: 'It is in the very nature of conservation that the "potential to conserve" itself is subject to early exhaustion'.

Three of the papers presented could be classified as belonging to the broad field of food and agriculture, although they were of widely different approach and scope.

Joseph Klatzman considered, one by one, the different inputs and other factors which influence — positively or negatively — the growth of agricultural output in the long run. Briefly, his conclusion was that, purely from a physical point of view, there are very considerable potentialities for higher output in those regions of the world where traditional agriculture is now predominant. As a cautious estimate for the relatively long run, Klatzman mentioned a total food production of four to five times the present world output, which should suffice for a satisfactory diet for a world population of 10—12 billions. Klatzman appeared to be far less optimistic as to whether the social and political conditions over the quarter-century ahead would permit the realisation of the physical possibilities.

The estimate just mentioned was based on the assumption that already-known techniques, and such technological progress as can now be envisaged with confidence, come to be widely applied. It was pointed out in the debate that there was an unavoidable downward bias in long-term estimates of this kind: The assumption that from now on no new scientific advance or technological breakthrough in agriculture will occur is necessary to avoid arbitrariness, but it is also a quite unrealistic assumption. However, the main issue in the discussion, initiated by Vernon W. Ruttan, was whether such estimates of future agricultural possibilities do require a formal model and a fully fledged econometric exercise, or whether experienced experts' judgement may be a better guide when really long-term estimates are involved.

A paper by Jean Waelbroeck and Associates dealt with the question of price incentives — or rather the lack of price incentives — in a South-Asian village. Behind this econometric study, undertaken for the World Bank, lay an understandable impatience with those mechanical and crude projections of agricultural output which dominate much of the current food-gap literature, and in which future supply and demand is determined without regard to the possible role of prices.

In order to amend this deplorable situation, Waelbroeck's econometric model — besides other improvements — simulates varying types of price policy. And the main results of this are quite striking: owing to the assumption of a highly elastic demand function for grain, the model predicts that an annual 1 per cent real increase in agricultural prices, continued over a period of ten years, would drastically improve India's foreign-trade balance for food.

As one would expect, the discussion of Jean Waelbroeck's paper, initiated by Yair Mundlak, drew attention to many points about the structure of the model and the estimated parameters. But the discussion, unfortunately, did not throw new light on the political conclusion implicit in Jean Waelbroeck's model, namely that an excessive and rigid inflation scare in Indian economic policy has tended to hinder the provision of adequate price incentives for agriculturalists and has thus held back the growth of agricultural output.

The third of this group of papers dealing with agricultural problems was a comprehensive study by Christopher J. Bliss and Nicholas Stern. Here, again, rural India was in focus. The study was a wide-ranging theoretical exploration of the consequences of the supposition – suggested long ago by Harvey Leibenstein – that increased food consumption by an agricultural worker may have a direct and immediate effect upon his efficiency. Like the paper by Waelbroeck, this one by Bliss and Stern, too, suggested possible kinds of economic policy for higher agricultural output. Wage subsidies easily come to mind as a possible solution, but the authors' discussion concludes that this is hardly a fruitful idea. On the other hand, the authors stress the wide scope and need for empirical research to find out how far the postulated link between food consumption and productivity actually exists.

The main discussant, Keith Griffin, took a rather critical attitude to this paper, and described it as reflecting a mechanical and individualistic attitude to poverty. This was, perhaps, the only head-on collision in our sessions, but unfortunately, there was no time to pursue that interesting controversy.

Closely related to the prospects for agricultural output in developing countries is of course the question of future population growth. We had before us a paper prepared for the Congress by Léon Tabah, director of the Population Division of the United Nations. At the Congress itself, Tabah was represented by his deputy, George Stolnitz.

Tabah's paper dealt primarily with a highly topical and tantalising question: Are we approaching a turning-point where the level of fertility in developing countries generally is beginning to recede significantly? Statistical evidence from many parts of the developing world does point to this possibility. It is understandable that both Léon Tabah in his paper and his deputy at our session avoided any strong assertion either way.

From the agricultural scene I now turn to problems of non-renewable industrial materials. In this field we had Marian Radetzki's study of long-term prospective demand and supply for three main metals – iron, aluminium and copper. Taken together, these three metals account for more than 80 per cent of the value of the thirteen most important metals.

The picture of long-term availabilities emerging from Radetzki's paper is reassuring: in all likelihood, we were told, the supplies of iron, aluminium, and copper would remain adequate in the very long run, so that future demand could be satisfied at real prices not much higher than those of the 1970s.

A paper by Alberto Quadrio-Curzio dealt intensively with the old 'dual' problem: how do the 'scarce' resources, generating rent, affect income distribution?

The paper considered this problem in two cases: (a) the 'induced' changes of income distribution arising from changes in the economy's level of activity; and (b) the 'autonomous' changes of income distribution due to exogenous changes of profit rate or wage rate. For both cases, Quadrio-Curzio shows that the presence of 'scarce resources', and hence of rent, so often ignored in contemporary analysis, heavily affects the wage/profit relationship and thereby the economic system's pattern of growth.

This group of papers, dealing mostly with non-renewable resources also includes one by the present rapporteur. Starting from Harold Hotelling's theory of exhaustible natural resources, the paper examines critically the usefulness and realism of the very concept of 'depletability'. The main contention is that scientific and technological progress since Hotelling's time has so much widened the scope for substitution that the very idea of existing 'funds' of minerals, etc., and of their 'depletion' becomes questionable.

The connection between the problems of natural resources and those of technological progress is a close one. In an important sense, natural resources are created by technical progress, and natural resources cannot be identified or defined, in an economically significant way, without implicit or explicit reference to the technologies which make them useful for human purposes.

We had a wide-ranging paper by Nathan Rosenberg, covering many aspects of technological change. In the 'era of substitutability' in which we were living, there was a pressing need for optimal public policies of research and development. Briefly stated, Rosenberg concluded that there was a good case for more extensive systems of public subsidies for R & D, so as to give more stress to longer-term research needs which risk to be neglected by business owing to too distant-pay-offs.

The other paper devoted to technological progress was by Partha Dasgupta and Joseph Stiglitz. It was a voluminous theoretical study of expenditure on research and development under different market structures. The starting point was a scepticism, fruitful as it turns out, towards Schumpeter's belief that monopoly and market power generally stimulate inventive activity. Since this contribution was the draft of a monograph, more than a mere paper, it would be hazardous, in this brief review, to try even to list the major results of the analysis.

To conclude this summary of the whole harvest of papers in Section III of the specialised programme, I think one can say that it had a great variety of themes and approaches, and also a reasonable degree of comprehensive coverage of the field. But this wide variety did not exclude considerable unity of keynote and basic approach.

IV   Prospects of Economic Growth, Economic Policies and Regulations

T. S. Khachaturov
ASSOCIATION FOR SOVIET ECONOMIC SCIENTIFIC
INSTITUTIONS, MOSCOW USSR

In our session we discussed nine invited papers and had ten contributed papers presented, which were also less fully discussed.

Every author of an invited paper had about twenty minutes for the presentation of his paper and each of the five or six discussants had five to six minutes for their comments.

Looking at the titles and contents of the invited papers, as listed in the programme, one might suppose that their subjects are so varied that it would be difficult to arrive at any general conclusions about the scientific results of Session IV as a whole. I will try to show that such a supposition would not be correct.

It is impossible to deny that the principal starting points of our contributors and discussants, their views and convictions, were very different, just as the basic principles of the political economy and philosophy of the east and west are different. But we did not discuss these basic differences. That does not mean that our discussions were not theoretical. Just the opposite. The main positive results of our papers and discussions were some theoretical generalisations on the basis of deductions from an analysis of facts and figures reflecting contemporary economic and socio-economic events – and not merely fruitless dogmatical speculations.

The new conditions in the world were stressed by Paul Streeten from the World Bank, Professor Perkins from Australia, Professor Stoleru, Secretary-of-State of France, Professor Simai from Hungary, and many discussants. What are the main features of the contemporary situation, according to the papers submitted? I will try to summarise them.

Among these features are very high rates of growth in many countries after the war during the 1960s and early 1970s, the appearance of new independent states which wish to be independent economically as well as politically, hatred of inequality and poverty and a new world economic order.

Recently the world economic situation has changed, and sad to say has changed rather for the worse. The high rates of growth are over. The era of cheap energy has ended. The gap between poor and rich countries has increased. All countries, with the exception of the socialist ones, suffer from unemployment. Instead of the traditional imbalance between national savings and national investment, there now exists imbalance between the surplus in some countries and the deficit in others (Stolezu). One new event is very damaging – the combination of unemployment and inflation. It is possible to add also increasing monopoly and oligopoly, backwardness in agriculture in many countries of the world, weak management and entrepreneurship, lack of horizontal and vertical co-ordination in planning, deficiencies of education. I enumerate some features of contemporary economics which were mentioned in the papers. As a result, the prospects of economic growth in the last quarter of the century are rather gloomy. Expectations of a new rise in the economy, as we can see, have not been realised. There are suggestions that the rates of growth will not exceed 2 per cent on average in the developed countries. It is very sad that, as a result of our work, we have few clear proposals as to what should be done in these circumstances. In some of the papers there was even the suggestion that as a result of the solution of one problem a series of new problems would appear. The creation of new jobs might in fact cause more unemployment — for example in the case of automation. Import restrictions, intended to reduce inequalities, might strengthen monopoly power. Policies designed to help the poor might benefit the upper and middle classes (Streeten).

In the papers and discussions it was argued that it was now impossible to use traditional economic remedies, such as reflation, devaluation, low prices, cheap credit (Stoleru). Some recommended the use of incomes policy. Others said that growth could now be determined by demand for goods. Others put forward the idea that it was useful to increase leisure rather than purchasing power. We discussed the necessity to meet, in the first place, the basic needs of the majority of the people, who are poor (Streeten). We also spoke of the use of financial measures for stimulating production growth (Perkins).

In the discussions, some criticism of these proposals was expressed. Speakers said that it was essential to define clearly what the basic needs were. In connection with this, it was necessary also to change the structure of production. This problem had not only an economic but also a political aspect.

As to demand, there were comments that the definition of demand was very important but that demand itself depended on production growth. In many countries there was insufficient demand due to deflationary policies, which were a real limit to growth. It was useful to take into account also the psychological aspect of economic development, which is often ignored (Weisglass). There is great dependence on confidence and expectation for the future growth of the economies of developed countries.

The proposition to impose a tightening of the money supply and the introduction of expansionary budgets by means of additional taxation and borrowing from the public — the so-called policy mix — (Perkins) might cut down productive investment, as the discussants argued (Didier). Maybe it is possible to increase government expenditure for R & D purposes, pushing the cost of production down and the productivity of industry up and by these means to fight inflation.

There was also discussion on the influence of international trade balance on the state of the world economy and, in particular, participation in a world organisation of raw materials markets; access to developed countries' markets (for developing countries), participation in technology markets; financial aid to narrow the gap between rich and poor nations (Stoleru).

Some speakers said that many countries were over-dependent on external trade. Such countries were therefore vulnerable in this respect and it was necessary to define how to help them to withstand such unfavourable situations (Simai).

The gap between rich and poor nations and how to fill this gap was the central idea of Professor Delivanis's paper on 'An Eventual Solution of Inter-dependent Bottlenecks Preventing Growth'. He proposed a new form of foreign aid. Discussions on his paper were centred on the scheme of aid proposed. Speakers thought that such aid could stimulate the economy, but, on the other hand, this aid would be an additional burden to the donor countries and could even deter their own development. Therefore such a scheme would seem to be inappropriate. The deficiencies, described in the paper, were well known, but as in other papers, there were no clear proposals as to what could be done for their removal. And that is the field for further research.

We also discussed a paper by Professor Tibor Scitovsky from the London School of Economics on the influence of consumer tastes on the economy of resources. It is a pity that the important economic problems involved in consumption receive much less attention from economists than the problems of production. Thus every new contribution in this field is to be welcomed. In this paper different life-styles were examined. It was evident that in many cases the changing of these styles could make a positive contribution to solving some of the problems of production and decreasing consumer waste. The author distinguished between the social and the personal comforts that could be obtained in various ways, and concluded that the satisfaction of personal comforts was more expensive for society than the satisfaction of social comforts. It is also likely that personal comforts, as was stated in the paper, generate on average more pollution than social comforts. The consumption of material goods is not the only way to obtain social and personal satisfaction. There are also many other categories of personal and social comfort and stimulation, including position in society, associations, titles, diplomas, and other distinctions, cultural and other needs. In the discussion of this interesting paper the following points were made:

(1) it is very difficult, if not impossible, to change consumer tastes without changing production and, moreover, changing the socio-economic system, and social order of life;
(2) social comfort in many cases is at the same time personal comfort, as is the case in socialist countries;
(3) market mechanisms can be used for changing tastes, but only to a limited extent;

Academician Aganbegyan gave an account of the perspectives for the development of Siberia. Basing himself on the facts and figures, and with the aid of slides, he described the tremendous possibilities for the exploitation of Siberia's rich resources, including a further increase in the oil and gas industry and the creation of huge new industrial complexes around electric power stations. Siberian industrial production was growing steadily by about 50–70 per cent every five years. During recent years special attention had been paid to the development of the infrastructure in this part of the country, including the Baykal-Amur railroad, pipelines and house-building.

Many questions were put to Professor Aganbegyan. One of the discussants was Luvsandorj from Mongolia, who spoke on the economic growth and resources of the Mongolian Republic. He had presented a paper describing the prospects of economic growth of Mongolia and showing that the country was rich in many kinds of natural resources. Given the age-structure of the population, its resources of manpower would be another favourable factor in the country's economic performance. Socialist economic integration and assistance from CMEA member countries had helped to cover the demand for financial means required for the fast economic growth of Mongolia.

We also had papers from Professor Morva on structural policy in the planned economy, in particular for long-term periods. Professor Miesankowsky spoke on the perspectives of economic growth, and his point of view was in turn criticised by Mr Ariki from Japan.

Of the ten contributed papers, some were very interesting; for example the papers of Tran Phuong, of the Socialist Republic of Vietnam, on the 'Strategy of Economic Development of Developing Countries – The Example of Vietnam', of Diejomach from Nigeria, of Stefani from Italy on the role of infrastructure and public services in the development of the urban economy in the existing circumstances of the lack of financial means of municipalities.

We would not claim that we have solved all or even most of the essential economic problems discussed, but I hope that our work contributed to the future research in the field of factors of economic growth. In general, the work of the Session was most profitable.

V   International Division of Labour and Co-operation in Economic Development

Irma Adelman
UNIVERSITY OF MARYLAND, USA

My task in summarising the discussions in Session V was complicated by two facts: one is that, for reasons which had nothing to do with the organisation of the Congress, I found myself being able to read the papers only at the Congress itself;[1] the other is that the discussions in this particular Session

---

[1] The specialised session was organised very actively by S. Chakravarty, who was due to chair it. But he was unfortunately unable to attend the Congress at the last moment because of a heart attack. I. Adelman was kind enough to accept to replace him on the spot – (*E. Malinvaud*).

were unusually polarised in terms of both the philosophies and techniques they reflected.

The discussion of the Session dealt with the international economic order particularly as it might affect the fate of developing countries. It reviewed some of the technical aspects of some possible reforms, and it also concentrated on the philosophy underlying the potential reforms.

Before addressing the technical economic issues, I shall spend a few moments on the philosophical ones and, in particular, I shall try to indicate what I think I learnt from the discussion concerning the role of the international economic order in economic development. In this I found the contribution made by Professor Pajestka to be the most fundamental. In his paper, he distinguished between a process of development for which the driving force and the major impetus comes from abroad, to which I shall refer as 'exogenous development', and its antithesis, a process of development for which the major impetus comes from internal forces, to which I shall refer as 'endogenous development'. As is clear from this brief characterisation, endogenous development is not to be confused with an autarkic approach to development.

It is I think fair to say that on the whole the development policy in the post-Second World War era has been based on the premise that the dynamic impetus for development has to be exogenous. Based on the experience of economic recovery from the Second World War in Europe and in Japan, the dynamics of development were first seen to come from international transfers of capital through trade and aid. Later the dynamic focus was shifted to international transfer of technology and to internal policies designed to rationalise the domestic system of incentives to enable developing countries to take full advantage of the impetus arising from the foreign sector. Domestic economies were made more responsive to foreign opportunities through changes in trade policy, through increased mobilisation of internal saving, through building up of physical infrastructure, and through industrialisation and investment policies. More sophisticated long-term versions of this policy stressed dynamic views of comparative advantage and the successive building up of factor endowments, especially human and physical capital, to change the nature of the production frontier and thereby change domestic productivity.

According to this view, if the dynamics of development are in fact induced exogenously, then the failures of the development process are also due primarily to exogenous forces. This explains some of the heat behind the clamour for a new international order. In this perspective, the reason for the failure of the development process of LDCs to deliver those benefits which they were supposed to deliver is seen as stemming primarily from the failures of the international economic order to operate so as to provide appropriate signals and opportunities for the development of LDCs and only secondarily to the failures of domestic policies to be appropriately adjusted so as to take advantage of the opportunities provided. The failures of the international economic order are attributed to inappropriate consumption patterns imported from abroad; inappropriate technology imported from abroad; the creation of a system of trade and payments which encourages *static* comparative advantage and specialisation in dualistic primary production; declining terms of trade; fluctuating export earnings; discouragement of local technology; and, last but not least, the encouragement of a dependency relationship for developing countries *vis-à-vis* developed countries. The failures of domestic policies are seen in the import substitution policies carried beyond the stage of primary import substitution — that is, into capital-intensive import substitution — and to inappropriate interest/wage/price ratios which encourage a distorted approach to the dynamics of comparative advantage and encourage growth with unemployment.

The model of exogenous development fails to take account of the importance of the initial conditions existing in the countries which inspired this theory of development. That is, this model tends to neglect the importance of pre-existing economic and socio-cultural institutions; the importance of pre-existing factor endowments, especially human and social capital; the importance of pre-existing institutions determining factor ownership patterns; and the catching-up effect. All of these were important for the countries in which the post-Second World War recovery proceeded.

In addition, as stressed by Pajestka, correctly in my view, the history of the development process of most currently developed countries is actually one of endogenous development. For the first-comers to development, England and Belgium, the dynamics of development came from technological change. In the later-comers, the dynamics of development came from government actions to promote institutional change and to implant endogenous technological dynamism. In both of these groups of countries, international trade played an important supporting role. It was used to support patterns of growth which were more industrialised and more urbanised than would have been possible in the absence of international trade and international investment. There is one group of countries among currently developed countries which did in fact undergo an exogenous development pattern for a large fraction of its history. This group consists of the land-abundant white-settler countries — the USA, Canada, Australia and New Zealand. But, at some point, even in these countries the weight of the dynamic impetus had to be shifted from exogenous development towards endogenous development.

In most currently developing countries, the dynamics of growth have in fact been exogenous throughout most of their histories. The capital, financial and human, for their development process came from abroad, as did the impetus for their growth and development. Their patterns of production, the institutions surrounding their factor and commodity markets, the nature of their infrastructure build-up, their patterns of factor expansion and of factor use, were all directed towards serving a role complementary to the development strategies of the colonial powers. But, as the experience of developed countries demonstrates, the proper answer to the sorry history of exploitation to which most developing countries have been subjected is not autarchic development. It is, rather, self-reliant development, in which the direction of structural change and growth is endogenous and the foreign sector is used to support the endogenously designed pattern of dynamic domestic change.

If that view of history is correct, then the new international economic order can in the long haul play at most a facilitating role in the development process. In the short-run, it can provide the exogenous shock which, if appropriately channelled, can provide the economies of LDCs with the necessary short-run impetus to growth. But it is only when and if the growth impetus is endogenised — I apologise for coining the word — that transition to the developed state will be possible. The endogenisation will have to provide, at the very least, the institutional, socio-cultural and factor-endowment preconditions that existed in currently developed countries by the mid-nineteenth century. These relate to socio-economic attitudes or networks and to the personal and institutional manner of responding to the challenges and opportunities presented by change. Their endogenisation will result in the dynamic forces for growth residing in the social, institutional and economic-technological structure of the country itself rather than in the external environments.

We now turn to the question of what is the international economic order. The international economic order is a system of international economic relations consisting of:

(1) a system of commodity flows which specifies patterns of trade, in terms of geographic and commodity composition;

(2) a system of payments which picks out an exchange-rate regime and a method of capital transfers;

(3) a system for establishing world prices, market or otherwise;

(4) a system for maintaining degrees of national or regional autonomy in the face of substantial international trade relations. This latter comprises measures for the decoupling of domestic from world prices, such as tariffs and subsidies; and measures for encouraging specialisation not in accord with present comparative advantage (in developed countries these measures are aimed at encouraging development according to past rather than present comparative advantage and in developing ones according to future rather than present comparative advantage);

(5) finally, measures aimed at regulating or decoupling from the international transmission of fluctuations in levels of economic activity and international prices.

The new international economic order calls for reform in all of these areas.

What is the new international economic order? First of all the new international economic order is not a specific system of proposals. Rather it is a clamour for reforms designed to effectuate a change in the purposes served by the international economic order. As emphasised by Richard Lang in particular, in the past the international economic order has served primarily the needs of development strategies of developed countries. It has consisted of a system of international economic relations resulting in the perpetuation of the underdeveloped status of developing countries. Some would put it more strongly and view the international economic order as a system of international economic relations directed towards the perpetuation of the dependent status of developing countries. It is admitted that in the international economic order there have been possibilities for mutual gains and that the successful developing countries are those which have taken advantage of these possibilities. But nevertheless, by and large, the world international economic order has not been arranged so as to maximise these possibilities.

The calls for reform argue that the international economic order should now be restructured so as to serve to a much larger extent the needs of development strategies of the *developing* countries. As Pajestka emphasises, this implies a *process* rather than a once and for all change; as Lang, Pajestka and Kohlmey stress, the successful implementation and operation of the new international economic order requires a change in the system of international power relations.

The justification for the new international economic order is primarily moral. It lies in the increasing income and quality of life gap between the majority of people in developed countries on the one hand, and the majority of people in developing ones, on the other. It is reinforced by the glaring, indeed shocking, failures of accelerated LDC growth in the past decades to have provided for increased satisfaction of basic human needs. But, for those not convinced by moral imperatives alone, the dynamics of population projections to the year 2000, which imply that four-fifths of the world's population will be in low-income developing countries, imply a veiled threat: reform *versus* armed confrontation.

We are now in a position to summarise the papers dealing with the more technical aspects relating to various policies for the reform of the international economic order. The papers would be grouped into one of the headings 1−5 describing the nature of the international system (see p. 255).

Several papers discussed the *commodity patterns of international trade:*

Balassa presented some statistical evidence in favour of the proposition that changes in the patterns of manufactured exports of developing countries can be expected to go through a set of typical dynamic sequences resulting from changes in their patterns of comparative advantage. As economies develop, their patterns of comparative advantage move from labour-intensive, to either skill-intensive or capital-intensive exports, depending on their past accumulation policies. If they have stressed physical capital (as have Brazil and Mexico) their future comparative advantage will be in capital-intensive exports. If they have stressed the build-up of human capital (as have Korea, Taiwan, Singapore and Hong Kong) their future comparative advantage will lie in skill-intensive exports. He argues that, in view of the existence of this hierarchy of specialisation, the demand constraints on the exports of developing countries are considerably less severe than one would think *a priori*. With countries progressing on the comparative advantage scale, their exports can supplant the exports of countries that graduate to a higher level. To the extent that one developing country replaces another in the imports of a particular commodity by the developed countries, the problem of adjustment in the latter group of countries does not arise. It is only where the products of newly graduating developing countries compete with the products of developed countries that demand constraints will be felt. Thus Balassa sees much scope for export-oriented policies in LDCs within the current international economic order.

Myint, looking at an earlier stage of economic development than Balassa, stressed the beneficial impact on economic development of primary exports. He argued that the expansion of simple exports from the traditional sector of an underdeveloped economy tends to promote development both directly and indirectly. The direct effect is due to a fuller and more effective utilisation of their under-utilised resources in the subsistence sector. The indirect effect stems from the induced extension and improvement of their domestic economic organisation. More generally, he concluded that free trade and export expansion policies tend to promote the economic development of LDCs.

Kreye, in a contributed paper, argued that certain technical developments will drastically alter the patterns of international division of labour. New technologies for the production of sophisticated products enable them to be produced with completely unskilled labour. Moreover, new communication and transport patterns enable a divorce in location between (a) the control and direction of production and the place of production; and (b) between the place where production occurs and the major markets. The combination of these forces will tend to give greater impetus to the location of manufacturing activity where the supply of cheap labour is.

With respect to *exchange rate regimes,* Corden considered the implications for growth, stability and the international division of labour of four exchange rate systems: the present system, that preceding the Bretton Woods system, and two polar theoretical systems – completely fixed rates and free floating rates. He concluded that their implications for growth were rather indirect. Exchange rates are monetary phenomena and the exchange rate regime is important mainly for affecting domestic monetary policy, and more generally domestic aggregate demand policies. The exchange rate regime influences the transmission of disturbances and of monetary trends between countries and the degree to which countries can carry on independent monetary policies. The effects of exchange rates on such matters as economic growth depend on how the internal demand policies affect economic growth. But the central issue turns out to be *not* the exchange rate–growth relationship, but rather the extent of integration or lack of integration of the world economy.

In a fixed rate system, economies are monetarily integrated and must inflate when the rest of the world inflates. Hence, in that system, the monetary policies of the major economies (the USA, Germany, Japan) will govern the economies of all other nations participating in international trade. By contrast, a flexible exchange rate system gives countries monetary independence; a country can inflate ahead of the rest of the world, reconciling its excess inflation with continuous depreciation of the currency, or it can follow a less inflationary policy than the rest of the world, appreciating its currency appropriately. Thus, Corden concludes that the movement from Bretton Woods to the present has increased the monetary independence of many countries. Nevertheless, domestic monetary policies are still affected by the outside world through external influences on domestic prices.

The final piece of research presented in this section concerned *the potential benefits to developing countries of indexing their prices* so as to keep their international terms of trade fixed.

Bénard used a simple aggregative, static model to examine this issue. The model employed consisted of (a) aggregate supply and demand functions to primary exports; (b) a cost function for a composite manufacturing good; and (c) an equilbrium condition which specified that demand equal supply for primary exports.

The sensitivity of the gains from indexation to variations in demand and supply, the evolution through time of these gains and their behaviour when a buffer-stock policy is followed for several years were also studied. The parameters of the model were estimated over the period 1955–74. These estimates led to the conclusion that for that period export price indexation for primary producers to manufactured-goods-import-prices would, for non-oil exporting developing countries, have been profitable. However, in order that a possible gain from indexation arise and stay, it is necessary that the growth rates both of developed and developing countries and the inflation rate of developed countries combine in a very specific way with the supply and demand elasticities for primary product exports. Possibilities for deriving gains from indexation would therefore appear to be unstable and very much affected by trade-cycle fluctuations, in particular. In addition, equilibrium with indexation implies that, in view of the decreed fixity of the international price ratio, another variable must adapt itself. This variable will probably be either the production capacity of exportables of primary products in developing countries or their GNPs. So, paradoxically, Bénard concluded that indexation, which aims at making developing countries escape from vulnerability to random shocks arising from fluctuations in world markets, will make them more rather than less vulnerable to such shocks by compelling their production to adapt to these fluctuations.

The overall import of the technical papers is that no panaceas can be expected from changes in specific features of the international economic order, and that there is much scope for gains to developing countries from appropriate export-oriented development in the present international economic order.

The conclusion from the philosphical papers is that the international economic order can provide the dynamic impetus for growth only for a rather limited period, that unless this dynamic impetus is supported by appropriate domestic policies in developing countries, and unless it is used to generate the internal structural changes necessary for growth with equity, long-term equitable development will not materialise.

VI   Japanese Economic Growth

S. Tsuru
HITSTSUBASHI UNIVERSITY, JAPAN

The Session had the advantage of focusing upon a particular country, Japan, and thus you might expect the chairman's job of summarising the discussions to be easy. But in actual fact, such was not the case. The geographical limitation meant that differing methodologies could more easily confront one another and also that a wide variety of subjects, so long as some mention was made of Japan, could be brought into the purview of the meeting.

However, we did try, in the planning stage of this Congress, to limit the points of focus to the following five problems:

(1) The examination of the factors which account for the unusually rapid rate of growth òf the Japanese economy.
(2) The relation between industrial organisation and economic growth; in particular, the question whether anti-monopoly regulations played an effective role or not.
(3) Critical appraisal of the commonly used index of economic growth, such as GNP, in the light of welfare considerations.
(4) Environmental problems as a concomitant of the process of rapid economic growth.
(5) Resource constraints on the Japanese economy, especially as regards energy and raw materials.

The first of these problems naturally invites comparative analysis and we were fortunate to have five highly interesting papers about it by Ohkawa, by Bronfenbrenner, by Jorgenson and Nishimizu, by Yukizawa, and by Zaneletti. Each one of these had a unique feature of its own; but one is struck by the differing emphases in accounting for the rapid rate of growth: one which tries to locate the proximate purely economic factors primarily responsible and the other which is more concerned with socio-political considerations. It is to be noted that this difference in emphasis does not necessarily coincide with the contrast in methodologies: one which makes use of econometric and national

accounts approaches and the other which is oriented more towards the
Marxian approach. It appears that more and more the first type of approach
has come to incorporate into its analysis historical and institutional factors
emphasising the importance of, for example, *sources* of R & D and the impact
of unions, etc.

The other set of contrasting methodologies is that between the so-called 'one-
sword' school and the 'literary' school. The former tries to explain the situation
with a theory that cuts through a vital point of the economy — a point so
vital that a push there would set the whole economy pulsating. The latter, on
the other hand, contents itself in arraying large numbers of 'factors responsible'
for the growth record. The latter school is often referred to by the term
'laundrylist' school.

A bold example of the 'one-sword' school for Japan's case was offered by
Bronfenbrenner, who regarded the marginal efficiency of capital as the big
sword. *Ex post facto* everyone can agree with this diagnosis; but the unique
aspect of Bronfenbrenner's analysis is that *ex ante* marginal efficiency could
be increased in Japan through the reduction of uncertainty because of the
peculiarly paternalistic attitudes of the government (Mugifumi and
Yamagoya).

Bronfenbrenner actually adds to this big sword a short sword of inflation
and a dagger of labour flexibility as important elements in the Japanese
growth process.

The historical impact of inflation on growth is, it is true, becoming a more
visible assembly point for very recent Japanese analytical work. However, it is
still less important as a topic than the direction and size of technological flows.
In regard to this problem, the eradication of the 'technology gap' leads to
speculation as to whether Japan, once a technology imitator, will become a
technology exporter. Sato's paper, dealing with this question in terms of
residuals in total factor productivity, comes out with the conclusion that
Japan still has far to go in international exchange of technology, with an
observation that 'this, however, touches upon one of the most fundamental
cultural traits of the Japanese, namely, their insularity'.

Whether 'insularity' is an important factor in the situation or not, Jorgenson
and Nishimizu came out with the conclusion that

> beginning in 1960 the level of Japanese technology moved up sharply
> relative to that in the US, reaching 90 per cent of the US level by 1970.
> Between 1970 and 1973 the level of Japanese technology actually over-
> took that in the US, so that by 1973 the level of technology at the
> aggregative level in Japan was very slightly ahead of that in the US.

How we can integrate this type of econometric analysis with that of the 'one-
sword' school is the challenge which, it appears to me, has not been answered
satisfactorily.

The problem of risk insurance by the government in the growth process was highlighted by Bronfenbrenner. But the question of the degree of market competition is highly relevant to the vigour of a capitalist economy. Was the record of rapid rate of growth of Japan helped by the existence of a high degree of competitive mechanism or not? Or, everything considered, was it due to the combination of a semi-monopoly structure with large-scale enterprises and the notorious administrative guidance by the government? Or, again, was it partly due to the co-existence of dual structures where small- and medium-scale firms were utilised to the advantage of rapid growth? Such are the important problems which call for our detailed analysis. The paper by Imai and Uekusa touched upon a major aspect of these allied problems, concentrating in particular upon the need for anti-monopoly policies in Japan from the standpoint of allocative efficiency. Size may contribute to the increase of research inputs in the economy's more innovative sectors; but size may not be attained without some degree of concentration. Here is the well-known dilemma which besets monopoly capitalism.

The income-doubling plan was officially announced by Ikeda in 1961; and so far as the statistics show, it was accomplished.

But, in retrospect, one cannot be certain if our living standard actually improved that much, as is indicated by the economists' index of *per capita* GNP. Even before Tobin and Nordhaus published their work on NNW, there were some studies in this country designed to modify the figure of GNP in such a way as to make it approximate more as an index of economic welfare. Kanamori's paper in this Congress well summarises what has been done more or less in official quarters.

There are many limitations on this type of approach and the author appeared to be perfectly aware of them. One of them, for example, is how to treat the matter of leisure time. There is a practical issue here: leisure time can be calculated as equivalent to real income and trade unions agree to such treatment, reduction of working hours without any change in *take-home pay* could be regarded as the case of an *increase* in real wage. But it will be extremely difficult to persuade workers to think in this way.

Concern for the environment is especially keen in Japan – because 'cars run fast on the narrow, muddy road splashing mud to pedestrians'.

We were fortunate in having two outstanding authorities on the subject giving their appraisal: Prud'homme, author of the OECD country review on Japanese environmental policy, and Miyamoto, a pioneer in the field in Japan. Throughout the discussion in our Session we were able to clear the deck, so to speak, to separate out the points of general agreement and those which needed more thrashing out.

As regards the former, it was agreed (i) that very considerable success was attained in Japan in controlling pollution, but much less success in securing a high level of amenity; (ii) that land planning was a relative failure (a problem

which was independently dealt with by Hanayama later); (iii) that popular
pressure on environment questions was an important factor in Japan.

But on two main issues further discussion was thought to be required:

(1) To what extent and how can we or should we make use of the market
    principles in our environmental policy?
(2) Is export of polluting industries to LDCs inadmissibly bad international
    behaviour or not?

Concern with resources problems in Japan is only natural and inevitable in
view of the meagre resource base of the country and the strain caused by an
extremely rapid rate of growth.

In connection with this group of problems we had five extremely interesting
papers by Kirby, Sakisaka, Nishikawa, Yasuba and Daly. The major issue
which cut across all these papers was: to what extent Japan could or should
depend on the free trade principle in the coming decades when the world
resources problem is likely to become more strained, at least compared with
1950s and 1960s.

On the one hand, Yasuba took the position that the resource constraint
had been deeply felt even in the early developmental stage of Japan's industrialisation and had led to all kinds of resource-saving creative technological
adaptation; although some ground for pessimism did exist for the coming
years, Japan should be able to meet this problem through technological innovations without making exaggerated appeal to external threats as in the
days of the so-called 'Have Nations *versus* Have-not Nations'. Sakisaka also, in
discussing the energy problem in particular, recommended strong governmental
efforts for R & D in the areas of solar energy, nuclear fusion and geothermal
energy.

On the other hand, however, Nishikawa was more inclined towards the
idea of abandoning the philosophy of international division of labour and
preferred the idea of Japan attempting to re-establish the primary sectors of
agriculture and fishing.

In a short summary like this I can hardly do justice to the contributors,
discussants and those who spoke from the floor, each one of whom reasoned
always with the necessary qualifications and a judicious choice of words. I
apologise to them for the bold stroke with which I have depicted the main
threads of arguments, which by necessity were packed within the limited
space of two days. At least, however, I can say, as a Japanese economist who
has worked in this field of economic growth and resource problems for the
past three decades, that the session was extremely worthwhile in making us
rethink the ideas to which we have been conventionally attached and also in
opening up new directions of research on the basis of comparison with the
experience of other countries. There is no better reward for an organiser of a
Congress like this than to be able to conclude with such words.

Appendix: Programme of the Specialised Sessions
(31 August and 1 September)

I PAST ECONOMIC GROWTH AND ITS MEASUREMENT

Sessions prepared and chaired by R. C. O. Matthews with the assistance of Moses Abramovitz, Odd Aukrust, Irving B. Kravis and Kazushi Ohkawa.

A Invited papers

Irma ADELMAN and Cynthia Taft MORRIS (USA)
   An inquiry into the course of poverty in the nineteenth and early twentieth centuries
Wilfred BECKERMAN (UK)
   Comparative growth rates of 'measurable economic welfare': some experimental calculations
René BERTRAND (OECD)
   Measuring growth in the economically advanced countries — problems and prospects (original in French)
Derek W. BLADES (OECD)
   What do we know about levels and growth of output in developing countries?: a critical analysis with special reference to Africa
Boris BLAZIC-METZNER and Götz SCHREIBER (World Bank)
   The measurement of economic growth in developing countries: problems, results, implications
G. SOROKIN (USSR)
   Methodological questions bearing on economic growth indicators
Hollis CHENERY and Moises SYRQUIN (World Bank)
   A comparative analysis of industrial growth
Phyllis DEANE (UK)
   Problems of measuring and interpreting rates of economic growth and levels of living in an industrial revolution
Donald McGRANAHAN, Eduardo PIZARRO and Claude RICHARD (UN, Geneva)
   The measurement of social development in relation to economic growth
Keith GRIFFIN and Azizur Rahman KHAN (ILO, Geneva)
   Real poverty in developing countries: an analysis of trends with special reference to contemporary Asia

David S. LANDES (USA)
  The 'Great Drain' and industrialisation: commodity flows from periphery
  to centre in historical perspective
Angus MADDISON (UK)
  Phases of capitalist development
Yair MUNDLAK (Israel)
  Agricultural growth in the context of economic growth
Theodore W. SCHULTZ (USA)
  On the economics of the increases in the value of human time over time

B *Contributed papers*

P. SICHERL (Yugoslavia)
  Growth and the time dimension of inequalities
Arun MAJUMDER (India)
  Retardation potentials of growth structure in colonial India, 1850–1940
T. R. G. BINGHAM (Finland)
  Structural change in the postwar Finish economy
K. Y. Edward CHEN (Hong Kong)
  Export expansion and economic growth in some Asian economies
A. VERCELLI (Italy)
  Link growth-distribution of income with particular reference to the postwar
  experience in Italy, US, UK and Japan

II FACTORS OF ECONOMIC GROWTH

Sessions prepared by C. von Weizsäcker with the assistance of Bela Balassa,
Ragnar Bentzel, J. Kornai, W. Nordhaus and Zdzislaw Sadowski. Sessions
chaired by Herbert Giersch.

A *Invited papers*

Ragnar BENTZEL (Sweden)
  A vintage model of Swedish economic growth from 1870 to 1975
Kenneth E. BOULDING (USA)
  Economic development as an evolutionary system
Gerhard FELS and Frank WEISS (FRG)
  Structural change in an open growing economy: the lesson of West Germany
Jørgen H. GELTING (Denmark)
  On the level of employment and the rate of economic growth
Josef GOLDMANN (Czechoslovakia)
  The role of investment in the context of the Kalecki model of economic
  growth under socialism
Paulo Roberto HADDAD (Brazil)
  Natural resources and regional development: lessons from the Brazilian
  experience

Evgeny KAPUSTIN (USSR)
  Economic growth and labour productivity
John W. KENDRICK (USA)
  Total investment, capital, and economic growth
Edwin MANSFIELD (USA)
  The role of technological change in US economic growth
Marian OSTROWSKI and Zdzislaw SADOWSKI (Poland)
  Growth factors and strategy choices in a semi-developed situation
Vernon W. RUTTAN, Hans P. BINSWANGER and Yujiro HAYAMI (USA)
  Induced innovation in agriculture
Erich STREISSLER (Austria)
  Models of investment dependent economic growth revisited.

B *Contributed papers*

Ranadev BANERJI (FRG)
  Inter-country differences in the average size of plants by industry: an
  attempted explanation using a capital intensity proxy
W. FRERICHS and K. KUBLER (FRG)
  Sectoral investment control as a factor of economic growth
Roland GRANIER et Paul DJONDANG (France)
  Quelques facteurs de la croissance à long terme dans les pays à développe-
  ment retardé, depuis 1950
Mieczyslaw NASILOWSKI (Poland)
  National income distribution as a factor of economic growth
M. TOMS (Czechoslovakia)
  Economic growth, choice of technology and socio-economic efficiency
D. Babatunda THOMAS (Nigerian in USA)
  An economic theory of international technology flows and productivity
  differences
Vittorio VALLI (Italy)
  Growth and crisis in an open economy: the Italian case
M. AUGUSTINOVICS (Hungary)
  Factors affecting long-term economic growth in Hungary, 1950–90

III RESOURCES FOR FUTURE ECONOMIC GROWTH

Sessions prepared by R. Solow with the assistance of Mogens Boserup,
J. Mirrlees and V. L. Urquidi. Sessions chaired by Mogens Boserup.

A *Invited papers*

A. ANCHISHKIN (USSR)
  Interaction of production factors and economic growth rates

C. J. BLISS (UK)
   Productivity wages and nutrition in the context of less developed countries
Mogens BOSERUP (Denmark)
   Are there really depletable resources?
Alberto QUADRIO-CURZIO (Italy)
   Rent, non-reproduced means of production, growth
Partha DASGUPTA and Joseph STIGLITZ (UK)
   Market structure and research and development
Bruno FRITSCH (Switzerland)
   The Zencap-Project: future capital requirements of alternative energy
   strategies — global perspectives
Joseph KLATZMANN (France)
   Resources for increasing world food production (original in French)
Tjalling C. KOOPMANS (USA)
   The transition from exhaustible to renewable or inexhaustible resources
Marc OSTERRIETH, Eric VERREYDT and Jean WAELBROECK (Belgium)
   Agriculture and growth in developing countries: an experimental study of
   the trade-off between agricultural prices and the agricultural trade balance.
Marian RADETZKI (Sweden)
   Will the long-run global supply of industrial minerals be adequate?: a case
   study of iron, aluminium and copper
Nathan ROSENBERG (USA)
   Technology, natural resources and economic growth
W. SASSIN and W. HÄFELE (Austria)
   Energy and future economic growth
Léon TABAH (UN)
   Are we at a turning point in the world demographic situation? (original in
   French)

B Contributed papers

Henry M. BOOKER (USA)
   Can man survive or merely exist in the next century?
Alessandro CIGNO (UK)
   Depletion of natural resources and accumulation of capital when population
   is endogenous
Lawrence W. COPITHORNE (Canada)
   The role of Canada's natural resource endowment in regional economic
   growth
F. CRIPPS (UK)
   On whether future economic growth will be limited by scarcity of natural
   resources
Oliver de la GRANDVILLE (France)
   Fundamental rules of optimal growth theory with exhaustible resources:
   a suggested interpretation

Trevor J. O. DICK (Canada)
   The specification problem in theories of resource-determined economic growth
James P. GANDER and L. T. PHILLIPS (USA)
   Technological change and raw materials
Markos MAMALAKIS (USA)
   The minerals theory of growth: the Latin American evidence
R. W. T. POMFRET (Canada)
   The staple theory and Canadian economic development
J.-P. BONVALLET (France)
   La croissance économique rend-elle inéluctable la concurrence entre l'homme et l'animal pour l'utilisation des resources alimentaires rares?
Akira TAKAYAMA (Japan)
   Optimal technological progress with natural resources

IV PROSPECTS OF ECONOMIC GROWTH, ECONOMIC POLICIES AND REGULATIONS

Sessions prepared and chaired by T. S. Khachaturov with the assistance of Herbert Giersch and J. Tinbergen.

A Invited papers

A. G. AGANBEGYAN (USSR)
   Development of Siberian resources and perspectives of the USSR economic growth
D. J. DELIVANIS (Greece)
   Eventual solution of interdependent bottlenecks preventing growth
M. MIESZCZANKOWSKI (Poland)
   Perspectives on economic growth of the developed countries – Marxist point of view
Tamás MORVA (Hungary)
   Factors of economic growth: structural policy
J. O. N. PERKINS (Australia)
   Macroeconomic policy and economic growth
Tibor SCITOVSKY (USA)
   Can changing consumers' tastes save resources?
Mihály SIMAI (Hungary)
   International economic relations and economic growth: problems and potentialities
Lionel STOLERU (France)
   Economic management with moderate growth (original in French)
Paul STREETEN (UK)
   Development ideas in historical perspective: the new interest in development

B Contributed papers

Syed M. AHSAN (Canada)
  Public policy and economic development in decentralised dual economies
Bodo D. GEMPER (FRG)
  The dangers and opportunities involved in the state's growing share of the
  gross national product in the maintenance of long-term economic growth
P. LUVSANDORJ (Mongolia)
  Economic growth and resources of the Mongolian People's Republic.
A. LOTFY (Egypt)
  La politique d'ouverture économique en Egypte
A. PARIKH (India)
  Effects of increased exports on output and employment in a developing
  and a developed country: a two-country multi-sectional analysis
Jeanne Marie PARLY and Danièle BLONDEL (France)
  L'inflation de la croissance
Giorgio STEFANI (Italy)
  Infrastructures and public services in the development of urban economy
R. Bercerill STRAFFON (Mexico)
  The perspectives of Latin American development
Tran PHUONG (Viet Nam)
  La stratégie du développement économique dans les conditions du sous-
  développement
A. WOS (Poland)
  The regulations of economic growth of Polish agriculture

*V INTERNATIONAL DIVISION OF LABOUR AND CO-OPERATION IN
ECONOMIC DEVELOPMENT*

Sessions prepared by Suklamov Chakravarty with the assistance of Irma
Adelman, M. Bruno and A. Lindbeck. Sessions chaired by Irma
Adleman.

A Invited papers

Bela BALASSA (USA – World Bank)
  A 'stages approach' to comparative advantage
Jean C. BENARD (France)
  A crude model of the effects of price indexation for developing countries'
  exports
Suklamoy CHAKRAVARTY (India)
  Development theory and the new international economic order
W. M. CORDEN (Australia)
  The exchange rate regime and the integration of the world economy

Boris S. FOMIN (USSR)

International division of labour and co-operation in economic development

Hendrik S. HOUTHAKKER (USA)

Structure and solution of The Heckscher-Ohlin model with the Cobb-Douglas production function

G. KOHLMEY (GDR)

International division of labour and international values: a socialist point of view

Rikard LANG (Yugoslavia)

The north—south relations and economic development

J. LESOURNE (France)

OECD/Interfutures research on international division of labour

H. MYINT (Burma)

Exports and economic development of less-developed countries

Józef PAJESTKA (Poland)

Factors of economic development and the new international economic order

B Contributed papers

Jamuna Prasad AGARWAL (FRG)

Foreign direct investment in the natural resources of developing countries — review and prospects

Takashi FUJII (Japan)

Formation of international economic policy co-operation and international collaboration in resources processing

Jacques E. GODCHOT (France)

La conférence sur la coopération internationale et le rapport RIO du Club de Rome

Hanns D. JACOBSEN (FRG)

Atlantic interdependence and economic development in the third countries

Otto KREYE (FRG)

The tendency towards a new international division of labour: worldwide utilisation of the labour force for world-market-oriented manufacturing

Pierre P. MAILLET (France)

Approvisionnement énergétique, localisation internationale des activités de production et commerce extérieur: scénarios exploratoires

Costin MURGESCU (Romania)

Le nouvel ordre économique international dans la conception du président Nicolas Ceasescu

Fabrizio ONIDA (Italy)

International trade and structure of demand—supply with reference to the industrial countries and particularly to Italy

Tudorel POSTOLACHE (Romania)

La croissance économique et la typologie des économies nationales dans le contexte de la création d'un nouvel ordre économique internationale

VI GROWTH AND RESOURCES PROBLEMS RELATED TO JAPAN

Sessions prepared by Shigeto Tsuru and chaired by Mark Perlman and Ronald Dore.

A Invited papers

Martin BRONFENBRENNER (USA)
  A 'marginal-efficiency' theory of Japanese economic growth
Donald J. DALY (Canada)
  Japanese economic development: the response to increased raw material prices, 1970–6
Yuzuru HANAYAMA (Japan)
  Urbanisation and land prices: the case of Tokyo
Ken'ichi IMAI and Masu UEKUSA (Japan)
  Industrial organisation and economic growth in Japan
Dale W. JORGENSON and Mieko NISHIMIZU (USA)
  US and Japanese economic growth, 1952–73: an international comparison
Hisao KANAMORI (Japan)
  Japanese economic growth and economic welfare
Stuart KIRBY (UK)
  Resource potential of continental East Asia for Japan's material need
Jun NISHIKAWA (Japan)
  'Resource constraints': a problem of the Japanese economy
Kazushi OHKAWA (Japan)
  Past economic growth: Japan's case in comparison with the western case
Rémy PRUD'HOMME (France)
  Appraisal of environmental policies in Japan
Masao SAKISAKA (Japan)
  Economic growth in Japan and energy
Kazuo SATO (USA)
  Did technical progress accelerate in Japan?: the fallacies of growth accounting
Yasukichi YASUBA (Japan)
  Resources in Japan's development
Kenzo YUKIZAWA (Japan)
  Relative productivity of labour in American and Japanese industry and market size, 1953–72

B Contributed papers

Tomotaka ISHIMINE (USA)
  Ocean resources: an analysis of conflicting interests
Ken'ichi MIYAMOTO (Japan)
  The environmental protection policy in Japan

Tasuku NOGUCHI (Japan)
    Costs and profits of economic growth
Kimio UNO (Japan)
    A social indicator approach to economic development
R. ZANELETTI (Italy)
    Capital accumulation and economic growth: a comparison of Italy and
    Japan
John C. O'BRIEN (USA)
    Economic growth and ethical progress — the western experience

Index

Entries in the Index in bold type under the names of participants in the Conference indicate their Papers or Discussions of their Papers. Entries in italic type indicate contributions by participants to the Discussions.